PSYCHOLOGY, MEDICINE &
CHRISTIAN HEALING

ALSO BY MORTON T. KELSEY

Tongue Speaking
God, Dreams and Revelation
Encounter with God
Healing and Christianity
Myth, History and Faith
The Christian and the Supernatural
The Other Side of Silence
Can Christians Be Educated
The Cross
Discernment
Dreams
Tales to Tell
The Age of Miracles
Afterlife
Adventure Inward
Reaching for the Real
Caring
Transcend
Prophetic Ministry
Christo-Psychology
Companions on the Inner Way
Resurrection
Christianity as Psychology
Sacrament of Sexuality

PSYCHOLOGY, MEDICINE & CHRISTIAN HEALING

A Revised and Expanded Edition of Healing & Christianity

MORTON T. KELSEY

HarperSanFrancisco

A Division of HarperCollins*Publishers*

Library of Congress Cataloging-in-Publication Data

Kelsey, Morton T.
    Psychology, medicine & Christian healing.

    Rev. and expanded ed. of: Healing and Christianity, [1973].
    Bibliography: p.
    Includes index.
    1. Spiritual healing. I. Kelsey, Morton T. Healing and Christianity. II. Title.
III. Title: Psychology, medicine, and Christian healing.
BT732.5.K4   1988   234'.13   87-46213
ISBN 0-06-064382-X
ISBN 0-06-064383-8 (pbk.)

91 92 HC 10 9 8 7 6 5 4 3

To my children—Myra, Chip, and John

Table of Contents

Preface

My introduction to the healing ministry was peculiar to say the least. As I shall point out later, the family in which I grew up had no belief in anything but medical healing. A brush with one of the healing sects at my mother's death left a very bitter taste in my mouth. My mother's sister accused my father of killing his wife by using medical methods to try to save her. My childhood was one sickness after the other; I know how evil sickness is. In seminary I carefully read through the New Testament in Greek with one of the finest Greek scholars of that time. No mention was made by that professor or any other that we should take the gospel and apostolic stories of healing seriously or that anything of that sort might happen in Christian communities today.

In 1946 I came to be assistant to the dean and later canon of Trinity Cathedral in Phoenix, Arizona. The dean was a very broadminded man. I noticed that those churches with healing services were drawing great crowds. A short service for the laying-on-of-hands for healing was to be found at the end of the Visitation of the Sick in the 1928 *Book of Common Prayer*. Anything in the Prayer Book is permissible. I asked Dean Carman if I might have a healing service following the Eucharist that I celebrated every Wednesday morning. He agreed. The number of people coming to the Wednesday service increased greatly. Some people were healed. The regular participants wanted to meet together after the service for a time of prayer, meditation, and fellowship. Some people from that original group are still close friends.

One day as I was picking up my car at the shop managed by one of the men of the group, he handed me a book. His wife told him that he shouldn't have given it to me, saying, "Morton isn't ready for that book." I am not always thrilled to receive books that other people think I should read, but I dutifully took it and went home, where I gave it to my wife. Some months later my wife, Barbara, was laid up with a cold and picked it up. She was entranced and read it straight through. When I came home, Barbara said to me, "Morton, you really should read this book. Either it speaks the truth or the person who wrote it is off the beam or lying." I did not make time to read it until three months later. When I finished the book, I realized that Barbara's judgment was correct. The book was Agnes Sanford's *The Healing Light*. I am a practical person and I decided to see if it worked.

An opportunity arose the very day that I finished the book. We were on vacation in a motel in Berkeley, California. When we retired Barbara complained of a headache. I decided to pray for her using the prayer from the Prayer Book that we used during the healing service at the Cathedral. I didn't want suggestion to play any part in this and so I put my arms around her in a husbandly fashion and prayed silently. Barbara suddenly said, "Morton, what have you done? My headache is gone." And it was as if the heavens opened and Barbara was flooded with Spirit. I was glad that I had read von Hugel's *The Mystical Element in Religion* and had some knowledge that such things could happen. The experience lingered on for several days.

When I went back to the Cathedral I found that my ministry at the hospital was more effective in providing healing than it ever was before or has been since. I knew then that healing and transformation could happen during the laying-on-of-hands. Even when physical or mental healing did not take place, a sense of peace and God's presence usually comforted both the patient and the family. We decided we wanted to meet the woman who had written *The Healing Light*. Barbara and I went to a meeting of Camps Farthest Out in Estes Park, Colorado, at which Agnes was speaking. Healing services were part of the program. She was humble, sincere, quiet, and touched many lives. We then invited her to come and speak at the Cathedral. We saw some remarkable healings as she visited the sick in the parish. She drew large crowds and made a deep impression on many people.

Agnes, Barbara, and I became fast friends. She came many times to St. Luke's Church to conduct healing missions, and we saw many more remarkable healings. Agnes then asked me to lecture at a series of conferences, the schools of pastoral care, which she and Edgar Sanford, her Episcopal priest husband, founded. The purpose of these conferences was to introduce clergy to the healing ministry. Finally she came to live in Monrovia, California, and became active in our parish. A memorial garden is dedicated to her memory at St. Luke's Church.

I became more and more active in the healing ministry. I became interested in Jungian psychology and found that my Jungian analyst friends were far more receptive to Agnes Sanford's ministry than most clergy. Indeed, as I began to understand the worldview of Jung, I saw that it had a meaningful place for both the healings of the New Testa-

ment and of Agnes Sanford and others who were reintroducing the
healing ministry into the mainline churches.

As I began to lecture on the subject, I realized that I needed more
information about healing in other religions, in the New Testament,
and in the church, both Eastern Orthodox and Western, from early
times until the present. I needed a book that provided a sound theological, psychological, and medical base upon which religious healings
might be understood. The only work that even came close to my spec-
ifications was Evelyn Frost's *Christian Healing*. This book, however, covered only a short period of the church's history and dealt with neither
depth psychology nor psychosomatic medicine. The author did not
point out the difference in worldview between Jesus and the early
church and most modern Western Christianity.

For twenty years I went on collecting material and, with the help of
Paisley Brown Roach, sifted through the history of the later church
fathers and of the church's relationship with medicine. I collected all
the books I could find on healing and religion. There were dozens of
good books with carefully detailed examples of religious healing. But I
could find no book that dealt with what was needed—an *understanding*
of the ups and down of healing in the Christian tradition, from Old
Testament times to the present. If Christian healing was to be as vital
a reality for people now as it was in the history of the church, then it
was necessary to offer a rationale for practicing healing in the church
today, as well as an account of healing in the church.

In the first edition of this book I tried to do just that, at the same
time considering why modern theology on the whole has avoided the
subject. After writing *Tongue Speaking* and *Dreams, The Dark Speech of the
Spirit* (now published as *God, Dreams, and Revelation*) and learning something about writing books, I read the manuscript that I had worked on
for years and totally rewrote it. I then sent it to my former publisher
who wrote to me that my manuscript was a fine treatment of the subject, but that the public was only interested in anecdotal stories about
healing. For two years the book wandered from publisher to publisher
until it was published by Harper & Row in 1973. It had wide circulation,
was picked up by one of the religious book clubs and was published in
England by SCM Press.

Francis MacNutt wrote me a fine appreciation of this work, saying
that he would not have been able to write his first book, *Healing*, with
confidence, had my book not been in print. And since the publication
of *Healing and Christianity* hundreds of books have been written on the
subject. In the last fifteen years many medical doctors have come to

believe that we have far more control over and influence upon our health than was once believed. Meditation, prayer, and faith have been suggested from the *medical* side as aids in conquering many of our diseases. With all this new information, the book needed to be brought up to date, and I was asked by an editor at Harper & Row to do just that. In order to show the vast amount of new material dealing with the relation of religion to psychological and to medical healing, I have retained the bibliography from the original edition and have added a new bibliography of books that have come to my attention since then.

I have just finished the task of completely rewriting *Healing and Christianity* a second time. A great deal of new material has been added and a slightly different worldview proposed from the original book. I realized that the book had been mistitled. It is really a statement about *Psychology, Medicine, & Christian Healing,* so I have given it this more appropriate title in its rewritten form. I have added a final chapter dealing specifically with how to begin a healing ministry in the church and have provided a model for the training of clergy and laypeople in undertaking a healing ministry. The original book provided the *why* of a healing ministry; this one provides some of the *how* as well. Agnes Sanford had complained when she first read *Healing and Christianity* that the practical suggestions for implementing a healing ministry were missing.

If I were to acknowledge those who have contributed to the writing of this book the list would be practically endless. Of course my first debt of gratitude is to Agnes Sanford. There are many different styles in the healing ministry, and mine is very similar to hers. The basic instructions on how to begin and carry out a healing ministry are based upon Agnes Sanford's approach. Paisley Roach worked with me through the original writings of *Healing and Christianity* and did much of the research in finding data about healing in the later church fathers. She also provided information on the history of the relation of medicine and Christianity and the development of psychosomatic medicine. She added many light touches and made many suggestions. Max Zeller and Hilde and James Kirsch provided an understanding of Jung that opened my mind to an alternative to the materialism in which I was trained. In a sense, they made it possible for me to read the New Testament and the writings of the early church with new openness and understanding.

During the period in which I was assembling this material for lectures, Dr. Leo Froke and I became good friends. With a background in literature, internal medicine, and psychiatry, he was a mine of information on all these subjects. He also read and checked the medical sections of the original manuscript. My own physician, the late Dr. Leland Hawkins, treated me with the kind of care and understanding that the best of modern medicine suggests is important for facilitating healing.

For the last twenty years I have served as a trustee for the Robert E. and May R. Wright Foundation of the Medical School of the University of Southern California. This foundation has provided many millions of dollars for research in arthritis, cancer, and heart disease. This position has brought me in touch with the top level of medical research of our time and has kept me abreast of medical developments.

Throughout this period John A. Sanford and I were closely associated. Both of us had the same Jungian background and developed similar worldviews. Most of the ideas presented here have been discussed with him. In the early 1960s, Dr. Ollie Backus came to St. Luke's as director of our program of religious education. She came with a keen interest in and knowledge about religious healing and had worked with the Unity Church. She provided an understanding of how we can help one another in developing a healing community. Even though she came from a totally different background, she confirmed the basic worldview that is presented in this book. Francis Whiting has been a support in my healing interest. He introduced me to Tommy Tyson and has been one of the richest sources of materials on the healing ministry. He also appreciated and validated the worldview presented here.

Early in my ministry at St. Luke's we started a healing service after a mission by Starr Daily. First Stuart Fitch came as an associate at St. Luke's and then Adam Lovekin and finally Cameron Harriot. Each of them had weekly healing services and prayer groups. Some people from Pentecostal churches were drawn to St. Luke's, and their experiences with healing and speaking in tongues helped us to avoid many pitfalls. Through forums and personal discussions we struggled with questions about healing, forging some of the answers presented here. The people of St. Luke's and their understanding support and interest in the subject have been the stuff of which this book is made. They became the proving ground for the answers that we offer. In nearly twenty years of healing ministry at St. Luke's, there were many complaints about many subjects, but virtually none about the healing ministry provided by the church.

Through these last forty years of interest in the healing ministry, it has been my privilege to know not only Agnes Sanford, but John and Ethel Banks, founders of the Order of St. Luke, Emily Gardner Neal, Francis MacNutt, Dennis and Matthew Linn, Theodore Dobson, Tommy Tyson, and the remarkable healing Benedictine community at Pecos, New Mexico, under the direction of Abbot David Geraets. I also became acquainted with the leaders of the charismatic movement at the University of Notre Dame and Ann Arbor, where the healing ministry was stressed. In 1970 I met Arnold Bittlinger, one of the leaders of the charismatic and healing movement in the Lutheran church in Germany and lectured many times at the ecumenical center of Schloss Craheim in Bavaria. Leon Joseph Cardinal Suenens, retired Archbishop of Malines, Belgium, and I were introduced by a mutual friend. I came to have great admiration and respect for this remarkable cleric, who was appointed by the pope to watch over the charismatic and healing movement in the Catholic Church. I have worked in the healing ministry with most of these people. They have all contributed to the insights of this book. When I use the editorial we, it is not just a convention.

Some of my finest colleagues in studying the subject of religious healing have been former students at the University of Notre Dame. They have been some of the most gifted people that I have met. One in particular, J. Andrew Canale, has been a friend of seventeen years. He has tested many of these ideas in his own life and in his psychological practice. He has also written several related books mentioned later. John Vara, John Whalen, John Neary, and Thomas Lischwe have also worked with me to provide a broader base for the material and ideas presented here.

My children were young when I was first writing this book, and they were patient through many hours I spent at the typewriter. One of them was vacationing with us during much of the time that I worked in the rewriting of this material. Barbara has been an incredible help in all my writing, reading and suggesting changes in my writing, checking and correcting many versions of the same material, until she knows it better than I.

The secretarial staff at Notre Dame, in particular the late Carmela Rulli, put the first draft into final form. Cindy Wesley has worked for months at her computer to produce this present manuscript that is old in many ways and very new in others.

One last and very important note: it is somewhat frightening to write on the subject of religious healing. It is almost like testing the fates. I am certainly not a paragon of physical health, although I am grateful that some of my best health and energy have come in these later years. I am not unusually gifted as a healer, as Agnes Sanford was, but I have experienced the effects of healing in my own life, ministered by others, and I have also seen the quickening power of new health come to some of those to whom I have ministered. I speak from the standpoint of the wounded healer, but I have seen the things of which I write.

Morton T. Kelsey

Gualala, California
Pentecost, 1987

CHAPTER 1

Is the Question Settled?

Not many things interest modern human beings quite as much as our health. We not only talk about it—in public as well as in private—but we spend a great deal of energy on it one way or another. In the United States alone hundreds of billions of dollars are spent to preserve health and prolong life.[1] Every welfare state, as part of its total program for the individual, provides all-inclusive medical care from birth to death. When my wife and I were visiting in New Zealand some years ago, we needed some medical attention and received excellent care. When we tried to pay for our treatment we found that they had no procedure for accepting our money.

People in the late twentieth century have experienced a resurgence of religious belief, often aggressively conservative religious belief. However, most people are more absorbed in staying alive and healthy than they once were in preparing for life after death. Even when the zest for living is gone, taking care of life in the here and now seems almost an obsession. It still does not occur to most people that religion itself might have some influence on this matter of mental and physical health, even though many medical professionals are suggesting this very idea. Yet until recently it was generally accepted that our religion, by affecting our relationship with spiritual powers, both good and evil, could have a powerful influence on health. It was believed that certain individuals were either official mediators of spiritual powers or were given special faculties by them and thus could affect the health of others profoundly.

---

[1] Richard Luecke, who works in urban ministry, told me that in 1985 11 percent of the GNP (one out of every nine consumer dollars) was spent on health care and 30 percent of that sum in the last year of life. In the last ten years little has been accomplished in lengthening life.

This point of view is found very clearly in the teachings of Jesus of Nazareth and in the practice of the early church.

Although this idea was generally abandoned by the western Protestant church after the Reformation, the question was seldom directly put: What is the place of the Christian idea of healing in the modern world? Instead, the sacramental and devotional practices directed toward healing were simply discouraged or discontinued, while theology turned its attention elsewhere. Today there is an almost total lack of theological support for such ideas or practice. Yet at the same time there are several indications that the question is not exactly settled. In fact, when it is asked directly we find, not that religious healing has finally died out in the Christian world, but rather that we have poked into a whole hornet's nest of divergent practices and ideas about it.

There is first of all the movement that started in the 1800s, spearheaded by New Thought and Christian Science. These groups have continued to grow. Then there are the Pentecostal churches, still one of the fastest-growing segments of Christendom. At first their revival of the healing ministry was only incidental to their emphasis on tongue speaking and other gifts of the Spirit. The early leaders were surprised to find healing occurring when converts were baptized and spoke in tongues. As a result, healing practices became a part of the Pentecostal way of life. This life-changing kind of Christianity has converted a large percentage of the people of South Korea to Christianity. Meanwhile services for healing had begun to appear in a few of the more orthodox Protestant churches, while among Catholics the occurrences at Lourdes and other shrines paved the way for the healing emphasis in the Catholic charismatic movement that has touched that church throughout the world. As we shall see later on, healing services and practices never ceased in the Greek, Russian, and other Orthodox churches.

In addition, our century has seen the growth of an essentially new interest in psychological healing, arising out of the relatively new professions of psychiatry and clinical psychology. These healing professions have found that it is quite possible to heal patients' neuroses by doing nothing other than talking with them. Such psychological treatment may also improve the patients' physical conditions as well. Sometimes a whole host of physiological problems, of hysterical or other origin, will disappear as a person's emotional maturity improves.

Finally, in the past thirty years or so, many physicians in other areas of medicine have come to realize that many physical illnesses have psychic roots as well as physical ones, and they have published some of their findings. With the growing realization that human beings cannot be treated piecemeal, medical doctors have begun to discuss the need to treat them as whole functioning organisms, including their social and religious life. It has even been suggested that medical schools offer courses on religious beliefs, to assist doctors in understanding and helping their patients.[2] In 1954 the Academy of Religion and Mental Health was founded for much the same purpose, and this group, with its own journal, continues the effort to establish a bridge between the healing and the religious professions.

But most orthodox clergy are not much interested in healing practices. The "orthodox" Christian, whether liberal or conservative, has little exposure to sacramental acts and little or no interest in physical or mental healing through religious means. This fact has been brought home to me emphatically on several occasions. One was the experience just a few years ago of a friend who was state commissioner of health in a large Eastern state. At his suggestion a group of doctors and clergy were called together to discuss the whole subject of spiritual healing. While the physicians on the whole were deeply involved in the discussion, the clergy who attended hardly treated the subject as a serious one.

At about the same time a similar meeting was called by a large Western hospital which has a department of religion and health. A selected group of clergy and medical men were invited to meet together and discuss the topic. All but one of the physicians responded, and 80 percent of them came, while barely 50 percent of the clergy even answered the letter, and less than 30 percent of them attended the meeting.

My wife, Barbara, and I have been in many different church groups over the last twenty years. Except for Pentecostal seminaries, we have found that, of the hundreds of Christian seminaries, less than half a dozen offer any courses in the religious dimensions of healing. In most seminaries the subject is dismissed with scorn.

What, then, *is* the place of healing in the Christianity of the modern world? What I have mentioned above suggests that there is quite a difference of opinion among Christians today on this subject. But there is far more than that. In reality, this difference over the value of sacramental or religious healing in the church is only one symptom of a fundamental division among Christians about how God acts in human

---

[2] Milton O. Kepler, M.D., "The Importance of Religion in Medical Education," *Journal of Religion and Health* (October 1968), pp. 358–60; see also Lester J. Evans, *The Crisis in Medical Education*, pp. 36–40. Note that full publishing data for references cited, if available in the Bibliography, will be omitted from the footnotes.

life. The points of view are so diametrically opposed and so deeply divided that they are often unspoken, each side simply accepting the validity of its own view without question.

Thus, in the Christian churches today we find two conflicting attitudes toward the ministry of healing of Jesus of Nazareth and the apostles—a ministry that was practically unbroken for the first thousand years of the church's life. On the one hand, we find an increasing interest in this spiritual ministry of healing. On the other are most Protestant churches today, where we find actual hostility to the practice of religious healing—hostility even to the idea of it. How has the church become so divided? Which point of view is nearer the heart of a vital Christianity? Which attitude fits better the knowledge we have of human beings and their world?

In order to find answers to these questions, we must sort out some complex and rather difficult material. We shall consider first of all the case against spiritual healing in the church—the outlook of probably by far the largest segment of modern Christianity. A short but revealing study of ancient ideas about healing follows, particularly as shown in the Old Testament. I shall then go on to outline the healing ministry of Jesus of Nazareth in relation to this cultural and religious background, showing what a radical innovation his ministry was in the contemporary religious scene. This will take us to a careful consideration of the actual preaching and practice of Jesus in regard to healing. We shall next examine the attitudes and practices of the early church, and then follow the status of healing through its later history.

We shall then turn to the medical profession to see what it has to tell us about the relation of the emotions, mind, and body, and whether the teaching and practice of Jesus and the early church make any sense in terms of modern medical practice. This will take us on to the relation of religion to human mental health and a consideration of modern psychological thought. We shall turn next to philosophy and theology to see whether there is any place for the healing ministry or action of the church in contemporary sophisticated thinking. We shall then look at the meaning of faith and the increasing medical evidence that faith in a loving God and the practice of love which flows from such a faith has important implications for our physical and mental health. In conclusion we shall offer some suggestions for initiating healing services in a church and for training clergy to lead such services.

It is strange—even ironic—to realize that this interest in the effect of spirit on our sick human bodies may make it necessary to reconsider the whole question of the place of spirit in human life and religion.

Since the source of such interest lies somewhat beyond the ordinary field of religion today, let us begin by looking carefully at the church's own arguments against a ministry of physical healing.

CHAPTER 2

The Case Against Christian Healing

Most modern Christian churches believe that they have nothing directly to do with healing the sick. They do not think that the church's action—its religious acts—have any direct effect on human health. It is true that religious groups do build hospitals and medical centers, but this does not differ from any other act of charity or compassion. Until recently many such hospitals did not even have chaplains to serve their patients. In fact, it has come to be widely believed that there is no particular relation between the practice of Christianity and sound health of mind and body.

Oddly enough, this constitutes an about-face in Christian belief. In the Roman communion it can be traced to about the tenth century, when the service of unction for healing was gradually transformed into extreme unction. Thus the sacrament for healing human bodies became a rite of passage for dying, a service to "save" the individuals for the next life and speed them quickly and easily into it. Still, it must be emphasized, healing interest was not dropped entirely from this major division of Christendom. But it shifted from the official sacramental action of the church as such to the efficacy of shrines and relics. We shall learn more about this later.

Among Protestants, who dismissed these later popular practices as so much popery and superstition, no action of the church was left, official or popular, dedicated to religious healing. What took over instead was quite different—so different that actual hostility developed to the idea that healing might or ought to take place within the church. Indeed, a rationale was developed to show why healing does not and *should not* take place as a function of Christianity.

In order to see just what reactions are involved here, we shall consider four different but overlapping views of healing within the modern Protestant church: first, the materialistic conviction that our bodies can be cared for adequately by medical and physical means alone and that religious help is superfluous. Next, the idea of sickness as God's direct and disciplinary gift, as expressed in the English Office of Visitation of the Sick. Then the conviction known as dispensationalism: the belief that God originally gave such ministries as healing only for the time being, in order to get the church established. And last, the point of view of rational materialism and existentialism so magnificently expressed in the theology of Bultmann: the understanding that there is no supernatural agency which can break into the autonomous physical world ruled by natural law. Since Bultmann and those who go along with him are in theological ascendancy at present, this all adds up to a very strong case against spiritual healing.

The "Orthodox" Medical Point of View

Well before the turn of the century it was apparent that the materialistic approach to human life would take over the healing professions lock, stock, and barrel. What was happening in the clinics of Berlin and Vienna as they became the medical centers of the world was not just a victory for physical medicine, but a rout of all uncertainty. Human illness could be dealt with like any other problem involving matter—a complex one, it is true, but quite susceptible to careful medical regulation. As the new century began, it even seemed that illness might be banished entirely, given enough knowledge about the body and its chemistry and a free hand for the scientist.

So successful was this approach that by 1956 the average American might expect to live twenty years longer than he could have hoped for in 1900; the death rate had dropped by an amount equal to one percent a year. In its 1960 study of the statistics, the National Health Foundation concluded:

Between 1900 and the present . . . the communicable diseases—gastritis, tuberculosis, and influenza and pneumonia—decreased sharply as causes of death and lost their places in the front ranks of major killers. They were replaced by heart disease, cancer, vascular lesions of the central nervous system, and accidents.

Although they were considerable in the first quarter of this century, the declines in mortality actually accelerated in the latter part of the second quarter. The improvement in infant and maternal mortality, and the decline of the communicable diseases . . . coincided generally with an acceleration in the pace of new medical advances, introduction of the sulfa drugs and the antibiotics and improvements in the standard of living. However, within the most recent period, the mortality rates generally have reached a plateau, and it may be that further declines will be slow, even though health progress steadily continues.[1]

With the emergence of the AIDS epidemic and the difficulties encountered in defeating it, a more sober attitude has arisen in many of us. Still we are hopeful that all such diseases can be brought under control by physical means.

Behind this amazing change in the health patterns in Americans, and also most western Europeans, is a point of view that can be put rather simply. The task of medicine is to heal the body, and since this physical mechanism (or an isolated part of it) responds to treatment, this is all that is important. The patient is essentially a set of assorted organs and physical processes working as a homeostatic unit that can be regulated by physical means: by surgery, drugs, hormones, rest, diet, and the like. Only the body is real and significant; the mind and emotions are merely mechanical functions of the brain and nerve cells. In fact, as techniques are more and more pinpointed, the causes of even mental and emotional illness will be isolated—in the brain or somewhere else—and the specific physical cure will be found even for them. Most of us, clergy included, have accepted this view of medical healing. Most criticism has generally come from doctors themselves, usually like the bit of satire written in the Twenties by Dr. F. G. Crookshank, a British physician. Discussing physical reactions to stress, he remarked: "I often wonder that some hardboiled and orthodox clinician does not describe emotional weeping as a 'new disease,' calling it paroxysmal lachrymation, and suggesting treatment by belladonna, astringent local applications, avoidance of sexual excess, tea, tobacco and alcohol, and a salt free diet with restriction of fluid intake, proceeding in the event of failure to early removal of the tear-glands."[2]

In the last thirty years the medical view has been changing. With the advance of psychiatry and the increasing importance of chronic illness, medicine is taking a new look at the factors that cause disease.[3]

---

[1] Odin W. Anderson and Monroe Lerner, *Measuring Health Levels in the United States, 1900–1958* (1960), p. 37.

[2] Quoted from the *British Journal of Medical Psychology* by Flanders Dunbar in her *Emotions and Bodily Changes* (1954), pp. 83–84.

[3] In reality this is not a very *new* look. It is the understanding of psychosomatic medicine, which can be traced as far back as Hippocrates. James Lynch in *The Language of the Heart* (1985) provides a sophisticated alternative hypothesis to the one described above.

Many physicians are giving very serious attention to the possibility that the mind and emotions of human beings have a significant effect upon their physical well being. But since this is a complex matter, often requiring medical background as well as psychological expertise, most people feel that it is foolish, if not downright dangerous, for the clergy to meddle in healing. Where the causes are purely physical, religious healing can have no effect except by encouraging or interfering with treatment. In the case of emotional or psychosomatic illness, the outlook is a little different, but even here the need is mostly for technical knowledge and analysis rather than for any change of attitude or belief.

The church has reasons of its own for being in general agreement with this conclusion. Ever since the Middle Ages a split has been growing between the concept of the human soul and the understanding of human physiology and psychology. Gradually the church has come to accept the idea that reality in the immediate world is derived from matter, which acts according to predetermined laws. With such materialism almost assumed, how can the soul, the nonmaterial, possibly affect the body? The answer seems obvious, and so the church must keep its efforts strictly divided.

There is a nonmaterial world in which the soul has eternal significance, and although it is somewhat difficult to pin down, the task of religion is certainly to save the soul for eternal life. But these efforts do not carry over to the immediate world, where our problems are being created and solved. Here the job of the church is to impart ethical and moral values by teaching and example or by social action—by building hospitals and providing social agencies, for instance. There is no way to bring in healing, nor any need to do so. We accept on faith that behavior in accordance with Christian gospel—that is, with parts of it—will have some effect on the later life of the soul.

Ignored or rationalized are other elements of the Christian message—the healings done by Jesus and his followers (which alone account for one fifth of the narrative portions of the gospels), the outpouring of the Holy Spirit along with other strange phenomena at Pentecost and in apostolic times, the dreams and visions, the references to angelic and evil spirits in the New Testament, indeed the whole emphasis on the interrelation of body, soul, and spirit. One begins to wonder how it is possible to take the ethical and moral teachings of Jesus seriously when nearly half the verses of the New Testament must be avoided because these other things—chiefly healing—intrude into them. In my book *Encounter With God* I provide a detailed analysis of these aspects of the New Testament. In lecturing I demonstrate this analysis with a copy of the New Testament in which these passages have been cut out with a razor. This demonstration is nearly always greeted with an explosion of laughter. It comes as a shock to most people to see that most of the powerful passages of scripture are cut out.

Modern Christians, however, have found several quite acceptable ways of avoiding the unmodern elements in these stories. One way is to hold that the New Testament writers were simply mistaken about the facts they were trying to describe; another is to suggest that the stories themselves were a later addition to the text by the more credulous early church; even though as Victor White shows in *God and the Unconscious* these stories about demons and healings belong to the earliest stratum of the gospel narrative.

In a world where miracles and demons were still part of the culture, legendary stories abounded, as well as pure leaps of the imagination and hearsay. Since we doubt healing to begin with, we simply cast doubt upon all such stories in the gospel narrative. When one's worldview has little place for religious healing, most instances tend to be discarded. However, biblical criticism after Bultmann is less quick to dismiss Jesus' healings out of hand in this way (see Appendix B).

A number of reasonable explanations are also given for the healings. The official view of our household was that these were not physical healings. The blind who were healed were merely hysterically blind; the lepers were just suffering from an allergy. I have heard many such explanations: the lame were psychologically bound; the dead were only in a coma or a catatonic state. For many people with some scientific knowledge this provides a satisfactory way of looking at the "irrational" elements in these stories. They seldom consider that psychological and psychosomatic diseases are often the most difficult to heal.

Another approach to such matters is simply to show how irrelevant they are, either by ignoring them entirely or by concentrating only on an allegorical meaning. For instance, the seventh volume of the *Interpreter's Bible* offers an excellent introduction to the New Testament, discussing everything from the life and teaching of Jesus to the cultural background and beliefs of the early church. This is probably as fine and comprehensive a survey of the Bible as anyone has made. Yet the two hundred and fifty pages given to introducing Christianity devote less than two pages to the healing ministry of Jesus and his followers. The book finds almost nothing to say about events which take up more than one-fifth of the entire text of the gospels and Acts. The recent *Encyclopedia of Religion*, edited by the late Mircea Eliade, looks at healings in a more realistic manner. In it I present a modern perspective for healing "miracles."

In the commentaries, many of these stories are also treated allegorically. It is suggested, for example, that, in healing the blind, Jesus was really trying to show that blindness of the spirit could be healed; or that his raising of the dead was actually a demonstration of the fact that one who is dead in spirit may find life again. By concentrating on a symbolic level of meaning, it is possible to deny Jesus' healings as actual fact.

Indeed, in one way or another a great many modern Christians seem to have reconciled some sort of belief in the New Testament with disbelief in the healings, which constitute a larger part of the New Testament narrative than any other single element. This kind of healing is apparently unknown today; there no longer seems to be any need for it. With its technical knowledge, modern medicine should be quite able to look directly at a sick body or mind and its various environments, diagnose the trouble, and correct it. There is no reason to worry about healing through the soul or human spirit. Indeed—spirit? Soul? Where, in what organ, would it be found?

But the reality of healing by spiritual means persists, and Christians have found other ways of looking at the problem. One of these is an older idea which is apt to creep into people's thinking today even though it seems passé. This notion is clearly expressed in the official service for the sick still found in *The Book of Common Prayer* of the Church of England.[4]

A Service for the Sick

In the English Office of the Visitation of the Sick we find sixteenth-century Christian thinking about illness clearly stated. This same attitude is still unconsciously influencing most Protestants today. In fact, this service expresses the outlook of popular modern Protestantism perhaps better than any other document.

The office is introduced by a rubric (a direction originally printed in red) which specifies: "When any person is sick, notice shall be given thereof to the Minister of the Parish; who coming into the sick person's

---

[4] It is difficult to believe that this service is still found in all copies of the English *Book of Common Prayer* and that the sixteenth-century views have not been officially changed. Such is the case, however, because British law requires parliament to ratify any changes, and that body is even more conservative religiously than the church.

house, shall say . . ." The minister—when ministers used the office—began by invoking God's mercy upon the miserable sufferer, and after the Lord's Prayer and a few versicles and responses, and then continued by saying:

Hear us, Almighty and most merciful God and Saviour; extend thy accustomed goodness to this thy servant who is grieved with sickness. . . . Sanctify, we beseech thee, *this thy fatherly correction to him; that the sense of his weakness may add strength to his faith, and seriousness to his repentance:* That, if it shall be thy good pleasure to restore him to his former health, he may lead the residue of his life in thy fear, and to thy glory: *or else, give him grace so to take thy visitation, that, after this painful life is ended,* he may dwell with thee in life everlasting; through Jesus Christ our Lord.[5]

One or both of the following exhortations was then read—perhaps to a person dying of cancer or parents watching their sick child gasp for breath. If the person was too sick to comprehend more, only the first was used.

Dearly beloved, know this, that Almighty God is the Lord of life and death, and of all things to them pertaining, as youth, strength, health, age, weakness, and sickness. Wherefore, *whatsoever your sickness is, know you certainly that it is God's visitation.* And for what cause soever this sickness is sent unto you: *whether it be to try your patience for the example of others, and that your faith may be found in the day of the Lord laudable, glorious, and honourable,* to the increase of glory and endless felicity; *or else it be sent unto you to correct and amend in you whatsoever doth offend the eyes of your heavenly Father;* know you certainly, that if you truly repent you of your sins, and bear your sickness patiently, trusting in God's mercy, for his dear Son Jesus Christ's sake, and *render unto him humble thanks for his fatherly visitation,* submitting yourself wholly unto his will, it shall turn to your profit, and help you forward in the right way that leadeth unto everlasting life.

If one had a chance of getting well, however, and might be redeemed by illness, the following advice was also read:

Take therefore in good part the chastisement of the Lord: For (as Saint Paul saith in the twelfth Chapter to the Hebrews) whom the Lord loveth he chasteneth, and scourgeth every son whom he receiveth. If ye endure chastening, God dealeth with you as with sons; for what son is he whom the father chasteneth not? *But if ye be without chastisement, whereof all are partakers, then are ye bastards,* and not sons. Furthermore, we have had fathers of our flesh, which corrected us, and we gave them reverence; shall we not much rather be in subjection unto the

---

[5] The italics throughout these quotations are mine.

Father of spirits, and live? For they verily for a few days chastened us *after their own pleasure; but he for our profit, that we might be partakers of his holiness.* These words, good brother, are written in holy Scripture *for our comfort and instruction; that we should patiently, and with thanksgiving, bear our heavenly Father's correction, whensoever by any manner of adversity it shall please his gracious goodness to visit us.* And there should be no greater comfort to Christian persons, than to be made like unto Christ, *by suffering patiently adversities, troubles, and sicknesses.* For he himself went not up to joy, but first he suffered pain; he entered not into his glory before he was crucified. So truly our way to eternal joy is to suffer here with Christ; and our door to enter into eternal life is gladly to die with Christ; that we may rise again from death, and dwell with Him in everlasting life. *Now therefore, taking your sickness, which is thus profitable for you, patiently,* I exhort you, in the Name of God, to remember the profession which you made unto God in your Baptism. And forasmuch as after this life there is an account to be given unto the righteous Judge, by whom all must by judged, without respect of persons, I require you to examine yourself and your estate, both towards God and man; so that, accusing and condemning yourself for your own faults, you may find mercy at our heavenly Father's hand for Christ's sake, and not be accused and condemned in that *fearful judgment.* Therefore I shall rehearse to you the Article of our Faith, that you may know whether you do believe as a Christian man should, or no.

The rubrics then required the priest to stop and examine the sick person to be certain that he really believed every part of the Apostle's Creed, and was truly repentant and ready to make restitution for anything he had done wrong. At this point the office was reinforced in the 1800s by a special prayer book for the sick, with complete forms of examination and instruction. One most enlightening story is found in the advice it offered ministers. A man who had had a heart attack confessed to the priest who was called that he had trouble believing in the incarnation; it took the priest several hours of prayer and instruction about the faith of learned men before he could go on with the office, and very soon after he left, the man died. This supplementary prayer book, which was used until nearly 1900, remarked that the case, of course, is "painful and unsatisfactory . . . but is here recorded to show the difficulties sometimes experienced in examinations of faith, and the means that may be taken in dealing with those difficulties."[6]

---

[6] *Visitatio Infirmorum* (1854), pp. ix–x. This volume of over eight hundred pages contains services, penitential Psalms and suggestions for almost every difficulty and affliction— all cast in the same intellectual rigidity about faith and morals.

Among the long forms of examination, one by John Kettlewell, called "the Trial and Judgment of the Soul," pp. 499–513, begins: "Are you persuaded that your present sickness is sent unto you by Almighty God? . . . And that all which you now suffer is

When the minister was satisfied of the sick person's faith, freedom from worldly cares and charity for all, he was to remind the patient to make a will, remembering the church, and pay all debts. Then the office concluded with a Psalm and brief prayers for mercy and such relief as seemed expedient to God.

This service is still the only official form of prayer for visiting the sick in the *Book of Common Prayer* in England and until 1928 the same was true of the Episcopal Church in America. The Office of Visitation in the 1928 American *Prayer Book* added a great deal of more comforting material. Some of the emphasis was shifted, leaving more to the discretion of the individual priest, but without suggesting to the clergy any fundamental need for changing their way of thinking. The two long exhortations I have quoted were deleted, but their essential meaning was shifted to a rubric, which retained the idea of sickness as a time to catch people and get their conscience and their faith straightened out. This is still the official statement of this church on its ministry to sick people.[7] There is little indication that the service should bring healing as well as comfort and strength.

---

far less than you have deserved to suffer? . . . Are you fully sensible and convinced now, how little there is in [all your possessions], and how soon you may be, or are likely to be taken from them?" Another form, based on baptismal vows, pp. 514–42, suggests an incredible number of specific questions, such as: "Have you not secretly rejoiced at the losses, crosses, disgraces, or death of any?" "Have you flattered with your lips, professing more love and respect to any than has been truly in your heart towards them?" After making the most of "lusts" and "wanton imaginings" it concludes: "Have you brought forth fruits meet for repentance, that is . . . more frequent and hearty devotions for your sins of ungodliness; almsgivings for your sins of unrighteousness; fasting for your sins of intemperance? If the tree of repentance bring not forth such fruits, it is neither lively, nor likely to be accepted." These forms were actually used for examining sick people in any condition short of dying. They seem to have been seriously proposed in a sincere belief that this was the best way to help a sick person.

[7] In the new services in the Episcopal Church, nothing remains of the pointed references to sickness and punishment for sin, but it is clear from the choice of New Testament passages, the place given to confession, and the care not to push spiritual healing, that this attitude is still at work. Aside from the brief optional prayer for laying on of hands, one is to pray mostly for the doctors and medical means of treatment, or else for strength and release from sin, and then for health. In the Church of Canada, where the Visitation Office was replaced in 1959 with an excellent set of services for "The Ministry to the Sick," the discussions occasioned by these services show that much the same thing is true there.

A casual reading of the Visitation of the Sick in the 1928 American *Prayer Book* would seem to indicate a belief in spiritual healing. This impression is derived largely from the addition of the Unction of the Sick in the 1928 revision of the *Book of Common Prayer* in the American Episcopal Church. However, this addition is neither historically nor organically related to the Visitation Office. Following the work of Percy Dearmer and

Of course, the words of the service are seldom read any more. Most branches of the Anglican church have displaced this service with a real healing service. But used or unused, it still stands as a major statement of the Christian attitude. Anyone who has done much pastoral work knows how thoroughly this outlook permeates the ways in which people respond when sickness strikes. Whether people express it religiously or medically or sociologically, the question is foremost: "Why did *I* get myself into this? How did *I* make a mistake that was so displeasing to God? How could I have been so sinful, or stupid, or clumsy?" When a child is involved, the parents' reasoning becomes even more clear. I have found this general attitude among most Christians throughout the North America, in Europe, and in a large part of the rest of the Christian world.

This moralistic relationship to God which the sixteenth-century church made so explicit in the Office of Visitation is still at work because it has not yet been replaced by a different point of view. The church has not yet come to rethinking the assumptions underlying this service.

Not long ago the Visitation Office was read as part of a paper on healing to a group of the rectors of large churches in one of the large Episcopal dioceses in this country. The reactions of these clergy were quite typical of modern clergy. None of them had ever used this service. None of them had read it through in many years. Yet a majority still supported its basic theology and were very hesitant about any need to change it.

If this is typical of what the church and its clergy feel about the relation of God and the church to the sick, and if it represents the unspoken view of the average Protestant and Catholic, then the following five conclusions are inevitable.

First, God is responsible for sickness. There is no indication that evil or what might be expressed as the devil or demons may be the cause of any of it. Since there is apparently no other place for it to come from, sickness, along with other adversity and calamity, even though pro-

---

others, the Anglican Bishops at Lambeth approved the idea of healing. Thus the service of unction was added, but in no way integrated into the stripped down version of the English prayer book, which was the basis of the American office. Two quite different ideas about healing are here superimposed upon each other, but molded into one service. Many of the clergy of the Episcopal Church find the visitation office ideas more congenial than those of the service of Unction of the Sick. Only a small number of Episcopal churches used the unction service, or the visitation office, but the basic attitude of most clergy followed that of the visitation office.

duced by material cause and effect must have been sent or allowed by God for a reason. A natural calamity is known in British law as an act of God.

Second, The reason must be that God as Father shows his love to us as human fathers are assumed to do—by giving their children needed correction and chastisement. According to this psychology, which we shall discuss later, the only way to change an individual is by education and punishment. Sickness, then, is seen as a natural punishment administered by God, and we become more dear to God the more he punishes us. In the words of the Visitation Office, those who receive no chastisement—the punishment of illness included—are bastards and not sons of God.

Third, God's purpose in sending sickness is threefold: sickness and death are punishment for breaking the commandments (Deut. 28:22–37; 2 Sam. 6:7–10); sickness shows human beings that they have sinned so that they may repent; and, because it tries human patience, sickness enables the sufferer to grow in faith and become more saintly. In other words, sickness is good—whether given to punish offenders, or to correct people in their evil ways, or to develop their faith—even such destructive diseases as cancer and mental illness.

Fourth, the minister's task then is to save a person's spiritual health and soul no matter what this does to the sufferer's mental or physical condition. There is really no better time for this intervention than when people are seriously ill—when they can be guided into repenting and set on the right track. If these ideas sound more like the arguments of the friends of Job than the spirit of the New Testament, this is not too important, since almost no one in the church articulates them any more. The trouble is, they leave a hollow echo in the depth of most Christians.

Fifth, the Christian minister is left with no healing function. Christianity has no particular mission toward our physical bodies, toward our physical and mental health. With sickness considered a cross sent by God to make people more aware of their defects and help them to become more mature, the church will obviously not undertake to remove it. Individuals are permitted to go to doctors, and churches may provide hospitals and medical missionaries, even though these actions are not quite consistent with this logic. The church itself, however, by its own religious and sacramental actions, certainly cannot oppose God's actions with an actual religious healing ministry. The church offers support and consolation which may have a healing effect, but in a secondary manner.

None of these approaches, however, has appealed very much to the more literal and fundamentalist churches, and so they have taken another tack. In doing so they have arrived at quite a different theory.

Healing and Dispensationalism

The theory of dispensationalism has appeared among the more conservative churches that cherish the historical value of the New Testament and wish to maintain it, but find that certain elements in it, such as the healing ministry, are no longer present in the church today. This can be explained, as they see it, by God's having given a special dispensation for these mighty works only for a particular period and purpose.

Luther faced the same problem when he had to admit that no one raised the dead any more or healed the sick. The day of miracles is past, he concluded, and the real gift of the Holy Spirit is to enlighten scripture, for "now that the apostles have preached the Word and have given their writings, and nothing more than what they have written remains to be revealed, no new and special revelation or miracle is necessary."[8] Or, in Calvin's words, "The gift of healing disappeared with the other miraculous powers which the Lord was pleased to give for a time, that it might render the new preaching of the gospel for ever wonderful. Therefore, even were we to grant that anointing was a sacrament of those powers which were then administered by the hands of the apostles, it pertains not to us, to whom no such powers have been committed."[9]

The influence of these two men can hardly be stressed too much. Practically all Protestant theology proceeds from one or the other of them. Whatever reason they had for rejecting miracles—whether they were reacting to an emphasis in the medieval church, or simply incorporating the views of Thomistic Scholasticism that had no place for divine intervention, or perhaps responding to the first whispers of so-

---

[8] *Sermons on the Gospel of St. John*, chapters 14–16, *Luther's Works*, 24:367. Although in the end Luther added another view of the experience of healing (see pp. 233 and 221–22), this did not happen until late in his life. In these earlier sermons, the sixteenth-century attitude toward healing and miracles is expressed with a vehemence and color which few other writers displayed. In fact, the same spirit is sometimes found in them as in the contemporary English Office of Visitation to the Sick. Luther expressed two attitudes towards healing. He never reconciled them, and the churches that were founded on his ministry followed the one more congenial to the worldview prevalent from the 1600s through the 1800s.

[9] John Calvin, *Institutes of the Christian Religion* IV.18 (1953), 2:636.

phisticated humanism—makes little difference. Calvin and Luther alike saw healing as a dispensation given only to early Christians, and the matter was settled for later orthodox Protestants. The fact that the church fathers up to Aquinas, as well as the Orthodox churches up to the present, had a different point of view was either unknown to them or not considered important.

The thinking of these Reformation giants has been continued in a refined way by that modern giant of theology, Karl Barth. More careful than either Luther or Calvin, he has not denied or affirmed the healing ministry for today. Instead, in the third volume of *Church Dogmatics, The Doctrine of Creation,* Barth presented the great German healer J. C. Blumhardt in a very positive light, particularly by comparison with Mrs. Eddy. But when he came to consider how the Holy Spirit and the gifts of the Spirit act in humans, he could see no real function for the spirit except to open our minds to understand and accept the original Biblical revelation.[10] Healing was dismissed by neglect rather than by denial. In his *Epistle to the Romans,* Barth makes no comment on verses 15:18–19 in which Paul writes that he preaches the gospel through "signs" and "wonders"—translations of the Greek words often used for the healing ministry.

For a long time this conclusion remained more or less implicit among Protestants. Most people simply accepted that there were two parts to God's history; that miraculous events like healing had happened in one of them, but would not happen again. It was assumed that no intelligent Christian of our age would encourage an interest in such things.

I had my first introduction to dispensationalism when I was ten years old. In a first flush of religious enthusiasm I read a simplified version of the Acts of the Apostles. I was entranced; this was better than my beloved *Wizard of Oz.* I went to my mother, the daughter and granddaughter of reformed ministers, and asked why Christians didn't do such things anymore. I was given the straight dispensational answer. God allowed such marvels to get the church started but once it was well established he removed this power. To my ears it sounded as if God baited a hook in order to get the church started and then took

---

[10] Barth's understanding of the work of the Holy Spirit is clearly shown in his discussions in *Church Dogmatics* (1936–1969), in various volumes, as follows: 1, *The Doctrine of the Word of God,* pt. 1, sec. 12.1, 526 ff.; 2, *The Doctrine of God,* pt. 2, secs. 33.1 and 34.3, 105–6, 118, and 249–50; 3, *The Doctrine of Creation,* pt. 4, secs. 54.3 and 55.1, 320–22 and 369–73 (including the discussion of Blumhardt); 4, *The Doctrine of Reconciliation,* pt. 1, 64.1 and 2, 648–49 and 666 ff.; pt. 2, 64.4 and 68.4, 320 ff., 648–49, and 825–28.

away the bait. I put the Bible aside and did not look at it again until I went to seminary thirteen years later. I was not interested in a God who acted this way.

But in time some serious questions were raised, and it became necessary to examine just what the church did mean by its rejection of miracles in current experience. One of these early formulations is found in a little volume from England, *The Silence of God*, written about the end of the last century by Sir Robert Anderson. In it he stated:

The dispensation of Law and covenant and promise—the distinctive privileges of the favoured people—was marked by the public display of Divine power upon earth. But the reign of grace has its correlative in the life of faith. Ours is the higher privilege, the greater blessedness of those "who have not seen and yet have believed." And walking by faith is the antithesis of walking by sight. If "signs and wonders" were vouchsafed to us, as in Pentecostal days, faith would sink to a lower lever, and the whole standard and character of the discipline of Christian life would by changed. The sufferings of Paul denote a higher faith than "the mighty deeds" of his earlier ministry. Not until miracles had ceased, and he had entered on the path of faith as we now tread it, was it revealed to him that his life was to be "a Pattern to them that should afterwards believe."[11]

In the end, when some quite intelligent Christians did become interested and actually involved in a healing ministry, taking the meaning of the New Testament stories seriously, the theory of dispensationalism was ready for use in specific rejection of miracles of healing.[12]

Probably the most specific explanation of dispensationalism in relation to healing was set down by Dr. Wade Boggs in 1956. His work, *Faith Healing and the Christian Faith*, is an excellent study of the difficulties raised for the practice of a healing ministry within the framework of modern orthodox Protestant Christianity. By sticking logically and consistently to the point of view that faith healing has no place in the modern Christian church, Dr. Boggs opens up a great many of the problems that must be faced.

His thesis is basically this: there is no doubt that Jesus spent a large portion of his ministry healing the sick, and it is also clear that the

---

[11] Sir Robert Anderson, *The Silence of God* (1952), pp. 153–54.

[12] Although the idea of divine dispensations is an old one theologically, the term *dispensationalism* has come into use quite recently and is not always employed in this sense. The theory of a Christian dispensation of grace is used by Pentecostal writers to signify that, from the founding of the church on, tongues, healing, and other gifts of the Holy Spirit have been available to all Christian believers. One of the basic differences between Pentecostal and fundamentalist thinking is the interpretation given to the word *dispensation*.

apostles healed the sick in both body and mind. But this was only a dispensation for the period of the New Testament. God permitted these healings to take place in order to establish the Christian church; once the reality of the new faith had been demonstrated, the dispensation was withdrawn. Thus the healing ministry, being given only for a special period, has no application to our time. And since the healing ministry of Jesus was given mainly to establish his message and to prepare the church to evangelize it, healing was not meant to relate to our situation. Even the apostles, Boggs remarks, made use of oil—the best medicinal agent available to them, which was partly responsible for their effectiveness.

Dr. Boggs points up the fact that in recent years most of the emphasis on religious healing has come from fringe groups about which there is reason to be skeptical. Christian Science (and Mrs. Eddy is certainly a controversial figure) is one example. New Thought with its dubious ancestry in the theory and practice of animal magnetism is another. The Pentecostal churches with their enthusiastic practices and disregard for the laws of hygiene form yet another class, and he discusses such figures as Oral Roberts, Little David, Aimee Semple McPherson, and others. The implication is that, because the ministry of healing has sometimes been associated with ridiculous practices and foolish persons, therefore that ministry is itself ridiculous.

On the practical side, Boggs calls attention to the tragic consequences that sometimes occur when faith healing takes the place of accepted medical practices. He deals specifically with the fact that people have died as a result of their refusal to have a doctor because this was against the belief of their sect. In addition, the connections seen in the Old Testament between sickness and sin and between sickness and God's displeasure are discussed at length, as well as Paul's mention of a thorn in his side, which is the only New Testament passage given much emphasis. All in all, the consistency of approach in the book allows it to state some difficult problems clearly and well.

The same approach has been brought up to date in a recently published book, *The Seduction of Christianity*, by David Hunt and T. A. McMahon. The authors state that any use of psychology or imagery is "shamanism" and not genuine Christian faith. Agnes Sanford, Robert Wise, Mother Teresa, Brother Lawrence, and the author of this book are analyzed as examples of Christians seduced by shamanism. The authors seem to be caught up in a worldview that has no place for God working in the world of today.

These are much the same problems as were faced by the American Lutheran Church in 1962, with the result that its two and a half million members were warned to steer clear of religious healing. A committee of doctors, ministers, and theologians appointed by the church looked very carefully at the "religious quackery" practiced by certain faith healers. Their report made three specific charges: faith healers often have desire enough for money and personal power to exploit human desperation; they ignore the God-given gift of proven scientific methods; and they generally blame their own failures on the sick person's lack of faith and so endanger the spiritual life of many. For these and certain theological reasons the committee concluded that, while God does sometimes perform miraculous cures, these should not be sought, since "it cannot be assumed that, because of Christ's victory in their lives, Christians can expect healing effects not available to other people."[13]

Unquestionably dispensationalism has faced a difficult problem. It has taken the New Testament seriously and rejected any ministry of religious healing to the sick in mind or body. The truth is, spiritual healing, whether within the church or by individuals outside it, is still not a familiar event in modern life, nor does the average person feel at all capable of it.

Existential Theology and Healing

From the same starting point, current religious philosophers have taken quite a different path to arrive at an even more conclusive interpretation of the whole problem. Philosophically the church has found itself in an equally tight spot. Liberal theology in the nineteenth century was bedded down, seemingly complacently, between the idealism of Hegel and the scientific naturalism of Darwin. But this was a crowded bed. It did not leave much room for human individuality or spiritual worth, and it was soon under severe attack from Kierkegaard on one side and Nietzsche on the other. Unfortunately neither of these thinkers was quite equipped for the role; but they provided thought at the right time, and it is to Kierkegaard and Nietzsche that many religious philosophers have turned in the effort to find some reasonable base for Christian faith in the sophisticated modern world. As a result, the two

---

[13] *Anointing and Healing: Statement*, adopted by the adjourned meeting of the 1960 convention of the United Lutheran Church in America, June 25–27, 1962, Detroit, Mich., p. 23.

schools of thinking which came to the fore—Christian existentialism and the "God is dead" movement—both make a complete case against Christian healing. They find no more place for it than did naturalism or Hegelian idealism.

Christian existentialism joins the ideas of Kierkegaard and the method of Hegel with the philosophy of Husserl.[14] For the followers of Husserl—Heidegger, Jaspers, Sartre, Marcel, Merleau-Ponty—nothing is real but the present moment of existence. Existentialism discards any idea of supernatural nonphysical reality existing apart from personal psychic material. It questions the value of history, and accepts as axiomatic a scientific understanding of the world as a closed and inevitably physical system. The course of nature cannot be broken into or interrupted by any powers beyond "existence"; instead meaning comes to human beings as they authentically live in this immediate, conscious situation. They then discover the ground of their being.

Kierkegaard also made it quite clear that the supernatural is beyond the historian's province and thus irrelevant in Christian thought. Only Christ who is known only paradoxically is of value, not Christ the healer.[15] Kierkegaard saw little of value to be found in the history of Jesus of Nazareth. Husserl followed much the same view in his discussion of mythical-religious ideas as opposed to scientific and theoretical ones. Husserl's statement—ex cathedra and without evidence—was that there is no value to the religious belief that higher powers can influence human life in this space-time existence.[16]

One large segment of Continental theology has accepted this point of view and tried to interpret the Christian message in these terms. Bonhoeffer, Tillich, and Bultmann were the leaders in this thinking, while Bishop Robinson and the early Bishop Pike popularized it in England and the United States. And so this has become a widely accepted way of thinking in Christian academic circles today.

This theology is quite satisfied that there is no basis for Christian healing in the known world. It would be a typical example of intervention into the natural order by supernatural powers, a breakthrough that changes the foregone conclusion. Bultmann, who is the cleverest and most consistent representative of this school, views the gospel accounts

---

[14] Husserl's philosophy, which he called phenomenology, stresses the careful description of phenomena in all domains of experience without regard to traditional epistemological questions.

[15] Søren Kierkegaard, *Training in Christianity* (1944), pp. 9–39.

[16] Edmund Husserl, *Phenomenology and the Crisis of Philosophy* (1965), pp. 169–172.

of healing as "mythology." These events, he holds, did not take place in actual fact, but were created by the faith of the early Christian community. Even the resurrection experience was a result of faith rather than a fact in the strictest sense.

As Bultmann expresses it,

The whole conception of the world which is presupposed in the preaching of Jesus as in the New Testament generally is mythological; i.e., the conception of the world as being structured in three stories, heaven, earth and hell; the conception of the intervention of supernatural powers in the course of events; and the conception of miracles, especially the conception of the intervention of supernatural powers in the inner life of the soul, the conception that men can be tempted and corrupted by the devil and possessed by evil spirits. This conception of the world we call mythological because it is different from the conception of the world which has been formed and developed by science since its inception in ancient Greece and which has been accepted by all modern men.[17]

In order for modern people to accept the Christian message, the *kerygma*, Bultmann finds it necessary to demythologize the early Christian documents. Only then can we appreciate Jesus Christ and experience the power of the early Christian community.

From this point of view all angels and demons, all extrasensory perceptions (for which there is now good scientific evidence), the experiences of prophecy and tongues, the value of dreams and visions, as well as every account of healing the demon-possessed and the physically ill, must simply be rejected. They did not happen as such. Obviously, since they did not happen then, there is no reason to believe that they happen now. If we believe that they do, or that they should, it is because we are still under the domination of a "mythological" point of view which is untenable in the modern world. Christian healing, therefore, has no place in today's Christianity, which is dealing with people where they are. It need not be considered, and any modern accounts of it are probably distortions of fact.

This point of view was carried to its logical conclusion in the radical theology of the "God is dead" movement. Hamilton, Altizer, and Van Buren did much of the talking for this school, which leaned heavily on Nietzsche.

Obviously, with God no longer active in the world, the basis for any spiritual reality of healing no longer existed either. It does not make much difference whether divine healing ever did exist, since there are

---

[17] *Jesus Christ and Mythology* (1958), p. 15.

no longer any terms in which this could be discussed. Religion—aside from direct activism, no longer directed by God—is a matter of waiting for the silent God to repeat himself once more.[18]

A Clean Sweep

Certainly most Christian thinking, both Catholic and Protestant, was been swept clean of any idea of Christian healing.[19] On the one hand the successes of medicine have made it unnecessary, and on the other, modern theology has made any belief in it untenable. First of all, the church has accepted the necessity of dealing with the natural world on its own natural, material terms. Then there has been an acceptance of sickness as a part of that world, put there by God. Dispensationalism has found a way to divide this world so that healing, once seen as one of the greatest divine gifts, no longer seems needed or even wholesome. Finally, most modern theology has made clear in ample reasoning why it did not happen at all.

Meanwhile the churches have gone on finding ways to adjust to a religion without the expectation of healing or other experiences of that nature. For a long time just talking about the nonmaterial soul and its salvation for a nonmaterial heaven was sufficient. To support this emphasis material things were produced. Hospitals were built to heal the sick by modern scientific methods, some hospitals without even a resident chaplain. Churches went on constructing buildings and conducting campaigns for money using modern business techniques. They went into public relations and advertising, emphasizing numbers and attendance, and even made use of billboards like the one picturing a beautiful little white church, with well-dressed parents and children and a caption two feet high: *It Is Smart to Go to Church.* Now churches have added television ministry and its problems to the list.

But today the awareness of huge dilemmas in our world has developed almost concurrently with a theology which has room only for a direct, outer materialistic way of solving difficulties. To find some more effective approach to people's problems, and something really to show for its morality, the church turned to social action. The emphasis then

---

[18] The historical development and present-day significance of these schools of thought are discussed in detail in my book, *Encounter with God* (1987).

[19] Thomist theology, once the basis for the official Roman Catholic position, is discussed in Chapter Nine. The new attitude toward healing developed during Vatican II is discussed in Chapter Ten. Process theology to which we shall refer later also has no place for spiritual healing.

was on the picket line or political activity, on meeting people and problems "just as they are." Religious healing does not fit in with either of
these atmospheres. It is neither smart nor social action-oriented—nor,
in fact, generally considered *possible*—and so is ignored by practically
the whole modern official Christian community. However, in the last
fifteen years the human psyche and spirit have received a new emphasis. If God can touch the human psyche, God can touch the body as
well, and both psychological and physical healing become a religious
possibility.

Let us take a fresh and honest look at the cultures that lie behind
our own—Hebrew and Greek as well as Christian—to discover what
they have to say about the value and reality of religious healing. Let us
then see what sense the gospel narrative makes on its own, and what
evidence there is in later and modern experience to bear it out.

CHAPTER 3

Religious Healing in the Ancient World

If we are to assess intelligently and critically the healing practices described in the New Testament and followed in the early church, these events must be seen in relation to the world in which they occurred. For one thing—perhaps strangely—we are so accustomed to the modern idea that healing is good that we forget how peculiarly Christian this idea is. It is surprising to find how much Jesus of Nazareth differed from the thinking of both his Judaic heritage and the Hellenistic world of which he was a part. His religious concern for the physical and mental welfare of women and men represented a departure. Although primitive peoples have always had their rites for relieving illness and pain, although other great faiths, such as Hinduism and Buddhism, have in certain areas developed elaborate rituals and practices dealing with physical health, it is nevertheless true that Jesus spoke and acted from a consistent and well-developed point of view which was new and quite at variance with the mainstream of Judaism and of official Greek and Roman religion.

Yahweh's Visitation

The Old Testament in general gives little thought to attempts to influence God's power over life and death. Deuteronomy 32:39 pretty well summarizes the basic attitude of most of the Old Testament: "It is I who deal death and life; when I have struck it is I who heal (and none can deliver from my hand)." This was essentially the same thing Yahweh is reported to have affirmed to Moses earlier, when he asked,

"Who makes him dumb or deaf, gives him sight or leaves him blind? Is it not I, Yahweh?" (Exod. 4:11) This understanding of good and evil was practically the theme of the prophets. "Does misfortune come to a city if Yahweh has not sent it?" Amos demanded (3:6), while in Isaiah 45:7 it was Yahweh who declared: "I make good fortune and create calamity, it is I, Yahweh, who do all this." God, the giver of all good things, was seen equally as the dispenser of misfortune and pain, including sickness of all kinds.

The hostile and destructive reactions of Yahweh did not always have a reason that human beings could understand morally, and strange disasters occurred. Jacob came away lame from wrestling with the angel (of Yahweh) the night before he was to meet Esau on his journey home (Gen. 32:32). Even more curious was the story of Moses coming directly from his encounter at the burning bush, when "Yahweh came to meet him and tried to kill him," and his wife interfered. Zipporah cut off the foreskin of their son and touched it to Moses' feet, and God let him live (Exod. 4:24–26). David was so displeased and fearful at seeing Uzziah struck down for merely steadying the ark as they were taking it to Jerusalem that he changed his plans and left it outside the citadel (2 Sam. 6:7–10; 1 Chron. 13:10–13). But unlike these events, sickness was mostly seen as God's rebuke for human sin.

Until very late in the history of Judaism there was so limited a conception of the afterlife that any reward or punishment coming to the individual had to be seen here and now. The shadowy existence of Sheol, or the Pit, was certainly no recompense for the disappointments of this life; as the psalmists reminded Yahweh on so many occasions, there was no praise for God from there. In addition, the dead human body was vile and unclean.[1] Since God's goodness had to show in this life if it was to be felt at all, human beings were led to overvalue this world and its immediate rewards and punishments. In the book of Deuteronomy this point of view is clearly and consistently developed. Health and wealth are the rewards of God, and sickness, poverty, and misfortune were divine punishments.

From the beginning the law went into detail about the kind of disease Yahweh would send upon those who did not live by his covenant. In Leviticus consumption, fever, and pestilence were enumerated, along with a variety of other penalties (26:16, 25), and in Deuteronomy the list was greatly extended and in the King James version colorful: "Yahweh will strike you down with Egyptian boils, with swellings in

---

[1] Even to come near a corpse could produce uncleanness in the living (Lev. 21:1–2).

the groin, with scurvy and the itch for which you will find no cure. Yahweh will strike you down with madness, blindness, distraction of mind, until you grope your way at noontide like a blind man groping in the dark, and your steps will lead you nowhere" (28:27–29). In fact, there was really no end to the ailments Yahweh could produce for the benefit of people who did not obey the letter of the Law. Besides these, burning fever, inflammation, all the diseases dreaded in Egypt, and every sickness "not mentioned in the Book of this Law" were promised in payment for sin (Deut. 28:22–61).

The connection between sickness and sin was borne out by the history. Beginning in Genesis, Pharaoh's whole household was struck down by severe plagues because Sarah was taken into his palace (12:17). When Abimelech unwittingly planned to take Sarah, Yahweh made all the women of his household barren (20:18). Because Onan wasted his ability to procreate when it was needed, Yahweh caused him to die as Er had for his offense (38:9–10). The plagues the Egyptians suffered for their hardness of heart included physical illness and ended with the death of their first-born (Exod. 9:8–10, 12:29). For her slander of Moses, Miriam was stricken with leprosy (Num. 12:10), and the same disease was inflicted on Gehazi for his avarice (2 Kings 5:26–27). When quail were provided for the Israelites in the wilderness, their gluttony angered Yahweh so much that he sent a plague from which many of them died (Num. 11:33).

After the Philistines captured the ark of God, wherever it was taken the townspeople suffered from tumors and were only relieved when the ark had been sent on its way (1 Sam. 5:6, 6:1–12). Because of his temerity in taking a census of the people, David was given a choice between famine, conquest, and plague. He accepted the last, and seventy thousand people died in Israel before God took pity on the country (2 Sam. 24:10–15; 1 Chron. 21:7–14). There is certainly no question how sickness was looked upon in this major strand of the Old Testament; it was sent by Yahweh to punish people for breaking the ritualistic or moral law.[2] Since the sick were tainted, no person could be a priest

---

[2] There are many more historical references to God's power to punish and direct people by striking them with sickness. For instance, Moses' hand was turned leprous and then restored (Exod. 4:6–7). Yahweh's angels struck blind the people who were threatening Lot's house (Gen. 19:11). Yahweh threatened the people of Israel with pestilence when they were rebelling against Moses and Aaron, struck down a few and then many, and later inflicted plague upon them when they turned to Baal of Peor (Num 14:11–12, 36–37, 17:12–15, 25:3–9, 17–18, 31:16). The seventy sons of Jeconiah were struck down because they did not rejoice at the return of the ark (1 Sam. 6:19). Yahweh determined the death of Jeroboam's child in order to wipe out the house of the unfaithful king (1

before Yahweh who was deformed or ill. Leviticus 21:18–23 is very clear:

. . . no man must come near [to make a food offering to God] if he has an infirmity such as blindness or lameness, if he is disfigured or deformed, if he has an injured foot or arm, if he is a hunchback or a dwarf, if he has a disease of the eyes or of the skin, if he has a running sore, or if he is a eunuch . . . he must not go near the veil or approach the altar, because he has an infirmity, and must not profane my holy things; for it is I, Yahweh, who have sanctified them.

Sickness represented a breach between Yahweh and the individual. Those assigned to be priests were no longer worthy to approach holy things once illness or physical handicap had shown them to be profaned by sin, or if they had touched a corpse.

This theory of illness was expressed in several ways in the Psalms. In those that cry to Yahweh for deliverance from enemies and foreign adversaries, sickness is included as one of the ills that seem to come from the Lord himself. Psalms 6, 22, 38, 39, 88, and 102 all express this despair about illness, praying for deliverance. Then there are the Psalms that call down a curse upon one's enemies, in which there are imprecations for disease as well as all other ills. In addition, Psalm 101 clearly spells out the thinking of Deuteronomy in theory, while 78 and 106 outline it in terms of history.

Throughout the book of Proverbs this basic theory runs like a recurring theme, warning that illness and misfortune follow upon sin—for example, from Proverbs 3:7–8 and 11–12:

Do not think of yourself as wise,
    fear Yahweh and turn your back on evil:
health-giving, this, to your body,
    relief to your bones.
My son, do not scorn correction from Yahweh,
    do not resent his rebuke;
for Yahweh reproves the man he loves,
    as a father checks a well-loved son.

Kings 14:10–14). Because he consulted Baalzebub, Ahaziah was refused healing by Yahweh (2 Kings 1:16). In answer to Elisha's prayer Yahweh struck the enemy blind and later restored their sight (2 Kings 6:18–20). Even though he had done what was pleasing to Yahweh, the king Uzziah was struck with leprosy (2 Kings 15:3–5). The later editors considered that this had happened because of his pride (2 Chron. 26:16–20). Sennacharib's army was struck down in the night by the angel of Yahweh (2 Kings 19:35; 2 Chron. 32:21; Isa. 37:36). For deserting Yahweh, Jehoram was struck down by an incurable disease of the bowels (2 Chron. 21:14–15).

Again and again one is told that to follow wisdom and the law will bring health and long life, while to do otherwise will result in misery, misfortune, sickness, and death.

Behind This Emphasis

Back of this concern with the disciplinary effect of disease rather than with healing were two most important factors. First was the stress upon the group. In much of the Old Testament there was so much emphasis upon the people of Israel as a whole that what happened to the individual was a secondary matter. For this reason the sin of David, for instance, was visited upon the whole of the people, and the Philistines all paid for the sin of their leaders in seizing the ark of Yahweh. Only in the later developments of the Old Testament, in Ezekiel and after, are individuals responsible for their own sins. Up to that time one had to suffer collective guilt as a matter of course.

The other principal reason for neglect of individual healing was the fact that any idea of a principal of evil or evil spirits as the cause of sickness and harm was rejected. This belief was common among most peoples at the time of the early Hebrews. Both the Egyptians and the Babylonians held that sickness resulted from the demonic ill will of various gods or evil spirits. The Persians with their well-developed dualism looked on disease as one activity of the powers of darkness. In the Vedic writings it is sometimes difficult to decide whether a noun refers to a sickness or to the demon who caused it, so closely are the two related. But much of the Old Testament was an attempt to bring the people of Israel to a worship of Yahweh alone, who was seen as the sole source of both good and evil, of sickness as well as health.

Demons had no place in the Old Testament, and its angels were merely messengers to carry out Yahweh's will. Any idea of spiritual powers independent of Yahweh in their action came only in the postexilic time.[3] Then the ideas of the Persians and Babylonians and Egyptians finally made inroads upon Hebrew thinking. Until this happened, there was no source from which sickness could come except Yahweh. And since real healing could come only from him, even Hebrew ideas of medicine were quite different in some respects from those found among other peoples.

---

[3] See Rivkah Schärf Kluger's *Satan in the Old Testament* (1967) on the Judaic concept of the origin of evil.

While the secular practice of medicine was discussed in other ancient religious writings, it was barely mentioned in the Old Testament. For instance, the Persians and the Chaldeans recorded the separation of medical practice into surgery, medicinal treatment, and prayer, indicating that all three were considered and discussed. Among Egyptian writings there is at least one long account of the diseases treated, which even goes into the fees received by the physician. But in the Old Testament physicians are hardly mentioned except in a derogatory way. The only reference in the historical records is in connection with the death of King Asa, and here it is made quite clear that Asa died for a good reason. A disease attacked him from head to foot, "and, what is more, he turned in his sickness, not to Yahweh, but to doctors" (2 Chron. 16:12). This is most probably an allusion to pagan physicians, probably the only ones to whom the early Hebrews could turn.

Since secular and religious practices of healing were very closely tied together, it seems clear that both were discouraged among the Hebrews. Those who practiced medical healing were also versed in divination and magic and probably had relations with other gods, and so came in for the same condemnation as the foreign interpreters of dreams. With sickness the direct "gift" of Yahweh, it is hardly logical that such secular means would be considered effective, or that healing of any kind would be much encouraged. For the most part it was spoken of only in connection with the priestly function of cleansing.

In fact, not until the apocryphal book of Ecclesiasticus, probably written in the century after Chronicles (about 190 B.C.), is there any other mention of physicians. In chapter 38 the first fifteen verses are devoted to the doctor. Sensible people will not despise medicines, according to this work, but since healing is a gift from the Most High, they will pay the doctor the honor and the fee that are due him. People are counseled, when sick, to cleanse themselves from sin, offer incense and a gift of fine flour, and also as rich an offering as they can afford, and "then let the doctor take over." Thus the words of wisdom conclude with the cheerful thought: "If a man sins in the eyes of his Maker, may he fall under the care of the doctor."

The same attitude continued to be expressed in the rabbinic schools of later Judaism. In the Mishnah, and also later in the Talmud, we find the conviction that sin is the root cause of illness. Rabbi Johnathan, for one, is quoted as saying: "Plague comes for seven sins, for bloodshed, perjury, unchasity, pride, embezzlement, pitilessness and slander" (*Babylonian Talmud, Arakin 161*). Almost the same thinking is found in *Sing-*

er's Prayer Book, published in London around 1900, which lists the seven kinds of punishment meted out for the seven types of sins.

It is true that there was healing among the Jews in Jesus' time, in spite of the fact that these incidents were looked upon with great suspicion by the rabbis. Still, people sought some relief from their sufferings, and so a form was used in which the healer whispered words adapted from Exodus 15:26: "If you listen carefully to the voice of Yahweh your God and do what is right in his eyes, if you pay attention to his commandments and keep his statutes, I shall inflict on you none of the evils that I inflicted on the Egyptians, for it is I, Yahweh, who give you healing." The main schools of Judaism considered the practice involved here akin to sorcery and magic and forbade it, but the Talmud attests to its use. In several places there are references to the fact that those who employ such measures will have no share in the world to come (*Mishnah 10:1; Babylonian Talmud, Sanhedrin 11 and 101a*). This is certainly consistent with the statement in the Talmud that Jesus was hanged on a tree on the Passover Eve because he practiced sorcery.

This whole attitude thus had its beginning in the teaching of the great prophets who first saw the righteousness of God. They taught a theory that supported a concern for righteousness. Later this teaching became a code in the book of Deuteronomy specifying illness for sin. As later editors who held to this view went through the sacred books, their sharpened pencils pointed up how this moral law was carried out in history. Now and then they did come across people whose lives did not fit the pattern—who were anything but moral, yet still kept their health and wealth—but they slipped over these disconcerting facts as lightly as possible. After all, no one holds onto life and property forever, and the exception only proves the rule. It is not hard to see the origin of the English Office of the Visitation to the Sick, of the idea of Dr. Wade Boggs's careful study or David Hunt's dismissal of healing; all express this Old Testament teaching.[4]

Another Strand

But the amazing thing about the Old Testament in this connection is that the central belief set forth above is not the only one expressed

---

[4] The problem of the authority of biblical revelations is not within the scope of this work. In Willard M. Swartley's *Slavery, Sabbath, Women and War* (1983) the very carefully considered position of the Mennonite Church is presented. The whole body of scripture needs to be evaluated in the light of Jesus' teachings and actions.

in it. Another strand of experience and belief about healing was just as carefully preserved, though it did not become part of the code accepted as directing the people of Israel. There are few areas where the difference between the Old and New Testaments is more marked than in the teaching about healing. The people of Israel took one direction, and yet—here is the greatness of our religious heritage—they took care not to erase from their records the experiences and signs that pointed another way.

Some years ago I was lecturing before a group of physicians interested in the dimensions of religion and faith in the healing process. I gave the above evidence and went on to say that Judaism had no vital place for religious healing. In the question period a rabbi got up and said: "You are correct about the lack of evidence for religious healing in the Old Testament." Then he added, "However, no Jew, not even the most conservative, takes the Old Testament literally. It is interpreted through the Mishnah, the Talmud and other teachers to apply to the present day. Only Christian fundamentalists use it without interpretation." I suggest that Jesus' teachings in the New Testament gives Christians the basis for their interpretation of healing in the Old Testament.

This other strand of belief about healing found in the Old Testament is not as wide or obvious as the teaching accepted by Hebrew leaders. It is expressed in certain healing stories, in some of the Psalms, in the hopes of certain passages of Isaiah, and in the gigantic protest of the book of Job. This element is the one Jesus followed, the base from which he acted.

As we have already seen, in the Old Testament there was no question, in theory, that Yahweh could heal. In several places remarkable instances were recorded. Some of the most touching and best-remembered stories are those in which children were given to women who were barren. Though barrenness was often considered the result of divine disfavor (Gen. 20:18, 30:2), a child was given as a particular gift of God to Sarah (Gen. 18:10, 14), to Manoah's wife, the mother of Samson (Judg. 13:5, 24), to Hannah, the mother of Samuel (1 Samuel 1:19–20), and to the Shunammite woman (2 Kings 4:16–17). There are also the beautiful stories of both Elijah and Elisha healing a child, which in so many ways carry the quality of the later healings of Jesus. No sin is imputed to the child or its mother, and these are acts of compassion through the power of Yahweh (1 Kings 17:17–23; 2 Kings 4:18–37). Elisha's cleansing Namaan of leprosy is another example of healing where no sin is attributed to the sick man (2 Kings 5:1–14).

There was also a strange story of raising from the dead, which took place just after the death of Elisha and involves the touching of relics, which in the Middle Ages became so prominent a theme. Some men were carrying a body out for burial, and as they came to Elisha's tomb a band of Moabite raiders appeared. The Israelites threw the body into the tomb and ran, and: "The man had no sooner touched the bones of Elisha than he came to life and stood up on his feet" (2 Kings 13:21).

Instances are recounted of healing after the proper sacrifices are made. A bronze serpent was fashioned that saved anyone bitten by the fiery serpents Yahweh sent (Num. 21:9). The Philistines, to obtain healing, delivered to the people of Israel golden models of the tumors and rats Yahweh had inflicted on them (1 Sam. 6:4–5). When Hezekiah prayed, he was saved from the death earlier decided by Yahweh; almost immediately Isaiah knew that Yahweh had relented and had a healing fig poultice placed on the king's ulcer (2 Kings 20:1–7; Isa. 38:1–6, 21). Twice a plague was halted, once by Aaron's act of atonement, again by David's prayer (Num. 16:47–50; II Sam. 24:10–25).

Finally, the apocryphal book of Tobit tells the delightful story of how Tobias, through the power of the angel Raphael, healed his father's blindness and defeated Asmodeus, the demon who was striking down Sarah's husbands.[5] Except for Job, these few are all the references to incidents of healing up to the New Testament. Interesting as the stories are, they are peripheral to the main thought of Hebrew scripture.

Yet the same theme is found scattered through the Psalms and the prophets. In Psalm 103 Yahweh is blessed for healing diseases, and Psalm 91 tells how God protects from all plague. Similar confidence in Yahweh as healer of mind and body and social and political condition is found in Psalms 41, 46, 62, 74, 116, 121, and 147. In certain Psalms, healing power is simply implied; others, like 73 and 94, protest that Yahweh has failed to reward goodness with health and mercy. Hosea also made clear that Yahweh had power to save people from evil—from plagues and death—but did not exercise it because of the people's wickedness (6:1–11, 13:12–15).

Isaiah referred in certain passages to the days of Yahweh when all the ills of humanity would be healed. The dead would rise, the deaf would hear, and the blind would see (26:19, 29:18, 61:1–11).

---

[5] The apocryphal books of the Bible are those found in the early Greek translation, the Septuagint, and not found in the Canonical Hebrew text. The early Christian Church used the Greek translation as its scripture.

Then the eyes of the blind shall be opened,
the ears of the deaf unsealed,
then the lame shall leap like a deer
and the tongues of the dumb sing for joy (35:5–6).

Although the day of Yahweh was seen by some as the end of time, when wrongs would all be righted, in the popular aspirations of the people it was also seen as the day of the Messiah—the one longed for—who would inaugurate the kingdom of heaven. Ezekiel's story of the valley of dry bones (chap. 37) was also an expression of healing. Though told as an allegory, it conveys what Ezekiel apparently knew of the power of Yahweh to heal.

The great protest against the Deuteronomic theory of sickness and healing is found in the story of Job. One of the main purposes of this book was simply to challenge the theory. Job was a righteous man; of this there was no doubt. We are taken into the very court of heaven to discover why he should suffer. He was firm and sincere in his religious profession, but in order to convince Satan of this—Satan, who is seen as one of the Sons of God—Job is overwhelmed with suffering and tragedy, with rebukes and illness.

Because these outer symptoms obviously indicate disfavor with God, Job is treated with scorn by his neighbors and even by children—unthinkable among the Hebrews while an older man was healthy. And so he ends up on the village dump, throwing ashes over his boils and scratching his sores with a potsherd. Even former friends turn upon him and plague him with their judgment, suggesting that he look for sins of which he knows he is not guilty. His wife leaves him with the comforting recommendation that he curse God and die. Unquestionably the reactions of Job's neighbors, children, wife, and friends represent the actual attitude of people in those days toward those struck down by adversity and serious illness. These were signs that people had lost God's favor, usually by their own wickedness. But Job, maintaining his innocence, was in the end justified by Yahweh.

The whole book is a profound discussion of the problem of evil. Job's was a voice crying in the wilderness. So much did later copyists disagree with this presentation and its basic outlook that they altered the text to bring it a little more in line with the orthodox Deuteronomic theory of the origin of suffering and sickness. Thus this strand of teaching was not a final, accepted development of Jewish thought about healing.

This, at any rate, was the strand of belief that Jesus brought forth—the understanding he developed, even though it put him at odds with the official religion of his people. His own orthodox tradition did not have much to offer when it came to creating a new attitude toward sickness and sick human beings. In order not to be naive about Jesus' inspiration in regard to healing, let us look at other possible antecedents very carefully.

Healing in the Hellenistic World

Did Jesus, then, receive the inspiration for his healing ministry as a package from the Hellenistic culture? If Greek paganism is examined carefully, the answer is equally clear: although there is some reason to see a kind of maturity in this culture, healing is not a part of its religious life. The early Greeks and Romans found ways to seek religious healing, just as the Hebrews did. There were several healing cults, including the well-developed cult of Aesculapius, which reached many people. Formal Western medical study undoubtedly had its beginning in the great Hippocratic school of ancient Greece. And as we have shown elsewhere, this school on the island of Cos evolved almost hand in hand with the growth of Aesculapian healing there.[6]

Plato recognized the prime need for curing the soul in order to find real healing of the body, and he also saw the importance of healing as one of the ways in which divine creative energy seizes and possesses human beings. All through the *Dialogues* he variously stressed the necessity of getting at disease by treating the whole person;[7] in the discussion of divine inspiration in the *Phaedrus* he listed healing along with prophecy, art, and love as ways in which he saw the divine breaking through into the physical.[8] It is clear that Plato accepted the kind of healing that came to be experienced in the temples of Aesculapius. But there was little development of this basic understanding until after the

---

[6] See my *God, Dreams, and Revelation* (1974), p. 71; also C. Kerényi, *Asklepios: Archetypal Image of the Physician's Existence* (1959), pp. 47–52.

[7] *Charmides* 156–57, *Symposium* 186, *Timaeus* 87–91, *Republic III* 408. In the *Charmides* Plato wrote: "For all good and evil, whether in the body or in human nature, originates . . . in the soul, and overflows from thence, as if from the head into the eyes. And therefore if the head and body are to be well, you must begin by curing the soul; that is the first thing. And the cure, my dear youth, has to be effected by the use of certain charms, and these charms are fair words; and by them temperance is implanted in the soul, and where temperance is, there health is speedily imparted, not only to the head, but to the whole body. And he who taught me the cure and the charm at the same time added a special direction: 'Let no one,' he said, 'persuade you to cure the head, until he has first given you his soul to be cured by the charm. For this,' he said, 'is the great error of our day in the treatment of the human body, that physicians separate the soul from the body'" (157).

[8] *Phaedrus* 244. Josef Pieper in *Love and Inspiration: A Study of Plato's Phaedrus* (1965) discusses this very important point in Plato's philosophy, pp. 58–65. See also Paul Friedländer's book, *Plato: An Introduction* (1964).

Christian church had appropriated Plato for its own and this implication of his thought was realized.

Greek polytheism made it unnecessary to integrate this insight into a more central place in Greek thinking, and there was no religious basis for it until the joining of Greek thought and primitive Christian experience in the church. With Aristotle, divine healing became impossible because of a metaphysics which rejected any elementary principle of evil in the world, and at the same time eliminated any other realm of reality which could intervene to offer healing. Here again Christianity picked up one strand of a culture and made it an integral factor of a new religious attitude which had its effect on the world for centuries.

In reality, there was only one major difference between the approach to sickness of the Greco-Roman world and that of Judaism. The Greeks looked upon disease as an affliction from the gods, and for the most part considered the sick as unlucky, tainted people to be shunned and avoided, just as did the Jews. But they connected this more with fate or destiny than with sin. The idea of human responsibility to God for moral actions—either as a whole people or later as an individual—was a Judaic one. The Greeks were subject to the gods, but not related to them by agreement or covenant. Thus sickness was seen as a matter more of luck or fate than as punishment for breaking an agreement—for misdoing or sin.

Throughout the literature of ancient Greece and Rome we find the idea that sick people were suffering from the displeasure of the gods. Like Yahweh, the same gods that brought disaster could sometimes turn about and bring healing. But there were only a few minor gods in whose shrines it was appropriate to ask for relief from sickness. There were the cults of Seraphis, Amphiaraus, Trophonios, and particularly Aesculapius.

It is true that the cult of Aesculapius, in particular, attracted many people in the Hellenistic period. The popularity of Aesculapian healing has been thoroughly demonstrated by modern archaeology. Yet there are few references in ancient writings to this cult, and it stood in contrast to the basic religious attitude of that world toward sickness. The temples in which the god was worshiped were strictly places of healing. The sick person came there to sleep in a bed called a "clinic" within the confines of the temple and to ask for a vision or dream from the god to heal him or show him the way to healing. All activity centered around this principal rite of "incubation."

Various symbolic acts seem to have contributed to the healings, such as the sacrifice of small animals in the rotunda near the altar, or in the mysterious labyrinth, at Epidaurus. Ritual bathing and even stadia and gymnasia stressed the importance of the body. One ritual involved harmless snakes viewed as agents of healing power. These snakes are today still the symbol of the medical profession in the caduceus. In great amphitheaters near the temples, drama became part of the ritual, with healing effect. Certainly there was no lack of meaning for the individual in these rites, and it is even suggested that they offered the expectation of a culminating religious experience.[9] Visiting Epidaurus several years ago I was touched by the beauty of the place and by the healing history that took place there. On the whole the Greeks, like the Chinese, went to doctors to maintain wellness but to the shrines for healing.

In fact, the myth of Aesculapius itself reveals a great deal about the place given to healing in Olympian Greek religion. We are told that he was the son of Apollo and the human princess Coronis, who was killed by the sun god because she could not hide from him her desire for a mortal man. Apollo, however, saved his son and entrusted him to the care of Chiron, the wise centaur whom Apollo himself had instructed in the arts. Aesculapius became a favorite pupil because of his preference for the gentle art of healing, and he surpassed his teacher as a physician, reputedly restoring even the dead to life. This drew the anger of the gods, and at Pluto's demand Zeus is said to have unleashed a thunderbolt and killed him.

Aesculapius came to be much honored by men, and in post-Homerian mythology was himself raised from the dead and received among the Olympians, although too late to become an equal of the gods. He remained specifically the healer. While the other gods were not particularly concerned with this, and still used their malicious powers, Aesculapius could be appealed to for relief of human misery. But his power was subject to the higher authority of the other, greater Olympians.

Although his temples were widely popular, as shown by the numerous inscriptions telling of cures, they represent more a split in the Greek mind and culture than a central element of Greek religion. In a later age this classical paganism is well represented by the Emperor Julian, the apostate, who scorned Christianity because it was interested in healing. The period in which Aesculapius became a god, and his temples places of pilgrimage, was also the time in which the intellectual leaders of Greece came to take the Homeric gods less seriously and the people turned from the worship of their fathers to a variety of cults. Plato foresaw this and in his later writings made a bid to stave it off.

---

[9] Kerényi, op.cit., pp. 38–39.

But what he could not fully comprehend was the great need of the people for a religion of caring about the whole person. Healing represented by the Aesculapian and other cults was an eddy alongside the stream of paganism.

Instead, a notion of the dichotomy of mind and body, known as Gnosticism, became one of the important currents of Greek thought. Out of this came a theory of the origin of human beings which held that they had been made when the *nous-psyche* (mind-soul) somehow became entrapped in the grosser body, the *physis*. This material part was nonessential.[10] Later, as Gnosticism matured, the body came to be viewed as positively evil, and salvation was seen as the liberation of the mind-soul from it, so that the valuable part of humans might have freedom and bliss.

And so in Gnosticism a point of view emerged in which healing of the body was clearly an unimportant matter. In some Gnostic asceticism the body was practically destroyed. Until the Council of Nicaea the church fathers were constantly fighting the influence of the Gnostic point of view on Christianity, because its low valuation of the body denied the idea of incarnation and the ministry, death, and resurrection of Jesus. In a later chapter we shall consider how far the Gnostic point of view has crept back into the teaching and practice of the church.

Healing at the Greek shrines was one expression of the longing for a god who cared about the bodies as well as the minds and souls of human beings, a god who was soon to become a reality to them. It is no wonder that these healing cults soon gave way to the vital practices of Jesus of Nazareth, who came among mortals to heal their bodies and minds along with their souls. Nor is it strange that Aesculapian and other shrines were so often transformed into Christian churches in the Greek world.[11]

Starting before the fifth century B.C.E. another point of view developed in which it was believed that certain individuals could mediate spiritual powers, bring back lost souls, and guide people through the experience of death. This has been the form of religion of a vast number

---

[10] An excellent study of this theory of Orphism and its effect upon later Greek thinking is found in Walter Wili, "The Orphic Mysteries and the Greek Spirit," *Papers from the Eranos Yearbooks 2, The Mysteries* (1955): 64–81. This paper draws together the evidence that supports the position above.

[11] Mary Hamilton, *Incubation (or the Cure of Disease in Pagan Temples and Christian Churches)*, pp. 109–10. See also C. A. Meier, *Ancient Incubation and Modern Psychotherapy* (1967), p. 20. Dr. Meier offers evidence of the effectiveness of the practice of incubation (sleeping in these shrines).

of human beings from the earliest days to the present time. The practices of some existing Siberian tribes still reflect the attitudes of this point of view as clearly as any one ethnic group. The mediators are called shamans. The customs of modern American Indians fall into the same category, as they are described by Carlos Castaneda in *The Teachings of Don Juan* and his other books, by John Neihardt in *Black Elk Speaks,* and by Franc Newcomb in *Hosteen Klah,* a description of Navajo healing.[12] The classic study of shamanism is Mircea Eliade's monumental work, *Shamanism.* Another work of the same compass is Violet MacDermot's, *The Cult of the Seer in the Ancient Middle East.* One might even say that in the writings of Plato one finds the philosophical statement of shamanism, of human beings as instruments of divine grace.

When we look at the ministry of Jesus, we see the contrast between his attitude and the official attitudes of Judaism and the Olympic gods. We find that his life and acts, his teaching and practice, are rather akin to a shamanism based on an intimate relationship with a loving god. As we shall see in our study of the early church, those who received the Holy Spirit after Jesus' resurrection were expected to become healing channels of God's love, as Jesus had been. In fact, an important study might be made comparing the ministry of Jesus with that of shamanism, but this is not the place for it.

Those who are taken aback by his healing ministry and would disregard or excise it from the New Testament record or from present-day emulation simply are ignorant of the experiences of healing universally known—and in great numbers—in most forms of shamanism. The shaman is the mediator between the individual and spiritual reality, both good and evil, and because of this the healer of diseases of mind and body. In stepping into his healing role Jesus picks up the prophetic and shamanistic strand of the Old Testament tradition already mentioned. Thus Jesus brings to new focus an aspect of religious life which had been neglected in the official religions of the day.[13]

---

[12] C. G. Jung noted the importance of *Black Elk Speaks* when it first appeared in print in the 1930s. John A. Sanford is conversant with the extensive literature on American Indian shamanism and healing. He deals with this data in *Healing and Wholeness* (1977) and in a novel, *The Song of the Meadowlark* (1986).

[13] See Appendix B where I have discussed two of the recent biblical critics, Norman Perrin and Günther Bornkamm, who support this point of view.

CHAPTER 4

The Unique Healing Ministry of Jesus of Nazareth

Modern medicine has tended to look back to Hippocrates and Galen as the only ancient source and inspiration of modern medical practice. But this presents a very incomplete picture. As one physician pointed out,

It has become traditional to identify modern doctors in spirit with a long line of historic greats reaching back to the impressive Hippocrates. This notable Greek, a veritable pinnacle in ancient medicine, often called the "Father of Medicine," largely set the pattern for current professional attitudes and relationships. But sometimes it is forgotten that medicine owes its greatest debt not to Hippocrates, but to Jesus. It was the humble Galilean who more than any other figure in history bequeathed to the healing arts their essential meaning and spirit. . . . Physicians would do well to remind themselves that without His spirit, medicine degenerates into depersonalized methodology, and its ethical code becomes a mere legal system. Jesus brings to methods and codes the corrective of love without which true healing is rarely actually possible. The spiritual "Father of Medicine" was not Hippocrates of the island of Cos, but Jesus of the town of Nazareth.[1]

Few religious leaders have had more influence on the basic ideas of our modern age then Jesus of Nazareth. The effect of his teaching, his thoughts, is felt not only by nine hundred million avowed Christians but among all peoples touched by Western civilization. Oddly enough, his thinking was in some respects the most materialistic of any of the important religious leaders, particularly in relation to health. The interest Jesus showed in the physical and mental health of human beings

---

[1] J. W. Provonsha, M.D., "The Healing Christ," *Current Medical Digest* (December 1959), p. 3. See Appendix A for Dr. Provonsha's complete article.

was greater than that of any other leader or religious system from Confucius through Hinduism and Buddhism to Islam. There is no doubt about what he thought of the value of healing our minds and bodies or about the way he put it into practice. The source material found in the New Testament is clear and consistent. Let us survey it briefly and then study certain aspects of it in detail.

The New Testament Record of Healing

An honest, unprejudiced reading of the first chapters of the Gospel of Mark shows that the ministry of Jesus was a ministry of preaching, teaching, and healing. Similar passages are found in Luke and Matthew. Jesus proclaimed, or preached, the Good News, the present reality of the kingdom of heaven, now accessible to all people.[2] He *taught* his hearers how to relate their lives to God and the kingdom; his teachings showed them how the various aspects of their thinking, their devotional practice, and their behavior related to the God now breaking into people's lives and into history in a new way. This new insight was interpreted in the religious language then current, the tradition of first century Judaism. And third, he healed: he brought physical and mental health to the sick in body and mind, those with physical affliction and those considered possessed by demons. Nearly one-fifth of the entire gospels is devoted to Jesus' healing and the discussions occasioned by it.[3] This emphasis is by far the greatest given to any one kind of experience in the narrative. It is startling to compare this emphasis on physical and mental healing with the scant attention given to moral healing. Very few examples of moral or ethical transformation are mentioned in

---

[2] The kingdom, as Jesus proclaimed it, may be viewed inwardly as well as eschatologically (as the final state of things). It is true that Jesus and his followers undoubtedly looked for the immediate coming of the kingdom in history. However, the statements about it may also be seen as referring to the kingdom within, or the kingdom breaking through now in history. In other words, eschatology need not refer only to the future; the idea of God acting at present and does not mean that he cannot also act in final things. This understanding of the dual meaning of Jesus' preaching was carefully developed by John A. Sanford as a part of the introduction to *The Kingdom Within* (1970). It was deleted by the original editor as too technical for the general reader. I have published this material as Appendix B in my book, *Afterlife: The Other Side of Dying* (1982). In this material Sanford also shows that this dual vision of the kingdom was the understanding of the great early Greek theologians.

[3] Out of the 3,779 verses in the four gospels, 727 relate specifically to the healing of physical and mental illness and the resurrection of the dead. In addition there are 165 verses that deal in general with eternal life, and also 31 general references to miracles that include healing. Complete lists of these references are found in the appendix of my book, *Encounter with God* (1987).

the gospels. There are the stories of Matthew, Zaccheus, the woman at the well of Sychar, and the woman of Luke 7:37 and John 8:3, which together originate the tradition of Mary Magdalene, and that is about all unless one considers the calling of disciples as examples of moral conversion. A transformation of the apostles occurred at Pentecost after the ascension, but there is little in the gospels which can be described as realization of "authentic being." There may well have been many moral transformations, but they are not recorded. Is it not possible that the belief in Jesus' moral healing has risen to take the place of those healings which we have been allowed to ignore?

Instead we find that everywhere Jesus went he functioned as a religious healer. Forty-one distinct instances of physical and mental healing are recorded in the four gospels (there are seventy-two accounts in all, including duplications), but this by no means represents the total. Many of these references summarize the healings of large numbers of people. Those described in detail are simply the more dramatic instances of this activity of Jesus—certainly an extensive ministry, to say the least.

It is also clear that Jesus sent his disciples out to continue this basic ministry (Mark 6:7–13; Matt. 10:5–10; Luke 9:1–6). The book of Acts records how well they carried out this commission. It is difficult to see how Bultmann, and many who follow him, can eliminate this entire ministry on theological and philosophical grounds by calling it mythology. It is particularly difficult when we realize, on one hand, that these stories form one of the earliest levels of the gospel tradition from the point of view of form criticism, and on the other, what a close relation modern medicine has shown between psyche and body and how much they interact with one another. In chapters ten and eleven we shall deal with this subject in more detail.

The importance of this ministry is expressed in a very striking way in Ethel Bank's booklet, *The Great Physician Calling*. This is simply a collection of healing stories from the gospels using the arrangement of Percy Dearmer's book, *Body and Soul* (1909).[4] Mrs. Banks combined sto-

---

[4] This tabulation of the healing works described in the gospels is as follows, arranged in the order listed by Dearmer, pp. 137–38.

No.	Healing	Matthew	Mark	Luke	John	Method
1.	Man with unclean spirit		1:23	4:33		Exorcism, word
2.	Peter's mother-in-law	8:14	1:30	4:38		Touch, word; prayer of friends

ries that obviously tell of the same healing, listing them as one instance. As one reads account after account in succession they demolish doubt

No.	Healing	Matthew	Mark	Luke	John	Method
3.	Multitudes	8:16	1:32	4:40		Touch, word; faith of friends
4.	Many demons		1:39			Preaching, exorcism
5.	A leper	8:2	1:40	5:12		Word, touch; leper's faith and Christ's compassion
6.	Man sick of the palsy	9:2	2:3	5:17		Word; faith of friends
7.	Man's withered hand	12:9	3:1	6:6		Word; obedient faith
8.	Multitudes	12:15	3:10			Exorcism, response to faith
9.	Gerasene demoniac	8:28	5:1	8:26		Word, exorcism
10.	Jairus' daughter	9:18	5:22	8:41		Word, touch; faith of father
11.	Woman with issue of blood	9:20	5:25	8:43		Touching His garment in faith
12.	A few sick folk	13:58	6:5			Touch (hindered by unbelief)
13.	Multitudes	14:34	6:55			Touch of His garment, friend's faith
14.	Syrophoenician's daughter	15:22	7:24			Resp. to mother's prayer, faith
15.	Deaf and dumb man		7:32			Word, touch; friend's prayer
16.	Blind man (Gradual healing)		8:22			Word, touch; friends' prayer
17.	Child with evil spirit	17:14	9:14	9:38		Word, touch; faith of father
18.	Blind Bartimaeus	20:30	10:46	18:35		Word, touch, compassion; faith
19.	Centurion's servant	8:5		7:2		Resp. to master's prayer, faith
20.	Two blind men	9:27				Word, touch; men's faith
21.	Dumb demoniac	9:32				Exorcism
22.	Blind and dumb demoniac	12:22		11:14		Exorcism
23.	Multitudes	4:23		6:17		Teaching, preaching, healing
24.	Multitudes	9:35				Teaching, preaching, healing
25.	Multitudes	11:4		7:21		Proof of John Bapt. in prison
26.	Multitudes	14:14		9:11	6:2	Compassion, resp. to need
27.	Great multitudes	15:30				Faith of friends
28.	Great multitudes	19:2				
29.	Blind and lame in temple	21:14				
30.	Widow's Son			7:11		Word, compassion

about this ministry, just as a jackhammer demolishes a concrete road. One begins to realize how much of the life of Christ was given to caring for the physical and mental ills of people and how fully he expected his disciples to go on with the same work.

There is even evidence outside the gospel narrative for this aspect of Jesus' ministry. In the *Talmud (Sanhedrin 43a)* we find the tradition that Jesus of Nazareth was hanged on a tree on Passover Eve because he practiced sorcery and that he was destroyed because he healed by calling upon evil forces rather than upon God. This tradition is confirmed in Mark 3:22.[5] Wherever Jesus went he was simply besieged by people who wanted to be healed. His family tried to seize him, saying that he was beside himself, and the Pharisees claimed he was possessed by Beelzebub and that it was by the prince of the demons that he cast out demons. Even his opponents did not contest the fact that Jesus healed; they only tried to cast doubts upon the agency through which he did it.

Jesus' ministry of healing is certainly in line with the constant emphasis in his teachings upon compassion and caring about one's neighbor. Certainly it is not out of character with that teaching. This stress on the importance of *agape*, love, is a most basic aspect of his teaching. One of the most concrete ways of expressing that love is through concern about another's physical and emotional condition, and the removal of torturing infirmities, physical hindrances, and the horror of mental or emotional illness. The story of the good Samaritan is an excellent case in point, whatever the means of healing. Where sickness was so prevalent and so little was actually known about curing it, healing was

No.	Healing	Matthew	Mark	Luke	John	Method
31.	Mary Magdalene & others			8:2		Exorcism
32.	Woman bound by Satan			13:10		Word, touch
33.	Man with dropsy			14:1		Touch
34.	Ten lepers			17:11		Word; faith of the men
35.	Malchus' ear			22:49		Touch
36.	Multitudes			5:15		
37.	Various persons			13:32		Exorcism, and not stated
38.	Nobleman's son				4:46	Word; father's faith
39.	Impotent man				5:2	Word; man's faith
40.	Man born blind				9:1	Word, touch
41.	Lazarus				11:1	Word

[5] Parallel passages are found in Matt. 12:24 and Luke 11:15.

an incomparable gift. People were touched by Jesus' ministry. It was a sign that God cared about people in their misery. The healings of Jesus, far from conflicting with his preaching of the kingdom of God, were instead referred to as a direct evidence of it. He stated specifically that his healing was a sign that the kingdom of heaven was breaking forth into this world. In answer to the charge that he was a sorcerer, he replied in Matthew 12:27–28, "And if it is through Beelzebub that I cast out devils, through whom do your own experts cast them out? Let them be your judges, then. But if it is through the Spirit of God that I cast devils out, then know that the kingdom of God has overtaken you."[6]

In much the same way Jesus answered the disciples of John when they came to inquire if he were the one who was to come or if they should look for another. By quoting the essence of Isaiah 35:5 and 61:1, he pointed to scripture and the messianic hope of both first and second Isaiah in these words: "Go back and tell John what you hear and see; the blind see again, and the lame walk, lepers are cleansed, and the deaf hear, and the dead are raised to life and the Good News is proclaimed to the poor" (Matt. 11:4–5).

According to this answer, the healing ministry was one basic credential and evidence that he was the messiah, the long-awaited messenger of the kingdom of heaven. His healings were the sign needed by John, who languished in prison at the time, to believe that Jesus was indeed the one who was to usher in the new age. The message was given to comfort John, to make him realize that he had not preached and baptized in vain. This aspect of Jesus' ministry was thus certainly not considered incidental or unimportant by the evangelists. They set down as one of his basic ideas that the power of God had broken through into our world and that physical and mental illness, the work of the power of Evil, were therefore being put to flight. In the final coming of the kingdom they would be eliminated entirely; Evil would be utterly defeated.

This theological attitude of Jesus marks one of the basic differences between the healings of Jesus and those in other ancient cultures, particularly in the Greek world. The Greek god Aesculapius was simply one divine power among many, a god who happened to be interested in healing. If Jesus saw himself as the messiah, then he represented God's essential nature and was God's specific messenger, and his healings therefore sprang from the essential nature of God. Sickness and demon possession were considered prime evidences of evil in the

---

[6] Quotations of Scripture are from the Jerusalem Bible unless otherwise noted.

world. By dealing with them as the messiah, the agent of God, Jesus laid the attitude of God toward sickness out on the counter where all could see it. We shall have more to say about this in the next chapter.

Underlying this healing attitude was a view of human beings quite different from that of most of the ancient world. Jesus had a surprisingly modern theory of human personality. Although implicit, his view of human nature was a unique and highly developed psychological point of view, consistent not only with his ministry but with his whole ethical attitude. His healing ministry was the natural result of this outlook.

The Psychology of Jesus

Each of us has a psychology, whether we know it or not, whether we call it by that name or not. Everyone has a pattern of acting toward other human beings; we show what we think about other people by the way we act toward them, even if we never consciously articulate the ideas embodied in our actions. While Jesus never expounded his psychological theory in so many words, it is not difficult to deduce from what he said and did. His teaching and his acts were of a piece, and both reveal a point of view very different from the popular attitude bequeathed to us by the rest of the ancient world. In order to see how different his outlook was, we must first of all sketch the view of personality which has been current in most societies from ancient Israel and Greece up to our own time.

According to this attitude the human personality is relatively simple and easy to understand. The basic assumption is that there is only one essential center to the human personality or psyche and that each of us is in control of that center of our being, able to determine our actions by our own conscious choice. If we have knowledge, therefore, of what is right or wrong, expedient or inexpedient, we will do the good or wise thing if our will is good, and the evil or foolishly inexpedient thing if our will is bad. *Therefore,* if (and this "if" is even larger than the first) we human beings do anything silly or evil or illegal with foreknowledge, this action must be the result of our essential desire to do the silly, evil, or illegal thing.

According to this idea of human personality, evil action is the result of our conscious ill will, and ill will can be changed only by punishment. If we punish people enough they will change. If they do not respond to punishment, then the will is irredeemably bad and there is no way to reach them, so they must be imprisoned, banished, or executed. In a nutshell, the implicit attitude at the bottom of our ordinary social structure is quite simple. We normally sane human beings are understood to be single integrated personalities, knowing what we are doing and why, and capable of controlling ourselves at all times if we really wish to. The task of society is to educate and to punish, and that is all. So long as we are not psychotic to the point of being unable to perceive reality, we are responsible for our actions. Even psychotics were held morally responsible for their action at many periods in human history.

What is never stated can hardly be questioned or criticized, which is the great danger of implicitly held beliefs. Because we do not set them forth in the open, in clear statements, we simply cannot see their implications. This enables us to hold completely inconsistent or even contradictory views. The very fact that we keep so many of our beliefs unstated—until we express them in action—is what allows so many of us to live and act inconsistently, at times with such tragic effect. We do not hold an unquestioned, unstated belief—it holds us. The unstated psychological theory sketched above is extremely significant, for as individuals and as a society we govern our actions and attitudes toward other people according to this theory. It forms the very ground of our sense of our own being, as well as of our relationship with our fellows.

Accepted from before the time of Christ down to the present, this basic view of our essential human nature is seldom challenged either by the person in the street or the average clergy. It is simply taken as a natural part of the social environment. Unless we have run into serious personal problems, have been faced with grave mental illness among those close to us, or have carefully studied the whole subject of emotional difficulties (and as a part of that study made clinical observations), few of us ever question our generally accepted psychological heritage. And the pity of it is that this idea of personality which is part of our worldview is tragically inadequate.

And yet on this theory legal practice is based. If it can be established that people breaking the law are capable of "knowing" what they were doing they then receive the full impact of the law's retribution. Because the law rests upon antiquated theory, people who are clearly emotionally incapable, by any modern medical standards, of controlling their actions are sent to prison and to death by the courts.

This same inadequate theory of personality is the basis on which our ineffective penal institutions have been created and maintained, which—far from reforming the criminal personality—serve more often as schools for crime. The only penal institutions that have lowered the rate of recidivism (the rate of return to prison by prisoners) are those that have broken entirely with the conventional psychological point of view.

The same theory of personality is no less responsible for many mental hospitals throughout the ages, which have taken mentally ill persons out of society but which healed almost none of them. Only as the hospitals have broken entirely with this rigid and ancient psychology have the people under treatment had a chance to recover. Today many psychotic people in our country who need hospital care have been turned out of them and so have come to make up at least half of the homeless people in the United States, because of the notion that drugs can provide adequate healing for the mentally ill. But sick people often don't take their prescribed drugs. And drugs do not work on all people; some people need loving attention as well as drugs to recover.

Nonetheless, the very old psychology implicit in modern Western society has had great and noted advocates. It was the theory of Socrates. He stressed the fact that you must know before you can do, and assumed that if you really knew, you would do the right thing unless your will was wrong. Nor did Plato ever come to grips with the question of how to change the basic core of human will. His theories apply only to the good will, which desired to do well. Plato saw eros, or love, which is capable of changing a person, as an irrational *gift*, rather than the product of human will. Hence the utter disillusionment in *The Laws*, where he relies only on law—almost dictatorship—to hold society together. Aristotle provided no basic change in the popular theory, which was also the personality theory of much of the Old Testament, reaching its ultimate expression in the book of Proverbs. Here wisdom is enough; if we get wisdom, and exalt wisdom, then we shall be brought to honor. For the Jews in general, morality was a relatively simple matter of education and good will, and fear was a most useful instrument to enforce the right way when good will was not present.

Jesus, on the other hand, treated human beings as much more complex. He believed and taught that, up to a point, we do have conscious control of our personality and that it should be exercised and developed. So much did Jesus stress the importance of conscious control, in fact, that it became one of the marks of a Christian society. In the societies influenced by Jesus' teachings, consciousness and the emphasis on personal responsibility has grown more than anywhere else in the world.

In addition, however, Jesus clearly believed that we humans could be influenced by "spiritual powers," that is, by psychic realities. He was himself driven by God into the wilderness. He repeatedly referred to the angels or messengers of God. While Jesus understood that we could be helped or enlightened and directed by these positive spiritual powers, he also believed that we could be possessed by alien powers, unclean spirits, evil spirits, demons, and satanic forces. No evidence exists that Jesus tried to change the popular way of alluding to these things, some of which we might now call psychological "complexes." Demonic spirits made people sick physically, mentally, and morally. They could not be controlled by the conscious will of the individual, once it had been overwhelmed by the alien power. The possessed (or demonized) people knew that they were not in control, but were unable to do much about it. It was a matter of possessing the will, not of knowledge alone.

The whole subject of Jesus' understanding of subtle and underlying modes of psychic or spiritual reality has been so completely ignored that one who begins to study is in virgin territory. It forms, however, such a basic part of Jesus' view of human personality that to ignore these references is to do violence to his psychological point of view and his whole understanding of human nature and of healing.[7]

The interested reader is referred to the Appendix in my book, *Tongue Speaking*, where all these nonphysical realities are carefully catalogued. We shall show later that Jesus' belief that such realities have an effect on human beings is not as absurd as was once believed. An understanding of the unconscious and the spiritual (psychoid) world as explained by Carl Jung gives modern minds some grasp of the worldview from which Jesus spoke and acted. In two recent books, *Christo-Psychology* (1982) and *Christianity as Psychology* (1986), I have shown how much the worldview of Jung and other modern thinkers have in common with Jesus' view of the universe. Without such an understanding, it is certainly not possible to make much sense of the healing ministry described in the New Testament.

Jesus also spoke of achieving the single eye, implying that human beings could be other than single-eyed, single-hearted, single-minded and that there might be various centers of personality. He spoke again and again—it is almost the keynote of the gospels—of losing one's life in order to find it. Whatever else this means, it certainly implies that there are various levels of personality, and that to gain the higher one of them the lower has to be made subject to it. The importance of these concepts can hardly be overestimated in seeking an understanding of

---

[7] I have discussed the subject of the demonic at length in *Discernment, A Study in Ecstasy and Evil* (1979).

Jesus and the New Testament. One has to put aside the centrality of one's own will so that God's will, God's Spirit, the Holy Spirit can become the center of one's life and personality. The human will or ego cannot stand against demonic infiltration unless one is endowed with the Holy Spirit. This again shows clearly the complexity Jesus saw in human personality.

By our own humanity, our own will, we cannot deal with the depth and complexity of the psychic life in which we participate. Single-handed, humanity cannot stand against the demonic. One reason Jesus was so responsive to sickness and sin was his sense that they result from our domination by spirits antagonistic to our deeper meaning and purpose. The only way to drive them out—to bring health of body, mind, and soul—was through the Holy Spirit, which is characterized by love. Thus the injunction of Jesus that we love one another as he loved us is not just an ethical maxim. It also has healing implications. Only a life characterized by love can give hospitality to the Spirit of God. As this Spirit resides in us we build up defenses against alien forces so that they cannot so easily attack and possess us. By the same Spirit we can help others mobilize their own personalities and so become free of similar domination. Love, as an invitation to God's Spirit and as an evidence of it, is one important agent which helps to free human beings from alien domination; it is healing to mind and body as well as moral in power.

Jesus' Point of View in Action

Jesus was fully human, living among down-trodden men and women in an occupied country. His attitude toward people who were caught in moral, mental, or physical illness was one of compassion. He was able to respond freely and directly because he knew that there were many causes of sickness and suffering beyond human control. Nowhere in the gospels is there any suggestion of Jesus asking sick people what they had done or whether they had sinned before healing them. Instead he took direct action to meet the need. Even the healing of the Gentile child, the daughter of the Canaanite (or Syrophoenician) woman in Matthew 15:22–28, was given freely.

Knowing the actualities that people encounter within the soul or psyche, Jesus had a clear point of view about them. He knew the reality of alien and evil "spirits" that can influence us (today this might be called possession by an archetype or complex) and also how the reality of God can touch an individual and not only eliminate the influence of such a spirit but put something else in its place. According to his point of view, we cannot always by our own will fight off the infiltration of alien, evil personality constellations that somehow or other get a foothold in us. As Jesus describes in Luke 11:24–26, a person can get rid of an evil spirit, but if that is all, the spirit can return to its old place, and "finding it swept and tidied, it then goes off and brings seven other spirits more wicked than itself, and they go in and set up house there, so that the person ends up by being worse than before."

Thus Jesus made clear that most people in their present condition do not deserve or need judgment and punishment, which only drive them further into despair and defeat, and further under the influence of evil. Only twice did he make any point of speaking to the sick about their sins, and the way he did it was striking in itself. One was the paralytic whom Jesus forgave before healing him (Matt. 9:2; Mark 2:5; Luke 5:20). The other was the man he healed at the pool of Bethesda, whom he then warned not to sin again or something worse might befall him (John 5:14).[8] People who were sick and in trouble morally needed understanding and compassion, not judgment and punishment. They were up against realities or forces which the human will could not handle on its own; they needed help, and Jesus responded to their need. Even Paul cried out that the things he did not want to do he did and those things he wanted to do, he was unable to do (Romans 7:15, 25).

Jesus' attitude toward sin and sickness was in opposition to almost the entire Judaic and Greek culture of his time. At least six of his healings were done on the Sabbath to show his own people how important it was to set aside statutes of external observance when there was an opportunity to help a sick or disabled person.[9] Thus Jesus' treatment of people was not just his own unique approach. It was intended as a general way for people to treat one another. As such, it was (and still

---

[8] Jesus' treatment of direct moral difficulty in Luke 7:48 and John 8:11 is the same. These four are the only accounts of his dealing directly with the sins of an individual. Judgment was for the establishment, for the self-righteous who kept the old order inflexible at the expense of other people's moral, mental, and physical health. Jesus' judgment, in fact, was largely reserved for those in a position to impose their ideas on others.

[9] These are the healings in Mark 1:21–27 (Luke 4:31–35), Mark 3:1–6 (Matthew 12:9–13, Luke 6:6–10), Luke 13:10–13, 14:1–4, John 5:2–10, and John 9:1–14. The account in Mark 1, also makes clear that the first recorded healing in the synagogue in Capernaum (1:23) was followed immediately by that of Peter's mother-in-law (1:29–31), and that this demonstration by Jesus of his willingness to break the law of the Sabbath for the sake of healing brought a crowd of sick people to him. The account in Luke 4 is also parallel.

is) a radically new attitude about how human beings should treat each other, with all sorts of implications beyond the healing ministry.

Jesus saw that one of his major tasks as the messiah was to defeat the realities of evil that could contaminate us and keep us from achieving our full potential in the kingdom of heaven. He saw himself in conflict with forces of evil. As Mark in particular shows in 1:24, 1:34, and 3:11, these demonic realities were equally aware that he was bent on dissolving their power. There was open warfare on a cosmic level, with physical and mental healing one of the things fought for. Failure to release human beings from these powers would have been unthinkable for those who saw them from Jesus' psychological and moral point of view. And failure to heal if one had the power would have been just as unthinkable.

If Jesus had any one mission, it was to bring the power and healing of God's creative, loving spirit to bear upon the moral, mental, and physical illnesses of the people around him. It was a matter of rescuing us from a situation in which we could not help ourselves. Jesus disclosed a new power, a ladder to bring us out of the pit of our brokenness and evil. Leaving people in their wretched condition so as to learn from it makes no sense in this psychological or moral framework. Judgment and punishment most often add to a burden already intolerable.

Jesus' healing actions flowed from his knowledge of our psychological nature and our moral situation as children of God. Modern medicine has adopted the same nonjudgmental attitude towards healing. The sick person is not to blame. Unless one understands Jesus' view of the human condition, it is difficult if not impossible to understand his healing ministry. It is also difficult to understand the kind of fellowship he formed around him and the injunctions he gave. The New Testament does not yield a wholly clear idea of when the end of the world was expected to come, but it is very clear that the disciples were to continue in their lives to manifest as much of God's healing spirit as they could.[10]

---

[10] One of the main gaps in the thinking of Barth and Bultmann is their neglect of this very fact. The disciples and the early church, as well as Jesus, did manifest the merciful action of God in a sinful and broken world by performing physical and mental healing. This deliberate disregard of an element so emphatically a part of the New Testament account—and in such bulk, with so many ramified allusions—derives of course from their belief that the entire record of healings from beginning to end, even including Jesus' teaching *about* healing, was mythology, in the sense of something made up to explain what we do not understand. On the other hand, if such things actually happened, then God is not as far from the human condition as Barth and Bultmann insist. Once the premise of the absolute separation between human beings and God is denied,

Present influence of the kingdom and its ultimate fulfillment were not inconsistent. The Spirit was now manifested in a limited way, particularly in healing; it would be manifest totally in the age to come. When that time came, the forces of evil would be completely routed and sickness would disappear.

With this background let us now turn to a detailed discussion of the healing ministry of Jesus.

---

the structure of dialectic theology falls apart. Is one to take experience or reason as the final criterion of truth? This is the question.

CHAPTER 5

What, How, and Why Did Jesus Heal?

When we actually look at the record of healing in the four gospels, it is apparent that the writers were describing the effect of Jesus' actions on quite a number of different diseases. The words they used were of course different from those of modern clinical diagnosis, but even so, many of the conditions are well enough identified to compare with diseases we know today.

What Did Jesus Heal?

Probably the most common ailment healed was mental illness, generally described in New Testament times as demon possession. Many sources tell of the radically changing times of the first century and how the collective pattern of life was breaking up, much as it is in our time. People found life without structure, without meaning to which they could cling. They could not cope with the uncertainties and complexities that faced them and so they disintegrated psychologically. Depth psychology shows how such factors contribute to mental illness. This kind of illness was described in the healings in Matthew 8:28–32, 15:22–28, and Mark 1:23–27, and their various parallels in other gospels, plus Luke 8:2, as well as in the six references to the authority given the disciples[1] and in nine of the many accounts of the healing of great numbers of people.[2]

---

[1] Matt. 10:1, 8; Mark 3:15 and 6:7; Luke 9:1 and 10:17–20.

[2] Matt. 4:24 and 8:16; Mark 1:32 and 39, 3:10–12, and 6:13; Luke 4:41, 6:18, and 7:21. The understanding of severe mental illness, schizophrenia in particular, as a reaction to the intolerable conditions under which people live is expounded in many of the writings of

One case of "demon possession" appears to have been epilepsy. This was the boy whom the disciples could not cure, described in Mark 9:17–27 (Matt. 17:14–18; Luke 9:38–42). Other physical disabilities appeared to those present as clear examples of demonic possession, as the result of psychogenic rather than physical causes. For example, the apparent cases of hysterical blindness or muteness in Matthew 9:32 and 12:22 are connected with demonic possession, and in Luke 11:14 the demon itself is described as being mute.

Several persons were healed of "leprosy." Of course, it may well be that some "lepers" were suffering from a variety of other diseases. Because of the dread nature of leprosy and the difficulty of distinguishing it clearly from other afflictions in its early stages, all these healings were considered of great importance, and with good reason. Leprosy is a curse still to be feared, as my wife and I observed when taken to a leper colony on a marshy manmade island off the coast of Sumatra. The Salvation Army captain who guided us told us that some of the people had been there forty years. But there is nothing in the record itself to raise doubt about the curing of true leprosy by Jesus. One story tells of ten lepers coming to him in a group. These accounts of the healing of persons described as lepers are found in Matthew 8:2–4, Mark 1:40–42, Luke 5:12–14, and Luke 17:12–15.

There are a number of examples of the healing of lameness, palsy, or paralysis, and other crippling infirmities. It is easy for us to overlook the vital importance of these healings. There was no such thing as unemployment compensation or disability insurance, of course, and any crippling disease that kept a person from earning a living worked impossible hardship, often on family and friends as well as on the individual.

Perhaps the most striking story is that of the paralytic who was lowered by his friends through the roof into Jesus' presence because they could not bring his litter in through the crowds. This is related in Mark 2:3–4 and Luke 5:18–19. In John 5:2–7 the sick man healed at the pool of Bethesda had apparently been lying there day in and day out for thirty-eight years, trying to get to the waters when they were said to be troubled by an angel. In Matthew 9:2–7 a paralytic was brought to Jesus stretched out on a bed. In at least one instance physical deterioration had taken place in the part that was restored; this is found in Matthew 12:9–13 (Mark 3:1–5 and Luke 6:6–10), where the man's hand

---

R. D. Laing. In *The Politics of Experience* (1968) he describes schizophrenia as the individual turning away from a disturbed, out-of-joint outer world to the inner world in search of healing and peace.

is described as "withered" or "shriveled." Some permanent damage might also be assumed in two of the women whom we are told Jesus healed. One was bent double; she had been disabled or "possessed by a spirit" for eighteen years (Luke 13:10–11). The other had suffered hemorrhages for twelve years (Matt. 9:20–22; Mark 5:25–29; Luke 8:43–44).

Two different accounts describe sickness involving fever. The first is the delightful story of Peter's mother-in-law, who was healed so that she could get up and wait on the group of disciples (recorded in the three synoptic gospels: Matthew 8:14–15; Mark 1:30–31; Luke 4:38–39). In the incident of the nobleman's son in John 4:47–53, we know that the boy's illness was attended by fever since a report reached the father of the precise hour at which the fever had left him.

Blindness was another curse of the Roman world, as it had been of every culture not reached by modern medicine and hygiene. Since it was one of the greatest tragedies that could happen to a human being in that world, it is no' wonder that so many examples are given of its healing. There is, first of all, the elaborate account of the man born blind in John 9, which takes the whole chapter. Then come the stories of the blind Bartimaeus in Mark 10:46–52 and Luke 18:35–42; of the two blind men in Matthew 20:30–34; of the man brought to Jesus at Bethsaida in Mark 8:22–25; of two blind men in Matthew 9:27–30; and finally of those who came to him in the temple in Matthew 21:14. In Mark 7:32–35 we also find the homely story of how Jesus healed a man who was deaf and had an impediment in his speech.

In the case of the person healed on the Sabbath in Luke 14:1–4, there was a cure of dropsy or edema. The single example of the healing of a wound occurred under most unusual circumstances: in Luke 22:50–51 when one of the disciples resisted Jesus' arrest in the garden of Gethsemani, the disciple struck out with a sword and injured the ear of Malchus, the high priest's servant, and Jesus healed it.

At one time the three accounts of raising from the dead were hard for people to accept, but we now have many examples of people who have been revived and tell of their experience. These are told in some detail. The reviving of Jairus's daughter is found in Matthew 9:18–25, Mark 5:22–43, and Luke 8:41–56. The raising of Lazarus in John 11 was a climactic event before the entry of Jesus into Jerusalem. And in Luke 7:11–15 an incident at Nain is related, when Jesus raised the widow's son from his bier. None of these stories mention the cause of death.

Aside from individual healings, there are also nineteen incidents in the first three gospels where it is said that numbers of people were healed, without much detail as to the disease concerned. Very likely the healings described separately were the more dramatic occurrences. But there were also cures of other conditions that cannot be identified at all.[3] And the last words of the Gospel of John tell us, "There were many other things that Jesus did; if all were written down, the world itself, I suppose, would not hold all the books that would have to be written" (21:25).

There does not seem to be much question about the drift of these passages. Where great crowds gathered there were people with a wide range of ailments. Naturally we do not find modern descriptive terms such as carcinoma, sarcoma, leukemia, typhoid, rheumatic fever, gangrene, or the like, but this does not justify the inference that the conditions Jesus healed were not serious or varied. On the other hand, neither can we attach modern labels to most of those illnesses, as some students have attempted to do. We have only popular descriptions from an age which had far less specific information about human disease than our own, and it is useless to try to identify them by current medical terms.

Still, some broad medical categories can help us in understanding the New Testament descriptions. We find three basically different classes of human illness. First, there is organic disease in which the structure or tissue of the body is damaged in some way. Second are the functional disorders, in which sickness results because one organ or part of the body is not working properly. Third is psychic or mental illness, which shows up as a disturbance of the personality. Brain damage is usually included here, although there is some question as to how much ordinary mental illness can be attributed to it. These three categories help us understand a good deal about the kinds of sickness spoken of in passages concerned with healing.

Under organic disease we find all the various disorders that result in direct damage to organic tissue, including wounds, foreign bodies, lesions, and resulting blood clots or hemorrhages; bacterial and viral infections; and growths of various kinds.[4] This group also embraces the

---

[3] Nine of these passages simply say that Jesus healed "all kinds of diseases" or that he healed those who were sick: Matt. 4:23, 9:35, 12:15, 14:14, 14:35–36, 19:2; Mark 6:5, 6:55–56; Luke 9:11. In six of them similar wording is used, but demon possession is also included: Matt. 8:16; Mark 1:32–34, 3:7–12; Luke 4:40–41, 6:17–18, 8:2. There are also four similar passages that variously include demon possession, lunacy, paralysis, and healing of the blind, the dumb, the lame and cripples: Matt. 4:24, 15:30, 21:14; Luke 7:21. In addition it is implied in Luke 5:15 that the sick among the crowds that gathered were being healed; Mark 1:39 tells that demons were cast out.

[4] The body has a natural defense system against bacterial and viral infections and even seems to attack and destroy malignant cells. An American Cancer Society film, *The*

deterioration that follows these invasions as well as that which results from long functional disturbance.

The second grouping comprises an almost infinite variety of disorders in which the malfunction of one part disturbs the whole organism. Nearly every organ may be affected: the heart or the entire cardiovascular system, the intestinal tract, the skin, the urinary system, the blood in its complex chemical and organic balance, indeed any part of the body. Many commonly recognized diseases, especially in their early stages, fall into this category: various heart diseases, high blood pressure, peptic ulcers, anemia, allergies, and so on. It is also clear that functional disease which continues unchecked can so damage the affected organ that it is permanently changed, and organic disease results.

Finally, mental illness may manifest itself in various ways, as psychosis, neurosis, or in hysteria. In psychosis the person can no longer distinguish inner reality from outer reality and the ego no longer has direction; often the person cannot function as a human being at all, and the illness may be marked by states of wild frenzy or catatonic stupor. Psychoneurosis, on the other hand, is the state of a troubled psyche, one which has not lost the ability to deal with inner conflict and is characterized by anxiety, compulsiveness, and depression. The neurotic, it has been said, worries about castles in the air, while the psychotic lives in them. And then there are the hysterias: purely psychogenic physical states such as hysterical blindness or paralysis. The hysterical person can copy reliably nearly any disease syndrome. There is little organic damage, only the unconscious idea that one cannot use that particular organ—an idea so deep that the person is literally unable to do so. While hysterical patients can be suggested out of this state or tricked in various ways to reveal the psychic cause of the problem, still they are genuinely ill and cannot just snap out of it.[5]

It has become increasingly clear in recent medical practice that destructive emotional causes or influences may play a part in any disease, whatever the class or immediate cause. Most of the work in psychoso-

---

Embattled Cell, a lapsed-time movie of living lung tissue, actually shows the various lines of defense the body provides. This film is available free from chapters of the American Cancer Society. AIDS is so destructive because it attacks the body's defense system. Only healings of organic diseases are considered miraculous by the medical board at Lourdes.

[5] One occurrence of hysterical illness in recent times involved more than one hundred of the medical personnel of London's Royal Free Hospital, two-thirds of them sick enough to require hospitalization. The hospital had to be closed for over two months ("Mass Hysteria," *Time*, January 26, 1970, pp. 59–61).

matic medicine has been done in the area of functional illnesses; the psychic origin of many of these disorders has been revealed, and it is here that psychosomatic medicine has had real success in finding new methods of cure. For while emotional sources may directly cause many malfunctionings of the body, or its failure to resist disease, the effect is still that of physical illness.

It is perfectly clear that the healings of Jesus occurred in all three of these medical categories of disease. But even more interesting is the fact that they occurred predominantly in the first and last groups. According to the gospel records Jesus did not heal many sicknesses that could be termed purely functional. We have no accounts of his healing headaches, backaches, stomach trouble, or muscular tension, although he undoubtedly must have, since such problems respond quite readily to suggestion and religious healing. It is quite possible that many functional diseases were among those spoken of generally when it is said that he healed the multitudes.

The great majority of the recorded healings of Jesus were either of the mentally ill or of physically damaged bodies and organic disease. It may be easier for us, because of the prevailing materialism of our time, to believe that Jesus could heal mental illness than to accept his physical healings, but those who have had experience with it know that this category of disease has been more resistant than any other to the advances of modern medicine. It can be moderated or controlled by drugs, but real healing is rare.

Recent studies indicate that slightly more than one person out of every five in the United States over eighteen suffers from at least one recognized psychiatric disorder during any six-month period.[6] There has been no great conquest of serious mental sickness, and neurosis can be conquered only by long and costly treatment, nor is this always successful. These healings are therefore just as impressive and startling as the physical ones, if not more so. Modern science has been able to care for and cure a great many types of physical illness, but it has done little for mental illness and many of its physical manifestations. For instance, although it is known that certain allergic reactions have a basically emotional cause, and the symptoms can often be controlled or temporarily relieved, psychiatrists are embarrassed by the fact that they can so seldom get at the psychic basis of the disorder and heal the disease. Psychological illness is not in fact easy to heal. A large portion

---

[6] These findings of National Institute of Mental Health were reported in *The San Francisco Chronicle*, October 3, 1984.

of the hospital beds in the United States are reserved for the mentally ill. Probably half of the homeless in our American cities, a dark blot on the American conscience, are people who were turned out of our mental hospitals when a mistaken enthusiasm for the effects of drug therapy resulted in their closing.

Many attempts have been made to explain away the healing ministry of Jesus as simply suggestion which relieved functional and hysterical symptoms. I know this well, for it is the idea upon which I was raised. There is no basis for it, however, in the actual records that have come down to us, nor is there any basis (other than the interpreter's inclination) for rationalizing the healings as mere suggestions to psychoneurotics. This may suit the modern mind, but it does not reflect the textual record. Most of the individual descriptions point out a pertinent fact which clearly characterizes the disease healed, such as the duration of bleeding in Mark 5:25, the crippling effect in Luke 5:18 and 6:6, or the severe psychotic state in Mark 5:2–5.

There is also agreement between the descriptions of individual healings and the several passages which speak of the healing of numbers of people, both of which make a distinction between physical illness and demon possession. This is shown in Mark 1:34, Matthew 4:24 and 8:16, and Luke 4:40–41 and 6:17–19. Nor is it possible to understand "the lame, the crippled, the blind, the dumb and many others" who were brought to Jesus, according to Matthew 15:30, as simply neurotics or only functionally disturbed. The words of the gospels are few, and they must be read as they are.

In fact, as we have shown, examples are given of the healing of physical disorders attributed to mental or psychic causes (demons), as in Matthew 9:32 and 12:22 and in Luke 11:14. When the disease was hysterical in nature, this seems to be how it was described. But purely hysterical illness is rather rare, and if Jesus' power was limited to alleviating this type of condition, he must have been on the lookout for such symptoms. If this were the case, there would be an implication of duplicity, and whatever else we may say about Jesus of Nazareth, this is patently absurd. This suggestion is out of character with the tone of the gospel narrative and would make mockery of Christianity, both religious and ethical.

In addition, we have a tendency to look upon people living in the first century as quite simple and naive, and to discount this ministry from our own superiority as people "come of age." But they were more sophisticated than we ordinarily realize. The authors of the gospels seem to have been quite aware of the distinction between purely functional disorders and organic disease. It is clear that the healing incidents recounted in detail were selected out of a wide range of possible ones, and in the telling conveyed the amazement of those who witnessed them. The fact is that the particular descriptions not only show that Jesus healed many different kinds of disease, but stress the types that are especially resistant to either medical knowledge or religious healing practice, then as now.

If we accept the stories at all, we must conclude that Jesus healed all kinds of disease and that we do not know how he did it, for we are still not able fully to follow in his steps. Most attempts to rationalize these miracles do not make sense, for they are based more upon wishful thinking (in a negative sort of way) than on the facts as stated in the stories themselves. While there may be uncertainty in certain instances, the plain sense of the gospels is that Jesus healed the most serious kinds of ailments, and that what he did had the effect of true healing, not just of alleviating symptoms.

The modern rejection of the healing stories is mostly a *blanket rejection* which is theological and—over and above our own inexperience and sense of impotence in the matter of healing—entirely theoretical. Most theologians may even take into account the newer understanding of recent medical practice and the fact that the stories themselves are most likely the earliest and most authentic in the gospels. But they still consider the whole idea of them untenable because it is "mythological." By a circular reasoning they simply assume that God does not touch human sickness and heal it. As C. S. Lewis pointed out in his excellent essay "Modern Theology and Biblical Criticism," this kind of rejection is very questionable.[7] It denies the idea of an experience offhand and on pure theory, instead of dealing with the experience itself on a basis of actual knowledge of it. And the fact is that we have little reason in modern life for direct knowledge of this kind of experience; what seems impossible to us must therefore have been impossible long ago and is not to be taken seriously. Bergson has pointed out there is no way to prove a *fact* untrue. However, in the fifteen years since this book was first published an enormous literature, much of it written by medical practitioners, has accumulated that shows that these healings do still occur.

---

[7] C. S. Lewis, *Christian Reflections* (1968), pp. 152–73. In my *Encounter with God: A Theology of Christian Experience* (1987), I discuss this whole subject in detail. In Appendix B, pp. 330–31, I quote two post-Bultmannian scholars, Günther Bornkamm and Norman Perrin, who show how fearful biblical scholars have been of tackling the problem of healing in the New Testament.

How Did Jesus Heal?

Jesus responded in different ways to the sick who came to him. He called upon the faith of the person who needed help, he touched the sick person, he uttered commands, he used various physical media. His healing methods were as diverse as the kinds of disease he healed. And as one analyzes his approach, comparing it with other possible methods, it appears that the healing of Jesus was largely sacramental in nature.

His most common means of healing was by speaking words and touching the sick person with his hand. Often he combined the two, although at times he used them separately. In the later history of the church, touching became known as a "laying on of hands." In only two instances is this method referred to alone. When Jesus was in Nazareth, he was hindered by the unbelief of the people; yet he cured a few by laying his hands on them (Mark 6:5). In the account of his healing of Malchus' wound, it is reported only that he touched it (Luke 22:51).

The use of words or commands was also perpetuated in the practice of exorcism. A number of times Jesus appears to have used only words, as in the raising of Lazarus (John 11:43), the healing of the ten lepers (Luke 17:14), the freeing of the Gerasene demoniac (Mark 5:8), the healing of the nobleman's son at a distance (John 4:50), and the restoration of the impotent man at the pool of Bethesda (John 5:8). In many instances the two means were used together. Jesus touched people—laid his hands upon them—and also spoke to them or to the spirit that seemed to possess them. Nearly half the examples of healing in the gospel record are characterized by this approach.

There are three instances of the use of saliva, alone or mixed with mud. Saliva was common as a healing remedy at the time, but Jesus used it not so much as a direct healing agent as a carrier of his personality and power. In the Gospel of Mark we are told of the man who was deaf and dumb: Jesus put his fingers in his ears, touched his tongue with his saliva, and then spoke the word *Ephphatha*—"Be opened!" (7:33–34). Much the same method was used for a blind man in Mark 8:23. In John 9:6–7 he mixed his saliva with earth, making a paste of it to rub on the blind man's eyes, and then told him to go and wash in the pool of Siloam.

Although the gospels do not mention Jesus using oil in healing, he probably did. Mark says that the disciples used oil when they were sent out by the master; they "cast out many devils, and anointed many sick people with oil and cured them" (6:13). This was certainly a common healing practice from the earliest times in the history of the church, and continues to be in Eastern Orthodox tradition.

Occasionally healing occurred as a person touched Jesus or his garments. The story of the woman who suffered from a hemorrhage is one clear example (Mark 5:25–34). In Mark 6:56 it is said that "wherever he went, to village, or town, or farm, they laid down the sick in the open spaces, begging him to let them touch even the fringe of his cloak. And all those who touched him were cured."

In raising Lazarus, Jesus prayed to God a prayer of thanks before commanding Lazarus to come out (John 11:41–44). In Matthew 15:25–28 it was the prayer of the Canaanite (or Syrophoenician) woman herself that initiated the healing of her daughter. While people often begged Jesus' help, and healing was freely given, in this instance the woman's humility and her own prayer were involved. Jesus was quite harsh with her—indeed, she may at first have been noisy and importunate—but she accepted his rebuke and continued to ask for help. This persistent humility which obtained its goal was also stressed in the parable of the widow before the unjust judge (Luke 18:1–5).

Several examples are given in which the faith of the individual was a potent factor in the healing. When Jesus spoke to the woman who had been healed of hemorrhaging, he told her, "*your* faith has restored you to health" (Mark 5:34, italics mine). When he restored the sight of the two blind men, he touched their eyes and said, "Your faith deserves it, so let this be done for you" (Matt. 9:29). Jesus put it up to the father of the epileptic boy that healing was possible for anyone who had faith, and the man cried out, "I do have faith. Help the little faith that I have" (Mark 9:23–24). In several instances the faith of a third person was the important factor. We see this in the stories of the court official's son in John 4:47–53 and the centurion's servant in Matthew 8:5–13. Again, the faith of the friends who brought the paralyzed man and lowered him down through the roof was a determining factor in Mark 2:3–11. We shall see later that faith releases the medically potent endorphins in the body.

As we have seen earlier, forgiveness of sins is twice mentioned in connection with healing. In the story of the paralyzed man brought by his friends, Jesus said to him, "My child, your sins are forgiven" (Mark 2:5). And after the man had been healed at the pool of Bethesda, Jesus later saw him in the temple and told him, "Now you are well again, be sure not to sin any more, or something worse may happen to you" (John 5:14). We shall have somewhat more to say later about the connection between sin and disease.

Four times the gospel narrative states that Jesus had compassion upon people and healed the sick. He felt sorry for the widow of Nain when he saw her standing beside the bier of her son (Luke 7:13). In Matthew 14:14 a large crowd had followed him to a lonely place, and he took pity on them and healed their sick. When he went up to Jerusalem for the last time, and the two blind men sitting by the road heard that Jesus was passing by and told him what they wanted, he had compassion on them and healed them (Matt. 20:34).

The fourth case was one of two strange instances in which anger appeared to be present at the time of healing. When the leper in Mark 1:40 came up to Jesus on his knees and said, "If you want to, you can cure me," Jesus was moved by compassion, by deep feeling apparently touched with sternness.[8] At least his final instruction to the man was direct and stern, as if he resented the man's doubt of his intention and desire to heal. Later he was clearly angry when he healed the man with the withered hand on the Sabbath (Mark 3:5), and it may be that this, and the reaction it evoked, contributed to both healings.

What, then, is the significance of these various actions of Jesus? In order to understand them in relation to the healing that resulted, one must look at them again from another standpoint, in this case to see his methods in relation to the various therapeutic practices of modern times. We have, first of all, healing which is purely medical and largely physical. This our age has developed to a fine art. It includes techniques to remove or repair an offending part, such as surgery, X-rays, radiation, and electroshock treatment for the mentally ill. Specific drugs help the body react favorably—digitalis for instance, or tranquilizers, hormones such as ACTH, even aspirin—as well as treatment by diet or rest. There are medicines, like the antihistamines and antibiotics, to aid in eliminating an offending substance or to bolster the body's natural defenses. Finally, there is prevention, by isolating, cleaning up, or inoculating against the source of disease. While these methods intervene directly to change something in the body, they are all basically ways of improving conditions under which the body itself constantly resists or

---

[8] The Greek word here for compassion, pity, sorrow—*splagchnizomai*—means to be moved in the bowels, originally by anger; later it carries the connotation of other feelings. The gospel writers used it in the parables to express the feeling of the master toward the unforgiving debtor, the Samaritan toward the beaten man, the father toward the prodigal, and his own feeling for the crowds like sheep without a shepherd (Matt. 18:27; Luke 10:33, 15:20; Matt. 9:36). Zechariah used a form of this word to speak of God's mercy in Luke 1:78. It describes Jesus' feeling toward the crowds when he provided the loaves and fishes (Matt. 15:32; Mark 6:34, 8:2). The father of the epileptic boy used it to ask compassion of Jesus (Mark 9:22).

adjusts to disease. In essence, medical healing consists in methods of promoting the recuperative power of the body itself.

A second mode of healing is psychological, either by suggestion or through some form of psychotherapy. As Flanders Dunbar has pointed out so well, suggestion (of which hypnosis is only an extreme form) almost always plays an important role in getting well. A physician's negative suggestions as to the course of a disease may bring about a negative conclusion to it, while positive suggestion is usually an important factor in mobilizing the body's recuperative powers. The results of suggestion in arousing a patient's inner healing powers have been described by Jerome Frank in his fascinating book, *Persuasion and Healing*, about which we shall have more to say in another chapter. Dr. Frank writes that "until the last few decades most medications prescribed by physicians were pharmacologically inert. That is, physicians were prescribing placebos without knowing it, so that, in a sense, the 'history of medical treatment until relatively recently is the history of the placebo effect,'"[9] Suggestion does have healing power. However, suggestion seldom cures the more seriously neurotic or psychotic patient; instead it often merely removes the symptom, leaving the underlying cause to pop up again in some other, often more serious guise. Nor is it possible to tell exactly how suggestion or hypnosis works.

Psychotherapy does sometimes enable seriously disturbed individuals to relate to other people and adjust to their own inner psychic life and also to outer reality, both physical and nonphysical. By removing anxiety and emotional conflicts, it can have a positive effect upon the body, sometimes curing illness. This method usually requires the cooperation of the patient and is a long and involved process, the success of which is, to say the least, difficult to predict.

There is a third kind of healing which, for want of a better word, may be called psychic healing. It is a power which seems to inhere in certain people and to emanate from them with effects upon the lives of others. Since it apparently works at the level of unconscious images or attitudes (and perhaps at times even more directly), this kind of power may be present without conscious desire or realization. Jung has called attention to an interesting case history of such a person described in a work entitled *The Reluctant Healer*.[10] Some of the novels of Charles Williams also deal with this power in a fascinating way. Such healing power has little relation to religion or morality; it may reside in individuals

---

[9] Jerome D. Frank, *Persuasion and Healing* (1969), p. 66.
[10] William J. MacMillan, *The Reluctant Healer* (1952).

with little conscious religious faith who may lead amoral lives. Since it takes place largely unconsciously, the healing involves little wish for transformation on either side.

Ordinary caring human touch appears to have a healing effect as Dr. James Lynch, professor of psychiatry at the University of Maryland Medical School, demonstrated clearly in his book, *The Broken Heart*. He surveys the literature showing that infants that are not held and fondled often waste away and die even in the most antiseptic environments. He also demonstrates that the very touch of a nurse taking the pulse of a patient monitored in an intensive care unit for heart conditions produces an improvement in the heart's action.

Finally, there is religious or sacramental healing, the result of the healer's conscious and deliberate relation to God. The healers as individuals are not viewed as the primary source of healing power. Rather they are seen as an agency through which the Spirit and power of God, the very creative force of the universe, is transmitted. The acts of healing depend on the power of God and are therefore sacramental. Spiritual healing is an outer and visible sign of particular grace, inward and spiritual, at work within both the healer and the one who seeks healing.

As we consider Jesus' actions in relation to each of these methods, the nature of his ministry becomes clearer. He used almost no methods that could be considered medically or physically effective. He did use saliva and mud, but hardly as effective physical remedies. When Dr. Boggs states: "Rather, the prayer of faith combined with the use of oil (the best medicine available) will save the sick person *when it is God's will*,"[11] he does not deal with the facts. Most of the healings we know anything about have been accomplished without the use of any active outer physical agents at all. It was not the intention of Jesus to be a physician, nor to ask his disciples to meddle in matters of medical healing. This was simply not his interest or concern. He showed no hostility to contemporary medical practice (though he might well have, considering the medical practices of the first century). Instead Jesus spoke of doctors quite positively in his important saying comparing those in good health who have no need of the physician with the sick who do (Matt. 9:12; Mark 2:17; Luke 5:31). This suggests a more sympathetic attitude toward secular healing than was shown by most of the Old Testament and by Judaism at that time.

Of course, Jesus used some psychological methods, but not in the general sense of modern practice. Undoubtedly he made use of sug-

---

[11] Wade H. Boggs, Jr., *Faith Healing and the Christian Faith* (1956), p. 158.

gestion in some way, but with permanent effect, while ours usually is not. He did not employ hypnotism or psychotherapy, always a lengthy process. His contacts with people were brief, and most of the healings appear to have been instantaneous. The only possible use of psychotherapy would have been with the disciples, who were not ill, or perhaps with some of the women among his followers. The disciples' continual companionship and discourse with Jesus may well have been a kind of group therapy, but this was not used for healing the sick. The latter, instead of joining his company, were usually told to return to their homes.

Thus little in modern psychological practices compares with Jesus' method, and where such unusual effects do occur, they are as much a mystery to the therapist as many of the actions of Jesus are to us. We still have no clear idea of how healing through suggestion or psychotherapy takes place. In the last analysis, we actually know very little about how the mind affects the body. We can call the methods of Jesus psychological, but in so doing we are more or less describing one unknown in terms of another and are not moving very far toward understanding what went on in Jesus' healings.

A personality of such power as Jesus would unquestionably have a psychic effect whether he intended it or not, but there is little evidence that he used personal psychic powers as such. He continually turned attention away from himself and toward the power that came through him. He spoke of himself as an agent: "if it is by the Spirit of God that I cast out demons . . ." He tried to keep people from spreading news of him as a healer and constantly referred to something within the healed individuals which had been effective. At no point is personal psychic power spoken of as a major aspect of his healings.

Instead, the methods Jesus used with such effect upon the sick were actions which appear to have done two things. They awakened the spirit that lay deep within these people, waiting to be touched.[12] And at the same time his actions, word, and attitudes brought contact with the Spirit of God, the creative force of reality, which helps human minds and bodies to move toward inner harmony and which recreates them. Deep spoke to deep, through sacramental action. The nature of his healing, its essential method, was sacramental, religious. Through

---

[12] It has been suggested to me that sacramental actions perhaps opened individuals so that the Spirit of God dwelling within them was released or drawn out. The laying on of hands would then appear to be a drawing out process as much as flowing in.

him the power of God touched the lives of people, and they were made whole. There is little more that one can say.

The belief of certain healing sects that Jesus taught a detailed method of mental healing is unfounded in the gospel record. It is true that he taught people about God, but his healings did not follow as the result of his sermons or teachings. His acts of healing did not reveal spiritual laws by which individuals might live and so escape from physical ills. Seldom in the four gospels did Jesus speak of spiritual laws in relation to physical healing. The latter was usually accomplished by something other than getting the right ideas about reality or morality into people's heads. It was not accomplished by knowledge of reality, or law, or occult science. There was little Gnosticism in Jesus.

While so much modern religious healing is based upon the idea of discovering and living by spiritual laws, as in *The Course in Miracles* or *Science and Health*, for example, such healing is generally quite different from the spirit in which Jesus healed. He was dealing with a dynamic reality, a spiritual personality, a living, loving God. He was not concerned with a mechanical spirituality, to be used as one follows the textbook laws of physics or mathematics. Such a conception of reality is far from the mind and attitude of Jesus. His way was to bring people into a faith relationship to the loving God by the various methods of touching, speaking commands, compassion, and forgiveness, so that the power of the living God might be more fully in touch with them and restore them. Then he set about teaching them.

In order to start the process, to break through any hindrances to healing, Jesus drew upon the faith of the individual and those around him, and on his own compassion and power to forgive. He combined these attitudes with various media—a touch or a word—to convey his own loving person and also God's sacramental action. Through the complex medium of his own personal concern and the sick person's faith, a physical event became a sacrament of God's creative power. If one can fully explain sacramental acts then one may be able to explain Jesus' healing. Somehow, through his actions, person, and attitudes the power of God made effective contact with individuals. When there was utter disbelief or lack of faith in a large group of people, little healing took place, as when he went home to visit in Nazareth (Mark 6:5).

When we realize that ordinary touch has such a healing and sustaining effect upon humans, it is difficult to separate psychic, psychological, and sacramental healing completely. When my wife was in the hospital after a disastrous accident on the docks at Yokohama, I used

Delores Krieger's method of placing the hands around (but not touching) the foot and prayed that my ordinary natural healing power (human psychic power if you will) might be enhanced and multiplied a million times through God's Holy Spirit. This action followed the sacrament of Eucharist. At times she would feel pain in the foot in which could usually feel nothing. The incredible human Jesus would have had more of the human healing power and infinitely more access to the ultimate source of creativity and healing.

Why Did Jesus Heal?

Still, the most important of these several questions is not what Jesus healed, or how he did it, but *why*. Some very important things can be learned about this question from a careful reading of the gospels, and there is a most cogent reason for Christians to find them out. For if as a Christian one believes in the incarnation, then Jesus' attitude toward illness will reveal the attitude of God toward it. Certainly no Christian discussion of God's attitude toward sickness and suffering is complete without taking this into account. I am well aware of the difficulties proposed by modern Biblical criticism, of trying to plumb the mind of Jesus. However, if we are careful we can come to some understanding of what seemed to be Jesus' rationale in healing.

The most important reason that Jesus healed was that he cared about people and suffered when they did. The root meaning of compassion is just this: to know suffering together. He could not care without wanting to show mercy and to help. He was opposed to sickness because it caused needless suffering. It is the same spirit that rises to indignation when one hears of sick people being turned away from a hospital because they cannot pay. In cultures where the spirit of Christ has not been felt, this compassion is often conspicuously lacking. The healing ministry is the logical result of the incarnation: God so loved the world that God gave the essence of the divine in Jesus to be a savior for struggling human beings. Jesus so loved that he healed. His healings were the authentication of his mission and his person. They flowed naturally from him because he was what he was. Père Jean Leclerq, the great Benedictine scholar, remarked to me after reading this book that the healing ministry of Jesus was one of the best evidences of the love of God that he knew.

Another of Jesus' reasons for healing seems to have been that he was hostile to what made people sick. He rebuked the forces that seemed to possess the mentally ill and expressed the same antagonism towards physical illness. In the Gospel of Mark the story of Jesus' ministry begins with his rebuking and casting out an unclean spirit (1:25). His attitude was the same in the story of the Gerasene demoniac (Mark 5:8). When he finally healed the epileptic boy, "he rebuked the unclean spirit. 'Deaf and dumb spirit,' he said, 'I command you: Come out of him and never enter him again'" (Mark 9:25). In the Sabbath day healing of the woman who had a spirit of infirmity, Jesus answered the indignant Pharisee, "And this woman, a daughter of Abraham whom Satan has held bound these eighteen years—was it not right to untie her bonds on the Sabbath day?" (Luke 13:16).

Jesus' underlying attitude was that the demon-possessed and the physically ill were under the influence or control of an evil power. Some evil source—demons, Satan, something destructive and uncreative, the very opposite of the Holy Spirit—seemed to have gained control or at least a partial influence over the sick person. Since Jesus by his very nature was opposed to this power and hostile to it, he wanted to bring it into subjection and to free human beings from their suffering.

He made clear in various ways the destructive and deteriorating effect of sickness on human beings: that it tears life down rather than building it up. Experience bears this out. More dispositions are soured and lives warped by illness than the contrary. Personally I am well aware of how much harder I have to work at being halfway decent to live with, and how often my wife and children have had to take cover, if I am sick any length of time. It is well and good to talk of the brave, patient souls who have developed through suffering, but the fine borderline at which disease ceases to be a destructive force and becomes a blessing is very hard to see.

God can turn evil to good, but this does not change the fact that many are simply destroyed by illness. For instance, the mentally ill who have disintegrated as egos cannot possibly benefit from their isolation. And many who have been great in spite of illness might well have been even greater had they lived out their lives as whole persons. What the world would have lost, had Paul been a helpless invalid or had Francis of Assisi died prematurely!

The "Christian" attitude that glories in sickness is completely alien to that of Jesus of Nazareth; it is aligned on the side of what he was fighting against. I very much suspect that those who glory in the benefits of illness have either known little of it in themselves or those dear to them, or else have serious masochistic tendencies. Sickness is a destructive and evil phenomenon, and Christ as the incarnation of creativity was dead set against it. Modern medical practice is a monument to the attitude of Jesus; it practices in his way while the churches often do not. Dr. Provonsha states this view well in Appendix A.

Shortly after the publication of the first edition of this book I was asked to speak to the pastoral care staff of a Catholic hospital, four priests and three nuns. After I finished each of them spoke much the same theme: What good things we have seen happen to people religiously after they entered the hospital. Something within me bristled as I heard the same idea again and again. Then I had an inspiration. I went around the group and asked each one if he or she had ever been really sick. None of them had. How dangerous to speak of the value of illness that we have never known. I also realized that my interests in healing grew out of a childhood wracked with one illness after another.

Healing was also a good work. It was like pulling an ox or an ass out of a pit—important and valuable enough to break the Sabbath to accomplish it. The valuable laws of the Sabbath, made to protect human beings from being overworked, could and should be broken to show mercy and healing.

When Jesus entered the synagogue on a Sabbath and found there a man with a withered hand, the authorities watched to see whether he would heal him, for evidently he seldom let sickness come his way without dealing with it. Jesus called the man, and then turned to those who hoped to catch him breaking the Sabbath and said, "Is it against the law on the Sabbath day to do good, or to do evil; to save life, or to kill?" But they said nothing. Grieved to find them so obstinate, he looked angrily around at them and said to the man, "Stretch out your hand" (Mark 1:21–26).

The obvious implication of all this is that it is good to heal human beings—important enough so that ritual laws should not stand in the way. Just as the ox has a right to live, the human has a right to be well. Women and men are valuable, and whatever contributes to their restoration and health is also valuable. You will also note that this was independent of whether the person was good or bad, rich or poor. These questions were not asked. Healing, per se, was good. There is no other sense that can be made of the gospel narrative.

When people came to Jesus with faith and humility, persistence and courage, as did the centurion, the nobleman, and the Canaanite woman, Jesus healed as a response to this trust. Often these qualities bring human beings to God. These attitudes were to be encouraged. When people came with them, Jesus did not let them down. He healed to build up and strengthen people with such traits. In the same way, when the father in Mark 9:24 was torn between doubt and belief, it appears that Jesus healed in part to help the man believe. The healing was in part his response to the man's request: "Help the little faith I have!"

There is strange passage in Mark 1:40 where Jesus is strongly moved by the leper's begging: "If you want to you can cure me." Could it be that Jesus was angry, and healed because the person doubted that he wished to make him well? Then there is the passage quoted above from Mark 3:4 in which he is angry at those who would stand in the way of a healing act; their hearts are hard because they are more interested in religious rules than in human beings. Again we see real hostility toward sickness and the forces that cause it, including those who obstruct healing.

In the story of the man born blind, Jesus said quite specifically that he healed so that the works of God might be displayed in people. He wanted human beings to know the love of their God and to rejoice in the Holy One. Blindness was an obstacle to rejoicing in God; sight in those who had been blind enabled them and others to turn to God in thanksgiving and joy. Healing, then, is one way of opening our eyes to the creative love of God, so that we who are healed or see healing performed begin to know the reality of the loving God and seek the divine fellowship. This has been my own experience. People who come to know the power of God through physical or emotional healing often want more of this God and spend more time with this divine Lover and become instruments of this God in the world. They become saints and often continue Jesus' healing ministry.

Third and finally, Jesus healed to help us toward transformation. He was quite conscious of the relation between our human failure and sickness and of our human need for spurs toward wholeness. We have seen that at least twice—when he healed the paralyzed man in Mark 2:5 and after healing the invalid who could not get to the waters in John 5:14—Jesus expressly equated sickness with inadequate living. He never, however, made our human inadequacy or lawlessness the sole or most important cause of sickness.

Sin and Sickness

If sin is understood as turning aside from God's way, failing to follow the way of wholeness or individuation,[13] there is good reason for

---

[13] The word *sin* is a very slippery word and means a great many different things to different people. One should be very careful how one uses it. This is not the place for an extended discussion of the subject, but some clarification is essential before we go

believing that this can lead to illness. People who lose their religious way, or have found none to follow, find themselves exposed to destructive spiritual forces that often trigger emotional disturbances. Living in a meaningless world that ends with the grave inevitably opens intelligent people to fear and hate; to mental distress, meaninglessness, and despair; to destructive emotions that are almost a catalogue of the cardinal sins. There is good evidence, as we shall see, that such emotional disturbances often produce or contribute to a variety of mental and physical illnesses.[14] There is clearly a very direct connection between sin and sickness, particularly if sin is understood as missing the spiritual mark.

Although some illness is caused by moral and religious failure, Jesus did not have any illusion that therefore it all originates in such failure. Nor did he hold that once people stepped off the way toward wholeness and were suffering for it, they ought to be made to endure the full burden of their mistake. Let us examine these two ideas that Jesus

---

further. The Greek word translated as sin in the Greek New Testament is *hamartia* and means missing the mark, failing to follow the direction that a life should be taking. In the early stages of human development evil was believed to fall upon the entire group if one of the group broke the tabus, the rules of dealing with the Sacred. One of the great contributions of the prophets of the Old Testament was the recognition that individuals were responsible for their own actions. Ezekiel makes this very clear. In Jesus' time the popular idea of sin meant breaking either the ritual or moral law as laid down in the Torah or law. Deuteronomy 28:21–29 lays out the disastrous consequences that God will pour out on those who break the commandments laid down there. People will be wiped out by enemies and natural calamities as well as by mental and physical illnesses of the most catastrophic kind if they do not follow all the commandments.

Jesus taught a different view of sin. He stated that the Law was devised to serve human beings; human beings were not made for the Law. He violated the Sabbath laws again and again, and he changed the law concerning divorce and helped to liberate women. For Jesus, righteousness and sin were not black and white opposites. People were righteous when they lived out the love displayed by the loving Abba who made the sun to shine on both good and evil people, when they ceased judging other people, when they remained in contact with the loving God and had that Spirit working within them. None of us live this way entirely; indeed those who received Jesus' most severe castigation were those who thought they were totally righteous. And the first beatitude is: Blessed are the beggars in the spirit, for theirs is the kingdom of heaven. And yet in most churches the sins of the flesh (sexual) are the most severely condemned, and the proud and the gossips with their malicious ill will often serve in high places.

Anthropologists have told of many examples of people dying when they have broken a tabu in a tabu culture of which they were an integral part. When people believe that they have incurred divine wrath in breaking what they conceive to be divine law, they can be so overcome by guilt and fear that this alone can cause mental and physical illness. The loving God revealed in Jesus of Nazareth wants to draw all people into the orbit of love, not to destroy the offender. The word sin has such bad connotations to most people that I use it as infrequently as possible.

[14] See Chapter Eleven for the medical evidence.

avoided. They are very important if we are to understand the current popular outlook and modern behavior based on it and how both differ from the attitude and actions of Jesus.

Deuteronomic Judaism affirmed that sickness was the result of sin—that it was one of God's punishments for disobedience to the divine law. Hellenistic thinking came to much the same conclusion: sickness was the direct result of the anger of the gods against people who got in their way or took liberties with the divine prerogative. This idea of chastisement by disease, which we have already discussed at some length, was also basic to the Teutonic paganism that overwhelmed the church from the sixth into the tenth century. In popular Islam, children born blind were considered cursed by God and shunned by most people.

While it is easy to see how people arrive at the idea that sickness *can* be caused by defiance of or unconscious trespass against God, this is no reason, as the book of Job so ably shows, to assert that all sickness is so caused. But most human beings hate incomplete knowledge, and so they transform it into final, unquestioned conclusions. Jesus did not fall into this trap. He specifically rejected the theory that all that ails humanity is caused by trespass against God.

In Luke 13:2–5 Jesus was speaking to a large group of people who came to tell him about the Galileans, whose blood Pilate had mingled with their sacrifices. Jesus went on to say: "Do you suppose these Galileans who suffered like that were greater sinners than any other Galileans? They were not, I tell you. No; but unless you repent you will all perish as they did. Or those eighteen on whom the tower at Siloam fell and killed them? Do you suppose that they were more guilty than all the other people living in Jerusalem? They were not, I tell you." How could this be stated any more clearly? There is no mistaking the sense: people who suffered tragedy were no *more* sinful than other people. And when the disciples questioned him in the same way about the man born blind, Jesus answered, "Neither he nor his parents sinned," adding, "he was born blind so that the works of God might be displayed in him." (John 9:3).

When he saw a need to speak of sin in connection with a healing, he did not say that this was the sole cause of the person's trouble. Jesus seemed to believe that a primary cause of sickness was a force of evil loose in the world which was hostile to God and the divine way. He believed that people sometimes fell into the hands of this power, which then exerted a destructive influence in their lives, morally, psychologically, and physically. You may call this force Satan, the devil, evil spirits, demons, autonomous complexes, or what you will; its exact source was never fully accounted for. But this understanding, this knowledge of the reality of such errant destructiveness is shot through the teaching and actions of Jesus.

Perhaps missing the moral and religious mark does leave an individual more open to the invasion of this power. Jesus did not discuss this relationship except when he suggested that it was emptiness that allowed a person, after being healed of an unclean spirit, to be possessed by seven other devils (Matt. 12:44–45). The person's defenses at that point were nil. In fact, the way Jesus treated people who were considered as sinners by society suggests that sin itself may be the result of an intrusion of the power of evil into the personality of women and men, so that the sinning and the sick person equally need God's presence, touch, and help. Indeed, the only way to be secure against the invasion of evil was to be filled with God's spirit.

The idea that God is bent on causing illness for sinners is still very much alive among today's Christians, however. As we have indicated, this attitude—the persistent feeling that much sickness must result from some basic error or fault on the part of the sick person—comes to us directly from the Middle Ages and the Reformation. This is one area of medieval thinking the reformers didn't reform. Instead they firmly preserved the medieval idea that human sickness is the result of breaking God's law. The thirteenth-century church, for instance, carefully kept a sick person from seeing a doctor until after the priest had come to hear and forgive sins. Church authorities in nineteenth-century England still thought this decree "wisely made."[15] And English clergy were given detailed instructions, based on references to Calvin, on how to bring sick people to realize God's purpose in making them suffer. Today many sincere Christians assume that somehow illness, borne properly, makes stronger and better Christians, without questioning why they believe such a thing (though this need not prevent them from visiting the doctor and doing their best to get well). They simply do not consider illness as coming from something other than God and being alien to God's love.

Yet this is uncomfortably close to the conclusion that, if sickness is caused by sin, it must be God's will for human beings and therefore relieving it is contrary to God's will. Behind this conclusion is the basic premise that God enjoys a very human anger against women and men

---

[15] *Visitatio Infirmorum: Or, Offices for the Clergy in Praying with, Directing, and Comforting the Sick, Infirm, and Afflicted*, 3rd ed. (1854), p. 323.

and loves them only when they are good, hating and punishing them when they are bad.[16] God must then be seen as interested not so much in keeping people corrected as in punishing them for punishment's sake. Sickness becomes a weapon the angry God reaches for when people overstep the way set out for them. Not many people today put this into words, or consider how completely Jesus avoids this attitude or how it denies the very essence of the spirit of Jesus. Francis McNutt has often stated that if a parent gave a child a little leukemia for being bad we would put him in jail and yet we attribute such actions to God.

The coming of Jesus, if indeed he was the incarnation of God, wipes out once and for all the notion that God puts sickness upon people because of divine wrath. Jesus' ministry of healing embodies the exact antithesis of this idea. He did not inquire whether people were good or bad, whether they had repented or were reforming, *before* he healed them. He loved women and men just as they were and wanted to help them out of their misery. If sin had contributed to that misery, Jesus' attitude appears to have been: once these people are healed, perhaps they will reflect and come to their senses, but as long as they are sick and suffering it is difficult for them to reach out to the loving God.

With essentially this point of view Jesus acted to express God's compassion toward people caught up in sin and sickness; he healed both. However, the gospel narratives contain ten times this number of physical and psychological healings than moral and religious ones. There was no hint of sitting back to wait for suffering to teach human beings their lesson and bring them back to relation with God; Jesus knew that healing could accomplish God's will in people far better. God through

---

[16] Many churchmen in the eighteenth and nineteenth centuries seem to have concluded that God liked them best when they were dead. The English book of prayers for visiting the sick, the *Visitatio Infirmorum* referred to in note 15, above, suggests this in service after service. It is particularly clear in the three-page exhortation "to a Child dangerously ill," which begins, "My dear Child, do not be afraid of death . . . To wicked people, indeed, to die is a very dreadful thing, for it takes them to those torments which await them in another life; but to the pure and good, death is only the way to pleasures so great, that if you could now plainly and clearly see them, you would, I am sure, be quite willing to leave this naughty world. For your soul, whenever it leaves this body of yours, will immediately return to GOD . . . Who loves you much better than even your dear parents here on earth." And: "Your body will not be long kept from these great pleasures, which GOD made it fit to enjoy," on and on to the minister's last words: "And now tell me, my child, when you thus think of the joys of the next world, and the miseries of this, whether you would not willingly change this present life for that happy one which is to come; and whether it will not be better for you, if GOD so require it, to hasten immediately to the presence of GOD, rather than by staying longer in this life to expose yourself to the danger of losing all these great delights, by falling into sin." *Ibid.*, pp. 394–95.

Christ is interested in whole, redeemed men and women, not in using them to satisfy divine anger. This is one of the fundamental conceptions of Jesus and vital Christianity. Jesus underwent crucifixion and resurrection for human beings *before* people thought of accepting God's way of love.

All the Wrong Reasons

Reasons are sometimes given for Jesus' healings for which there is little if any support in the gospel record. We have discussed some of these in Chapter Two. Let us now look at them in the light of the material in this chapter, beginning with the notion that illness is the best time to catch people off base and get them on the path toward their greatest spiritual development—one way God uses to trip people up when they are going astray. There may be some truth in this. In time of illness people can sometimes be more open, and those who are more or less conscious can, by reflection, let disease or emotional problems help to show them where they have wandered from the track. But while this may be found to happen in psychological practice and under religious direction, it does not mean that sickness itself is God's will. The first task is to get over it, not to bear it patiently. As Jesus demonstrated in helping people on their way toward wholeness, it is not the illness itself but the *healing* that is a stepping stone toward repentance and change. Jesus first healed. And if healing failed in that effect—well, converting people *is* a challenge.

There is also the idea among Christians that Jesus came to provide a do-it-yourself manual for human beings, that his primary purpose, so to speak, was to teach ingenuity, self-reliance, and the one right method of spiritual healing so as to avoid sickness. This does not tally with the record on the whole. As we have seen, his healing practices varied, and he made no explicit suggestion that people should learn to get along without physicians. Nor, of course, did he recommend that they do without God's healing and rely entirely on medical practice. Instead Jesus dignified intelligence as a way for humankind to deal with their problems, while increasing their reliance upon God.

The notion that his healings were intended only to point the way to salvation—to ultimate wholeness in another life—has even less foundation in the gospel story. However, this idea completely ignores the fact that healings actually occurred, and that they were effective in bringing new life right then, *as well as* in confirming the expectation of life to come. Essentially everything we know of Jesus of Nazareth underlines the importance of this present life, both in its own relation to God and as a way of touching the kingdom of heaven in preparation for the future. Jesus certainly did not seem to be healing in order to make an allegorical statement of something quite different.

Finally, some churches believe that Jesus healed merely to help people take his mission seriously. They are persuaded that his purpose was to reveal his spiritual authority, confirm his divinity. Hence the church continued to heal until this was well established, and then the power was withdrawn from human beings. Many Christians seriously hold this theory which, as we have seen is one aspect of dispensationalism.

Seldom was this the attitude of Jesus. Far from using his healings as signs of power, he seemed embarrassed by them and told people not to speak of them. At times he even gave the impression that he would rather not have performed healings from a tactical point of view. But it was his nature to be hostile to illness and to have mercy on the sick; it appears almost as if he could not help himself. As the incarnation of a loving God, he had the authority, desire, and power to heal; it was as if healing were an obligation he had to accept, if he was to fulfill his destiny.

We also know that in his temptation Jesus rejected once and for all the idea of using miracles as a sideshow attraction, a way of astonishing people into taking spiritual reality seriously. He repelled the suggestion of the devil to jump from the top of the Temple to demonstrate that he would be held up on the hands of the angels, so that people would see and be awed into belief (Matt. 4:5–7). His healing miracles were not done merely to impress the populace; they were rather the natural reaction of his spirit to sickness and suffering in the world and his desire for God's grace to be known in those he touched. When the Pharisees, on the other hand, wanted him to produce a sign, he replied, "It is an evil and unfaithful generation that asks for a sign! The only sign it will be given is the sign of the prophet Jonah" (Matt. 12:39). However, when all is said and done, the healings described in the gospels (and so carefully ignored by most Biblical critics) do show a loving power let loose in the world and gave Jesus the kind of stature that later convinced Christians that in him they had met not only a truly whole human being, but also the very essence of God as well.

Practical Conclusions

What were the reasons, then, that Jesus spent so much of his ministry healing sick people, and what conclusions can we draw from this?

He was a real human being and yet he carried the essence of God's nature (and so they called him the son of God). He knew what it is to be a human being in all of its glory and agony, and he cared about human beings whom God had created in the divine image. He was hostile to anything that marred that image—particularly the destructive aspects of spiritual reality which resulted in sickness. Illness hindered people from achieving their full human potential, and he wanted them to have life, and that abundantly, so that they might "glorify and enjoy God forever."

There is more than just academic interest in this. The attitude of Jesus and his healing ministry offer some very practical considerations for the life of the church. Our analysis suggests four principal conclusions for Christian groups, which we shall consider further as we look at healing in the history of the church.

First, the Christian who goes around saying that sickness is God's will has not fully understood the life and teaching of Christ. A large part, perhaps even the major part, of Jesus' ministry was devoted to healing the sick just because it was indeed God's will that they should be well and not ill. God in Christ was opposed to sickness and to what makes people sick; one reason he was in the world was to heal it.

Second, health of mind and body and Christianity cannot be separated. It may be possible to separate health of mind and body from other religions, but not from Christianity; they are in a corporate relationship. Whether God wants perfect health for all people at all times one cannot be sure, but it is certain that God wants wholeness and salvation for each individual. Jesus came into the world in order to give people a better chance at wholeness at *life* and to save those lost in despair and psychological darkness. It is dangerous, if not downright deadly, to judge of any other people that their sickness is good for them; in fact it is even dangerous to judge this about one's self. Instead, the task of Christians is to use whatever means they can to bring wholeness and health without first judging—in other words, with just about the same interest and concern that good medical doctors bring to those who need them.

Can you imagine Jesus of Nazareth saying to anyone, "Oh, go your way and make something of your sickness! It is better for you than the mischief you have been getting into." Although he could be quite harsh when it was needed, this was not his tone toward the sick, or even toward individuals generally. Instead his criticism was most often directed to the people who thought they had attained religious perfection. But his response to the sick was to heal them. In the next chapter we shall look at Paul's actions, and also what he said and did not say about having a thorn in the flesh. Later we shall compare these things with some of our own opinions and our actions or lack of action.

Third, for all practical purposes the aim in founding the church was to make it possible to carry on the ministry of Christ while they waited for the coming of the kingdom. On one hand Christians who are actually followers of Christ—in whom his spirit is still working—have good reason to want their ministry and its healing activity to continue. And on the other, there seems to be only one good way to keep this spirit alive in people, and that is to be touched by and to help carry out that same activity and ministry.

Jesus gathered together a band of disciples to carry on his work after he was gone. While he was still with them, he started them out with the same ministry as his own. In Mark 6:7, Matthew 10:5–8, and Luke 9:1 we have the account of his sending out his disciples and giving them authority to cast out demons, preach, heal the sick, cleanse lepers, and raise the dead. The disciples returned ecstatic with joy and amazement because of their success. In Luke 10 we are told that Jesus selected seventy-two others and sent them out with similar instructions. They too reported phenomenal success, and Jesus said: "I watched Satan fall like lightning from heaven. Yes, I have given you power to tread underfoot serpents and scorpions and the whole strength of the enemy; nothing shall ever hurt you. Yet do not rejoice that the Spirits submit to you; rejoice rather that your names are written in heaven" (10:18–20). If one writes this off as mythology and says that Jesus and his followers were *only* interested in the life to come (eschatology), one does real violence to the text.

In John 14:12–14 Jesus expressed the same essential attitude when he said:

I tell you most solemnly,
whoever believes in me
will perform the same works as I do myself;
he will perform even great works,
because I am going to the Father.
Whatever you ask for in my name I will do,
so that the Father may be glorified in the Son.
If you ask for anything in my name,
I will do it.

It is hard to see how followers who really accepted such a commission could come back later and ask whether it was God's will or not that sick people be healed sacramentally.

Fourth, Jesus' ministry was to preach, teach, and heal. It was to be the same ministry for his disciples and for his church. In other words, his followers were to proclaim the presence of the Kingdom of God. They were to show the evidence of the kingdom operative at the present time. And finally, in some very specific ways, they were to bring the healing power of God to bear on the mental and physical illness of their time. The commissions would seem to be the same for the church in our time, unless the words of the New Testament have been superseded by later authority.

Beyond all the embroideries and inventions that must have crept into so large and long a tradition, the core of real expectation and experience seems undeniable. As we shall note presently, when Paul wrote to the Galatians reminding them of healings they had already witnessed, he had nothing to gain in his missionary labors by pointing to something false and unconvincing which would at once discredit him.

CHAPTER 6

Signs, Wonders, and Mighty Works

We turn now to the first organized group of Christians, to see what they actually did about all this. The books and letters that contain the record of the first Christian churches, taken together, do not make a very long work. But besides recording the persons, places, experiences, and specific problems that arose and were solved, these books contain some of the most important thinking that has been done by Christians. As the apostles carried the new faith to the centers of the Gentile world, Paul and others set down for the new churches much of their basic understanding of Christian experiences, including healing. The passages about healing are brief and to the point, and one has to know where to look to put the whole story together.

Any serious study of healing in the early church should begin with three brief references in the letters of Paul. They occur in three of the earliest letters to different congregations: the Galatians, the Corinthians, and the Romans. Few serious modern scholars deny Paul's authorship of these letters. They are authentic, firsthand accounts of what was happening among Christians twenty to thirty years after the resurrection, written by a leader who left his imprint on all organized Christianity from then on. In his exegesis on 2 Corinthians 12:12 in the *Interpreter's Bible*, Floyd Filson has remarked significantly: "Writing to churches that would have challenged him had he falsified the facts, Paul refers unhestitatingly to such miracles [as healing]; he knows that even his enemies cannot deny their occurrence. In other words, the study of miracles must begin by accepting the fact that many such remarkable events happened. Moreover, this verse implies clearly that other true apostles were doing similar *mighty works*."[1] Although the word *healing* itself is not used in these three places, there is essential agreement among scholars, as Filson suggests, that this is the plain meaning in the Greek. Let us look at these passages in which healing is referred to as one important action of the true apostle of Christ.

Writing to the Galatians who were turning away from his teaching, Paul asked, "Does God give you the Spirit so freely and work miracles among you because you practice the Law, or because you believed what was preached to you?" (3:5). To the Corinthians, who were in conflict with him on many subjects, Paul was opening his heart about what it meant to be an apostle; toward the end of this second letter he stated one of the clearest confirmations of his authentic ministry: "You have seen done among you all the things that mark the true apostle, unfailingly produced: the signs, the marvels, the miracles" (12:12). In the following year he put together his careful reasoning about Christian experience in a letter to the Romans, in conclusion commending his ministry to them and saying, "What I am presuming to speak of, of course, is only what Christ himself has done to win the allegiance of the pagans, using what I have said and done by the power of signs and wonders, by the power of the Holy Spirit" (15:18–19).

Paul used here the Greek word *dúnamis*, translated as miracle and power, *semeîon*, or sign, and *teras*, marvels or wonders. All three were also used again and again in the gospels and Acts to refer to the miracles done by Jesus and later by the apostles, very often miracles of healing. The translation of these words is not consistent, particularly in the King James version, and it is worthwhile to look at their meaning in the original Greek.

Words and Acts of Power

Dúnamis (δυναμις), which means power or ability, is the word from which "dynamite" and "dynamic" are derived. Any power may be implied, from the power of money to that of medicine or of mathematical exponents. It is that essential force or energy which can effectively accomplish some result; something of the same sense is conveyed by the English word dynamics. It is also commonly used in the phrase "the power of God" (or of Christ or the Holy Spirit), and in this sense it refers to divine or spiritual power, as in the doxology of the Lord's Prayer.

---

[1] *The Interpreter's Bible*, 10:411. Emphasis from the original.

Since *dúnamis* may also refer to the action accomplished, it often means "miracle," the action accomplished by some extraordinary power, in Paul's words "by the power of God." The miracle, in other words, is the concrete expression of that particular power. The gospels, Acts, and Paul's letters all used this word in the same way to speak of the more than ordinary happenings, the "mighty works" or signs and wonders, particularly healings, by which divine power manifests itself.[2]

Semeîon (σημειον), or distinguishing mark, carries much the same significance as the English word *sign*. In the New Testament it is used almost exclusively to speak of unusual events that display divine, or sometimes demonic, power.[3] Particularly in the Gospel of John the healing miracles are spoken of as signs of Jesus' divine calling and mission. In these passages and also throughout Acts, this word is used to refer to healings as significant evidence of divine power breaking through and making contact with people in the human realm. In a few places it was also used to describe portents in the heavens, as in Luke 21:11, or in the simpler sense of an ordinary sign, like the kiss given by Judas as a sign for the soldiers to act in Matthew 26:48.

Teras (τερας), is used only with the word *sign* (*semeîon*) in the New Testament, in the phrase "signs and wonders" or "marvels."[4] Basically it means a portentous event or prodigy, a happening that excites wonder and awe. This word is particularly interesting because the specific way it is used in the New Testament reveals how a meaning in classic Greek was given a new Christian sense. To the Greeks an event in nature—a thunderbolt, a snake, the wind—rightly timed, could be a prodigy in itself. A god had caused the wind to rise before their ship, a serpent to drop onto the altar at the sacrifice. To Christian writers a prodigy was not separate from its significance as being a sign of Christ or the Holy Spirit. "Wonders" were spoken of, not as wonders in themselves, but in conjunction with the signs and evidences that Jesus gave, and those the apostles continued to perform in his spirit. And except

---

[2] *Dúnamis* in the sense of miracle, a mighty or wondrous work that is a sign of divine power, occurs in Matt. 7:22, 11:20, 21, 23, 13:54, 58; Mark 6:2, 5, 14, 9:39; Luke 10:13, 19:37; Acts 2:22, 8:13, 19:11; 1 Cor. 12:10, 28, 29; 2 Cor. 12:12; Gal. 3:5; 1 Thess. 1:11, 2:9 (satanic power); Heb. 2:4.

[3] *Semeîon* as a miracle, a sign of divine intervention, occurs in Matt. 12:38, 39, 16:4; Mark 8:11, 12, 16:17; Luke 11:16, 29, 30, 21:7, 11; John 2:11, 8, 23, 3:2, 4:54, 6:2, 14, 26, 30, 7:31, 9:16, 10:41, 11:47, 12:18, 37, 20:30; Acts 4:16, 22, 8:6; in conjunction with *teras*, marvel or wonder, it is found in Matt. 24:24; Mark 13:22; John 4:48; Acts 2:19, 22, 43, 4:30, 5:12, 6:8, 7:36, 8:13, 14:3, 15:12; Rom. 15:19; 2 Cor. 12:12; 2 Thess. 2:9 (satanic sign); Heb. 2:4.

[4] See note 3, above.

for two references to Old Testament events and to false Christs, the wonders described were all miracles of healing.

Thus it is clear what Paul was speaking of when he wrote simply about miracles in Galatians and emphasized signs and wonders in Romans and 2 Corinthians. Healing, he told these congregations, is a sign by which they could know that the Holy Spirit was working in them in the here and now; it was one important test of a true apostle of Christ.[5] Then, in his first letter to the Corinthians, Paul referred directly to the ministry of healing as a special *charisma* or gift of the Holy Spirit. Twice in the twelfth chapter he catalogued the gifts. To some people, he wrote, "gifts of healing [are given] by the one Spirit" (12:9), and again, in conclusion, he wrote, "And God has appointed in the church first apostles, second prophets, third teachers, then workers of miracles, then healers, helpers, administrators, speakers in various kinds of tongues. Are all apostles? Are all prophets? Are all teachers? Do all work miracles? Do all possess gifts of healing?" (12:28–30). Here Paul specifically relates the ministry of healing through sacramental or spiritual means to the power of God. Healing, representing the Spirit's presence, has the dignity of a Christian profession.

In this discussion Paul used one of the common words for healing or remedy (*iáma*), found in medical literature as well as other writings. He spoke of gifts (*charísmata*) of healing in much the same way that Luke wrote about miracles or signs of healing, using *semeîon* with *iásis*, a word from the same root as *iáma* in Acts 4:22. In Paul's writing *charísmata* (χαρισματα) was used to signify those divine gifts which give Christians special powers beyond ordinary human capabilities. In the case of gifts of healing, the ordinary word for curing or restoring to health was given a special, Christian sense, and this was one of four such basic words which we should recognize. All four, given here in the verb form, were used in an essentially similar way throughout the gospels and Acts.

Iáomai (ιάομαι), to heal or cure, was almost exclusively a medical term in Greek usage. Like such words in our own language, however, it could extend to the healing of moral wounds or sickness. Indeed, as far as the Greek language goes, it may have had a peculiar application in pagan usage to breaking the religious tabus and incurring divine

---

[5] Barth in his *Epistle to the Romans* (1963) makes no comment on this verse, as Paul's statement in Romans 15:19 does not fit into Barth's worldview. This seems to me like ostrich biblical criticism.

displeasure and so resulting in sickness, both physical and psychological.

Therapeúō (θεραπεύō), from which our English word therapy is derived, was another common word for medical treatment and healing. The original meaning was to give care or service of various kinds, including serving the gods. By adoption it came to mean heal, restore, or cure.

Hugiaínō (ὑγιαινο), to be in good health, was taken from the name of the goddess of health, Hygeia, and has given us the English word hygiene. This word could be used to refer to a healthy or sound state either of the body or of political or religious affairs. It was a basic word in Greek medical usage.

Sōzō (σώζω), to preserve or keep from harm, to rescue, save from death, was used in a variety of senses, including the medical, in classical Greek. It carried the meaning of healing in the sense of saving a person from illness or death. Since in the Greek mind the saving of the body implied moving one step on the way toward salvation of the entire being, this word was related by implication to the whole idea of salvation. From it the theological word soteriology, or the study of salvation, is derived. The compound word *diasōzō* (διασώζω), [combining the meanings of "through" and "preserve"], to bring safely through some danger or preserve through danger, was similar in meaning and usage.

These, then, are the words used all through the gospels and Acts to record that, wherever Jesus, and later other people, brought his Spirit through their ministry, healings occurred.[6] Such miracles were spoken

---

[6] These words used in the sense of healing disease, are found in the following places in the New Testament:

Iáomai, 'iáma, 'iásis: Matt. 8:8, 13, 15:28;
    Mark 5:29;
    Luke 5:17, 6:17, 19, 7:7, 8:47, 9:2, 11, 42, 13:32, 14:4, 17:15, 22:51;
    John 4:47, 5:13;
    Acts 3:11, 4:22, 30, 9:34, 10:38, 28:8;
    1 Cor. 12:9, 28, 30;
    James 5:16;
Therapeúō, therapeía: Matt. 4:23, 24, 8:7, 16, 9:35, 10:1, 8, 12:10, 15, 22, 14:14, 15:30, 17:16, 18, 19:2, 21:14;
    Mark 1:34, 3:2, 10, 15, 6:5, 13;
    Luke 4:23, 40, 5:15, 6:7, 18, 7:21, 8:2, 43, 9:1, 6, 11, 10:9, 13:14, 14:3;
    John 5:10;
    Acts 4:14, 5:16, 8:7, 28:9;
Hugiaínō, hugiés: Matt. 12:13, 15:31;
    Mark 3:5, 5:34;
    Luke 5:31, 6:10, 7:10 (healthy), 15:27;

of simply as healings or cures, being made whole and healthy, saved
from sickness and disease. They were stated in the same words Hippocrates and Galen used, both in description of the incidents themselves and also in the discussion of gifts in 1 Corinthians and in the
instructions about healing in the letter of James. The fact that these
events were supernatural or religious in nature is known simply from
the accounts of what was said and done at the time they were happening, and because they were spoken of as "miracles," "works of power,"
or "signs and wonders."

Besides these specific references to healing and gifts of healing, other statements in the Epistles express the conviction that humankind
had been under the influence of various forces of evil. Paul spoke of
these forces as demons or idols, sovereignties, elements, powers, the
flesh, the law, sin, death, dominions, and so on.[7] One of the primary
results of their domination over human beings was sickness. And one
of the reasons for the coming of Christ in Paul's theology was to rescue
people from this domination and set them free both from evil forces
and from the illness—moral, social, mental, and physical—that came in
their wake.

This idea of sickness is suggested in Galatians, where he wrote:
"Formerly, when you did not know God, you were in bondage to
beings that by nature are no gods; but now that you have come to know
God, or rather to be known by God, how can you turn back again to
the *weak* and beggarly elemental spirits, whose slaves you want to be
once more?" (4:8–9—italics mine). Paul used here the Greek word *as-
thenes* (ἀσθένης) to speak of elements that are weak, sick, or diseased.
This is the same word that occurs in various places in his own writings
and in the gospels and Acts to describe people who were sick.[8]

John 5:4, 6, 9, 11, 14, 15, 7:23;
    Acts 4:10;
Sōzō, diasōzō: Matt. 9:21, 22, 14:36;
    Mark 5:23, 28, 34, 6:56, 10:52;
    Luke 7:3, 8:36, 48, 50, 17:19, 18:42;
    John 11:12;
    Acts 4:9, 14:9;
    James 5:15.
In addition, in raisings from the dead, it was simply said that the dead arose, with the
implication that they were then whole. The command Jesus gave to the daughter of Jairus
was "Wake up," and to Lazarus "Come out," while Peter simply said to Tabitha, "Arise."
[7] See Appendix A in my book on tongue speaking for a complete listing of these colorful
    names, *Tongue Speaking: The History and Meaning of Charismatic Experience* (1981) pp. 237–
    43. See also Walter Wink, *Naming the Powers: The Language of Power in the New Testament*
    (1985) for a definitive description of the "powers."
[8] Other examples are Mark 6:56; Luke 4:40; John 4:46, 11:1, 3; Acts 9:37, 19:12; Paul's

Other statements of this basic conviction are found in 1 Corinthians 15:24 and in Romans 6:11 and 8:38. In Colossians Paul wrote: "He has overriden the Law . . . he has done away with it by nailing it to the Cross; and so he got rid of the Sovereignties and the Powers, and paraded them in public, behind him in his triumphal procession." (2:14:15). The author of the letter to the Ephesians expressed the same idea: "For it is not against human enemies that we have to struggle, but against the Sovereignties and the Powers who originate the darkness in this world, the spiritual army of evil in the heavens" (6:12). Hebrews also states that: "Since all the children share the same blood and flesh, he too shared equally in it, so that by his death he could take away all the power of the devil, who had power over death, and set free all those who had been held in slavery all their lives by the fear of death" (2:14–15).

As we shall see, these ideas of metaphysical evil make a good deal more sense than the nineteenth century world believed possible. Basically it was the contention of Paul and the other writers that forces of evil existed which could not be grappled with by physical means alone and which sapped and destroyed human life. The Christian as a follower of Christ had a means to oppose these damaging forces that had been defeated in the crucifixion and resurrection of Jesus.

Another Point of View

The only passages in the letters that suggest any other point of view about the value of healing are the famous "thorn in the flesh" passage in 2 Corinthians 12:7 and the references to illness in 1 Corinthians 11:29–30, Philippians 2:26–27, 1 Timothy 5:23, and 2 Timothy 4:20. Let us look at the simpler references to illness first and then turn to Paul's description of his own trouble, which is quoted by nearly everyone who believes that the healing ministry should not be a part of Christian practice today.

Paul gave a stern warning to the Corinthians about the casual way they were partaking of the Lord's supper. He told them that any one who shares in it "without recognizing the Body [of Christ] is eating and drinking his own condemnation. In fact that is why many of you are

---

letters in Phil. 2:26; 1 Tim. 5:23; 2 Tim. 4:20; 1 Cor. 11:30; also James 5:14 (including noun and verb form). In translating Gal. 4:9, for some reason the Jerusalem Bible omits the specifically descriptive words and refers only to "elemental things . . . that can do nothing and give nothing."

weak and ill and some of you have died" (1 Cor. 11:29–30). He then went on to say that the reason for punishment like that was "to correct us and stop us from being condemned with the world." Irreverence toward the sacred was seen here as resulting in sickness, which could only be relieved by reforming and getting back into relationship with God. This is the most pointed such judgment in the New Testament outside the book of Revelation and the story of Ananias and Sapphira in Acts 9. Sickness is tied to irreverence much as it was in most of the Old Testament. In Acts, however, the illustration is even more graphic. After Ananias and Sapphira had defrauded the Christian community, each came in separately, lied about it, and there in front of the apostles fell down dead. As it says in Acts, "This made a profound impression on the whole Church" (Acts 5:11).[9]

Then there are three places in which Paul speaks about the illness of those close to him. He reports to the Philippians that his "brother" and fellow worker Epaphroditus has recovered after being so sick that he almost died. The congregation had had news of his illness and were worried; Paul reassures them that he will soon be back with them (2:25–28). There is no contradiction here, for as far as I know no one seriously suggests that Christians are perfect and never fall ill, but only that they can often be healed by physical, psychological, and spiritual means. The means of healing are simply not mentioned in this instance, and we have no way of knowing whether they were religious or medicinal.

In another letter Paul advises Timothy, who had trouble with his stomach, to drink a little wine to relieve the ailment and help his digestion[10] (1 Timothy 5:23). There is nothing here of contradiction to Christian healing. Paul simply recommends a remedy of long standing. If one believes that God heals directly by contact with the spirit, this in no way implies that God does not provide healing through thoroughly physical and medical means. In the second letter Paul tells Timothy that

---

[9] These deaths appear to be examples of tabu deaths, a phenomenon which is studied and discussed by scientists today. For instance, Dr. Jerome D. Frank, who taught psychiatry at John Hopkins Medical School, has included a discussion of the subject in his *Persuasion and Healing* (1969), pp. 61, 230–34, giving references to both anthropological and physiological studies of similar deaths. See also Herman Feifel, ed., *The Meaning of Death* (1959), pp. 302–13. It must also be remembered that the Hellenistic (Greek and Roman) and Hebrew culture perceived God as punishing people with sickness. I wonder if Paul in 1 Corinthians 11:29–30 was not following more the attitude of his culture than the teaching and practice of Jesus.

[10] The question of whether or not Paul was actually the writer of all parts of these letters does not matter greatly; they are early Christian documents and represent some of the concerns of the early church, whoever the writer was.

he has left Trophimus sick in Miletus (4:20). There is no reason to suppose that he was not in the process of getting well.

The passage in 2 Corinthians is important enough to quote in full. Paul wrote: "In view of the extraordinary nature of these revelations, to stop me from getting too proud I was given a thorn in the flesh, an angel of Satan to beat me and stop me from getting too proud! About this thing I have pleaded with the Lord three times for it to leave me, but he has said, "My grace is enough for you: my power is at its best in weakness" (12:7–9). Twice he repeated that the trouble, whatever it was, was given him because he became too proud or puffed up, and his discomfort kept his feet on the ground so that he would not be carried away by his own importance. It was a messenger of Satan which prevented self-inflation, itself a malady that resulted in self-centeredness rather than letting his experiences keep him God-centered.

Paul did not say that God had sent the malady or that it was a good thing. He only made clear that God did not take it away because it gave Paul the weakness, humility, and poverty of spirit which he needed for God to be manifest in his life. I am sure that God would have preferred Paul without his pride *and* his thorn. But even if it is assumed from this passage that God was responsible for the ailment, this did not keep Paul from healing other people and commending the healing ministry. It is therefore not an argument for others to shy away from the ministry of healing in the Christian church; it cannot be generalized as a basis for Christian action.

The Classic Healing Text

In the letter of James we find the classic New Testament text on spiritual healing. The church has pondered and studied it for centuries, and the later practice of anointing the sick was largely based on it. But outside of the Pentecostal churches and other churches influenced by them, it is not often considered seriously today as a basis of action; students in seminary seldom, if ever, study these words. James wrote, probably to Jewish Christians all over the empire: "If one of you is ill, he should send for the elders of the church, and they must anoint him with oil in the name of the Lord and pray over him. The prayer of faith will save the sick man and the Lord will raise him up again; and if he has committed any sins, he will be forgiven. So confess your sins to one another, and pray for one another, and this will cure you" (5:14–16).

For centuries the Roman Catholic church officially interpreted this passage to mean the act of saving a person from spiritual death, and supported this meaning with the translation from the Vulgate. It was upon this understanding that the practice of extreme unction was based. Instead of the Latin words *curo* or *sano*, which commonly meant to heal or cure medically, only the word *salvo*, to save, was used in the Vulgate to translate "save" or "heal" or "cure" in this passage. This was a word that came into Latin only in Christian times and carried the peculiar modern meaning of salvation, rather than the meaning of the ordinary words in common usage that referred to physical or mental healing.[11] The idea of being saved from spiritual death cannot be supported, however, by the original Greek text. The sense of the words in Greek is healed, cured, saved from illness or death. Modern Roman Catholicism has returned to this meaning and has returned to the use of anointing and the laying on of hands for healing. While there may be some question as to who was the actual author of this letter, there is no one who doubts its early Christian inspiration and authorship.

This passage is worth considering carefully. First we notice that Christian healing is no longer described as a special gift, a unique *charisma* which God gives to certain individuals; it has now become the official action of the church officer as such. Thus what was once exclusively a *charisma* is now a sacrament which any qualified church official may administer. Second, anointing for healing was given a firm foundation in this passage, and in the West the practice did continue as an integral part of the church's ministry for nearly a thousand years. In the Orthodox church it is still a central religious practice. Finally, not only was anointing directed, but this was done in a certain relation to forgiveness of sin. The anointing and healing came first; confession and forgiveness might well go along with the healing actions or follow them, but they were not necessarily prerequisite for the healing itself.

In at least one official modern document an attitude toward healing has been expressed that is very similar to this passage from the letter of James. The Anglican report on the healing at Lambeth in 1930 took the following position: "Within the Church . . . systems of healing based on the redemptive work of our Lord . . . all spring from a belief in the fundamental principle that the power to exercise spiritual healing is taught by Christ to be the natural heritage of Christian people who are living in fellowship with God, and is part of the ministry of Christ

---

[11] The Latin word *salvo* was probably first used by Lactantius in the third or fourth century A.D.

through His Body the Church."[12] The Anglican bishops assembled at this Lambeth Conference commended the statement to their church without a dissenting vote. The resolution still called for "a fuller understanding of the intimate connection between moral and spiritual disorders and mental and physical ills," but it stressed a ministry to the whole person. For the first time that I know of, a modern mainline church acknowledged in an official pronouncement that unction and laying on of hands can have a direct effect on the body.

Largely through the effort of one woman, Anne Hancock, the United Church of Christ meeting in its annual official national assembly approved a resolution that Christian healing was an organic part of Christian ministry and should be studied and practiced in churches of this denomination. Mrs. Hancock first brought the matter to her local church and then to the Vermont Synod of that church, where it was approved in 1978. It was then presented and approved by the twelfth General Synod of the United Church of Christ in June 1979.[13]

In contrast, the letter of James represented the practice of the whole church. As Luke says in Acts by way of preface to what the apostles did after Pentecost, "The many miracles and signs worked through the apostles made a deep impression on everyone . . . Day by day the Lord added to their community those destined to be saved" (2:43, 47).

The Healing Ministry of the Apostles

The healing practice referred to in the letters of the New Testament is borne out all through the book of Acts,[14] which is to say, wherever Christianity was taken during all the early years of the church's life. Since there is no work that looks at these healings with respect to the categories of illness and since these healings were by *followers* of Jesus, we present a complete summary of the examples given in Acts.

---

[12] *The Ministry of Healing: Report of the Committee Appointed in Accordance with Resolution 63 of the Lambeth Conference, 1920* (1924), p. 13 and *The Lambeth Conference, 1930* pp. 61–62, also pp. 182–83.

[13] The Vermont Overture and resolution of the twelfth General Synod are reproduced in Appendix C.

[14] Chapter 19 of Percy Dearmer's excellent work, *Body and Soul* (1909) offers a very fine analysis of the healing ministry recorded in Acts. Appendices D and E in *Power Healing* by John Wimber and Kevin Springer (1987) provide a more modern and more easily accessible analysis of the healings in Acts. This book is also an up-to-date and sophisticated treatment of Christian healing from the perspective of the more conservative Christian tradition.

This ministry of the apostles began after Pentecost with the healing of a man who had been lame all his life. As Peter and John were going into the Temple for prayers, the man begged them for money. They told him, "Look at us," and when he did, Peter said,

"I have neither silver nor gold, but I will give you what I have: in the name of Jesus Christ the Nazarene, walk!" Peter then took him by the hand and helped him to stand up. Instantly his feet and ankles became firm, he jumped up, stood, and began to walk, and then he went with them into the Temple, walking and jumping and praising God. Everyone could see him walking and praising God, and they recognized him as the man who used to sit begging at the Beautiful Gate of the Temple. They were all astonished and unable to explain what had happened to him (3:6–10).

A similar healing of a cripple who had never walked occurred in Paul's ministry in the town of Lystra. While Paul was preaching this man managed to catch his eye, and Paul realized immediately that he had faith to be cured. He simply called out in a loud voice, "Get to your feet—stand up," and the cripple jumped up and started to walk. The crowds were so amazed that they thought Paul and Barnabas must be gods disguised as men, and called them Zeus and Hermes. The two had all they could do to keep the people from offering a sacrifice to them (14:8–12).

In two instances details are given about the healing of particular diseases, one paralysis and the other dysentery. When Peter came to visit the Christians in Lydda, he found there a man named Aeneas who had been paralyzed and bedridden for eight years. Peter said to him, "Aeneas, Jesus Christ cures you: get up and fold up your sleeping mat," and the man at once arose. Everyone who lived there, and in the next town as well, saw him, and they were all converted to the Lord (9:32–35).

In the other instance the healing came through the actions of Paul. This was after their shipwreck on the island of Malta. Publius, the chief official of the island, took them into his home, and when Paul found that his host's father was in bed suffering from feverish attacks and dysentery, he went in to him and prayed. When he laid his hands on the old man, he was healed (28:8).

Twice Paul himself was miraculously saved. Just before this healing, when they had got safely to shore, Paul was putting sticks on a fire and a poisonous snake, attracted by the heat, fastened itself on him. The natives saw the creature hanging from his hand and decided he must be a murderer; he had escaped the sea, but divine vengeance had caught up with him.[15] Paul shook the snake off, and they waited a long time for him to swell up and die. When nothing happened, they changed their minds and concluded instead that he was a god (28:3–6). These last two stories come from the "we" section of Acts and are probably eyewitness accounts.

Again in Lystra, some Jews hounded the apostles and turned the townspeople against them. Paul was stoned and dragged outside the town, apparently dead. But when the apostles gathered close around him, he got up, and on the following day he and Barnabas went on to the next town (14:19–20).

One story is told of the healing of demon possession, and on another occasion the negative power of demons is referred to. In Philippi the apostles met a slave-girl who had a spirit of divination and made a great deal of money for her masters by telling fortunes. She annoyed Paul by following them everywhere and shouting, "Here are the servants of the Most High God; they have come to tell you how to be saved!" Paul finally faced her and ordered the spirit in the name of Jesus Christ to leave her, and it came out and left her whole. As a result she lost her soothsaying ability and her masters lost their profit. They took Silas and Paul into court and had them flogged and jailed (16:16–24). Demons or evil spirits are also mentioned three times in passages telling how the apostles healed large numbers of people.

There is a refreshing reverse twist in the story of the demon and the seven sons of Sceva. Jewish exorcists were going about casting out demons "by the Jesus whose spokesman is Paul," and these sons of the high priest had found that this practice was effective. But one day an evil spirit answered back, "Jesus I recognize, and I know who Paul is, but who are you?" Instead of coming out of the man, the spirit made him jump on them and beat them until they ran from the house naked and mauled (19:13–16). These men found it was dangerous to imitate apostolic methods without the apostolic Spirit and power. This is the difference between magic and healing; trying to control spiritual powers, rather than relating to them, can lead to destruction. Modern science comes perilously close to magic when it seeks to control nature without an accompanying spirit of humility and awe: the result is a bomb, either psychic or atomic.

The healing of blindness is represented by the story of Paul and Ananias, almost too well known to need discussion. Whatever the

---

[15] This story expresses well the popular belief at that time of illness and disaster as God's punishment for wrongdoing.

cause of his blindness on the Damascus road, Paul's sight was completely restored when Ananias, somewhat reluctantly, laid his hands upon him so that he might receive his sight (9:17). There is also an instance of blindness used as punishment for working against God. When the governor of Cyprus was about to be converted to Christianity, the sorcerer, Bar-Jesus, tried to interfere, and for this was struck blind (13:6–11). This incident parallels the story of Ananias and Sapphira and Paul's warning to the Corinthians about punishing themselves with sickness for their misuse of the Lord's Supper. While this account is the opposite of a healing, it does demonstrate the intimate connection between religion and health.

Once, and perhaps later in a second instance, a person was raised from the dead. The first of these was Tabitha, or Dorcas, who died in Joppa where she had done many kind things for people. The widows who prepared her body for burial were even wearing clothes she had made for them. When the disciples there heard that Peter was nearby in Lydda, they sent for him to come in a hurry. He came immediately, and putting the mourners outside knelt down and prayed; then he turned to the dead woman and said, "Tabitha, stand up." She opened her eyes, and when she saw Peter she sat up, and Peter helped her to her feet (9:36–41).

The other incident is that of Eutychus, who was sitting in a third-story window listening to Paul preach when he fell asleep and tumbled out to the ground. This story, which is not really clear as to whether the young man was dead or badly injured, must be a warning for those who sleep through sermons. It relates that the people rushed down and picked him up as dead. But Paul embraced him and then said, "Don't get so excited. His life is in him." The group then ate and talked until morning, and happily took Eutychus back home with them alive and well (20:8–12).

In addition to these specific healings, described in some detail, there are ten passages in Acts which refer to the healing of large numbers of people by the apostles. Most of these passages simply seem to reinforce, as briefly as possible, what everyone was aware of already:

> Acts 2:43. Awe came upon every soul, and many signs and wonders took place through the apostles.

> Acts 5:12. And many signs and wonders happened among the people by the hands of the apostles.

Acts 5:15. The sick were brought out on beds and couches into the street so that at Peter's coming his shadow might fall on some of them. And a crowd from the cities around Jerusalem also came bringing their sick and those beset by unclean spirits, and they were all cured.

Acts 6:8. And Stephen, full of faith and power, worked great miracles and signs among the people.

Acts 8:6. And the crowds with one mind listened to the things Philip said when they heard and saw the miracles he did. For unclean spirits, crying with a loud voice, came out of many who were possessed by them, and many that were paralyzed and lame were cured. And the joy was great in that city.

Acts 8:13. And Simon also believed, and having been baptized, stayed by Philip, because he was amazed to see the signs and great works of power being done.

Acts 14:3. Therefore . . . [Paul and Barnabas] stayed there a long time, speaking boldly with reliance on the Lord, who gave witness to the message of his grace by causing signs and miracles to be done through their hands.

Acts 15:12. The crowds kept still and heard Barnabas and Paul telling what signs and miracles God had done among the people through them.

Acts 19:11. And God worked unusual works of power by the hands of Paul, so that if even handkerchiefs or aprons from next to his skin were brought to the sick, the diseases left them and the wicked spirits came out of them.

Acts 28:9. [After the healing of Malta], all the rest on the island who had diseases came and were cured.[16]

---

[16] I have made my own translation of these statements from the Greek. The reader not familiar with Greek may consult *The Interlinear Literal Translation of the Greek New Testament* by George Ricker Berry (1960).

All of One Piece

Reading one after another the stories of these events in Acts, one is struck by the same quality of expectation, the same experience of power as is found in Paul's letters and in James. Those of us who would take the New Testament seriously must deal with these experiences that the apostles reported. The person who ignores them, or thinks of them as unimportant later additions to the text, can hardly consider the letters of Paul as they were written, using precisely the same words about miracles of healing. Nor can the events themselves be studied seriously if they are dismissed as mythology, pure and simple, on philosophical and theological grounds. The apostles, in actuality, seem to have started with and continued the ministry of healing that Jesus had commended to them.

Geddes MacGregor has stated in his exegesis on Acts in the *Interpreter's Bible:* "There can be no question that the first Christians lived in daily expectation of 'miracles,' and may therefore well have experienced them; and Luke is just as likely as any alleged later editor to record miracles in full good faith."[17] While this is scarcely an all-out plug for spiritual healing, it as an honest effort to face the facts given in the text.

Indeed the entire body of evidence of the early church is of one piece. In a simple, almost offhand way it affirms that Jesus' ministry was continued among his followers. They did not go out of their way to make a point of the matter. It just *was*. Of course it was important, for it offered the evidence that the Holy Spirit was working through them. It means something to sick people to get well, and large numbers of pagans who were healed turned with joy and amazement to the church. Not all were converted, any more than all of the ten lepers returned to give thanks to Jesus after their healing, but this ministry was one means of evangelization. After all, if simple, ordinary people have access to divine power, it is impressive; and on the basis of Acts and the epistles, taken together, we can come to no other conclusion. Jesus' followers seemed to have a power and Spirit more than their own, which worked through them and gave them uncommon resources to deal with the physical and mental illnesses of sick women and men.

Two somewhat different views of how the healing gift of the spirit was operating in the church are found in Acts. In some sources, the power to heal was viewed as bestowed directly on certain people as

---

[17] *Interpreter's Bible* 9:53.

their vocation—a nontransferable grace or charisma. This view prevails in Paul's letter to the Corinthians. Elsewhere it was considered a function of the church as a corporate entity. The individual then mediated the spiritual power of the church. In this case any ordained member of the group had the power; most likely any Christian did, simply by virtue of being a part of the redeemed community. This is the general idea expressed in the letter of James.

Whatever the theory about how the gift of healing was received, we find the apostles using the same basic sacramental approach to it as Jesus. Some word, a touch, or a material element such as oil was believed to convey the power of the Spirit that was channeled through the Christian. The words or touch were important as an outward and visible sign of an inner grace, a spiritual energy. The sacramental acts were only outward carriers of the Spirit that wished to heal. The healer's contact with the Holy Spirit had to be maintained or the action became meaningless. This was not magic where healers manipulated spiritual energy for their goals, but rather human beings used as instruments by the healing, loving Spirit of God.[18]

We have seen examples of exorcism and other commands, of invoking the name of Jesus, of touching, laying on of hands, and anointing. There are also examples of people healed by contact with the clothing of an apostle. As in the healings of Jesus, the faith of the sick person is sometimes mentioned, and we must assume that the compassion of the healer was involved, although these factors seem to play a lesser part in the actions of the apostles. As time went on there was apparently less and less of the personal element in the healings and less psychological emphasis or understanding. They became more strictly sacramental; yet from the records there is little evidence that they were any less effective.

There is no indication, as some authors suggest, that sacramental healing was implemented by the apostles through medical means. But neither is there any suggestion that medical practices of healing were

---

[18] In James Hastings' *Encyclopedia of Religion and Ethics*, published about 1915, scant attention is paid to the subject of healing miracles in Christianity. The subject is discussed under magic for non-Christians. Wimber (*op. cit*, p. 9) shows how little space is given to the subject in *The New Dictionary of New Testament Theology* and *The New Catholic Encyclopedia*. The *Encyclopedia of Religion* (1987), edited by the late Mircea Eliade, has a worldview capable of dealing with the subject of miracles and has an article on miracles written by the author of this book. It is the first such extensive work of modern times to view spiritual reality as a real part of our total universe. A definitive study of medicine and miracles of healing in the New Testament, is to be found in *Medicine, Miracle and Magic in New Testament Times* (1987) by Howard Clark Kee.

discouraged. There is no evidence for the contention of some healing groups that Christians had to avoid medicine or other external methods if they were to receive spiritual healing. As far as we know, the church in those early years never suggested that spiritual healing was a higher method, and physical methods of a lower order. The church had been commissioned by its Lord to heal, and so it healed. It distilled the essence of Jesus' actions and perpetuated them, and this continued to work even through people who were not noted for a special healing gift.

If we ask why the apostles healed, we find one very simple answer: obedience. Their master had told them to do it, and so they did. It was doubtless natural for them was to continue the ministry they had seen in their teacher and learned from him, of which healing was a large part. It became one aspect of being a Christian. Beyond this the apostles themselves do not seem to have pursued the matter. It did not occur to them to ask, "Is it God's will that this person should be healed, or not?"

An attitude of good will towards others is so normal in modern Western civilization that we seldom realize what a new thing in ancient times was the wish to help others, to extend beyond the limits of one's own family or tribe the compassion and help due to others within those limits. Basically, these people had learned to love, and to care for themselves and others by being cared for in a new way, which they had learned was God's way. They had been in contact with God's spirit in Jesus, and when they became filled with the Holy Spirit themselves, they were then filled with love, *agape*. In the letters of Paul love and the Holy Spirit are practically interchangeable and can be substituted for each other with practically no change in his meaning. The Spirit that had touched the disciples through Jesus and the Holy Spirit that now filled them were the same, and they continued to express it. As Jesus had shown love by healing and ministering to people, finally offering his life as a ransom for those in bondage to evil, just so the disciples continued the same kind of caring. As followers of Jesus they loved one another as Jesus had loved them. The misery of human sickness touched their hearts as it had their master's, and they wanted to relieve as much of the suffering and sin and lostness of human beings as they could.

The apostles did not pause to consider whether they *should* heal, any more than they stopped to ponder whether they should bear love toward other people regardless of race, class, sex, or bondage or whether they should relieve the distress of widows and orphans. From the actual text it does not appear that a choice ever occurred to them. Nor does it appear that they worried about their occasional failure to heal. Very likely they wondered at times about their own inadequacy, as in the story of the epileptic boy in Mark 9, but their failures did not cause them doubts about their practice.

The record also makes clear the great difference between Jesus and his disciples in their relation to God. In the pages of Acts the apostles who carried on the ministry of healing are revealed as ordinary men. When they stretched forth their hands to heal, these men who had known Jesus were sharing with other people like themselves the gift they had received from God. The story in Acts 3 shows their basic approach.

It is also clear that the people whom Jesus sent out to heal understood this ministry in a way that is as relevant to our lives today as it was then. If the same Spirit is in the church today as in that time, then the same things can happen once again. Unless one dismisses the entire record of healings as fiction, or restricts it by a framework such as dispensationalism, no other conclusion is possible. We must acknowledge that a major part of the gospel account is devoted to healings. Aside from the many individual incidents related, we are told that great crowds gathered around Jesus from the earliest moments of his ministry, so that he was hard pressed to find time to sleep or pray, and—again and again—that he healed them; that the people came from all the region around, both city and country, from the sea to the eastern mountains, even considerable distances, sometimes at the cost of fatigue and exhaustion; that he took refuge at times on the hillsides, across the lake, or in the middle of the night to find privacy; that he healed a great variety of ailments; that he repeatedly commanded his disciples to heal, and instructed them in how they should go out to do so; that his answer to a deputation from John in prison mentioned healing; that what Herod had heard about him was along this line, making him want to see a "miracle" at Jesus' hands.

It is rather hard to believe that this person was, on the contrary, merely a charismatic lecturer on ethics and religion, about whom a tremendous and complex legend grew up quite specifically at odds with what he really was and did. If we find in modern life any experience that bears out the possibilities of healing so abundantly set forth in the gospel record (and down through the centuries), we would be rather silly not to look into it.

It is true that in Acts and the epistles the moralistic theory of health found in the Old Testament began to be reintroduced in small doses.

There is no doubt that Paul and the author of Acts attributed certain sicknesses to a person's transgression. Examples include Paul's blindness on the Damascus road, the blindness of the sorcerer Bar-Jesus, the sicknesses and deaths of the Corinthian Christians, the deaths of Ananias and Sapphira, and Paul's thorn in the flesh. Yet there is no suggestion that, because this was the case, Christians should cease their healing activity. Whether these afflictions were due to a demonic agency to which these people had exposed themselves or to the action of God is not stated clearly, and the door is opened once again to the less compassionate theory of the Old Testament, a possibility not found in the acts or sayings of Jesus. In his own healing ministry Jesus was apparently perfectly consistent with his principle: judge not lest you be judged. The more moralistic attitude toward healing became undoubtedly one way of reinforcing authority. But only after many more generations would the older attitude fully reemerge and begin to blot out the whole healing ministry. Instead, this ministry continued as the church grew.

The disciples of Jesus attracted other people like themselves into the fellowship of the risen Christ. These men and women went out to the far corners of the Roman Empire and even beyond it, preaching, teaching, and healing. No small part of the impression Christianity made upon that empire came from the healing ministry of these earliest ambassadors of Christ.

CHAPTER 7

The Expectation of Every Christian

To trace what actually happened about healing in the history of the church involves research enough to fill a book rather than a chapter or two. Because of the skepticism mentioned earlier, the subject has simply been ignored by the scholarly world in modern times. Even the New Testament record of healing in the apostolic church, where it was so obviously important, has rarely been discussed. When I first wrote this book fifteen years ago I could find only one careful study done about thirty years earlier dealing with the continuing ministry in the postapostolic church. However, there is a great library of Christian writing dating from the middle of the second century and continuing for the next thirteen or fourteen centuries; some of the documents are still only available in Latin and Greek, and since references to various incidents are scattered all through several hundred volumes, not many people have really known to what extent the healing ministry continued in the early years of the church.

The one important study is *Christian Healing*, by Evelyn Frost, which covers the earliest records of the church after the New Testament, from about the year 100 to 250.[1] Dr. Frost's work has made the whole approach to the history of healing practices in the church easier. She has not only examined piece by piece the several thick volumes of this early

---

[1] Evelyn Frost, *Christian Healing: A Consideration of the Place of Spiritual Healing in the Church of To-day in the Light of the Doctrine and Practice of the Ante-Nicene Church* (1940). This book is important for anyone who wants an understanding of the place of healing in the early Christian church. It shows clearly that the practices of healing described in the New Testament continued without interruption for the next two centuries.

literature, turning up a quantity of valuable references, but has pointed out the centrality of sacramental healing.

The sober quality of the writing and the large number of healings recorded by early Christians continues the New Testament record and stands firm against any attempt to turn this body of experience into myth or mere fancy—to say nothing of the fact that spiritual healing has continued into modern times. The witnesses we have selected are careful writers, as different from the superstitious tale tellers of the ancient world as the New Testament is from the overblown accounts found in the apocryphal gospels, letters, and acts of the various saints. In Appendix B Norman Perrin has pointed out how sober and sane the New Testament is by comparison with much of this literature. A compelling trait of the New Testament, in great contrast with much contemporary writing, is its very simple and matter-of-fact tone.

Undoubtedly there has been some elaboration in the material we are about to present, and many of the stories of healing will in any case seem fantastic to readers brought up in a rationally materialistic modern world. Yet, then as now, the witness is there. We give the record of that time as it comes down to us.

A Vital Church

The church experienced a time of great vitality during the two hundred years following the apostolic period recorded in the New Testament. Starting from small bands of Christians, usually centered in the big cities, it grew to a vast spiritual fellowship reaching into nearly every corner of the Roman Empire. Evidences of Christianity dating from this era are found in Britain, Switzerland, North Africa, along the Danube, and far into the East, carried by the ambassadors of Christ wherever the Romans went and even beyond. Part of the vital faith these Christians brought with them was the conviction that their God was a loving, caring, healing God who expected a healing ministry from Christian followers.

Christianity spread in spite of the fact that it was a proscribed religion up until the Edict of Milan in 313 c.e. Christianity probably became illegal during the time of Nero, about the middle of the first century. From then on Christians were always in danger if they were discovered. It was not a continuous persecution, however. For years Christians were tolerated, until one emperor or another, needing a domestic scapegoat on whom to project current fears and anxieties, would settle upon the Christians. They served the same purpose that the Jews did in Nazi Germany, and anything might happen to an individual Christian. One person might suffer minor legal penalties while another was condemned to torture and death. A man convicted of being a Christian could be executed and his children sold into slavery. For nearly three hundred years anyone who took part in the new religion lived with danger, almost from day to day. In spite of this, the church grew and flourished. Indeed, as we shall see, torture and death gave Christians an opportunity to manifest an important form of both spiritual and physical poise and strength, which was an expression of inner joy and certainty about eternal life that roused the wonder and envy of those who saw them die.

Obviously one did not become a Christian during this period merely from intellectual curiosity or fanciful whim. It required real conviction. Jung once pointed out to me that conviction means literally "to be conquered by." These early Christians had been conquered by the love of a caring God revealed in the crucified and risen Jesus of Nazareth. In return the church was careful to screen newcomers to the fellowship. It was vital not to betray the secrecy of meeting places and rites, and there was constant danger that someone might be accepted who, carelessly or for money, would become an informer. As a result few asked or were accepted who were not deeply moved to become Christian.

For much of this time Christians were also the target of personal hatred and ridicule, a by-product of persecution and ensuing secrecy. Almost anything evil was believed of them. Stories were circulated about sexual orgies and drunken brawls, of how they sacrificed babies for the strange feasts they held. It is no wonder that the earliest groups separated themselves from the world, often actually going underground. Records of this period are almost nonexistent. Much of the knowledge we have of the church for the first hundred years after the day of Pentecost depends on archaeological findings and a few references in the Talmud and contemporary Roman writers. Both the New Testament and the seven or eight authentic documents that remain from around the year 100 were written to inform and instruct the Christian community, not the outside world. For a long time, in fact, early Christians stayed apart from the world because of their belief that the world itself was about to end.

But as persecution continued year after year and the end of the world still did not come, Christians began to turn to the pagan world in an effort to justify their position. More and more pagans were drawn into the church, and for them the change of outlook was much greater than it had been for converts from Judaism. For most pagans Christianity demanded an about-face in moral point of view as well as burning religious conviction. One of the real tasks of church leaders was to develop a method of training new converts. As late as the third century, three years of training as catechumens was often required in preparation for baptism. Consequently, few people came into the church in this period who were not both well-trained and conquered by the risen Christ.

As a result, the church of the second and third centuries retained the vitality of the apostolic age. It also prepared women and men to be leaders who knew at first hand what Christianity could offer to pagan life and saw ways of reaching the pagan world. From about the middle of the second century on, these early leaders, now termed "apologists," began to express the Christian message in ways that the pagan world and its philosophers would understand. These writings show that the healing ministry was continuing in much the same way as in apostolic days. They show that healing was part of a total framework in which Christians were educated: a reality of religious experience in which they participated, either directly or indirectly. And indeed, if they were to follow the teachings of Christ as handed down, it is hard to see how they could do otherwise. Materialistic disbelief was not yet—by many centuries— a norm in the world.

There was trouble, however, and not only from the outside. Along with persecution, the church was also soon faced by heresy within, and some of the most important efforts of new Christian thinkers were directed toward combatting Gnostic tendencies. Early in the second century, Greek Gnosticism was already attracted to the figure of Jesus. Groups of Gnostic Christians, know as Docetists, began to preach a Christianity quite at variance with the gospels. The entire physical world was seen as the creation of an evil demiurge, directly opposed to the God of Christ; from this point of view the human body itself was an evil. Thus any idea of incarnation appeared unthinkable. The physical Jesus was seen as an illusion, so there could have been no crucifixion in the real sense. Because Christ had come to give a teaching, a system of knowledge or *gnosis* through which human beings could save themselves, any idea of atonement also disappeared in these systems.

Some of the Gnostics were outstanding thinkers. The writings of Valentinus and the excerpts we have of Basilides still make interesting reading today as one follows the intricate maze of speculation that captivated the intellectuals of the time. But the early leaders saw the dangers of these ideas. Later, Augustine was taken in by them and like them came to feel that what one did with one's physical body made no real moral difference.[2] According to this line of thought, the body had so little value that it did not need to be considered morally or in any significant way. Thus Christian thinkers were forced to argue with vigor to defend the value of the body and the idea of the incarnation, the resurrection of Jesus and of the human body, as well as the atonement and the outpouring of God's love in filling Christians with the Holy Spirit. To these people who had found healing and new meaning in life in the risen Jesus who had transformed their lives, defeating Gnosticism was as much a matter of life and death as persecution from the outside.[3]

Let us first look briefly at these leaders whose thinking was so crucial for the church's life and growth. Let us note how they spoke of experiences of healing, and then how their understanding of healing developed as they began to explain the reality of their faith to a hostile world.

The Early Christian Thinkers and Their Evidence

The first of the Christians who produced formal defenses of their faith, or apologies, were converts who lived and wrote in Rome: Quadratus early in the second century and Justin Martyr, who taught philosophy there until he was executed for being a Christian about 165 C.E. At Carthage in North Africa, Tertullian and Cyprian became two of the church's most influential converts, writing until well into the third century. During the same period two other important leaders emerged in the great intellectual center of Alexandria: Clement had been drawn there from a pagan background in Athens, while his brilliant follower Origen was a native, born into a Christian home. Irenaeus, originally from the church in Smyrna, lived in Gaul and wrote voluminously through the latter part of the second century.

---

[2] For nine years Augustine stayed with the Gnostic Manicheans as a hearer and, after he finally broke away and entered the church, some of their ideas about the human body and sexuality stayed with him.

[3] For the reader who wishes more detailed information on this period, an excellent study of the background and the struggle that resulted is found in Hans Lietzmann's *A History of the Early Church* (1961); see particularly Chapter Fifteen, pp. 264–75. Also, for an interesting study of some later, contrasting source material, see E. R. Dodds, *Pagan and Christian in an Age of Anxiety* (1965). For the reader who wishes to go to the sources themselves, W. B. Eerdmann Publishing Company has provided these writings in the ten volumes of *The Ante-Nicene Fathers* (various dates).

These were educated men, often drawn to Christianity after wide experience in the pagan schools and in the world. Indeed, they were men of culture, even intellectual sophistication. While it is possible to think of some of the New Testament writers as intellectually unsophisticated (far as this is from the truth for all of them), the same idea cannot be made to fit these leaders of the church. Tertullian, for instance, was a first-rate jurist and wrote Latin as polished as any of his most cultivated contemporaries. Origen had one of the best minds of his day and was admired by non-Christians as well as Christians. The Christian school in Alexandria at that time was one of the most respected intellectual centers in the entire empire.

The writings of these men show quite clearly the way they expressed their belief in one loving God. They wrote about all kinds of experience that showed how God had acted and continued to act in Christian lives, including much that was lively and down-to-earth. Healing of physical illness and the ability to relieve "demon possession" are spoken of again and again in the more important works and referred to in some way by all these writers. Justin Martyr, for example, wrote in his "apology" addressed to the emperor in Rome, referring to the significance of Jesus as man and Savior: "For numberless demoniacs throughout the whole world, and in your city, many of our Christian men exorcizing them in the Name of Jesus Christ . . . have healed and do heal, rendering helpless and driving the possessing devils out of the men, though they could not be cured by all the other exorcists, and those who used incantations and drugs."[4]

Origen wrote his great treatise *Against Celsus* to take pagan thinking apart piece by piece, and here he spoke in several places of how Christians "expel evil spirits, and perform many cures," many of which he had himself witnessed. Or again, "the name of Jesus can still remove distractions from the minds of men, and expel demons, and also take away diseases."[5] Several such statements occur in this work, which was written especially for the intellectual leaders of the pagan community. Cyprian told in one of his letters how baptism itself was sometimes the means by which a serious illness was cured, and that there were Christians living on and giving their lives to the church because of such an experience.[6]

---

[4] Justin Martyr, *Second Apology: To the Roman Senate*, 6. Unless otherwise noted, references to the works of these Fathers are taken from *The Ante-Nicene Fathers* (various dates).
[5] Origen, *Against Celsus* I.46 and 67.
[6] Cyprian, *Epistle* 75.15.

In a telling protest written to the proconsul in North Africa during the persecutions there, Tertullian cited facts even more specific:

All this [that is, the number of times Roman officials simply dismissed charges against Christians] might be officially brought under your notice, and by the very advocates, who are themselves also under obligations to us, although in court they give their voice as it suits them. The clerk of one of them, who was liable to be thrown upon the ground by an evil spirit, was set free from his affliction; as was also the relative of another, and the little boy of a third. And how many men of rank (to say nothing of common people) have been delivered from devils, and healed of diseases! Even Severus himself, the father of Antonine [the emperor], was graciously mindful of the Christians; for he sought out the Christian Proculus, surnamed Torpacion, the steward of Euhodias, and in gratitude for his having once cured him by anointing, he kept him in his palace till the day of his death.[7]

Thus there is no question that the ministry of healing continued in the church. These men, whose evidence we shall consider in more detail later, were writing for a skeptical public who made no bones about their attitude toward Christianity: that the world would be better off if these annoying Christians were simply eliminated. The Christian writers were well aware of this. They were also well informed for their time, well enough to be sure of the facts they presented. From all parts of the church and out of their many different backgrounds, they spoke of healing in much the same way. It was simply a fact of Christian experience which pagan officials could verify if they wished.

At the same time they did not talk very much about individual healings, or give names very often. Of course, there were not many emperors whose names could be produced as Antonine was by Tertullian, and most ordinary citizens were not anxious to have their names connected with the Christians. Origen once commented that there were many instances he could set down from his own experience, but he saw no point in giving nonbelievers another chance to ridicule Christians for imagining things like healing.[8] Irenaeus, who offered the most impressive list of the kinds of healing to be seen in the church of his time, said explicitly that Christians were not practicing deception on people. The followers of Gnosticism, for whom he was writing, simply did not

---

[7] Tertullian, *To Scapula* 4. Severus until his death was co-emperor with his son Caracalla, who was often called "Antonine" because he tried to pattern his rule after Marcus Aurelius Antoninus. Severus was vilified by contemporary historians, and the picture we have of Caracalla was probably created in part in the same way.

[8] Origen, *op. cit.* I.46.

believe such things were possible. The body was not significant enough to heal.

In different ways, the thinking of both pagans and Gnostic Christians shut out the idea of healing accomplished directly by God. Magic they could accept, but the idea and experience of a loving God reaching out to heal through human instruments was as effectively blocked as it is for most people today. And so Christian thinkers tackled this problem, for there was no point in talking about experiences that people could not even see. The set out to provide an understanding of reality that would bring into focus the superstitious materialism of most pagans and the Gnostic rejection of the material world. What they did in the end was to produce the theological and philosophical foundation on which Christians would build and through which the Christian world would expand for a thousand years. Let us look carefully at this approach as it relates to various ideas people have held about the human body and soul.

Theology and Healing in the Early Church

Christian theology as it is now understood first developed during the second century by joining contemporary philosophy with Christian experience. Theology then and now is an attempt to relate religious experience to the rest of one's experience and knowledge. This effort to fit religious experience into the total framework of life and thought usually does not take place until a religion is questioned—until people try to explain to others who disagree with them what they really believe and try to practice. There is little developed theology in the New Testament. Indeed one of the problems of biblical critics is the fact that the risen Jesus was so much a reality that early Christians were not careful to distinguish between the actions of the historical Jesus and the actions of the risen Jesus among them. It contains, instead, the raw material of theology: that is, the experience upon which a theology is based. In describing it the New Testament writers all express an implicit theology, but its explicit development came with the effort of the apologists to justify and explain their faith to a hostile world and a divided church.

Justin Martyr was the first to unite the intellectual method and worldview of Plato with the life and experience he had discovered in the Christian community. The importance of Plato to Christian theology is seldom recognized today.[9] It is well to remember that the philosophic framework was provided by Plato's carefully expressed notion of a non-physical and eternal world which shapes and directs the physical world. He refined and stated the belief commonly held in most cultures that human beings are caught between the physical world, which they perceive through their senses, and a nonphysical world with which the soul, or nonphysical nature, is in constant interaction. Plato tried to show how the tangible world, of which the human body is a part, constantly interacts with a world of Ideas, spirits, demons, and deities. In this framework the Old Testament descriptions of direct human dealings with God made good sense, as did the dreams and visions, the healings, prophecies, and angels and demons of the New Testament. Plato could be called the philosopher of the shamanistic experience, the experience that human beings can be in touch with both a physical and a spiritual dimension of reality.[10]

From this knowledge of Plato and from his own Christian experience, Justin saw that what Plato had conceived intellectually Christians now knew as concrete reality, though without realizing its full philosophical and theological significance. The thinkers who came after Justin took the same basic approach, developing a consistent body of theological conclusions. This basic understanding of two worlds in interaction was the philosophic foundation of their ideas and of Christian thinking for the next thousand years. Four of these central ideas are directly connected with healing and are so significant that they make a healing ministry practically imperative for the Christian church.

All four ideas originated in the experience of the apostles with the human Jesus, which continued to be expressed in relationships within the church. This experience of Jesus had struck deep into their lives and minds. Although they were unprepared for the resurrection, they could look back to intimations they had had of Jesus' more than human nature. The living, resurrected Christ continued to appear to them. They believed first of all that this human being had *truly incarnated* the God of the Hebrew people. Second, because of this and because their Hebrew background they saw *human flesh and body as essentially good*. As

---

[9] Few modern theologians have a broad background in the history of philosophy. Knowing only contemporary views, they occasionally spend their time reinventing the wheel, an argument for requiring seminary education to include a semester's course in the history of philosophy.

[10] Mircea Eliade's *Shamanism: Archaic Techniques of Ecstasy* (1970) is the definitive analysis of this experience.

a result they believed that the human body and life in the here and now had eternal significance.

Third, the early church valued remembered events and fresh experience, so that in the second century the early creeds began to state formally the idea of *the resurrection of human bodies*. Finally, the concept of *the atonement* was also developed at this time, comprehending Christ's incarnation, life, death, resurrection, ascension, and bestowal of the Holy Spirit upon his followers as the sequence that defeated the forces of evil which had dominated human beings.[11] Each of these ideas represented an utter rejection of the Gnostic speculation of the time. Their importance for a theology of healing can hardly be overestimated. Let us look at the effect they had upon the theory and practice of the church.

As Evelyn Frost has pointed out, the early church inherited the high valuation of the body from Hellenistic Judaism.[12] This belief was almost unique in the ancient world. To most Greek and Oriental thinkers, the soul was the only salvageable part of human beings. We have already suggested the Greek understanding, expressed in the myth of a cosmic catastrophe or explosion of the pleroma that trapped the soul in pieces of evil matter.[13] Hellenism for the most part saw little real value in the body itself. The soul was so separated from it that what people did with their bodies in this world had little effect on what happened to their souls.

The elaborate embalming rituals of Egypt expressed the same essential thought in a different form. The religion of the Egyptians was almost entirely otherworldly in its emphasis. While that future life was viewed in a very physical way, still it was quite separate from this physical life and infinitely more important. Thus the kings of Upper Egypt (as well as the Emperors of China until recent times) spent much of their lives and substance erecting temples and tombs to prepare their place on the other side of this life.

The idea of interdependence of soul and body grew up in Judaism. Until very late the Hebrews had little belief in a worthwhile afterlife. If good were to be experienced, it had to be known in the here and now. Those who contributed to the earthly misery of their fellow human beings came under severe censure of the prophets. Later Judaism cod-

---

[11] This view of the atonement, the ransom theory (as distinguished from the Anselmic satisfaction theory, which seems hardly Christian to me), dominated the life of the first ten centuries of Christian thought as shown by Gustav Aulén in *Christus Victor* (1951).

[12] *Op. cit.*, pp. 20–27.

[13] See our discussion pp. 38–39.

ified these insights, and we find a value placed upon this world, the physical body, and morality—upon human relationships and material things—that is rare in religions which have not sprung from the Judeo-Christian heritage. The physical body and human existence in the physical world were supremely valued by God.

It was, then, not by chance that morality, codes of behavior for interaction with our fellow human beings, assumed such an important place in the thinking of this people. The moral emphasis was one the ancient world was hungering for, and all over that world Gentiles flocked to the Hebrew synagogues. Although many of these people did not embrace the ritual law, these "God-fearers" took seriously the ethical side of Judaism. Such groups provided ready-made congregations to which the Christian teaching appealed.

Nor was it by chance that among these people, with one foot in Judaism and the other in the pagan world, the idea of the incarnation took hold. They were aware of the Hebrew value of the body, and the Greek notion of the gods consorting with human beings was certainly not foreign to them. If the incarnation was true, then the body was good and valuable enough to incarnate not only the human soul but the very reality of God. Tertullian put it well in his treatise on resurrection when he wrote:

For, whatever was the form and expression which was then given to the clay [by the Creator], Christ was in His thoughts, as one day to become man, because the Word, too, was to be both clay and flesh, even as the earth was then . . . To what purpose is it to bandy about the name *earth*, as that of a sordid and grovelling element, with the view of tarnishing the origin of the flesh, when . . . it would be requisite that the dignity of the Maker should be taken into consideration. . . . It was quite allowable for God that He should clear the gold of our flesh from all the taints . . . of its *native* clay, by purging the original substance of its dross.[14]

It is not flesh or earth that is evil, but something that happens to it when it falls under the domination of "death" and the forces of evil. The soul is even more subject to this evil than the body, and passes its corruption on to the latter.[15]

---

[14] Tertullian, *On the Resurrection of the Flesh* 6.

[15] Evelyn Frost (*op. cit.*, pp. 71–86), cites a great number of passages from the ante-Nicene thinkers relating to the ideas discussed here. Among them, those that deal primarily with the value of the body, and also how it becomes subject to evil, are *The Epistle of Barnabas* 6; Justin Martyr, fragments of the lost work *On the Resurrection* 7–8, and fragment found in Leontius, *Against Eutychians* II; Theophilus of Antioch, *To Autolycus* II.25; Irenaeus, *Against Heresies* III.23.5 ff.; Tertullian (besides the above passage), *Against*

The incarnation gave tremendous significance to the physical body, a significance which carried over to the afterlife. The result was the doctrine of the resurrection of the body. But this was not held naively as in some of the more Biblically literalistic sects today. We tend to laugh at the belief. Some of the notions we impute to the thinkers of the early church are really quite funny. I remember, for instance, a housekeeper in our family who worried about the resurrection of the body because her husband had lost a leg in France, and she wondered how the Lord would get him together again. But these ancients were sophisticated men whose understanding was very different. Their main point was that the body has eternal significance and that out of it a resurrected form arises, not physical as we know it, but somewhat as a seed germinates and grows into a plant.[16]

The implications of this thinking for Christian healing were great. The body had real intrinsic value, not merely because it was associated with the soul, but in its own right. Thus healing the body was a valid act; it became a good work whether the soul was influenced or not. (How different from the official position of the church in the Middle Ages!) It should be noted, however, that healing the body was believed almost inevitably to affect the soul, while healing the soul affected the body; the two were inextricably joined. The sharp sense of separateness which is current today (when we can hardly say that we *have* such a thing as a soul), and which was current in the pagan world, simply did not exit for early Christians.[17]

Equally important for healing was the understanding of evil and the saving work of Christ. It was believed that human disobedience in Adam resulted in "death," which was more than simple physical dissolution of the body. In this first falling away an alien and destructive

---

Marcion II.4 ff.; Methodius, *Discourse on the Resurrection* I.11; and also the references in note 17 below.

[16] I have shown in *Afterlife: The Other Side of Dying* (1980) that most of these thinkers believed in *both* the immortality of the soul and the resurrection of the body as two different aspects of Christian life after death.

[17] The close relation between body and soul was stressed by most of these writers, as in Clement of Rome, *First Epistle: To the Corinthians* 26; Ignatius, *Epistles to the Magnesians* 13, *To the Smyrneans* 13; *The Pastor of Hermas* III.5.6–7; Clement of Alexandria, *The Instructor* I.2 and III.12; Athenagoras, *Treatise on the Resurrection of the Dead* 15; Irenaeus, *Against Heresies* IV.20.4, V.3.3, 6.1–2, 8.1. Also in discussions of the resurrection pointing up the importance of the body and of healing: Justin Martyr, *The First Apology* 18–19 and fragments of the lost work *On the Resurrection* 4–5 and 9–10; *The Second Epistle of Clement* (An Ancient Homily) 9; Tatian, *To the Greeks* 6, 16, and 20; Theophilus of Antioch, *To Autolycus* I.7 and II.26; Origen, *Against Celsus* V.19 and VII.32; Methodius, *Discourse on the Resurrection* I.12–13.

spirit tempted and entered human life and gained power over humanity, corrupting both body and soul. The term *death* referred to this metaphysical entity as well as to the resulting condition. It was an uncreative, disintegrating force directly opposed to God. Through human disobedience the door was opened so that death could possess human life. This destructive spirit, "death," obtained control over human beings and turned them away from God and the Holy, or creative, Spirit. Its power was expressed in human life spiritually by immorality of all kinds and by mental illness, and physically by bodily disease and physical death. Illness was not the will of the loving God, but directly and antagonistically opposed to it.

Then on Golgotha Christ met the forces of "death," submitted to them, and conquered them. Through the crucifixion and resurrection of Jesus, the power of "death" (the Evil One) was defeated, so that by following Jesus' way people could be saved from *both* immoral living *and* from psychological and physical sickness. The early church knew these forces which Christ defeated. They had dominated humankind up to that time and still ruled most people. They were described in the New Testament, particularly by Paul, as "dominions," "thrones," "principalities," "spiritual wickedness," "the dragon," "death," and a variety of other colorful names.[18]

To the thinkers of the church these forces were not merely concepts; they were concrete and powerful entities. As Gustav Aulen has shown conclusively, up to the seventh century the atonement was seen by nearly all the church thinkers in terms of a victory over just such actual spiritual beings of some sort.[19] And as we shall see, even for later thinkers the idea of spiritual entities or elements outside the personality that affect the human psyche and body is not quite so absurd as most people

---

[18] For a complete catalogue of these passages, see Appendix A in my book *Tongue Speaking: An Experiment in Spiritual Experience*. See also Walter Wink, *op. cit.*, for a definitive study of these destructive entities.

[19] Gustav Aulén, *Christus Victor: An Historical Study of the Three Main Types of the Idea of the Atonement* (1951). This understanding of "death," of its effect, and of the Christian attitude toward it was developed by many church fathers. It is found in Clement, *The First Epistle: To the Corinthians* 3 ff., 9, 24, 44–45; *The Epistle of Barnabas* 16; Ignatius, *Epistle to the Ephesians* 19; Polycarp, *Epistle to the Philippians* 10; the *Epistle to Diognetus* 10; Justin Martyr, *Dialogue with Trypho* 124; Tatian, *To the Greeks* 12 ff.; Irenaeus, *Against Heresies* III.19.1, 23.6–7, IV.33.4, 38.3–4, 39.1, V.7.2, 12.1 ff., and 24.4; Tertullian, *On the Soul* 52, *On the Flesh of Christ* 6, 17, *On the Resurrection of the Flesh* 47–8, *Apology* 50, *Against Marcion* I.22, *Antidote for the Scorpion's Sting* 6, *On Idolatry* 14, and *Ad Nationes* I.19; Clement of Alexandria, *Exhortation to the Heathen* 11–12, *Stromata* II.9, IV.7, and VI.9; Origen, *Against Celsus* VI.36, 44, and VII.32; Hippolytus, *Refutation of All Heresies* IX.19; Cyprian, *On the Lapsed* 26 ff., *Epistles* X.2, XX.2, XXVI.1, and LIV.17; Lactantius, *The Divine Institutes* II.13, 16, and IV.27.

feel it to be. The studies of Jung have helped us to take a fresh look at these things, as I have shown in *Discernment, A Study in Ecstasy and Evil*.

With the understanding that the effect of these forces in the actual physical world was disease, corruption, and dissolution of both body and soul, healing was the natural result of Jesus' having lived and conquered these very forces. In the words of that time, "How can they maintain that the flesh is incapable of receiving the life which flows from Him, when it received healing from Him? For life is brought about through healing, and incorruption through life. He, therefore, who confers healing, the same does also confer life; and He . . . [who gives] life, also surrounds His own handiwork with incorruption."[20] Jesus by his nature had brought life and healing to the people he encountered. He had also shown that the power of God's Spirit moving through him was greater than the power of the Evil One by rescuing human beings from sickness and immorality caused by it, and finally by defeating it on the cross. Ultimately it was thought, when the spirit of God gains complete control in the world, these forces of evil will be ruled out entirely and illness will disappear. In the meantime, Irenaeus wrote, "As He suffered, so also is He alive, and life-giving, and healing all our infirmity."[21] In the same vein, Clement of Alexandria wrote, "He freely bestows life on you . . . He Who expels destruction and pursues death . . . He Who builds up the Temple of God in men, that He may cause God to take up His abode in men."[22] And Tertullian wrote, "without hesitation accept . . . what you have seen already on every side; nor doubt that God, Whom you have discovered to be the restorer of all things, is likewise the reviver of the flesh."[23] Within the church the

---

[20] Irenaeus, *Against Heresies* V.12.6.

[21] Irenaeus, *Fragment 52* from the lost writing.

[22] Clement of Alexandria, *Exhortation to the Heathen* 11.

[23] Tertullian, *On the Resurrection of the Flesh* 12. There are a great many of these passages about the saving action of Christ, the atonement, and the effect on humans here and now, their flesh, and their diseases, bodily and otherwise. They are also found in *The Epistle of Barnabas* 16; Ignatius, *Epistles to the Smyrneans* 5, *to the Ephesians* 3, 7–8, and 17, *to the Magnesians* 1 and 5, *to the Philadelphians* 9, *to the Trallians* 9; the *Epistle to Diognetus* 9; Justin Martyr, *The Second Apology* 13, *Dialogue with Trypho* 17 and 30, fragments of the lost work *On the Resurrection* 10; Theophilus of Antioch, *To Autolycus* I.7; Athenagoras, *A Plea for the Christians* 10; Irenaeus, *Against Heresies* III.18.4, IV.20.2 and 4 ff., 33.4, 38.1, V.3.1.ff., 6.1–2, 11.2; Tertullian, *Of Patience* 15, *To His Wife* II.3, *On the Flesh of Christ* 6, *On the Resurrection of the Flesh* 34, 37, 54, and 57–58; Clement of Alexandria, *Tractate: Who Is the Rich Man That Shall Be Saved?* 37, *Stromata* IV.7, V.11, and VII.11; Hippolytus, *Treatise Against Boron and Helix*, esp. Fragment 2, *Discourse on the Holy Theophany* 7–8; Origen, *Against Celsus* VII.32; Cyprian, *An Exhortation to Mar-*

Spirit of Christ still lived. It was available to Christians, ready to indwell those who followed Jesus. The first and major battle with the forces of evil had been won. Since the devil was still around, particularly in the dark corners, the church had ways to continue the fight. It could also offer healing for the bodies and minds as well as the souls of human beings just as Jesus had done in his time.[24]

Naturally the early church sought out the sick to care for them and heal them, just as it sought out the lost and broken morally and tried to bring them new life. Healing was rescuing human beings from the domination of the enemy. This was the natural function of Christians as members of the body of Christ. It was not by chance that Christian churches came to be regarded as healing shrines competitive with the shrines of Aesculapius and other Greek gods. It was also natural that in many places the Christian churches took over the function of those temples as the pagan religion died out, and that Christian shrines often appeared on the site of former pagan temples. The great cathedral at Chartres was built over a spring sacred to Diana and was a healing shrine for centuries before it was a Christian church.

In confrontation with the pagan world, the uniqueness of Christianity was clear. Celsus, who warned second-century pagans about the dangers of the new religion, sneered at Christians because sick and derelict people were acceptable to their God, who would not cast them off, and who indeed had sent his son to serve them.[25] Almost two centuries later the emperor Julian the Apostate gave much the same picture of fourth-century pagans and Christians when he wrote: "These impious Galileans give themselves to this kind of humanity: as men allure children with a cake, so they . . . bring converts to their impiety. . . . Now we can see what makes Christians such powerful enemies of our gods. It is the brotherly love which they manifest toward strangers and toward the sick and the poor."[26] These writers represent well the attitude toward the human body and human sickness discussed above. It was the underlying outlook of the Hellenistic world in which Christianity grew up, expressed in the mystery cults and in philosophies like the later Pythagoreanism and the Docetism and Gnosticism both inside and outside the church. They were all views which separated the mind

---

tyrdom 10, *Epistles* 74.2–3 and 76.2; Methodius, *Oration Concerning Simeon and Anna* 1 and 5, *Homily on the Cross and Passion of Christ* 1.

[24] Lance Webb gives a good picture of the early church in his novel *Onesimus* (1984).

[25] Origen, *Against Celsus* III.71 ff. Much of the work of Celsus is extant because Origen refuted it point by point, quoting whole sections.

[26] Juliani Imperatoris; *Quae Supersunt Praeter Reliquias apud Cyrillum: Omnia*, 1:391–92.

or soul from the grosser body, concerning themselves only with the part of the human being that they considered valuable and eternal. These approaches to life involved either secret rites to unite the believer with a bodiless god or the achievement of higher and higher levels of esoteric knowledge. They found no particular value in healing the body. Instead, they concentrated on freeing the soul from its prison, the physical world.[27]

The church stood firm against both of these efforts. It continued to see salvation as the redemption of the total human being, not just liberation from the body. The Hebrew idea that God created the world, that it was good, and that it was meant to be good, was never lost to the mainstream of Christian thought. The value of the body and the saving action of Christ for both body and soul remained a cardinal doctrine of the early church. (Since one's thinking is likely to have quite an influence on one's ultimate behavior, the actual theology of the body in today's church would be an interesting study.) In the second and third centuries, at any rate, Christians acted upon their belief that the Spirit of God would work through them and through the sacraments to save people physically and spiritually. As a result, what they had to say theologically kept alluding to experiences of healing then happening in the church. These writers set down some facts about the healing they themselves had seen.

The Facts About Healing

Many sources document the prevailing acceptance of healing as a norm in the Christian church. In the very early and imaginative *Shepherd of Hermas* we find a fascinating reference to those who did *not* undertake to relieve illness and distress in the Christian way. "He therefore," Hermas wrote, "that knows the calamity of such a man, and does not free him from it, commits a great sin, and is guilty of his blood."[28] Indeed the healing of physical illness was seen in this period as telling evidence that the spirit of Christ was actually present and at work among Christians. Since both bodily and mental illness were a sign of

---

[27] Plato is often overlooked by many Christian thinkers because in some of his work he devalues matter and the body as gross and resistant to *Ideas* or spiritual influences. Some Roman Catholic religious orders used this aspect of his thinking to support all sorts of abuses to the body. The early Christian thinkers knew their Plato too well to do this.

[28] *The Shepherd of Hermas* III.X.4 in *The Apostolic Fathers*, trans. Archbishop William Wake (1909), 1:299.

domination by some evil entity, the power to heal disease was prime evidence that the opposite spirit, the Spirit of God, was operating through the healer. Thus the healing of "demon possession" was often spoken of in conjunction with curing illness from other causes.

Quadratus, one of the earliest apologists, wrote in Rome that the works of the Savior had continued to his time and that the continued presence of people who had been healed left no question as to the reality of physical healing. Justin Martyr tells in several places how Christians healed in the name of Jesus Christ, driving out demons and all kinds of evil spirits. Writing about the *charismata*, the special gifts of spiritual power God pours out upon believers, he calls attention to the power to heal as one of the particular gifts that was received and used.

Theophilus of Antioch specified the physical healing of human beings he had witnessed as particular evidence that the resurrection was beginning to work in them and that death was being put to flight; he also spoke of the fact that demons were sometimes exorcised and confessed their demonic nature. Tertullian, as we have seen, explicitly identified persons who had been healed and testified to their great number and the wide range of physical and mental diseases represented. Elsewhere he says that God could, and sometimes did, recall the souls of human beings to their bodies.[29]

In the *Acts of S. Eugenia*, who is portrayed as so close to God that she could cast out devils, it is told how a certain noblewoman of Alexandria was healed of a recurring fever when Eugenia prayed over her. And Minucius Felix, who wrote about the end of the second century, describes the exorcism of demons in these words: "Since they themselves are the witnesses that they are demons, believe them when they confess the truth of themselves; for when abjured by the only and true God, unwillingly the wretched beings shudder in their bodies, and either at once leap forth, or vanish by degrees, as the faith of the sufferer assists or the grace of the healer inspires."[30]

Perhaps the most interesting discussion of healing among the ante-Nicene writers comes from Irenaeus in Gaul, who probably wrote more

---

[29] References to healing by these various writers are found in Quadratus, *Apology* (fragment); Justin Martyr, *Second Apology: To the Roman Senate* 6, *Dialogue with Trypho* 30, 39, 76, and 85; Theophilus of Antioch, *To Autolycus* I.13 and II.8; Tertullian, *To Scapula* 4, *The Soul's Testimony* 3, *The Shows* (or *De Spectaculis*) 26 and 29, *Apology* 23 and 27, and *On the Soul* 57. Also Tatian, *To the Greeks* 17–18 and 20; while in the earliest Clementine literature an instruction is found for Christians to visit the sick as bearers of the Holy Spirit and healing (*First Epistle Concerning Virginity* 12).

[30] Minucius Felix, *The Octavius* 27. Also *Acts of S. Eugenia* 10–11. See also Edgar J. Goodspeed, *The Story of Eugenia and Philip* (1931), pp. 80–81.

freely because he was somewhat removed from the danger of persecution that faced most of these thinkers. In *Against Heresies*, one of his telling points was that heretics were not able to accomplish the miracles of healing that Christians could perform. They did not have access to the power of God and so could not heal. One wonders what he would say of modern Christianity, liberal and fundamental.

Irenaeus attested to almost the same range of healings as we have found in the gospels and Acts. All kinds of bodily infirmity as well as many different diseases had been cured. The damage from external accidents had been repaired. He had seen the exorcism of all sorts of demons. He even describes the raising of the dead. His pagan readers were well aware of these miracles of healing, as he makes clear, since this was often the path to conversion for pagans, as well as the means of bringing bodily health to both Christians and non-Christians. He also mentions that no fee was charged for healing performed by Christians, a practice quite different from that of the pagan temples of healing such as Epidaurus and Pergamum.[31]

There is no indication that Irenaeus viewed any disease as incurable or any healing as against God's will. Indeed the whole attitude he voiced was that healing is a natural activity of Christians as they express the creative power of God, given them as members of Christ by the Holy Spirit. But fifty years or so later Cyprian was complaining that the church lacked strength in prayer because it was growing more worldly and so giving power to the enemy. Appropriately enough, this passage comes from his book, *On the Lapsed*. Even so, Cyprian discussed in other passages the means by which healing continued to take place within the church.

At the same time Origen also showed that the gift of healing extended even to Greeks and barbarians who came to believe in Jesus Christ, and these people sometimes performed amazing cures by invoking the name of Jesus. "For by these means," he wrote, "we too have seen many persons freed from grievous calamities, and from distractions of mind, and madness, and countless other ills, which could be cured neither by men nor devils."[32] Origen saw that the name of Jesus (or a person's belief in Jesus) could bring about a complete change

---

[31] Irenaeus' discussions of healing are found in *Against Heresies* II.6.2, 10.4, 31.2, 32.4–5, and III.5.2.

[32] Origen, *Against Celsus* III.24; also I.6, 25, 46–47, and 67, II.8 and 33, III.24, 28, and 36, VII.35. References in Cyprian's works occur in *On the Lapsed* 6–7; *On the Vanity of Idols* 7; and *Epistle* 75.12–13 and 15–16. There are similar statements in Hippolytus, *Scholia on Daniel* X.16; Dionysius of Alexandria, *Epistle* XII, *To the Alexandrians* 4; and Clement of Alexandria, *Who Is the Rich Man That Shall Be Saved?* 34.

even in the human body, by removing a diseased condition. In one place he adds that demons were even driven out of the bodies of animals which were suffering from injury inflicted on them by evil spirits.

Finally, at the beginning of the fourth century, both Arnobius and his pupil Lactantius wrote about healing. While Arnobius spoke mainly of Jesus and his apostles, his point was that none of Jesus' healings were so miraculous or astonishing that he did not freely put them within the power of the humble and rustic women and men who followed him. Arnobius' implication is clear, and Lactantius added what he had seen in the church in his time, writing: "As He Himself before His passion put to confusion demons by His word and command, so now, by the name and sign of the same passion, unclean spirits, having insinuated themselves into the bodies of men, are driven out, when racked and tormented, and confessing themselves to be demons, they yield themselves to God, who harasses them."[33]

Several methods of healing are mentioned in the various writings cited, and we find practices very similar to those recorded of Jesus and the apostles. Prayer along with laying hands on the sick is specifically mentioned; undoubtedly oil was used. Sometimes prayer alone was effective; or again, the result was obtained by calling on the name of the Lord or even mentioning some fact of Jesus' life. In one place Irenaeus speaks of the prayer and fasting of an entire church as effective in raising a person from the dead.

Nearly all the ante-Nicene Fathers note the successful use of exorcism. During those powerful years of the church's life the Christian group was recognized for its ability to treat the mentally sick or "demon-possessed." The church, as its early writings show, was the place to which people came to find this help. Exorcism was so much a part of its life that the writers of the time give little thought to defending it; they mostly write about the results. It appears, however, that it was performed in several ways. One method was to rebuke the evil spirit in the name of Jesus Christ. Another was to touch or lay hands upon the possessed people; a third way was to breathe upon them. Sometimes stories of Jesus may have been told, and holy water was probably used.[34]

---

[33] Lactantius, *Epitome of the Divine Institutes* 51. See also *The Divine Institutes* II.16 and V.22; Arnobius, *Against the Heathen* I.48 ff.; Victorinus of Petau, *On the Creation of the World*. Many stories of healings also occur all through the apocryphal works and religious romances of this time. While these do not give firm evidence of healings, they do give a picture of the mental horizon of the time as to the fact of healing and its prevalence.

[34] Aside from mental illness, which we shall consider in Chapter Eleven, exorcism may

Exorcism was not only a priestly function, but in the third century specially selected lay people were trained for it. In fact, the order of exorcists soon grew so large that one bishop in Rome complained that they outnumbered the priests.[35] During this period candidates for baptism were all exorcised, and vestiges of this practice are found in the Roman sacrament of baptism today.

The sacraments were also considered a direct source of healing. Cyprian, discussing the fact that wicked spirits no longer found a home in the bodies of Christians who were coming to know the Holy Spirit after baptism, wrote, "This, finally, in very fact we also experience, that those who are baptized by urgent necessity in sickness, and obtain grace, are free from the unclean spirit wherewith they were previously moved, and live in the Church in praise and honour."[36] One of the most dramatic healings I have witnessed followed my baptism of a premature infant who was dying. Her veins had collapsed and so intravenous feeding was no longer possible. Edgar Sanford, a priest and cofounder with Agnes Sanford of the Schools of Pastoral Care, also reported similar experiences.

The same direct effects were known to flow from the forgiveness of sins and from the Communion itself, which was spoken of as a renewal of flesh and blood. Besides the sacramental actions of exorcism and laying on of hands, the sign of the cross (the *sphragis*) was also generally used to provide protective and authoritative healing power when one felt danger from evil spirits. Evidence for this effect of sacramental action which conveyed grace to body as well as soul, is found in most of the works cited below.[37] I have myself found the wearing of the cross

have more relevance for our day than most of us have considered. One should look at the evidence from recent times presented by Leon Christiani in his *Evidences of Satan in the Modern World* (1962); and in *Demonism Verified and Analyzed*, (1922, reprinted 1963), by Hugh W. White. White, Agnes Sanford's father, was a missionary in China. William P. Blatty mentions other standard sources in *The Exorcist* (1971). Navajo rituals have been found successful in treating schizophrenia when modern medical help had failed. At the same time we should not be overwhelmed by fear of the demonic. I have discussed this whole matter as length in *Discernment: A Study in Ecstasy and Evil.*

[35] About the end of the fourth century, abuses and a changing church led to the abolition of the order and transferred this function to the priesthood.

[36] Cyprian, *Epistle* 75.15–16.

[37] For instance, *The Epistle of Barnabas* 6 and 16; Justin Martyr, *Dialogue with Trypho* 14, *The First Apology* 66; Irenaeus, *Against Heresies*, various places, particularly IV.18.5, V.2.2–2 and 11.1; Tertullian, *On Baptism* 5, *To His Wife* II.5; Clement of Alexandria, *Stromata* I.20 and II.11; Origen, *Against Celsus* VI.48; Hippolytus, *Discourse on the Holy Theophany* 8; Cyprian, *Demonstration of the Apostolic Preaching* 97, *On the Dress of Virgins* 2; Vincentius of Thibaris in *The Seventh Council of Carthage under Cyprian (A.D. 258)*; and the *Recognitions of Clement* II.71 and IV.17. A story is also told by Gregory of Nyssa, a careful

an incredible help in times of psychological crises. One of the most startling psychological changes I have observed in my ministry occurred when I was prompted to take a cross from around my neck and place it over the head of a deeply disturbed young man.

The Victorious Christians

For nearly three centuries this healing, centrally experienced, was an indispensable ingredient of Christian life. The same strengthening force was at work, not only in dealing with physical and mental disease, but in meeting persecution. A truly supernatural power was given to these men and women to meet slow and agonizing death, without repudiating Christianity. Thus the martyrs, too, were continuous evidence of a power able to strengthen them beyond normal expectations and of the Christian's relation to the source of that power.

There are many examples of the belief that the Spirit of God enabled the martyrs to withstand and overcome the torture to which they were subjected by the pagan world. Ignatius on his way to martyrdom testified to the amazing resource upon which these women and men drew in their trials. The author of the *Epistle to Diognetus* expressed the conviction of almost all contemporary witnesses: "Dost thou not see men and women cast to wild beasts in order that they may deny their Lord, and yet they are not conquered? . . . These seem not to be the deeds of a human being, these things are the power of God; these are the signs of His presence."[38]

Cyprian, writing during the Decian persecutions, told of instance after instance of the power of Christians to stand above and be victorious over torture and death. Gregory Thaumaturgus, an eyewitness of these martyrdoms, wrote in *A Discourse on All the Saints*, "And if any one believes not that death is abolished . . . let him look on the martyrs disporting themselves in the presence of death, and taking up the jubilant strain of the victory of Christ. O, the marvel! Since the hour when

---

writer, about a deacon in this period who arrived at a certain city late one day and insisted on taking a bath. He was told that a demon visited the public baths at night and inflicted incurable diseases or other harm on anyone who entered. Finally he was given the key and went in to meet the terrifying visions of the demon, but in each room he made the sign of the cross, and the demon left. When he came out unharmed, the guard could hardly believe his eyes (S. Gregorii Nysseni, *De Vita S. Gregorii Thaumaturgi*, in *Patrologiae Graecae* 46 (1869), col. 951).

[38] *The Epistle to Diognetus* 7, *Apostolic Fathers*, 2:187.

Christ despoiled Hades, men (and women) have danced in triumph over death."[39]

One finds the same conviction, the same power, in the specific accounts of martyrdoms. The pagans who witnessed them were amazed and stunned by the casual way in which Christians met death, not just stoically but with a joyous abandon. This power, vividly evident, was a crucial factor in drawing many pagans to the Christian church. These people had such conviction, such strength and joy, that neither torture nor death affected them. And the men and women who saw it, and hungered for such serenity and conviction, were drawn to the group which could give these gifts. The blood of martyrs was indeed the seed of the church, for here was manifest the reality of a power over agony of mind and body, and joyful equanimity in death.

It is amazing to me that a careful writer like Barth, who knew the writings of the early church could have missed the importance of these writings and stated that these healings and superhuman gifts ceased with New Testament times. However, most of the students of these writings also missed the importance attributed to dreams by these writers, as I have shown in *God, Dreams, and Revelation*. What we do not view as important or what does not fit into our worldview, we often do not see.

Strength given by God was both reality and necessity for these men and women who outthought, outlived, and outdied the ancient world. But the era was ending. What place would this power over sickness and persecution find in everyday life as the world became less hostile to Christianity?

---

[39] Gregory Thaumaturgus, *A Discourse on All the Saints*, as translated in Evelyn Frost, *op. cit.*, p. 55. There is, however, some question as to the authorship of the work.

CHAPTER 8

Healing in the Victorious Church

With the victory of Constantine and the Edict of Milan in 313, persecution of the church almost ceased, and this freedom opened up a new
era in the church's life. In a very short time the tables were turned and
Christianity became an accepted religion and then the established religion of the empire. Religious freedom seems to act as an intoxicant on
some people, and elements within the church reacted to Constantine's
acceptance of Christianity with a rash of heretical doctrines and ideas.
Besides the Arians, who wanted to make doctrine about Christ more
rationally acceptable and less paradoxical, there were dozens of other
groups, now almost forgotten, each intent on proving it had the right
line of reasoning to explain Christian experience. Great leaders arose
to bring order out of this theological chaos. A burst of activity and
creativity brought a flow of new literary work.

Few clergy and fewer lay Christians are acquainted with these leaders or their writings, most of which are preserved in the magnificent
edition of J. P. Migne. The three hundred volumes of this library contain
letters, sermons, theological studies, and biblical commentaries, only a
small number of which have been translated from the original Greek
and Latin in which they were printed in the nineteenth century.

Scholars have mined this material and produced hundreds of books
and articles about the theological ideas of these thinkers who set the
mold for later Christian thought. But none of the scholarly work deals
with the attitudes of the early church fathers toward healing or dreams,
visions or demons. Until my book, *God, Dreams and Revelation*, no one
in recent years had examined the writings of these church leaders with
regard to dreams and visions. Yet the early Christian leaders believed

that God used these means to touch and interact with humans. Dr. Frost's study covers interest in healing in the church up to the victory of Constantine, but there her record comes to an end. No one has continued her work, and the modern explorer of the subject is in virgin territory. The prejudices of the nineteenth century against healing in the church did not encourage patristic scholarship in these areas. Seldom do we study what we think is nonsense. Indeed, when scholars came upon passages which told of healings, they either ignored them or wrote condescending notes. Even the words "healing," "dreams," and "vision" are not to be found in the comprehensive indices of those volumes that the nineteenth century scholars thought worthy of translation, works now republished by Eerdmann.

As one plunges into the voluminous literary remains of the victorious church, one finds there the same essential practice and theory that began in the New Testament and continued through the dark days of persecution. One change may be observed, however. The church was now flooded with nominal Christians who found that membership brought favor rather than disfavor. This climate does not generate militant enthusiasm, commitment, or works of healing and yet where vitality of faith and dedication were found, the record shows that healing continued as in the preceding age.

The materials on the subject from this period might well be the substance of an entire book. We shall try to present the evidence of the Christian empire and its writers at this time in one chapter, as briefly as possible, selecting only those acknowledged as the greatest thinkers and avoiding secondary writers. Exhaustive reference to the sources is required throughout, since the material is not gathered together anywhere else.

The Doctors of the Church

The Christian church emerged from underground life to become one of the most important institutions in the Byzantine Empire; it now produced some of its greatest minds. There were a host of problems. In addition to theological confusion, its new position in the empire posed several insistent questions. What was to be the relation of the church to the imperial government? What was the Christian's role as a legal citizen or servant of the empire? How did Christians reconcile themselves to the world? If Christianity was to survive its adoption by emperors, it had to rework its theology, its ethics, its educational methods, and its political theory and thus develop a secure intellectual base.

The great Athanasius broke ground for other thinkers and laid the foundation for all subsequent orthodox Christian thinking. Almost single handedly he defended the trinitarian faith against the emperor and Arian bishops. His long life span, from 296 until 393, saw orthodoxy solidly accepted. In the East he was followed by four men of culture, intellectual power, and saintliness. Together they forged the structure of dogmatic Christianity, which has changed but little in the Eastern Orthodox Church since their time. Three were known as the great Cappadocians: Basil the Great (329–379), his brother Gregory of Nyssa (331?–396), and their friend Gregory of Nazianzus (329?–389). All were theologians—they were considered the finest minds of their time, Christian or pagan. John Chrysostom (345–407), known as "the goldenmouth" for his eloquence, was the greatest preacher of the time and popularized the ideas of the other three. All four were bishops and directed the practical affairs of the church as well. And they all recorded the practice of healing in the church and had a place for it in their theology.

Meanwhile the West produced four men in the same general period who were later acclaimed as doctors of the church. The saintly Ambrose (340?–397) was an effective bishop and the interpreter of the conclusions of Eastern Orthodoxy for the West. He was followed by Augustine (354–430), whose education was second only to Basil's and whose intellectual contribution to Christianity is immense. His voluminous writings set the direction of the Western church for the next thousand years. Jerome (340–420), one of the less attractive figures of this period, was the scholar among the doctors of the church. He translated the Bible from the original Hebrew and Greek into Latin—the Vulgate—and thus left his imprint on all Western Christians. The fourth illustrious doctor of the West, Gregory the Great, came nearly two centuries later. He was born in 540 and lived into the early part of the seventh century. Two other important figures came from roughly the same period: Sulpitious Severus, the biographer of St. Martin of Tours, one of the most popular of all wonder-workers, and John Cassian, who set forth much of the thought behind Western monasticism. Although we find accounts of healing among these various men, they viewed it from quite different angles, which eventually made a great difference.

These ten men started from a common intellectual point of view. All built upon the theological foundations of the postapostolic thinkers described in the last chapter. They accepted a basically Platonic worldview. They saw human beings in relationship with physical and spiritual reality. They believed in the destructive elements of the spiritual world which they called demons, as well as in the positive, angelic aspects of it. Only one of these thinkers perceived either the demonic or angelic in a physically absurd concrete manner. They believed that demons attacked the human pysche directly, bringing physical and mental illness. They accepted the crucifixion and resurrection as events indissolubly linked, through which the demonic host was defeated, and they believed that those who were filled with the spirit of Christ had power to turn back demonic attack and to provide healing in mind and body for those who sought it.

Healing itself was considered one of the evidences that creative spiritual powers were working through human beings. These theologians accepted Plato's basic thinking on the subject. Plato's thought is indeed quite in line with much of modern science, as we shall see presently. In fact, one psychiatrist who read this manuscript remarked that it might well serve as an historical introduction to the study of psychosomatic medicine. Many of the incidents these pioneers of Christian theology relate will be very difficult for the modern reader to accept— particularly those who are still immersed in the almost wholly materialistic worldview of the nineteenth and early twentieth centuries. Those, however, who have gone out of their way to witness and verify the healings of Agnes Sanford or Kathryn Kuhlman, for example, will realize that these healings are the same kind of thing that the early writers observed and recorded—writers who were sophisticated and brilliant thinkers and who laid the intellectual foundations of all mainline Christianity.

Four historians are responsible for recording the events of the first six centuries of the church's life. None of them draw any particular attention to the healings they described, but all occasionally include them in their histories. Eusebius was the first of the four. His work is a sober and careful account of the first years in the life of the church. Without his record we would know but little of the earliest centuries of Christian history. He was a contemporary and friend of Constantine, the first Christian emperor, and he tells in some detail of Constantine's conversion experience. The historians Sozomen and Socrates Scholasticus continue the record of Eusebius, building upon his narrative and adding materials from the following centuries. Finally Theoderet draws upon them all and carries the account on into his own time. These successive writers show no particular fascination with the miraculous, but occasional healings are a part of the history they record. They are certainly no more credulous than the secular historians of their age.

Socrates, for instance, tells how Maruthas, the Bishop of Mesopotamia, cured the Persian king of headaches which his magi had not been able to relieve, and how Maruthas was permitted in consequence to establish churches wherever he wished in Persia.[1] Sozomen tells of an attorney who was healed in the great church built by Constantine in his new capital. This man was unable to retain any food, and his physicians were baffled. Half dead, he had his servants carry him into the church, praying earnestly either to die or to be freed of the illness. In the night a divine power appeared to him and told him to dip his foot in honey, wine, and pepper. Against the wishes of his physicians, he did as he was told and was cured.[2] These two instances are more or less typical of those that recur in the historical tradition.

Healing and Desert Solitude

Discouraged with the worldliness of the church, increasing numbers of women and men went into the deserts of Egypt to recover the quality of life of the first Christians. The writings of these people demonstrate an intense inner life and the expectation of healings. These beginnings of Christian monasticism in Egypt are not very well known today. Monastic orders in the West soon took quite a different direction. Even the Eastern Christian tradition, under the direct influence of the "desert fathers," came to look back more to their interpreters than to the desert monks. Until the present century the "histories" that recounted these beginnings were available only in rewritten, rearranged, often interpolated or interwoven versions so confused that they appeared to have little if any relation to fact. Most students simply scoffed at the experiences set forth; even Antony was assumed to be a fictional character, whose life could not have been written by the great Athanasius.

About the end of the last century, however, Cuthbert Butler carefully analyzed the most important of these histories, the *Historia Lausiaca*

---

[1] Socrates Scholasticus, *Ecclesiastical History* VII.8. Unless otherwise noted, references to the historians and Fathers of the church are found in *A Select Library of the Nicene and Post-Nicene Fathers of the Christian Church* (various dates).

[2] Sozomen, *Ecclesiastical History* II.3. The following references locate all the healings we have found in these historians: Eusebius, *The Church History* I.13; IV.3; V.7; VII.18; Socrates Scholasticus, *Ecclesiastical History* I.17, 19, 20; IV.23, 24, 27; and VII.4; Sozomen, *Ecclesiastical History* II.1, 6, 7; III.14; IV.3, 16; V.21; VI.16, 20, 28 and 29; VII.27; Theodoret, *Ecclesiastical History* I.17, 23; IV.14, 16 and 18; also, *The Sayings of the Fathers* V.37, and *History of the Monks of Egypt* 6, in Helen Waddell, *The Desert Fathers* (1936), pp. 66 and 115–16.

of Palladius.[3] Once its text had been extricated from other source materials, most of the problems about dates and the movements of persons were soon resolved. Palladius himself was authentic enough. He was in Egypt for about twelve years and after that went to Bithynia, where he was consecrated bishop. He was present at a synod in Constantinople in 400, and for his support of Chrysostom—particularly in Rome in 405—he was exiled for several years.

Palladius had come to Alexandria as a monk in 388, and after some time there joined one of the colonies in the Nitrian desert for over a year. Twenty years later he set down what he remembered of these first monks and what he had been told by their disciples. The stories he related were homely, often earthy, sometimes derogatory. He did not dwell much on beliefs or dramatize their experiences; he recounted how these hermits tried to conquer all desire for physical satisfaction and described their world of visions and healing and power over demons. Both men and women stayed alone for years praying and working, sometimes in cells like tombs. They kept themselves from sleep or fasted for long periods, ate only dry bread or raw food, and wore only rags. Some never bathed in order not to be reminded of the sexual practices that went on in the public baths. As Palladius told it, some of them found complete dependence on Christ and the Holy Spirit. Some became so tenderhearted that they spent all their time caring for the needs of others; some were given powers of healing or prophecy.

Palladius described a number of healings in detail, including at least three that had happened in his presence. One of these occurred after he had been in the desert for some time, when a young boy possessed by an evil spirit was brought to Macarius there.[4] The latter put a hand on the boy's head and the other over his heart, and prayed; the boy's body became inflamed and swelled, until he seemed suspended in air. Suddenly he cried out, water poured from his body, and it returned to normal size. Marcarius put him in his father's arms, cured, with a caution not to give him meat or wine for forty days. (Similar occurrences are reported in many cultures, although they are difficult for many moderns to believe.) The old monk then revealed to Palladius his own

---

[3] The story of this painstaking research is found in Vol. 1 of his work, *The Lausiac History of Palladius* (1967), and the resulting reconstructed text makes up Vol. 2. The material that follows comes largely from this work. The name "Lausiac History" came from Palladius' dedication of his book to Lausus, an official of the empire.

[4] This was Macarius of Alexandria, a monk who was apparently the mainstay of those who lived in this area.

temptation at one time to go to Rome and show off his gift for curing the sick and how he had struggled to resist it, wearing himself out by carrying heavy loads across the sand. There were countless instances of his ridding people of demons; one was a noble woman brought from Thessaly who had been paralyzed for several years and was cured when he anointed her with oil and prayed over her for twenty days. On another occasion Palladius begged Macarius to help a certain priest who had sinned; he healed a cancerous growth on the man and also induced him to promise that he would live differently.[5]

Palladius relates the stories of several other monks who had power to heal and cast out demons.[6] He did not glorify the lives of these women and men, but showed that for most of them the struggle in dreams, or with demons who even did them bodily mischief, or with an inflated ego, was constant. He tells of hearing the old Macarius in his cell muttering to himself, "What do you want, you old man of evil? . . . Come, you white-haired old glutton, how long shall I be with you?"[7] He tells of quarrels and weaknesses; there were failures and near-failures, and some fell ill in the desert. Isidore of Scete, for instance, took care of a certain convert, Moses, who had given up a life of temptation and troublemaking. He was sick for a year, but finally regained strength. The great Isidore then said, "Stop contending with demons and do not bother them, for there are limits of bravery as well as in ascetic practice." The convert Moses replied, "I shall not stop before my fantasy of demons ceases." Isidore said, "In the name of Jesus Christ, your dreams have vanished. Now receive Communion confidently. You were subjected to this for your own good, so that you might not boast of overcoming passion." Later Moses said he no longer suffered anything. He was deemed worthy of power over demons and said to have less fear of demons than we have of flies.[8]

These desert fathers tried to do what they felt Jesus Christ wanted people to do. Their lives left a record of healing and of encounters in which the spiritual realm deeply penetrated the Christianity of their age, an influence felt throughout the Eastern church, and also in the West for a long time. The record of Palladius is difficult to accept, but

---

[5] Butler, *op. cit.*, 2:58–70.
[6] *Ibid.*, pp. 48, 55, 57, 81, 83, 104, 113, 119, 121. Besides these there are other references to healing and casting out demons on pp. 47, 51, 57–58, 89–90 (the story of a demon or temptation cast out in a dream), 108, 115, 131, 132, and 152.
[7] *Ibid.*, p. 66.
[8] *Ibid.*, p. 70.

it cannot be totally dismissed as mere fancy. Other reliable authors have set down the same kinds of things, and experiences similar to these are still recorded today.

Convincing support for these accounts is found in the writings of Athanasius himself. It was late in life before he took time from his political and theological labors to write specifically on the desert monks and healing. He had taken refuge earlier with the monks in the Egyptian desert and was asked to write about Antony after his death. His *Life of St. Antony*, set down about 357, was soon referred to as "a rule of monastic life in the form of a narrative."[9] In this deeply perceptive work Athanasius quoted, quite casually, the words of the old saint about his own healings and those of other monks: "We must not boast of casting out devils, nor be elated at the healing of diseases, nor should we admire only the person who casts out devils, and account that one useless who does not. . . . To work miracles is not ours; that is the Saviour's work. At any rate, He said to His disciples: 'But do not rejoice in this, that the spirits are subject to you; rejoice rather in this, that your names are written in heaven.'"[10] For this pillar of the church, as for the desert fathers who were considered the founders of monasticism, healing was simply one expression of Christian devotion to the risen Jesus, to be used as the opportunity arose. He took for granted that such things happened, as did other Christians of his time. But Athanasius was in a peculiar position to appreciate it, for he saw all aspects of the church in its struggle with the Arians.

Healing Among the Leaders

Few serious modern Christian theologians would lightly reject the theological reasoning of St. Basil or his close friend, Gregory of Nazianzus, yet these men also wrote of Christian healing. Is there any sound reason to ignore their thinking on that subject? Both had a good knowledge of medicine for their time—Basil, indeed, had some medical training—and with their health none too good, both had a direct interest in practical medicine.[11] Gregory also had reason to be aware of the brilliant

---

[9] Gregory of Nazianzen, *Oration XXI*, On the Great Athanasius, Bishop of Alexandria 5, quoted by Johannes Quasten, in his *Patrology* (1960), 3:40.

[10] St. Athanasius, *Life of Saint Anthony* 38, in Roy J. Deferrari, ed., *Early Christian Biographies* (1952), pp. 169–70.

[11] Numerous references to both medicine and religious healing in Gregory's writings are found in Sister Mary Emily Keenan's article, "St. Gregory of Nazianzus and Early Byzantine Medicine," *Bulletin of the History of Medicine* 9 (January 1941): 8–30.

medical career of his brother Caesarius, while Basil founded and maintained a large hospital outside Caesarea, probably the first public institution devoted to free care of the sick. At the same time, the two men
were equally committed to the reality of healing through Christ. Again
and again Gregory showed his understanding of the "deep roots" of
disease and how closely the church's task with people was allied to the
job of the medical practitioner.

Gregory related two incidents of healing in Basil's public life. The
first occurred when he was about to be exiled by the emperor Valens,
whose small son was suddenly sick and in pain. When physicians could
not help the baby, the emperor had a change of heart and called for
Basil, who came immediately; according to the reports of those present,
the boy began to improve at once, but later died because his father was
overanxious and asked the physicians to try their treatment again. The
other incident also occurred during a personal conflict between Basil
and Bishop Eusebius, who then fell ill and called for Basil. He went
willingly, and Eusebius confessed that he had been in the wrong and
asked to be saved. According to Gregory, Eusebius's life was indeed
restored; the bishop never ceased to wonder at Basil's power.[12]

Gregory also recounts some remarkable healings in his immediate
family. One instance was widely known locally. His sister Gorgonia was
dragged by a team of mules and so frightfully injured that no one
thought she could recover; she was saved by the prayers of the congregation. Years later she had a second experience, which was understand-
ably not spoke of outside the family while she lived. Gregory describes
her illness as a burning fever alternating with periods of deathlike
coma, with only brief remissions. He recounts how it continued in spite
of prayers and all that several physicians could do. One night, in the
middle of the night, she somehow made her way into the church and
in despair took some of the reserved sacrament in her hand and knelt,
grasping the altar. Crying out that she would hold on until she was
made whole, she rubbed the precious substance on her body, and at
last stood up, refreshed and stronger. She knew she was saved and
again began a miraculous recovery.[13]

Another account describes a similar healing of his father. On one
Easter eve the elder Gregory was dangerously ill. The church was filled
with people praying for his recovery as his son began the service. Just
as the bread and wine were set out and all was quiet for the prayers of

---

[12] Gregory Nazianzen, *Oration XLIII*, The Panegyric on S. Basil, 54–55.
[13] Gregory Nazianzen, *Oration VII*, On his Sister Gorgonia, 15–18.

consecration, the old bishop suddenly awoke and called out to his servant, who came running. He asked to be helped to his knees, and there beside the bed joined his people in celebration of the great rite. After pronouncing the final thanksgiving and blessing, he asked for food and then went to sleep quietly. On the next Sunday he was at the altar again to join his clergy in offering thanks for the miracle of his recovery and renewed vigor. As Gregory says, summing up the qualities of his father's life and the kind of events that filled it, "What wonder if he was thought worthy of the miracles by which God establishes true religion?"[14]

Several other events of this kind appear in Gregory's writing.[15] In his theological poems the healing miracles of the Bible are made vividly alive. This fascinating family was so deeply at home in the reality of the spiritual world that healing could be sought and received naturally as a gift from God. It is no wonder that Gregory of Nazianzus was in so many ways one pivot on whom the establishment of an Orthodox faith came to depend.

In telling how Gregory of Nazianzus took over in Constantinople at the end of the Arian controversy, the historian Sozomen adds an account of the healing of a pregnant woman in Gregory's church. He concludes that at least in this Orthodox church, "the power of God was there manifested, and was helpful both in waking visions and in dreams, often for the relief of many diseases and for those afflicted by some sudden transmutation in their affairs."[16] This kind of healing was seldom reported among the Arians whom Gregory replaced.

St. Basil was interested in practical matters and therefore in healing. In his work, *The Long Rules*, one of the most important treatises on monastic life, he considered "whether recourse to the medical art is in keeping with the practice of piety." His thinking has a modern ring to it. Medical science has been given to human beings by God, he contended, to be used when necessary, but not to the exclusion of spiritual healing. Just as the Lord sometimes healed merely by uttering a command and sometimes by physical touch, so "He sometimes cures us

---

[14] Gregory Nazianzen, *Oration XVIII*, On the Death of His Father, 27–31.

[15] During one of her rare illnesses, Gregory's mother dreamed that he had brought her a "basket of pure white loaves" which he blessed at the altar and then fed to her. The vision was so real that when he stopped by in the morning to ask how she was, she was surprised that he did not know how much better she felt. With the kindness that seems spontaneous in this family, Gregory conspired with her maids to keep her from knowing it had been a dream, lest the knowledge throw her back into depression. *Ibid.*, 30.

[16] Sozomen, *Ecclesiastical History* VII.5.

secretly and without visible means when He judges this mode of treatment beneficial to our souls; and again He wills that we use material remedies for our ills."[17]

He discussed the various natural remedies provided by medicine, implying that these are also gifts for which God is to be thanked, remarking that "to reject entirely the benefits to be derived from this art is the sign of a petty nature." On the other hand, there were reasons why a person might suffer sickness or fail to be healed. In considering them Basil did not deny either kind of healing to anyone, except possibly to a saint like Paul. It might be necessary, he said, for saints to suffer some infirmity in order to know that they were human, but "those who have contracted illness by living improperly should make use of the healing of their body as a type and exemplar, so to speak, for the cure of their soul."[18] In other words, saints and sinners alike might expect to suffer for their sins, but redemption, for sinners at least, was very much like the healing of physical illness. The expectation of healing as a normal Christian phenomenon apparently continued throughout Basil's active life. In his late sermon on "The Forty Holy Martyrs," for instance, he instructed his people: "Here is found a pious woman praying for her children, the return of her husband, his recovery when sick: let your prayers be made with the martyrs!"[19]

A Theology of Healing

The rest of what we know about these three men comes from Gregory of Nyssa, younger brother of Basil the Great. He resisted entering the priesthood, taking up rhetoric instead. Then came his famous conversion experience.[20] Finally the younger Gregory took his place in the church. The thinking of these three men—Basil, his friend Gregory of Nazianzus, and his brother Gregory of Nyssa—is so similar that any one of them can practically speak for the others. Indeed, Gregory of Nyssa finished his brother's important work, Hexaemeron, after Basil's death.

In The Making of Man, his thorough discussion of the healing miracles of Jesus revealed his understanding of the way human faith and theology develop, starting from basic facts such as healing. Then in

---

[17] Saint Basil, The Long Rules Q. 55, in his Ascetical Works (1950), p. 332.
[18] Ibid., pp. 333 and 336.
[19] S. Basilii Magni, In Sanctos Quadraginta Martyres 8; Patrologiae Graecae 31 (1885), col. 523.
[20] This is described in my book, God, Dreams, and Revelation, p. 135.

three very interesting subsequent works he described certain healings quite carefully. One was a sermon which also told about the dream that first brought him into the church, a dream that occurred at the shrine of the forty martyrs. These were Christians in the last major persecution who had stood by their faith even when the Roman army forced them to stand in an icy pond and so freeze to death.

Gregory told how nearby soldiers would bring their sick and injured men to the shrine. One night a lame soldier was in the shrine with several other men. He poured out prayers to God and to the martyrs, and in the night had a vision of a fine-looking man who said to him, "Lame one, do you need a cure? Give me your foot that I may touch it." As the soldier dreamed of dragging his leg forward, there was a wrenching noise and then a sound of violent impact that roused the others. The soldier awoke and stood up, cured. This was a man whom Gregory knew and had stayed with, who told everyone he met about the kindness of the martyrs and of his fellow soldiers.[21]

Soon after Basil died in 379, Gregory made a trip to their sister's retreat to find comfort. But she too was near death, and so, with the urging of those close to her, he began to write the *Life of St. Macrina*. This beautiful story was almost finished when a man, a military leader of the area, came to him to say, "Let me tell you what kind of good came out of her life, and how much there was of it." And he went on to tell what happened when he and his wife were visiting Macrina's convent.

There was with us our little girl who was suffering from an eye ailment resulting from an infectious sickness. It was a terrible and pitiful thing to see her as the membrane around the pupil was swollen and whitened by the disease. . . . I went to the men's quarters to be with the holy one. After an interval of time . . . we were getting ready to leave . . . but the blessed one would not let my wife go, and [Macrina] said she would not give up my daughter, whom she was holding in her arms, until she had given them a meal and offered them the wealth of philosophy. She kissed the child as one might expect and put her lips on her eyes and, when she noticed the diseased pupil, she said, "If you do me the favor of remaining for dinner, I will give you a return in keeping with this honor." When the child's mother asked what it was, the great lady replied, "I have some medicine which is especially effective in curing eye disease." . . . we gladly remained and . . . started the journey home bright and happy. Each

---

[21] S. Gregorii Nysseni, *In Quadraginta Martyres*, in *Patrologiae Graecae* 46 (1863), col. 783. Gregory preached three sermons on the "forty martyrs," showing how he knew that they were still alive and active in people's lives. In his *Oratio Laudatoria Sancti Ac Magni Martyris Theodori* he invoked the help of St. Theodore again and again.

of us told his own story on the way. . . . [My wife] was telling everything in order, as if going through a treatise, and when she came to the point at which the medicine was promised, interrupting the narrative she said, "What have we done? How did we forget the promise, the medicine for the eyes?" I was annoyed at our thoughtlessness, and quickly sent one of my men back to ask for the medicine, when the child who happened to be in her nurse's arms, looked at her mother, and the mother fixing her gaze on the child's eyes, said, "Stop being upset by our carelessness." She said this in a loud voice, joyfully and fearfully. "Nothing of what was promised to us has been omitted, but the true medicine that heals diseases, the cure that comes from prayer, this she has given us, and it has already worked; nothing at all is left of the disease of the eyes." As she said this, she took our child and put her in my arms and I, also, then comprehended the miracles in the gospel which I had not believed before and I said, "What a great thing it is for sight to be restored to the blind by the hand of God, if now His handmaiden makes such cures and has done such a thing through faith in Him, a fact no less impressive than these miracles."[22]

As Gregory noted, this was but one of several such miracles in Macrina's life that were talked about locally.

Gregory Thaumaturgus (the "wonder-worker") came to Cappadocia in the days of persecution. His life and power made a tremendous impression, particularly on the families of the three great Cappadocians. No wonder Gregory of Nyssa wrote a life of the saint. In it he gave an eyewitness account of the casting out of a demon that was tormenting an adolescent boy, who then stood quiet and whole before a crowd of country people. In addition, his power against sickness of all kinds was known throughout the region.[23] Basil gives much the same account of this Gregory in brief form in his work, On the Spirit.

Gregory of Nyssa was the only one of the Eastern theologians who made a definite statement relating healing to his total theology. In two of his most important works, The Great Catechism and On the Making of Man, he referred to it as the main door through which a knowledge of God reaches human beings. First, in considering "the way Deity is mingled with humanity," he proposed unequivocally that, although the subject was unapproachable by the processes of reasoning, yet "the miracles recorded permit us not to entertain a doubt that God was born in the nature of man."[24] As he went on to show, this is so because

[22] Saint Gregory of Nyssa, The Life of St. Macrina, in his Ascetical Works (1967), pp. 188–89.

[23] S. Gregorii Nysseni, De Vita S. Gregorii Thaumaturgi, in Patrologiae Graecae 46 (1863), cols. 942–43; also 922–23 and 950–51, where these healing powers are also considered.

[24] Gregory of Nyssa, The Great Catechism XI.

healing is as much a divine gift as life itself. Later in the same work he considered how one can be certain that deity is present when called upon to enter into the elements used for baptism. And again he concluded that the ability to perform miracles is one evidence that the baptismal water has indeed conferred grace upon the baptized.[25]

On the Making of Man describes in graphic terms a number of the healings of Jesus, showing how central they were to faith in his resurrection: they opened people's eyes to knowledge that the resurrection was a possibility.[26] Thus healing miracles were in the same category as the most important event in Christian history, only a little lower in the scale.

Healing from Another Perspective

A few years later, John Chrysostom in Antioch brought into the eastern church a different experience and contribution. He was well educated and became the favorite of his teacher, the renowned Libanius.[27] Before the age of twenty he was a successful lawyer in the city, already earning his appelation of "golden-mouth." Then Meletius was made bishop of Antioch, and apparently Chrysostom and the older man were drawn to each other. The youth abandoned the law and turned his life entirely to the church. First in Antioch and later in Constantinople, where not even Christians were very deeply concerned about morality, he preached the gospel and ministered to people.

From then on his consuming interest was to see the gospel lived, primarily in his own monastic life, and then, when his health declined, through moral commitment to it as a member of a lay order. He constantly preached moral commitment to the gospel as the only base from which Christian experience could spring. People came to listen, many of whom were far more at home in the baths and the theater than in church. When he applied the same truths to the empress and was banished for speaking out, they even followed him to his place of exile. He preached with sympathy, but never avoided hard conclusions, and there

---

[25] *Ibid.*, XXXIV.

[26] *On the Making of Man* XXV.6–10. Similar reasoning is presented in *On the Soul and the Resurrection*.

[27] This was the great classical scholar, friend of the pagan Emperor Julian, who had returned to Antioch after years in Athens and Constantinople.

was no question about the response. To this day Eastern Orthodox thinking still bases its doctrine on his moral teachings.[28]

At the same time, Chrysostom did not overlook the reality of healing or the expectation of actual miracles in his own time. He discussed the healings of Jesus and the apostles as few other writers did. In discussing the miracles in Acts he never lost sight of the fact that they were performed, and continued to be done, not by human beings but by God, whose power is always the same. The healing at the Beautiful Gate, he held, succeeded because these Christians called upon God for the things they ought to ask of God.[29] In his work written to comfort the monk Stagirius, who was suffering from severe depression with psychotic episodes, he put the emphasis entirely upon demons as the cause of the illness.[30]

Chrysostom never tired of mentioning the miracles he had known personally at the shrine of St. Babylas the martyr, near Antioch. In his treatise on the power of the martyr against the actions of Emperor Julian, he spoke of "the miracles . . . performed daily by the holy martyrs."[31] Once in a while he also gives details of a healing he knows of, such as the boy who was healed more than once by God's direct help. Left inarticulate after a fever, nothing the physicians did helped the boy. Finally, when his mother was in despair and prayed, God loosed the boy's tongue. Another time the boy's eyes were so affected by thick discharge that no hope was held for saving his sight. Again, in response to prayer, God alone produced a miraculous recovery.[32]

But looking for the immediate action of the divine in ordinary life was not Chrysostom's strongest point. He was more likely to complain, as he once did, of finding the sanctuary lamp empty when someone had run out of consecrated oil and wanted to anoint a sick friend. Or he might mention how much trouble the physicians were spared when

---

[28] See, for instance, *The Pedalion* (or "Rudder"), trans. Cummings (1957). This basic reference book of Greek Orthodox faith alludes to Chrysostom again and again.

[29] St. Chrysostom, *A Commentary on the Acts of the Apostles*, Homily X. Also, for instance, *ibid.*, Homily I; *The Homilies on the Statues* X.7 and I.5–6, where the illness of Paul and others are considered, first by proving their fully human nature and second as *permitted* (not caused) by God; finally, as no hindrance nor even embarrassment to them. They went right on healing and doing other works without becoming indifferent or powerless.

[30] S. Joannis Chrysostomi, *Ad Stagirium a Daemone Vexatum* I.1, in *Patrologiae Graecae* 47 (1863), col. 425–26.

[31] St. Chrysostom, *A Commentary on the Acts of the Apostles*, Homily XXXVIII.

[32] St. Chrysostom, *A Commentary on the Acts of the Apostles*, Homily XXXVIII.

patients recovered as a result of sleep and prayer.[33] Chrysostom knew almost too much about carelessness of both Christians and pagans in dealing with spiritual concerns.

In a lecture on the holy martyrs to men and women preparing for baptism, Chrysostom refers in passing to healing. The bodies of the martyrs have been left on earth so that Christians may reach out to them and so receive the greatest possible healing for either soul or body. The martyrs do not require the time and money it takes to procure the services of a physician, for "if we stand beside them with faith, whether our sickness be of the body or the soul, we will not leave their tombs without the healing of which we stood in need . . . here we need none of these things, neither the long journey, nor the trouble, nor the going back and forth, nor the expense; it is enough that we bring a loyal faith, that we shed warm tears and have a sober soul, for us to find forthwith a cure of our soul and healing for our body."[34] Chrysostom goes on to note prayers that have been answered: a husband brought back from far away, a frightfully sick child made healthy.

These four men, combining the intellectual, practical, moral, and intuitive approaches, worked together to produce a theology of healing that has remained alive in the Eastern church through the centuries. We shall see that this belief was enshrined in the records of public worship which have come down to us.

Liturgy and Healing

The forms of worship used by the early church may not seem an exciting study, but, if we are to understand Christian life at that time, it is essential. The importance of healing is clearly underlined in the liturgy of the church. The words and motions of the Eucharist carried the meaning of atonement and resurrection, of joining soul and mind and body in a kind of health that would last into life after death. With the comparatively recent discovery of the *Apostolic Tradition of Hippolytus,* written about 215, we now have a good picture of how the idea of healing developed in early liturgies and how much it was an ingredient of ordinary life.

The early church orders of service were practical handbooks of Christian worship and often a good deal more. One of the principal sources on the early churches, they describe the local forms of worship

---

[33] St. Chrysostom, *The Homilies on the Statues,* Homily VIII.1.
[34] St. John Chrysostom, *Baptismal Instructions* VII.5–6 (1963), p. 106.

and suggest the meaning then attached to these forms. They include moral instruction; some are even presented as the picture of an ideal Christian community. Except for the earliest—the *Didache*, which grew out of a Jewish instruction for converts to Judaism—all give specific directions for healing practices in connection with the central acts of Christian worship.[35]

From the first the sacraments were expected to bring life and health. Even in the *Didache*, the formal prayers offering the bread and wine for the Eucharist include thanks first for life and then for life eternal. A century later, when Hippolytus came to set down the tradition in Rome, oil reserved for the sick could also be offered at Communion, and thanks were given: "as at the offering of the bread and wine . . . in the same general manner, saying, 'That sanctifying this oil, O God, wherewith thou didst anoint kings, priests and prophets, thou wouldest grant health to them who use it and partake of it, so that it may bestow comfort on all who taste it and health on all who use it.'"[36]

As other liturgies became fixed, the same expectation was found in the words of the Eucharist in widely scattered areas from Gaul to Egypt, and the sacrament itself was offered as "the specific medicine of life unto the healing of every illness."[37] As we have seen, this expectation might also attach to baptism, and preparation for baptism was closely associated with healing.

At first the commission to heal was seen as a special gift or *charisma*, much as Paul had spoken of it. The individual who received this gift did not need to be ordained, as the *Apostolic Tradition of Hippolytus* clearly shows in the direction: "If anyone says, 'I have received the gift of healing,' hands shall not be laid upon him; the deed shall make manifest if he speaks the truth."[38] A century later it was apparently common for persons who received the gift of healing to ask to become priests,

---

[35] Careful studies of Christian rituals to the present time, particularly in relation to healing, are found in W. K. Lowther Clarke's *Liturgy and Worship* (1954). The section on "Visitation of the Sick" is especially valuable, and we are indebted to this study for many of the references that follow. See also Jean Daniélou, *The Bible and Liturgy* (1956), for important insights about healing in connection with the biblical origins of various Christian rites.

The various service books are discussed by Burton Scott Easton in *The Apostolic Tradition of Hippolytus* (1962), pp. 9–24. See also Bernard Botte, O.S.B., ed., *La Tradition Apostolique* [Hippolyte de Rome]: *D'Après Les Anciennes Versions* (1968), and Gregory Dix, ed., *The Treatise on the Apostolic Tradition of St. Hippolytus of Rome* (1968).

[36] *Apostolic Tradition of Hippolytus* I.5, in Easton, *op. cit.*, pp. 36–37.

[37] *Bishop Sarapion's Prayer-Book* I.I.c. ed. John Wordsworth, Bishop of Salisbury (1923), p. 63.

[38] *Apostolic Tradition of Hippolytus* I.15, Easton, *op. cit.*, p. 41.

and the later *Canons of Hippolytus* directed that the facts be definitely proved before a healer was ordained. The *Apostolic Constitutions* also provided for the ordination of exorcists and healers.[39]

By this time the clergy were instructed in the importance of visiting the sick, which Hippolytus had only mentioned. The *Canons* point out that visits by the bishop are "a great thing for the sick man. . . . He recovers from his disease when a Bishop comes to him, particularly if he prays over him." Public prayers and visits by the clergy are directed, with the clear intent to promote healing.

This intention is also found in the prayers for ordination, from deacons to bishops. There were prayers asking God to grant a deacon power over demons and to fill a presbyter "with the gifts of healing," and to give a presbyter or a bishop "a mild spirit, and power to remit sins, and grant to him power to loose all bonds of the iniquity of demons [by exorcism], and to heal all diseases, and to beat down Satan under his feet quickly." It became more and more understood that the gift of healing was conferred by the sacramental action of the church. What had been a *charisma* given to individuals was becoming a part of the priestly office, to be sought and used through the sacraments.

Lay Christians still continued to heal, but on a different basis. Besides services for visiting the sick, there were also prayers for sanctifying the oil and other objects which might be used to convey healing. *Bishop Sarapion's Prayer-Book* and the *Apostolic Constitutions* both provided special prayers at the Eucharist for blessing oil, bread, or even water for the sick, which were then taken to sick persons to heal them. Oil in particular was a substance that could heal once sanctified by the church. The shrines of the martyrs, both in the Eastern church and in North Africa, had come to have the same power. People believed that in the remains of a martyr holiness and therefore healing were present through the sacrament of their devotion and death.

People began taking the consecrated oil, bread, and so forth home to use when needed. By the fifth century this controversial practice prompted Innocent I to write to one of his bishops that Christians not only had the definite right, when sick, to be anointed by the clergy with holy oil, but also "to use it themselves for anointing in their own need, or in the need of members of their households." Three hundred years later in England, when the Venerable Bede discussed the needs

---

[39] References to the *Canons of Hippolytus* (p. 53) are from Clarke, *op. cit.*, pp. 475–79; those to the *Apostolic Constitutions* are taken from *The Ante-Nicene Fathers* VII. 26, pp. 491–94.

of the sick in his exegesis on the letter of James, he supported the same practice for his people, citing the pope's letter as confirmation.[40]

This use of consecrated oil by ordinary Christians became fixed in Western liturgy through the forms for preparing candidates for baptism. In Hippolytus's time new Christians, who had been exorcised daily during their final preparations, were anointed twice on Easter Sunday, the day of baptism. The "oil of exorcism" was used first, and then the "oil of thanksgiving," or chrism. As the rituals developed in Rome, these oils, as well as oil for anointing the sick, were blessed by the pope (and elsewhere by a bishop) at the Chrismal Mass on the Thursday before Easter. Mgr. Louis Duchesne has carefully described this practice:

Towards the end of the Canon the faithful brought small vessels of oil to be blessed for their own use. This was the oil for anointing the sick, and the faithful could make use of it themselves. It served also for extreme unction. The vessels containing it were placed on the balustrade. . . . and brought to the altar where the Pope blessed them, using the following formulary:

"Send forth from the heavens, Thou who art our Lord, Thy Holy Spirit, the Comforter, into this fat oil to bring forth, as from green wood, things worthy for restoration of mind and body; let Thy Holy blessing protect in mind and body, in soul and spirit, all who are anointed, all who taste or carry it away, doing away with all pain, all infirmity, all sickness of mind and body, blessing them as Thou didst anoint Thy priests, kings, prophets and martyrs with Thy perfect unction, O Master, bringing it to continue permanent in our flesh, in the name of our Lord and Master Jesus Christ."[41]

After the Communion the greater vessels of oil were blessed, as is still done on Holy Thursday. This Mass has been celebrated with high ceremony since about the sixth century. With its inclusion in the *Pontifical*, the service book for Catholic bishops, the basic idea of anointing for healing was given a place in the liturgy, where it remained for several centuries.

There was another form for healing, however, also found in the older service books that have come down to us from the Roman tradi-

---

[40] Innocentii I Papae, *Epistola*, XXV.8 in *Patrologiae Latinae* 20 (1845), cols. 560-61. Also, Venerabilis Bedae, *Super Epistolas Catholicas: Expositio Super Divi Jacobi Epistolam* V, in *Patrologiae Latinae* 93 (1862), col. 39. For further evidence of this practice, see Hastings's *Encyclopedia of Religion and Ethics*, Vol. 5: 672–73.

[41] Mgr. Louis Duchesne, *Christian Worship: Its Origin and Evolution* (1919), pp. 305–06. The prayer is given in our translation from the Latin used by Duchesne. See also Michel Andrieu, *Les Ordines Romani du Haut Moyen Âge* (1931–1948), 3:468–69.

tion. This was a form for visiting, anointing, and laying hands on the sick, which undoubtedly originated in the early church orders of service. The Eastern liturgy, starting from the same forms of Hippolytus, provided a similar service, which is still in use today. But in the West the healing element or meaning was gradually laid aside, and the service itself, while continuing in use, was transformed.

The oldest copy at present known of a Western service for visiting the sick comes from the library of a monastery in northern France. It is part of a fairly complete service book dating from before the reign of Charlemagne, and varies greatly from the later versions.[42] The contrast reflects the gradual change from a service for healing to a service to speed the dying. Until at least the eleventh century the intention was definitely to heal. This earliest version called for several priests and members of the congregation to take part and pray with the sick. They began by exorcising unclean spirits and blessing water and salt, which were mixed and sprinkled over the house. The prayers that follow are reminiscent of New Testament healings and leave no doubt that the object of the prayers is physical healing.

The sick person then knelt for laying on of hands, which suggests that recovery may already have begun. The person was anointed on the throat, chest, and back, "and also," the service reads, "let them be more thoroughly and liberally anointed where the pain is more threatening." Besides general prayers of thanksgiving, the sick were told to pray for their own recovery; only then did they make their confession, if any, and receive Communion. Finally, priests and "ministers" were directed to come back for seven days to bring Communion; they were to repeat any part of the office that seemed advisable until the sick person recovered.

It is hard to understand how this service could become a preparation for death, and in the East this did not happen. Instead the healing practices and attitude of the primitive church continued in the eastern liturgy. The *Euchologion*, the service book for most Orthodox churches, which had its beginnings in the early centuries of Christianity, still today provides a congregational healing service, performed if possible in church by seven priests. But if necessary, any single person may represent the whole church. Anyone seriously ill may be anointed,

---

[42] This copy of the "Orationes ad visitandum infirmum" is found in the *Liber Sacramentorum* (Sancti Gregorii Magni), in *Patrologiae Latinae* 78 (1895), cols. 231–36. There is a preface, written by Hugo Menard about 1645, carefully describing the various manuscripts, and four variations of the service, down to the tenth century, are compared in detail (cols. 15–24 and 519–42).

whether in danger of death or not, and the service is performed as many times as needed.[43] In practice, the Eastern rite of unction has been neglected and sometimes mixed with local superstition, but the understanding still remains that the Holy Spirit, operating through the body of the church, can and does heal the sick. There is little essential difference between the understanding of Greek service books, the thinking of early doctors of the Eastern church, and the popular practice in most Orthodox churches today. The same thinking and practice continues much as in the day of the Eastern doctors of the church. Interesting confirmation of this healing tradition is also found in the Russian church right up to the time of Czar Nicholas II.[44] We turn now to the Western church, where a different kind of attitude developed, an attitude toward healing that made a great difference in those churches with Western European roots.

Healing in the West

The development of Augustine's thought holds special interest for the understanding of Christian healing. He was the preeminent theologian in the West for nearly a thousand years. In his early writings he stated quite specifically that Christians are not to look for continuance of the healing gift. Then something happened, his skepticism gave way to belief in Christ's healing power, and he frankly admitted that he had been wrong. In the *Confessions* he acknowledged the important part played in his conversion by Athanasius's *Life of Antony*. At that time, however, physical healing among the distant desert fathers did not seem important to him. Nearly forty years later in 424, when his greatest work, *The City of God*, was nearing completion, his outlook changed.

In an important final section of that work, he describes miracles of healing in his own diocese of Hippo Regius, and how he instituted the recording and attesting of miracles there, because, he wrote,

---

[43] See the *Service Book of the Holy Orthodox-Catholic Apostolic Church* [*The Euchologion*, Tikhon ed.] (1922), pp. 332–44; also Aimé Georges Martimort, *L'Église en Prière: Introduction à la Liturgie* (1961), p. 96. Richard and Eva Blum, *Health and Healing in Rural Greece* (1965), pp. 208–16, also offer the most interesting present-day confirmation of these facts. Mary Hamilton has written a fascinating study, *Incubation* (1906), of the practice in the Greek Islands in the early years of the twentieth century, showing how the practices described by the Greek doctors of the church still continue. Visiting Greece in 1974 I found that I could still buy metal replicas of parts of the body which one left as a thanks offering at a holy place when a healing had taken place. Many holy places were covered with them.

[44] This was drawn to my attention in *Not All Vanity* by Agnes de Stoeckl (1950), sent to me by Dr. Ray St. Clair Dwyer.

I realized how many miracles were occurring in our own day and which were so like the miracles of old and also how wrong it would be to allow the memory of these marvels of divine power to perish from among our people. It is only two years ago that the keeping of records was begun here in Hippo, and already, at this writing, we have nearly seventy attested miracles.[45]

The City of God was completed in 426. The following year, three years before he died, Augustine wrote in the *Retractions* (more properly the "Revisions"):

I also said, *These miracles are not allowed to continue into our time, lest the soul should always require things that can be seen, and by becoming accustomed to them mankind should grow cold towards the very thing whose novelty had made men glow with fire.* (*De Vera Religione*, cap. 25, nn. 46, 47, italics added.) It is indeed true: that not everyone today who has hands laid on them in baptism thus receives the Holy Spirit so as to speak in tongues; nor are the sick always healed by having the shadow of the promise of Christ pass across them; and if such things were once done, it is clear that they afterwards ceased.

But what I said should not be taken as understanding that no miracles are believed to happen today in the name of Christ. For at the very time I wrote this book I already knew that, by approaching the bodies of the two martyrs of Milan, a blind man in that same city was given back his sight; and so many other things of this kind have happened, even in this present time, that it is not possible for us either to know of all of them or to count up all of those that we do have knowledge of.[46]

What had happened to change his view? The story, which must be pieced together partly from sources still in Latin, begins with the discovery in 415 of the bones venerated as relics of St. Stephen the martyr. One of several shrines containing these relics was placed in Augustine's church in Hippo. In 424, two weeks before Easter, a brother and sister came to Hippo, both suffering from convulsive seizures. They gave a sad account of parental rejection and came each day to pray at the shrine for healing. On Easter morning before the service the young man was in the crowded church, praying as he held onto the screen around the reliquary.

Augustine was still in the vestibule, ready for the processional, when the young man fell down as if dead. People near were filled with fear. But the next moment he got up and stood staring back at them, perfectly normal and quite cured. When one after another had run to

---

[45] Saint Augustine, *The City of God* XXII.8 (1954), p. 445.

[46] S. Augustini, *Retractationum* I.13.7, in *Patrologiae Latinae* 32 (1877), cols. 604–05. Another section (*ibid.*, I.14.15, col. 607), referring to *On the Advantage of Believing* 16.34, retracts a similar statement about miracles in much the same way. The miracle mentioned above as occurring in Milan is told in the *Confessions* IX.7.16 and is described on p. 188, below.

tell Augustine about it, the church finally quieted down for the service. In his sermon the bishop did little more than mention what had happened, but the young man stayed with him for dinner and they talked at length.

In the days following, Augustine preached about St. Stephen, the healing, and other martyrs and healings. On the third day after Easter he read the young man's statement, while both brother and sister stood on the choir steps where the whole congregation could see them—one quiet and normal, the other still trembling convulsively. Augustine then asked them to sit down, and was giving his sermon about the healing when he was interrupted by loud cries. The young woman had gone straight to the shrine to pray, and exactly the same thing had happened to her. Once more she stood before the people, this time healed, and in Augustine's own words, "Praise to God was shouted so loud that my ears could scarcely stand the din. But, of course, the main point was that, in the hearts of all this clamoring crowd, there burned that faith in Christ for which the martyr Stephen shed his blood."[47] In this last section of his final great work Augustine paid his dues in full to the reality of healing. It was one of the ways, he now saw, that people find how true the gospel really is, particularly the resurrection.

The City of God describes this experience, but to follow the development of Augustine's understanding of healing, one must look in other places, particularly in his daily sermons recorded at the time.[48] He continued to preach about healing. By the time *The City of God* was completed in 426 he had witnessed another remarkable instance, which was also observed by the physicians of the man concerned, who had been preparing him for an operation which then was not required. Augustine also knew personally and in detail of several other incidents. Some occurred in Uzalum, where his friend Evodius was bishop, others in Calama, where attested records had been kept for some years; in both places shrines had been dedicated to St. Stephen.[49] Just before his death Augustine himself, it was recorded, became a healer of others who

---

[47] *City of God*, p. 450.

[48] S. Augustini Episcopi, *Sermo CCCXVII–CCCXXIV* in *Patrologiae Latinae* 38 (1841), cols. 1435-47. See also F. van der Meer, *Augustine the Bishop: The Life and Work of a Father of the Church* (1961), pp. 549–54, for a complete but critical account. In addition, in 425 Augustine sent some relics of St. Stephen to another bishop and wrote him suggesting that they be honored as they had been in Hippo. *Letters (204–270)* 212 (1956), pp. 51–52.

[49] *City of God*, pp. 484–92. The discovery of Stephen's relics through the vision of Lucian is told in *Epistola: Luciana ad Omnen Ecclesiam*, and several of the miracles at Uzalum are described in *De Miraculis: Sancti Stephani Protomartyris*, written for Evodius by an unknown author, in *Patrologiae Latinae* 41 (1900), cols. 807–18 and 833–54.

came to him. The incident occurred during his last illness, after *The City of God* was completed. His biographer, Possidius, mentions how Augustine prayed with tears and supplication for certain demoniacs, and they were freed from possession. He then relates that after Augustine fell ill

a certain man came with a sick relative and asked him to lay his hand upon him that he might be cured. Augustine replied that, if he had any such power, he certainly would have first applied it to himself. Thereupon his visitor replied that he had had a vision and in his sleep had heard these words: "Go to Bishop Augustine, that he may lay his hand upon him, and he will be healed!" When Augustine learned this, he did not delay doing it and immediately the Lord caused the sick man to depart from him healed.[50]

For Augustine, as for Gregory of Nazianzus, dreams were closely associated with healing.

The very first healing mentioned by Augustine was also linked with a visionary experience. This was the vision that revealed to Ambrose, Bishop of Milan, where he would find the hidden bodies of the martyrs Gervasius and Protasius. When they were found, he had them placed in his new church, and a service was held in their honor. As the bodies were being laid on their biers, Severus, who had been blind for many years and was well known in Milan, begged to touch his handkerchief to the biers. He did so, and put it to his eyes, and his sight was immediately restored. At the same time many people who were possessed by unclean spirits were cured.

These events, which took place in Milan before Augustine's baptism, are recounted both in *The Confessions* and in the *Life of St. Ambrose* by Paulinus, who had been Ambrose's secretary as well as his friend and protégé.[51] Paulinus recorded several other healing miracles connected with Ambrose, including bringing a dead child to life again. Paulinus also tells of Ambrose's great power over unclean spirits. And then there is the story of Nicentius, a notary who was so crippled by pain in his feet that he was rarely seen in public. But when he attended to church one day and came up to the altar to receive the sacrament, the bishop accidently stepped on his foot. He cried out in pain and heard Ambrose say, "Go and be well henceforth!" At the death of Ambrose he came weeping to say that from then on he had had no more pain.

---

[50] Possidius, *Life of St. Augustine* 29, in *Early Christian Biographies* (1952), p. 111.

[51] St. Augustine, *The Confessions* IX (VII).16 (as well as in *The City of God* XXII.8 and in certain later sermons); Paulinus, *Life of St. Ambrose* 5.14, in *Early Christian Biographies* 41.

Paulinus also reports a healing involving the remains of martyrs and a vision of Ambrose after his death. A blind man dreamed of seeing people in white disembark from a ship. When the man learned that one of them was the dead bishop, he prayed to him to be cured. In the dream Ambrose told him to go to Milan on a certain day and contact his "brothers" who were coming there. The man went, and on that day the bodies of Sisinius and Alexander, who had died in a recent persecution, were being carried to the church. He touched the bier and was given his sight.[52]

Sulpitius Severus wrote about St. Martin of Tours, who lived far to the north in Gaul and who is credited with remarkable healing powers. St. Martin was also responsible for establishing monasticism and thus education in the heart of what is now France. (Martin's biographer, Sulpitius Severus, was almost equally interesting. He was a gifted and successful lawyer. At the peak of his career, after the death of his wife, he withdrew from the active world to become a follower of the saint.)

Sulpitius's little book, The Life of St. Martin, dwells far more on the miraculous than most of the Eastern records to which we have referred, and its emphasis on this aspect of the saint's life is difficult for the modern reader to accept. It is as if our gospels had recorded healings and little else; one wonders in fact if the author's enthusiasm did not sometimes run away with him. On the other hand, the actual accounts of healing are not very different from those of New Testament times. I once suggested to Ethel Banks, one of the founders of the Order of St. Luke, that the order reprint The Life of St. Martin so that it would be more easily available. She replied that people were not ready for it.

Martin had been a soldier in the Roman army, but he was an unusual soldier in that he desired to live a Christian life. Probably the best-known incident of his career is when he cut his only garment in two pieces, so that he might share it with a freezing beggar. That night he dreamed Christ appeared to him clad in the half of his cloak that he had given away. When he was released from the army and became attached to the church, he did not feel worthy of serving at the altar. His bishop wisely appointed him to be an exorcist and thus to learn in a more humble position.

Martin's whole story is remarkable, simply because he cared so deeply about both God and human beings. His healings, miraculous as they were, seemed to flow naturally from this depth of spirit. On one

---

[52] Paulinus, Life of St. Ambrose 8.28, 9.44, 10.52; other healings are told in 3.10, 6.21, and 9.44. In Early Christian Biographies 38–39, 45–46, 50, 60, 64.

occasion, returning to the monastery of which he had become head, Martin found the brothers mourning for a young follower who had died after a brief fever. Sulpitius relates that at first he wept.

Then laying hold, as it were, of the Holy Spirit, with the whole powers of his mind, he orders the others to quit the cell in which the body was lying; and bolting the door, he stretched himself at full length on the dead limbs of the departed brother. Having given himself for some time to earnest prayer, and perceiving by means of the Spirit of God that power was present, he then rose up for a little, and gazing on the countenance of the deceased, he waited without misgiving for the result of his prayer and of the mercy of the Lord. And scarcely had the space of two hours elapsed, when he saw the dead man begin to move a little in all his members, and to tremble with his eyes opened. . . . Then indeed, turning to the Lord with a loud voice and giving thanks, he filled the cell with his ejaculations.[53]

There is a similar quality in the other stories. In one of them he maintained physical contact with a paralyzed girl until, little by little, her body gained strength and she walked. On another occasion, to get control of a demoniac who tried to bite anyone who came near, he put his own fingers into the man's mouth, saying to the demon, "If you have a power, devour these," and the man drew back as if burned, without hurting him. Then the cure could begin.[54]

According to Sulpitius, pagans who were healed by Martin often returned to prepare for baptism, and regarded him with extraordinary affection. But apparently there were some in the church who did not. Later, in his Dialogues of Sulpitius Severus, the author found it necessary to defend Martin's gifts and to emphasize again his patience and the interest and love he showed for others. Sulpitius saw people denying the gift of healing and seemed to sense that it might be lost and the experiences forgotten. He continued to describe the incidents he knew, comparing them to what was being said of the monks in the Egyptian desert and insisting that this kind of experience should be listened to.

Beginning of a New Attitude

Despite the parallel experiences in the Western church, understanding did not develop around them as it did in the East. The events that Augustine witnessed in his own church, which brought home to him the reality of healing, came near the end of his life. He mentions these

---

[53] Sulpitius Severus, Life of St. Martin VII.
[54] Ibid., XVI, XVII; other healings are told in XVIII and XIX.

events in only two of his writings, and even then he does little more than present them as facts. Elsewhere in his works, his discussions of miracles, important as they were, treat them more as wonders of the natural world than as evidence of the power of the loving God to heal human sickness.

Writing about the same time, Jerome addressed the subject of healing but it was not part of his personal experience. He nevertheless accepted the reality of such experience: his letters referred again and again to the miracles of Jesus and others as if he were seeing them as he walked with the disciples on sacred ground. But healing as a present possibility he knew mainly through the lives of others.

Jerome early became interested in the desert monks. We have a letter written to his friend Rufinus congratulating him for having gone to visit the famous desert monk, Macarius.[55] Soon Jerome retired to a nearby colony himself for five years, and in this period his *Life of Paulus the First Hermit* was written, an account of certain wonderful events that Paulus had experienced. The monks in Egypt stirred Jerome's imagination; ten years later he made a visit to their abodes.

His party included Paula, who was to be his friend and helper for the rest of her life. Through her eyes perhaps more than his own, he saw "the Lord's glory manifested in . . . the Macarii" (Macarius of Egypt and Macarius of Alexandria, whose gift of healing was, if anything, even better known) and these "other pillars of Christ." Nearly twenty years later he wrote vividly of how they sought out each cell, finding Christ himself in these Christians.

After leaving Egypt they went directly to Bethlehem, where Jerome and Paula founded a monastery and convent side by side. A few years later Jerome wrote the book that expressed his knowledge of the reality on which monasticism was based. This was the *Life of St. Hilarion*, who was born in Palestine, became a disciple of Antony, and returned to the desert near Gaza. Jerome tells how, after years of solitude and after withstanding all kinds of demonic visions, Hilarion's reputation spread and people who needed healing began coming to him. One woman had been childless for fifteen years; he told her to have faith and wept for her, and within a year she came to show him her baby. He visited three little boys consumed by fever, made the sign of the cross over their beds, and saw that almost immediately they began to sweat and to

[55] St. Jerome, *Letter* III.2, To Rufinus, the Monk. This was Macarius of Egypt whose story was told in various works, one of them the *Historia Monachorum*, translated by Rufinus. See Butler, *Lausiac History* 1:15 ff. and 2:55–56.

recover. Hilarion also saw a man who had been seized by a demon and made rigid. When the man signified to Hilarion that he would live as a Christian, he was left free and healthy.

There are many other stories. Soon, Jerome recorded, crowds began to find Hilarion wherever he went. "Even the blessed Antony" gladly corresponded with him and told sick people about him. As Hilarion's followers increased, they founded monasteries all over Palestine, and miracle after miracle continued in his life and even after his death. Thus Jerome, like Augustine, acknowledged the reality of healing suddenly and completely. But unlike Augustine's *City of God*, Jerome's story of Hilarion told of events in the lives of others rather than of events that happened around or through himself.

Jerome's most vital contribution to Christianity was the Vulgate— that great work of scholarship which made the Bible available in the common tongue of the Western church. In it his use of the strictly theological word *salvo* to translate both "save" (and thus heal or make whole) and "cure" in James 5:14 was strangely similar to the way he turned the Old Testament prohibition against "soothsaying" into a command to pay no attention to dreams.[56] Whatever his personal reasons, Jerome helped to turn the church's attention away from healing, focusing it on what healing represented symbolically.

Even Ambrose, from whose presence healing seemed to flow naturally, took this approach in his writings. In his work on the sacraments he describes Namaan's healing in the Jordan, not to show that healing is possible for Christians, but to demonstrate the sanctification and curing of sins available in baptism.[57] For the most part Ambrose did not discuss healing.

---

[56] See pp. 115–16; also my book *Dreams: The Dark Speech of the Spirit*, p. 159n. In the case of dreams, Jerome had had hot words with his former friend Rufinus over his own failure to adhere inflexibly to the literal direction of this great conversion dream. It seems very likely that he suffered real guilt over the accusations of Rufinus and allowed this to determine, more or less unconsciously, his translation of these particular Old Testament passages.

In the matter of healing, it would seem Jerome had run-ins with some of the desert monks. Palladius tells of a Theban named Posidonius who had spent some time in a monastery outside Bethlehem and who expressed his opinion of Jerome quite freely. Palladius had a high regard of this Posidonius, with whom he lived for a year there near Bethlehem; he reported: "I knew of this prophecy made by this man: A priest, Jerome, dwelt in the same place; he was a man of good birth and well gifted in Latin letters, but he had such a disposition that it eclipsed his learning. Posidonius had lived with him a goodly number of days and he whispered into my ear: 'The fine Paula who takes care of him is going to die and escape his meanness, I believe,'" in Butler, *Lausiac History* 36.6, 41.2, 2:104 and 118.

[57] St. Ambrose, *The Sacraments* I.5.13 ff., in his *Theological and Dogmatic Works* (1963), p. 274.

One writer of some importance in the Western church at this time did express his ideas about healing. John Cassian spent several years among the monks in Egypt and also around Bethlehem, and he interpreted the thinking of the desert fathers for Western Christians. His works had a significant influence on the growth of monasticism in the West; Cassian's *Conferences* was one of the books specified by St. Benedict, for example, to be read aloud each day to the assembled brothers. A discussion of the divine gift of healing occurs in it, based on three accounts of miracles among the desert monks. These are prefaced by the statement that "we have never found that those works and signs were affected by our fathers; nay, rather when they did possess them by the grace of the Holy Spirit they would never use them, unless perhaps extreme and unavoidable necessity drove them to do so."[58]

These miracles, as Cassian saw it, were performed to demonstrate the power of the Lord to heretics or scoffers, or because a monk was "pestered" for healing. He thus expressed the most correct theology—the works were accomplished by the compassion of the Lord and not the merit of monks—but he himself seemed to have learned little about compassion. From this point on, the purpose of his discussion is clear. It was necessary to warn the church about the dangers of using the gift of healing. If Christians were not fully aware of them, they might lose not only their humility but also their inward purity and perfect chastity. Indeed, the implication was that people could lose their very soul by too much attention to healing human sickness.

We cannot be sure, of course, what lay behind this drift of reasoning, which continued in the church. Perhaps it sprang, in part, from an obscure contradiction between severe ascetic practices, so widely recognized as necessary to produce purity and humility, and the deep response to the ordinary needs and suffering of people—"the compassion of the Lord," which opens the way for divine healing to become a natural event in human life. Desert and monastery alike perhaps to some extent removed devout Christians unwittingly from fertile contact with the common needs of their contemporaries. Where mortification of the flesh was highly valued (a theme nowhere emphasized by Jesus), the ready healing of the flesh must have been increasingly felt as an anomaly. Nor do we know how far the growing climate of vague disapproval toward easing the pains of the flesh served as an alibi for something much more profound and hidden: sheer loss of ability—and perhaps any deep desire—to be a channel for divine compassion to do its healing work.

---

[58] John Cassian, *The Conferences*, The Second Conference of Abbot Nesteros XV.2.

At any rate, the attitude which Cassian typified grew in the monasteries until it was picked up and enshrined by the last notable doctor of the early Western church, Gregory the Great, in his *Book of Pastoral Rule*. This was one of the finest works on pastoral care to be found in the West. It was highly admired in Gregory's time. His special emissary to England, Augustine of Canterbury, took it with him as the basis for the new church there. Three hundred years later Alfred had it translated into the West Saxon tongue, and a copy was sent to every bishop in the kingdom. By the command of Charlemagne in successive councils, this book was to be studied by every bishop in Gaul along with the New Testament and the canons of the fathers. From the end of the ninth century, a copy of the *Pastoral Rules* was put into the hands of bishops at the altar during their consecration, along with the New Testament and the *Book of Canons*.

Gregory the Great, who was Bishop of Rome from 590 to 604, lived in a difficult period. Civilization had begun to crumble. Italy had been conquered and overrun by barbarians and partly reconquered by Byzantium. The Eastern regent resided at Ravenna, not Rome, and travel between them depended on the whims of the Lombard invaders. Life was uncertain at best, and God's wrath seemed more apparent than God's love. People could hardly imagine the pleasant days of the fourth century.

In such times it was no wonder that Gregory saw illness as one more way in which God chastises faithful Christians. "The sick are to be admonished that they feel themselves to be sons of God in that the scourge of discipline chastises them." He understood illness as one more blow of the hammer in shaping the stones of humanity to be placed in the heavenly wall on the other side. Sickness brings people to themselves so that they can ponder their sins and repent. Gregory compared the flesh with Balaam's ass, which stopped in its tracks because the angel of God stood in the way; just so the body, slowed by affliction, reveals the presence of God which the mind does not perceive. And last of all, "who with sound understanding can be ungrateful for being himself smitten, when even He who lived here without sin went not hence without a scourge?"[59]

Gregory's letters suggest that he practiced what he preached. He wrote to Marinianus, Bishop of Ravenna, about his own agony from the gout that plagued the last years of his life, and asked the bishop to "implore for me the compassion of divine loving-kindness, that it would

---

[59] Gregory the Great, *The Book of Pastoral Rule* II.13.

mercifully mitigate towards me the scourges of its smiting, and grant me patience to endure, lest . . . my heart break out into impatience from excessive weariness, and the guilt which might have been well cured through stripes be increased by murmuring."[60] He attributed the sickness of Venantius to his having left the monastery. In a letter to Rusticiana in Constantinople he told several tales of the demons that persecuted monks who thought of leaving their vocation, and even how a horse revealed two runaway monks by refusing to pass the tomb in which they were hiding. On the other hand, he enjoined Marinianus to follow his physician's advice during an illness, even at the cost of pastoral duties or fasts and devotions, and also sent relics to help abate the ravages of an epidemic in Ravenna. Gregory, as we shall see, was well aware of divine intervention, but tended to see it manifested as divine wrath unleashed in order to produce penitence. And when he did describe miracles, he did not discriminate between reasonably possible stories and tales which the most credulous would have difficulty in believing. One does not find in him the intellectual depth and critical understanding of Augustine or Basil.

With Gregory's point of view and practice, Western thinking about healing had come full circle. Sickness was no longer understood as the malicious work of demons or the Evil One, to be countered in every instance. Instead, it was a mark of God's correction, sometimes inflicted by the negative powers with divine approval, to bring moral renewal. There was no question about God's *power* to heal or ability to intervene, but only of God's *will* to heal. Only the righteous were likely to find healing. We find in Gregory's attitude the theme that grew more and more prevalent in the West until it was fully expressed in the English Office of the Visitation of the Sick. Here the Old Testament view of sickness largely displaced that of Jesus, the apostles and the early church, both East and West.

With Jerome, Cassian, and Gregory there was no question whatever as to the *possibility* of healing through the spirit, but rather of its advisability. Along with nearly all other church fathers, these men shared the implicit Platonic view of the world in which it was perfectly natural for the spiritual realm to influence the physical one. The views of Augustine of Hippo, in particular, about miracles predominated until Aquinas and Scholasticism took over nearly a thousand years later. To Augustine, miracles were not a hypothetical intervention of God contrary to the divine natural law, as later thinkers held. Although Western

---

[60] *Epistles* of St. Gregory the Great XI.32; also XI.30, 33, 36, 40, and 46.

thinkers did not spell out the specific implications of their worldview for healing, miracles were no problem to Augustine or the other church fathers, since they continued to live in a world where such things were expected. He did not in fact say much in his writings about healing miracles, probably because of his late appreciation of their frequency and value.[61]

Thus, with almost no clear emphasis on the importance of healing from a theological point of view, the Western church moved into the turmoil and confusion of the seventh and eighth centuries dominated by the pervasive influence of Gregory, who saw illness largely as a scourge of God. There were also other forces at work, which we shall discuss briefly as we examine the attitude toward healing that developed in Western Christianity for the next twelve hundred years.

---

[61] A careful study of Augustine's treatment of miracles, with exhaustive references, is found in Louis Monden's *Signs and Wonders* (1966), pp. 41–65. Father Monden sketches the difference between this point of view and that of Aquinas, showing how much more congenial the Augustinian framework is to an appreciation and understanding of healing miracles.

CHAPTER 9

Healing in Western Christianity

As already suggested, a great gulf developed between the Western Christian attitude toward healing and that of the early church and the renowned Eastern doctors of the church. Indeed, the difference is so pronounced that one wonders how two such divergent views could have developed within the same institution. This is even more puzzling when one realizes that the point of view of the early church was largely a simple continuation of the understanding found in the New Testament in the practice of Jesus and his immediate followers. How did so great a change in attitude toward Christian healing come about? What historical influences produced it? We have seen the beginnings of these causes. Let us now examine them in more detail.

Finding even some of the answers to such questions has been a fascinating pursuit over many years. If we are to see whether healing has a place in modern Christian activity, we must understand how the change took place. If the influences that led to the gradual elimination of a ministry of religious healing in the West grow out of the essence of the gospel, then this Christian practice should be discouraged or rejected. If, however, the factors responsible for the change are peripheral or contrary to the central meaning of the gospel, then an effort should be made to reintroduce healing as a part of present-day Western Christian theory and practice.

Three Reasons for Change

Tracing the historical development of a concept over a period of a thousand years is a complex and difficult task. After twenty years of work, I found the pieces came together in a pattern, and I venture to offer some tentative answers. Three main factors seem to have produced the change. First, there was a subtle and gradual alteration in the popular view of the nature of God and of humanity. This was associated with the decline of civilization in the West and the barbarian conquests. Second, there was a major shift in theological thinking, in which the worldview of Aristotle replaced that of Plato. This resulted in a theology which had little place for any direct and natural contact between God and human beings, hence little room for healing. Third, throughout these years people continued to believe in the miraculous and exhibited a lively and uncritical interest in healing miracles. Separated from theological understanding and criticism, this became more and more fanciful until it was difficult to believe many of the stories told during this period.

It is difficult for most of us to imagine living in a profoundly disintegrating civilization. The worst historical disasters of recent times have been followed by some kind of restoration and rebuilding. But in the sixth and seventh centuries, as Western civilization began to crumble, disaster followed disaster, and there was no renewal. Great cities of several hundred thousand people, like Aquileia, simply ceased to exist. Hundreds of other prosperous cities, from Italy to Britain and from Switzerland to Spain were deserted and remained only piles of rubble, soon totally forgotten. Plagues swept over Europe, sometimes killing fifty percent of the population of some areas.

From the time of Constantine and even before, the barbarians—some pagan, some Arian—hammered away at all sides of the western Roman Empire. Rome was plundered and finally fell. For a while the emperors based at the nearly impregnable city of Byzantium tried to resist the incursions of semi-civilized tribes in the West, but soon their attention was diverted elsewhere. Shortly after the death of Pope Gregory the Great, the Arabs came to a sense of national and religious identity and swept away much of the Roman Empire, all of the Middle East and North Africa, and most of Spain. Arab pirates gained control of the Mediterranean, and commerce simply disappeared, as did the urban civilization based upon it. The collapse was nearly complete. Indeed, the church was the only major institution to survive the chaos.

In such conditions it is not strange the people should become less confident of God's love and mercy and think more vividly of the wrathful aspect of the Godhead. We saw the beginning of this tendency in Cassian and Jerome, then even more markedly in Gregory the Great.

As things grew worse, people all but forgot God's love and concern for human beings, which was so much the essence of the message of Jesus. As education disappeared, few could read the Gospels even enough to hear what the teaching had been. The liturgy was often in a language unknown to the worshiper. With the end of persecution under Constantine, less committed Christians flooded the church.

Imagine what changes were wrought, when mass baptism of entire tribes followed the conversion of the chiefs or kings! The Christianity of such nominal converts was totally different from the commitment of those who had followed Jesus or who spent three years as catechumens before being allowed full membership in the church. The faith of many of these people was little more than their pagan religion with a new label. The Teutonic gods did not present a pleasant demeanor. As far as I have been able to discover, there were few shamans among these pagans to ameliorate the effects of their stern gods. And so the Lombards, Goths, and Franks took over a dying civilization, only to be overrun by the Normans and the Danes. When life itself appears so grim, of what use is a little bodily healing? Death is not so horrible under these conditions; it is almost a blessing if it comes quickly.

Within this context a new view developed of the relation of healing to God. The important thing was not to find some comfort in this life—that could hardly be expected—but rather to insure a good existence after death. Care of the soul became much more significant than care of the body: a saved soul brought one to the bliss of heaven—the body and this life were relatively unimportant. Since sickness was the result of God's wrath at the sins of humans, it was actually a valuable indicator of one's inner state, and from this viewpoint it was downright stupid to cure the physical body without finding out what was wrong in the soul and healing that. In addition, if suffering enabled people to share in the crucifixion, then ameliorating such suffering would be questionable. Curing the body without curing the soul was valueless, if not dangerous. Any kind of healing began to be treated with suspicion, whether secular or religious: the idea of compassion for people afflicted through no fault of their own was nearly lost.

With the emphasis on the next life, a profound change took place in the sacrament of healing. Its meaning shifted gradually to healing the soul in preparation for heaven. Unction for healing became unction for dying, a final cleansing which practically guaranteed, at least in the popular mind, that people would arrive in good condition and on the right path when they reached the other side. Following Jerome's translation of the word "heal" as "save," the medieval church developed its understanding of the sacrament of extreme unction, which remained until Vatican II in 1962.

Meanwhile a transformation took place in the intellectual climate of Western Europe. The philosophical base of most influential Western thinkers shifted from Plato to Aristotle. Even the best-educated people in Western Europe could not read Greek; even a genius like Aquinas never read most of the Platonic dialogues, because they were not available in Latin. Plato's work was available largely through popularizers like Chalcidius, who presented a one-sided and otherwordly version of it.[1]

Whole generations of women and men forgot that Plato had stressed the importance of this life as well as the next. Because they needed a point of view which gave value to the present world, the theologians turned to Aristotle, who provided just such an outlook. So, as medieval civilization pulled out of the Dark Ages, it turned more and more to the thinking of Aristotle, which had already formed a foundation for the brilliant Arab culture to the south.

Several Neoplatonic writings were accepted at this time as the work of Aristotle, and this made him far more palatable to the church. Boethius had translated Aristotle's logic (the *Organon*), providing an educational curriculum for western Europe for centuries to come. Many of the converted barbarians were not pure pagans, but Aristotelian Arians. Conditions were ripe for the emergence of a new worldview based on the thinking of Aristotle, a view which came to dominate the outlook of all western Europeans: prince and scholar, tradesman and pauper alike. Some scholars have called it Scholasticism, but it is more correctly defined as the Aristotelio-medieval worldview.[2] All of life and experience were part of a logically certain system ranging from a geocentric astronomy to the logical necessity of the Sermon on the Mount. This worldview had the full support of a powerful and authoritarian church, and any deviation from this total view was heresy. At the same time, a schism developed between the Eastern and Western churches, and anything Greek was viewed as practically heretical. Fertilization of European thought by sophisticated Platonic thought ceased. Instead of learning from the East, western crusaders sacked Constantinople,

---

[1] The importance of Chalcidius and others like him is described in my book, *God, Dreams, and Revelation* (1974), p. 155–58.

[2] I have described this at length in the appendices of my book, *Afterlife: The Other Side of Dying* (1980).

hacked the jewels from the altar of St. Sophia and occupied it to bring the heretics to true faith!

The most gifted exponent of this worldview was St. Thomas Aquinas. Humanity has produced few greater geniuses; he made an heroic attempt to build Christian thought and practice upon an Aristotelian foundation. And this made a great difference in attitude toward healing. If God is known primarily through intellectual activity rather than experience, there is little place for any gifts of the Spirit. As described by Paul, they fit more easily into a Platonic worldview than an Aristotelian one. The medieval church developed a final and certain total outlook based on past revelation elaborated by human reason; it needed nothing more. There was no need for God to continue to communicate with human beings. One might expect further revelations or healings, but only under extraordinary supernatural conditions. Thus the theologians supplied good reasoning to back up the more general shift away from the practice of religious healing. A closer look at the thinking of Aquinas and his followers will show how pervasive this change in attitude really was.[3]

Meanwhile, however—and paradoxically—healings continued to occur throughout most of this period. James Michael Lee, the well-known Catholic educator, once said to me: The Catholic Church has an Aristotelian head and a Platonic heart. The two do not always operate in concert. From the time of Gregory, reports of healings continue. In the end, several attested miracles, usually healings, were required before a person could be declared a saint. As Chaucer reminds us in the *Canterbury Tales*, pilgrimages to shrines developed into a universal pastime. The trade in relics was brisk and profitable. It has been suggested that enough fragments of the true cross were available by the end of the Middle Ages to construct a fair-sized church. Cut off from critical scrutiny, miracles of healing proliferated, and it became difficult to tell genuine from exaggerated or picturesquely fabricated instances. Books containing the more outrageous stories have circulated in every century down to our own.[4] No wonder many serious Christians have doubted

---

[3] I have described this development of thought in detail in *Encounter with God: A Theology of Christian Experience* (1987). The reader who wishes to pursue the change from Platonic to Aristotelian thought is referred to this work.

[4] For instance, in *The Dialogues on Miracle,* written by Caesarius of Heisterbach about 1220 to 1235, trans. H. von E. Scott and C. C. Swinton Bland (1929), there are many stories of miracles occurring in outer, physical substances. Two centuries later when the Dominican priest Johannes Herolt (Discipulus, ca. 1440) compiled the *Miracles of the Blessed Virgin Mary*, trans. C. C. Swinton Bland (1928), his emphasis was even more on tangible aspects of the miraculous. Many stories of this kind, down into the nineteenth century,

the existence of genuine healing at all. In fact, these stories have driven many people who otherwise consider themselves Christians to adopt an agnostic point of view about the miracles of Jesus. Can we, however, assume that all these accounts and the entire phenomenon of healing are fanciful? Again and again life has a way of bringing us up short with reality. In addition to my own firsthand experience in a ministry of healing and in teaching that ministry to clergy and lay people of every church affiliation, I frequently hear from others of experiences of God that resulted in healing. Once people know that I am open to the idea that God still touches human lives, they want to tell of their experiences. At a conference at Kanuga in 1986, nearly a quarter of the two hundred participants wrote accounts of religious experiences, many of them healings, that had transformed their lives. Let us, then, look more closely at the forces which have led to a disregard for religious healing and then see how persistent the gift has been throughout the ages, among most trustworthy and reliable Christian witnesses.

From Healing to Forgiveness of Sins

By the time of Charlemagne, as we have seen, the Western church was beginning to transform unction for healing into unction as preparation for death.[5] We can trace this change step by step. A similar restriction also applied to visiting, exorcising, and laying hands on the sick. The Council of Chalon-sur-Saone in 813 reserved the administration of unction to priests and priests alone. At Metz in 847 and Pavia in 850 the idea was clearly expressed that unction had more to do with forgiveness of sins than with bodily healing. The service soon reflected the change in thinking.[6]

In two copies of services from the ninth and tenth centuries, almost the first words of the priest as he entered the homes of the sick was to remind them of their sins. One version called first for confession, while the other version instructed the priest first to make a cross of ashes on

---

found in E. Cobham Brewer's *A Dictionary of Miracles, Imitative, Realistic and Dogmatic* (1885), republished in 1901.

[5] Charlemagne's ecclesiastical adviser, Theodulf, who was Bishop of Orleans about 815, seems to have been the first to issue a general instruction which stressed the administration of unction as a preparation for death, putting this aspect before healing (Theodulfus Aurelianensis Episcopus, *Capitulare*, in *Patrologiae Latinae* [1864], cols. 220–44).

[6] Cited by Percy Dearmer, *Body and Soul* (1909), pp. 220–21; also W. K. Lowther Clarke, *Liturgy and Worship* (1954), p. 492.

the sick person's breast and to cover the person with a hair shirt. The priest then read one or more of the seven penitential Psalms and anointed the patient with holy water (no longer blessed in the patient's presence), at points indicating each of the five senses, with a prayer to expiate and repair anything illicit, offensive, or harmful. The priest was to return with Communion, but out of five variations of the service only one retained the direction to "repeat any other rite"—perhaps fortunately for the patient.

Strangely enough, the words still expressed an intent to heal. Even in the eleventh-century service the priest might begin by stressing the healings in the New Testament to remind the people of God's love and kindness, and then, just before his Communion, ask God to free them of sickness so that "confirming them in strength, upholding them in power, you may restore them to the altars of your holy church with no good thing lacking for full health."[7] But in this same version, as in all others of the period, the actions that had shown care for people in their immediate illness are replaced by those that negate healing, with emphasis on sin and penitential Psalms and anointing for fault of the senses. The final act was to lay a hair shirt on the floor, place individuals on it, and sign them with ashes, asking them to think how they would soon return to ashes. With the question, "Are ashes and hair cloth pleasing to you as evidence of your penitence before God in the day of Judgment?" and the sick person's formal response, "They are pleasing," the priest turned away and the service ended.

Certainly by this time the change was nearly complete. Most of the order for visiting the sick was better calculated to produce anxiety and tension than to awaken forces for healing. Before long it would be given the name of a final sacrament for the dying. There is no doubt concerning the origin of the rite of extreme unction or its original meaning, but this was soon forgotten. Sin and sickness were linked together in what was almost an assumed connection. No one considered the very different teaching of Jesus of Nazareth who had expressly denied an exclusive connection.

In all the records I have scanned, I find no mention of a formal sacrament of healing. Instead, by the thirteenth century the order for

---

[7] *Patrologiae Latinae* 78 (1985), cols. 1017–23; also 138 (1880), cols. 987–1002 (*Monumenta Liturgica*). The evolution of the rite of extreme unction from these various services for the sick is detailed by Aimé Georges Martimort, *L'Église en Prière: Introduction à la Liturgie* (1961), pp. 580–94. The later manuscripts are also listed by Michael Andrieu, *Les Ordines Romani du Haut Moyen Âge* (1931–48), 1 (see Index under *infirmus*).

visiting and anointing the sick was becoming known as *unctio extrema*, one of the seven sacraments named by Peter Lombard in 1151.[8] The healing effect of unction was never denied; there may well have been cures as a result. But the church was fast coming to the position that it was to be administered principally (or *only*) at the point of death, for the purpose of securing "a spiritual advantage."[9]

The theologians finished what the councils started. Those who completed the *Summa Theological* for Aquinas added this final touch: "Extreme Unction is a spiritual remedy, since it avails for the remission of sins, according to James 5:15. Therefore it is a sacrament. . . . Now the effect intended in the administration of the sacraments is the healing of the disease of sin" (III-Supp.29.1). Since the other sacraments took ample care of the sins of the living, the only purpose of anointing the sick was that "it prepares a person for glory immediately" at the time of death. The church did not deny that healing might happen, but it did not expect that the spiritual would affect the physical body.[10]

In 1551 the Council of Trent legally defined unction a service only for those in danger of death, and healing ceased to exist as an official rite of the Catholic Church until very recent time. And yet people frequented shrines and wore amulets for healing. As Jesus came to be seen more as a judge than a compassionate healer, devotions to Mary grew to fill the human need for divine comfort. The practice of compassion passed from official church action to popular devotions at places like Chartres and Lourdes. The church indeed had an Aristotelian head but a Platonic heart.

Much the same attitude toward other gifts of the Holy Spirit continued up until the Second Vatican Council in 1962. As far as the gifts described by Paul are concerned, there was a special rule for saints, in which a gift like healing might be a sign of extraordinary holiness. But for ordinary people, some of these gifts were even considered unquestionably a mark of demonic possession.[11] Certainly the Spirit had little

---

[8] Around 1150, it appears, the first pronouncement about seven sacraments that included a sacrament of extreme unction was made in Peter Lombard's *Sentences,* which was one of the principal works studied by all theological students at the time of Aquinas (Petri Lombardi, *Sententiarum* IV.23.1–2, in *Patrologiae Latinae* 192 [1880], col. 899).

[9] As John Peckham, Archbishop of Canterbury, for instance, held in his *Constitutions of 1281;* quoted from Lyndewode's *Provinciale* in Dearmer, *op. cit.* pp. 221–22.

[10] Thirty years ago a good friend in the Catholic Church told me how puzzled her parish priest was after he had administered unction on two occasions to a dying uncle, whose condition immediately improved.

[11] "Signs of possession are the following: ability to speak with some facility in a strange tongue or to understand it when spoken by another; the faculty of divulging future

room to operate in the official church during these centuries. In addition, during this pre-Reformation period, the Catholic Church did not confine itself to liturgy; it began to legislate about medical healing as well.

The Church and Medical Healing

In the beginning of the twelfth century the church promulgated several decrees which in the end restricted medical healing as well as spiritual healing. The first general council in the West, the First Lateran in 1123, attempted to control the growing power of the monasteries: monks were forbidden to hold public Masses or offer penance, with a further proviso that they must not consecrate holy oil, administer unction, or even visit the sick (Canon 17). Henceforth, in the church a single, authoritarian approach to sickness was encouraged. However, many religious orders continued these practices.

When monks began to study medicine and law to make money on the side, this too was soundly condemned. The Second Lateran Council in 1139 held not only that the cure of souls was being neglected, but that the monks "thus make themselves physicians of human bodies. Since an impure eye is the messenger of an impure heart, those things about which good people blush to speak, religion ought not to treat"[12] (Canon 9). But in the meantime some members of the itinerant orders found that surgery could be practiced profitably, even without training. The Council of Tours handled this problem in 1163 by simply prohibiting church people from practising surgery at all, on the ground that "the church abhors the shedding of blood"; consequently, as medicine developed, surgery was left behind to become a barber's trade. The separation of medicine and surgery hindered the growth of both disciplines.

Medicine cannot develop without the study of anatomy. Medieval physicians, forbidden to practice human dissection, cut up pigs to find out how the human system worked. Galen, the ancient medical authority, had asserted that human anatomy was similar to that of pigs. The reason for prohibiting dissection was strange indeed. During the Crusades a peculiar practice developed of boiling and macerating the bod-

---

and hidden events; display of powers which are beyond the subject's age and natural condition . . . " (section on Exorcism, *The Roman Ritual* [1952], 2:169).

[12] Rev. H. J. Schroeder, O.P., *Disciplinary Decrees of the General Councils* (1937), pp. 201–02.

ies of men who died far from home, so that their bones could be brought back for burial. In 1300 Boniface VIII issued a papal bull prohibiting the practice. Since about this time human bodies were beginning to be used for medical dissection, the similarity was almost too striking to avoid. Human dissection was forbidden, and even when the ban was eventually relaxed, schools had to fight to obtain one or two bodies a year for the study of human anatomy. No wonder there was antagonism between physicians and the church; the wonder is that the hostility was not more pronounced.

In 1215 the Fourth Lateran Council, on the premise that "bodily infirmity is sometimes caused by sin," decreed that when physicians were called to take care of a sick person, their first duty was to call for the priest. The decree explained that after spiritual health was restored, bodily medicine might be applied beneficially, "for the cause being removed the effect will pass away." It then went on to say, "If any physician shall transgress this decree after it has been published by the bishops, let him be cut off from the Church till he has made suitable satisfaction for his transgression."[13] From this time on, doctors ran a personal risk in caring for the sick at all.

The worst was yet to come as the Catholic Church backed up its moral thinking on the subject of illness by putting the burden on physicians to enforce penance on the sick. From 1566 on, to obtain a license to practice medicine, Roman Catholic doctors were required to swear that they would stop seeing patients on the third day unless they had confessed their sins and had a statement signed by a confessor to show for it. The Roman Synod renewed this decree in 1725 with added penalties. For continuing to care for patients who had not confessed their sins, the eighteenth-century Catholic physician was permanently removed from the practice of medicine, ejected from medical societies, and bore "forever the stigma of infamy."[14] Small wonder that physicians have so often pointed to religious and moral tension as a major cause of mental and other illness.

In *A Distant Mirror: The Calamitous Fourteenth Century*, Barbara Tuchman describes the attitude in Europe when the Black Death struck there. Some students believe that nearly a third of the world's population died. The deaths in Europe probably amounted to over twenty million. In some cities more than four hundred people died each day.

---

[13] *Ibid.*, pp. 263–64.
[14] *Loc. cit.* We have read of a French physician sentenced under this canon in the 1700s, but have not discovered the original reference.

Medicine could do nothing to stanch the plague. The pope stated in a bull dated September 1348 that the plague came from God: "this pestilence with which God is afflicting the Christian people." The Christian Emperor at Byzantium wrote that this was not "a natural affliction" but "a chastisement from Heaven." And according to Piers Plowman, "these pestilences were for pure sin."

Medicine began to look with suspicion on the church and its attitudes and developed its own view of human bodies as strictly material. Obviously, such thinking has little relation to the Christian idea of wholeness of soul, mind, and body, or to the acts of Jesus. It is hard to see how the church ever reconciled it with the original Christian theology. But then, through the efforts of a singular man theology itself was changed, and the way most Christians thought of their relation to God was altered.

Aquinas and Healing

Many people find theology dull, and Scholastic theology even duller. The interminable questions and answers, the logical subtlety and the hair-splitting distinctions tax the patience of the general reader and many modern theologians as well. However, when a theology finally takes hold in a culture, it has deep and pervasive influence.

Thomas Aquinas was not the only theologian to write from an Aristotelian base, but he was the best, and his thinking finally became standard for the Catholic Church. His influence was so great that it can hardly be measured. His work affected the secular world as well as the religious; in fact, his writing was one of the factors that probably made possible the development of science in the Western world.

However, Aquinas had no real place for religious healing in his systematic thought, and his basic ideas gradually gained acceptance among Protestant thinkers as well as Catholic theologians. It is impossible to understand the intellectual rejection of the healing ministry in modern times without following his reasoning closely. There is again no study of the subject to which to refer the reader, and so of necessity we must present some rather uninspiring prose to reveal the conscious reasons for this rejections.

St. Thomas lived and wrote in the golden age of medieval civilization, in the latter half of the thirteenth century. He died at the age of forty-nine, after producing an incredible quantity of work. He began to teach and write just as the church was coming to realize that the new philosophy of Aristotle was in the Western universities to stay. When the writings of Aristotle began to appear in Europe, around 1200, the church at first tried to prohibit entirely the study of his physical, psychological, and metaphysical works, because they were so clearly inconsistent with the Christian understanding of the world.[15] Aristotle thought focused on the physical world and set up a closed, naturalistic system in which Christianity could have little or no effect, as some theologians saw clearly.

But by Aquinas's time students and faculties alike were observing and thinking about the world in Aristotelian terms, and Aquinas began almost immediately to teach and work with these ideas. Aquinas did not attempt to show that Christianity and Aristotle each offered valid descriptions of the world from different viewpoints. Besides commentaries on them, he wrote his two main religious treatises to show that, by rational understanding, Christianity could fit into a world just about as Aristotle described it. He first wrote a book devoted to converting the Aristotelian Arabs in nearby Spain, the *Summa Contra Gentiles*. He then produced a handbook of religious knowledge which would be relevant to the Aristotelian thinking of his time, and this was the *Summa Theologica*, one of the principal foundations of Western thought. In it, step by step, he developed an understanding of God, of creation, and of human nature within a natural order of cause and effect. Actual experiences of God's power, or anything else outside this natural order, were placed in the realm of the supernatural. Aquinas referred to medical healing in many places, but he never once mentioned Christian healing as any part of Christian life after the time of the apostles.[16] In the last part of the book, when he finally came to the manifestation of Christ through the sacraments of the church, he discussed the miracles of Christ and referred to such events in relation to penance.

In Part III, in the two questions on Christ's miracles, Aquinas said practically everything he had to say about healing. His interest was

---

[15] F. C. Copleston's *Aquinas* (1961), pp. 59–67 gives an interesting account of this period and the opinions of various theologians about the "pagan philosopher." But Aristotle's works on logic, known as the *Organon*, had been available in Latin and used all through the Middle Ages; there was no objection to these or to his *Ethics*.

[16] The references that follow are taken from St. Thomas Aquinas, *The "Summa Theologica"* literally translated by the Fathers of the English Dominican Province (various dates), in which the purely physical causes of healing by medical or "natural" means are alluded to at I.13.2, 5, 6, 16.6, 57.3, 62.4, 87.2, and 117.1; II-I.5.5, 8.3, 9.4, 12.3, 19.8, 33.4, 51.1, 79.4, 87.6, 101.3, and 109.5; II-II.1.1, 20.1, 24.10, 27.3, 6, and 33.7; III.15.6, 60.1, and 65.1, as well as other places. In the quotations that follow there is no way to avoid Aquinas's sexist language.

very limited. The main question he asked was why miracles occurred at all, and his explanation was that Christ worked them primarily in order to prove his teaching to human beings. Because Jesus' teaching was supernatural, it surpassed human reason, and therefore the show of divine power was required so that people could take this teaching on faith. And second, the miracles were needed to demonstrate the divinity of Christ. This was essentially Aquinas's whole point about the healings and other miracles. It is strange that the Aquinas, who wrote with such perception about the primacy of love and compassion, did not see that Christ's healings were inspired more by love than as instructive demonstrations.

It is equally strange that Aquinas allotted such a brief portion of the *Summa* to the consideration of healing and exorcism, in sharp contrast to the treatment accorded these phenomena in the four gospels, Acts, and the epistles. In one of the briefest statements in the entire *Summa Theologica*, he approved the miracles "worked in spiritual substances" (exorcism or the casting out of demons) and those "worked on human beings" (physical healing) (III.44.1). Then he remarked that Christ came especially for the salvation of human souls: "Consequently, He allowed the demons, that He cast out, to do man some harm, either in his body or in his goods, for the salvation of man's soul—namely, for man's instruction" (44.1, Ad. 4). This is quite a change from the Christ who came to combat the Evil One and his forces and died in his battle to defeat the power of Evil.

While it was also "fitting that Christ, by miraculously healing men in particular, should prove Himself to be the universal and spiritual Saviour of all," (44.3), Aquinas took a great deal more trouble to show that Christ worked miracles on the soul, because "in man the soul is of more import than the body." He cited several passages to demonstrate that Christ changed the minds of men and women not only by giving them righteousness and wisdom "which pertains to the end of miracles, but also by outwardly drawing men to Himself, or by terrifying or stupefying them, which pertains to the miraculous itself." Finally he cited Chrysostom to drive home his point: "By how much a soul is of more account than a body, by so much is the forgiving of sins a greater work than healing the body; but because the one is unseen He does the lesser and more manifest thing in order to prove the greater and more unseen" (III.44.3, Ad. 1 and 3). Like so many people who use proof texts, this great thinker does not give the other side of Chrysostom's thinking and he did not read Greek!

Aquinas and the Gifts of the Spirit

One wonders what difference it might have made in our present thinking about healing if Augustine had been struck by the experience of healing earlier and had built his theology from the beginning on its importance. For Aquinas, Augustine was *the* theologian, as Aristotle was *the* philosopher. If Aquinas had been forced to consider over and over again the amazement and conviction of which Augustine wrote in the final chapters of the *City of God,* he might have noticed something missing from the careful philosophic tower he was building.

Instead, Western thinkers had developed a theology based largely on experiences other than healing, and along the way a new idea emerged about the gifts of the Holy Spirit. Gregory the Great, in his *Morals on the Book of Job,* suggested that there were seven of these: wisdom, science, understanding, counsel, fortitude, piety, and fear. These replaced the healing, miracles, prophecy, and others described by Paul in I Corinthians.[17] When Aquinas came to his one main discussion of the subject, he chose the list suggested by Gregory (II-I.68–70). These gifts, he held, were the perfections that disposed human beings "to be moved by God" (II-I.68.1) toward "the Divine good which is known by the intellect alone" (II-II.24.1). He then turned to look at evil habits, vice, and the law, which finally brought him to a separate section on grace.

At this point the ideas of Paul about the Holy Spirit could not be avoided. But Aquinas partitioned them off. There was first sanctifying grace, which was noble because it made human beings pleasing to God. Then there was gratuitous grace, including the charismata or gifts discussed by Paul (II-I.111.1). The real purpose of these gifts was to produce an effective teacher, for one could only lead another person to God by instructing him (II-I.111.4). Certain outer equipment was needed to teach. Perfect knowledge of divine things was necessary, so there were "faith," "the word of knowledge," and "the word of wisdom." To provide proof when argument failed, there were "the grace of healing," "miracles," "prophecy," and "discerning of spirits." Finally, to supply the proper idiom and expression of meaning, there were "tongues" and "the interpretation of tongues."

It was impossible for Aquinas within his worldview to see that human beings can be influenced *naturally* in other ways than through the

---

[17] S. Gregorii Magni, *Moralium Libri, sive Expositio in Librum B. Job* 1.27 and 2.49, in *Patrologiae Latinae* 75 (1902), cols. 543–44 and 592–94.

intellect and sense experience. The complexities of the teaching process and the importance of emotions and the unconscious in meaningful communication were beyond his grasp. He believed that the saints performed true miracles, but not so much out of compassion for human suffering as to confirm the knowledge of salvation[18] (II-II.178.1). And this was practically, although not quite, Aquinas's final word about healing, or indeed about any other way in which spiritual power could work through human beings. Thus Aquinas demonstrated clearly that people in this life were part of the physical world, and their experiences, even their dreams, were limited to it.[19] We were given our human senses and the ability to reason from sense experience because these were our natural capacities for receiving experience. If God or any supernatural experience touched us, it had to come intellectually or else through some physical and sensory means.

Aquinas then came to the sacrament of penance (III.84–90). He had worked almost steadily for six years on the *Summa*, and here he was faced with a question that had to be wrestled with personally as well as intellectually. First of all, the validity of penance did not operate through any material object. No water, bread, wine, or even oil was made divine by the priest's action. No substance inside a person was supposed to change if the penance was effective. Instead, penance consisted in removing something from the body. If sins were removed when priests said: "I absolve thee," then by a simple human action, speaking ordinary words, the priest accomplished the work of God. Aquinas knew what it meant to be a priest and—with nothing holy in his hands to carry the power of Christ—to face a person who needed help. And so he looked again at the healings accomplished by the apostles simply through a word of command. He realized that penance and healing had much in common, and discussed the healing of the man at the Beautiful Gate (Acts 3:6) in this light (III.84.4). He even considered whether the laying on of hands would make the words more effective.

---

[18] It is at this point that the modern reader has the greatest trouble in understanding Aquinas. It is difficult for most of us to comprehend how concern with our soul's salvation would not also involve care for our suffering human bodies. Most of us cannot separate mind, body, and emotions. The idea of touching one of them without touching and affecting the others is nearly unthinkable. Aquinas was, however, more at home in discussing immutable essences than process. The idea that mind and spirit, emotion and body, were in constant interaction and flux was beyond him. It is for this reason that his ideas seem so foreign and unreal to many moderns, whether Catholic or Protestant.

[19] See my book, *Dreams*, pp. 173–83, for a more complete discussion of the effect of Aristotelian philosophy upon our understanding of the processes by which we receive knowledge; see also my book, *Encounter with God*, Chapter Four.

He then took up the healing efficacy of the human touch, particularly the touch of a "sanctified man's hand," and asserted that such a touch might heal the physical body (III.84.5).

For the first time Aquinas came close to suggesting that human beings might share the Spirit with each other in a nonintellectual way. But he skirted the idea and went back to penance. It was not meant to confer grace, but only to eliminate sins. Here he arrived at questions even closer to home. Did penance restore a person to ecclesiastical dignity? What effect did it have on works conceived without charity? And then on the morning of December 6, 1273, while saying Mass, Aquinas experienced something which made him from that moment leave his own monumental work where it stood, unfinished. "I can write no more," he told his friends. "All that I have written seems like so much straw compared with what I have seen and what has been revealed to me."

Many writers have spoken of this experience. But we know of no one who has looked at it in relation to Aquinas's understanding of how we know and interact with God and the realm of the Spirit. No one, as far as we know, has asked why the experience was so important, or why it came at just that time, only a few days after he had expressly stated that there was no connection between forgiveness of sins (penance) and the direct experience of the grace of God. We suggest that once he had begun to look directly at the question of human desire and need for direct awareness of God's grace, he was given an immediate vision of the healing and love which God offers to any who truly desire the divine presence. This was bestowed, not because God wanted to save his soul, but just because Abba loves and wants to express that love. There is more communication in love than in any intellectual process.

Unquestionably something of the grace, love, and healing of God spoke directly to Aquinas from within. Whether one calls it the Self or the Holy Spirit or God communicating with him, certainly a revelation from beyond his intellect or physical senses came through to him. Is this supernatural, or is it the natural way in which God responds to us when we allow it? Where would Aquinas put this experience in his system? He had met that of which he could not speak. Three months later, starting on a mission for the pope, he fell ill and died. The *Summa* was finished and its Aristotelian view rounded out by other less gifted Scholastics. Gradually its ideas were accepted, until, for modern human beings, the separation from God seems complete—unless one has an experience like that of Aquinas himself.

Some may question the importance of Aquinas and his thinking. For nearly a hundred years he was the *official* theologian of the Roman Catholic Church. By 1969, when I came to Notre Dame, liberated Catholics were singing "Let old Aquinas be forgot" to the tune of *Auld Lang Syne*. Aquinas and Aristotle have nonetheless become a part of Western civilization and must be dealt with if we are to look at Christian healing as natural phenomena. In addition Scholastic thinking had an enormous influence on Protestant thought.

The Reformers and Healing

The Protestant Reformation changed many aspects of church life and practice, but it never attacked the worldview of the Scholastics against whom it revolted. Among Protestants this still has not changed much.[20] The leaders of the Reformation worked to rid the church of superfluous practices such as unction and indulgences. They did not realize that the whole base of Christian theology needed to be rethought if Christian *experience* was to be central to *church doctrine*. Then, too, Calvin and Luther were almost as much concerned to maintain *religious certainty* as the Scholastics of the Council of Trent.

Luther clearly believed that the great miracles like healing were given in the beginning simply so that church people could later do "greater works than these" by teaching, converting, and saving people spiritually. Writing for parents about the fine things that could be expected of a son who entered the church, he went on to say:

Thus Paul says in Romans 8 that God will raise up our mortal bodies because of his Spirit which dwells in us. Now how are men helped to this faith and to this beginning of the resurrection of the body except through the office of preaching and the word of God, the office your son performs? Is this not an immeasurably greater and more glorious work and miracle than if he were in a bodily or temporal way to raise the dead again to life, or help the blind, deaf, dumb, and leprous herein the world, in this transitory life?[21]

---

[20] I have discussed the similarity between the reformers and the Scholastics in the matter of basic philosophy in some detail in *Tongue Speaking*, pp. 186–93. Those interested in the evidence will find it there. One writer has said that the reformers moved the cars around in the train but kept most of the cars. Theologically, it was the same train.

[21] "A Sermon on Keeping Children in School," *Luther's Works* 46 (1967) pp. 224–25. There is an interesting discussion of this problem by Louis Monden, J.J., in *Signs and Wonders: A Study of the Miraculous Element in Religion* (1966), pp. 295–98, with various references. Also in other volumes of *Luther's Works*, 8:182–83, 23:220–21 and 375–76, 37:76–77.

In fact, Luther rarely missed an opportunity to show that the "real miracles" were not visible ones.

Calvin was even more explicit when he came to discuss unction. There was simply no way it could be a sacrament of any miraculous power such as healing. These gifts, he said, were only temporary to begin with, because they were needed to make the preaching of the gospel wonderful. Calvin spared no argument to show that extreme unction was "neither a ceremony appointed by God, nor has any promise."[22] Those who used anointing were partly to blame for the fact that healing had ceased, since they performed the rite too late to cure or even to bring solace. But this was secondary to the image of an authoritarian God who had no interest in keeping the power to heal alive on earth.

In fact, neither Calvin nor Luther had much interest in *how* a relation comes about between God and humans. Despite Luther's interest in Plato and Augustine and his outspoken rejection of Aristotle, philosophy was not his main interest any more than was psychology. For the most part, both Calvin and Luther simply accepted the growing view that human experiences of the ordinary world were in one category and experiences of God and the spiritual world in another. While God had worked at one time in the ordinary physical world, and could enter it at any time, this was no longer necessary. The coming of Christ had made the salvation of the human soul available without direct experience of God, and the physical world worked on its own innate laws. The two sacraments of Baptism and Holy Communion provided a bridge, and no other miracle was needed. Faith in the saving power of Jesus Christ was more noble than asking for experience or evidence, although, like Augustine and perhaps Aquinas, Luther too seems to have changed his mind about healing love of the Holy Spirit in his final years.

On the other hand, there was no lack of divine action in the external world if people refused to abide by the rules or turned away from the sacraments. In England, as we have seen, where the break was more with the discipline of Rome than with Roman tradition, sickness came to be viewed as a particular punishment given by God for our good. There was probably no worse place in the Christian world to be sick and destitute than in England in the seventeenth and eighteenth centuries. The monasteries, which had provided healing and also physical care for the sick and the destitute, declined in numbers and support on

---

[22] John Calvin, *Institutes of the Christian Religion* IV.19.20 (1953), 2:638.

the Continent in a divided church, but in England they were wiped out entirely when it was to the political advantage of Henry VIII, who needed money for a navy. Luther's followers were at least told to visit the sick, while Calvin made the hospital in Geneva a major responsibility of his local church. In England, however, the sick were not only left to private care, but in 1552 anointing was dropped from the Order for Visitation, leaving English Christians with the idea firmly planted that even their peccadilloes would bring on gout, if not something much worse.

Healing in Modern Churches

Since the time of the reformers, innumerable practical actions have been taken by Christians and church groups to deal with physical and mental sickness. Christian hospitals and clinics and medical schools have been established wherever Protestant missionaries have gone. By a strange quirk of logic it is permissible to remove medically the results of human sins, but it is not quite correct to believe that God will do it if asked in prayer or invoked through sacraments.

When I wrote my first book in the early 1970s, few local churches, denominations, or seminaries expressed any interest in sacramental healing as a viable practice for Christians today. However, in the last seventeen years wide popular interest has developed in the subject through the influence of the charismatic movement in the church. Also, medicine has come to see the importance of faith in the healing process, which has led to many books on the subject.

Some groups do meet to pray for the sick, and some individual ministers use unction or the laying-on-of-hands sacramentally for healing.[23] Many major Christian bodies have made official studies of the effectiveness of religious healing and the need for it today.[24] The reports

---

[23] These churches have been listed from time to time in *Sharing*, the journal published by the International Order of St. Luke.

[24] These are *The Relation of Christian Faith to Health*, United Presbyterian Church (1960); *Anointing and Healing: Statement*, United Lutheran Church in America (1962); *Christian Faith and the Ministry of Healing*, American Lutheran Church (1965); *Handbook on the Healing Ministry of the Church*, Church of Canada (n.d.); and the *Report of the Bishop of Toronto's Commission on the Church's Ministry of Healing* (1968). There are various reports also from the Church of England, including *The Ministry of Healing* (1924), sections on spiritual healing in *The Lambeth Conference: 1930;* and *The Church's Ministry of Healing* (1958). In addition, there is a study by the Standing Liturgical commission of the Protestant Episcopal Church, *Prayer Book Studies III: The Order for the Ministration to the Sick*, that is present in a different form in the current *Book of Common Prayer*. We have already referred to the change of attitude in the Roman Catholic Church following

all offer a good understanding of facts and ample reasoning, and all recommend the practice of healing by the Christian church today. And yet only a small fraction of the local churches offer a regular healing service, and most ministers have never participated in such a service, for the subject is seldom ever directly mentioned in church seminaries.

Most major modern churches still do not have an official theology with a place for the direct action of God in any of the gifts of the spirit, healing included. My book, *Encounter with God: A Theology of Christian Experience*, presents a theological framework in which healing is integral to Christian life. The church speaks of miracles as if they were a public exhibition once staged, but ignores the desire of an incredibly compassionate God to reach out to human beings here and now in transforming experiences of grace *and* healing. The almost unbelievable power of God to love, to care for the created world, has been pushed further and further out of the picture. Two major theologians of twentieth century theology convey this very plainly. Barth, who speaks for the more fundamentalist and orthodox believers, has written:

It is strange but true that fundamentally and in general practice we cannot say more of the Holy Spirit and His work than that He is the power in which Jesus Christ attests Himself . . . creating in man response and obedience. We describe Him as His awakening power. Later we will have to describe Him as His quickening and enlightening power . . . How gladly we would hear and know and say something more, something more precise, something more palpable concerning the way in which the work of the Holy Spirit is done![25]

Some writers find these ideas of Barth quite inadequate. John Wimber, in his book *Power Healing*, provides a moving personal document of the effect of dispensationalism on many conservative Christians. The popular *Scofield Reference Bible* promoted this point of view, which became dogma with many Bible students and in many Bible colleges. Wimber also reveals how the orthodox Christian idea of God's love involves what one does about a healing ministry.

Bultmann puts the case against healing somewhat more bluntly for liberal and existential theology. He questions the reality of the healing experiences contained in the New Testament. They are examples of myth, that he describes as the breaking through of a more than physical order into the physical world. Such impossibilities must be eliminated from the New Testament narrative if Christians are to get on with the

---

Vatican II. See the pastoral letter, *Health and Health Care* of the American Catholic Bishops, Nov. 19, 1981.
[25] Karl Barth, *Church Dogmatics* 4, *The Doctrine of Reconciliation* (1958), pt. 1:648.

task of authentic living in the here and now. Speaking about actual experience of the Holy Spirit and how it fitted into this system, he said to a friend: "In my entire life I have never been able to get to first base so far as the Holy Ghost is concerned" ("Ich habe in meinem ganzen Leben mit dem Heiligen Geist nichts anfangen können").[26] Barth said miracles of healing don't happen any more; Bultmann maintained that they didn't happen in the New Testament either. Even the magnificent and influential Dietrich Bonhoeffer wrote, in *Letters from Prison*, that since human beings have come of age and can understand and manage the physical world so efficiently, they no longer need a God who works directly in the physical world to help them in their helplessness. I have seen nothing significant on the healing ministry written by process theologians. In spite of all this, individual Christians throughout the ages have attested to the healing power of God. This is true of nearly every age and every part of the splintered church. Let us look at the evidence.

A Persistent Gift in a Struggling Church

For the first several centuries after the fall of Rome there is little difference between the Western record of healing and the practices of the Eastern church. Not many accounts survive of elaborate sacramental healings, although exorcism is often mentioned and oil was certainly used by individuals for anointing. The following material is a sample from the records to show the persistence of the healing gift. I do not go into detail because the people involved were not the most influential leaders of the church.

One of the earliest descriptions of healing was written about 510 by Ennodius, Bishop of Pavia, to a friend. Ennodius was desperately ill with a fever, and his physician told him there was no remedy. He wrote, "My hopes increased when the help of man failed. I addressed myself with tears to the heavenly physician, and anointed my dying body with some blessed oil as a remedy against the fever . . . and in that instant the fever left me . . . God had heard my prayer."[27]

Apparently the oil for anointing often came from the shrine of a saint, from the lamps kept burning in those places. Gregory of Tours wrote of several healings produced by oil from various shrines of St.

---

[26] From a personal letter written by the friend to whom Bultmann was speaking.
[27] Ennodii Felicis, *Epistolarum* VIII.4, Ennodius (ad) Fausto, in *Patrologiae Latinae* 63 (1882), col. 141.

Martin.[28] This Gregory, who was Bishop of Tours from 573 to 594, is one of the best sources of information as to practices connected with these shrines. He was carried, critically ill, to Tours, where he was healed at the tomb of St. Martin. Gregory described many other healings of those who kept watch and prayed at the shrines of saints. Several of these stories concern his own experience or that of his family. He also wrote about the effective power of relics and the need to care for them properly.[29] The matter of relics is particularly difficult for modern people to accept, since we still like to avoid the fact that medical "relics" (placebos, or sugar pills) produce amazing cures in our own time. Placebos operate on suggestion, assisted by the patients' faith that something is working with them toward healing. How placebos go about actually affecting the body is a matter still shrouded in nearly total mystery.

Gregory also mentions that sleeping in the shrines of saints and martyrs—"incubation"—was practiced quite frequently. Such a practice was common among the Greeks in Epidarus, centuries before Christ. A Swiss psychiatrist C. A. Meier, has written a study, *Ancient Incubation and Modern Psychotherapy*, which suggests that there may be some significance in the practice. Gregory tells how a woman who had lain paralyzed for eighteen years was brought to the basilica of St. Julien in Vienne, hoping that she might at least beg during the vigils. But in the night she dreamed of a striking figure of a man who asked why she was not keeping watch with the others. When she explained, he seemed to pick her up and carry her right up to the tomb, where "she made her prayer, still quite asleep; at the same time it seemed to her that many chains fell away from parts of her body. Awakened by the noise, she saw that she had recovered the fullest health. Immediately she got up and began to offer thanks in a loud voice, to the amazement of everyone."[30] For Gregory, who knew the experience of healing himself, such happenings were simple facts of Christian life.

---

[28] *De Virtutibus Sancti Martini* I.15 and II.32; *De Gloria Beatorum Confessorum* 9 in Georges Florent Gregoire, *Les Livres des Miracles et Autres Opuscules* (1860), 2:48–49, 146–48, and 360–63. Other references to the same practice are cited by Percy Dearmer, *op. cit.*, pp. 256–57.

[29] *Libri Miraculorum* II.9, Gregoire, *op. cit.*, 1:323. The personal accounts are found in the *Libri Miraculorum* II.24–25, *De Virtutibus Sancti Martini* I.32–33, II.1–2, II.60, III.1 and 10, and IV.1–2; *ibid.*, 1:350–52; 2:74–77, 92 ff., 188 ff., 196–97, 208–09, and 274–77.

[30] It is interesting that Gregory came from an influential senatorial family which had also produced many of the bishops of this area. Once as a small child, when his father was sick, he had dreamed of the remedy that would cure the ailment (*De Gloria Beatorum Confessorum* 60, *ibid.*, 2:420–22).

Meanwhile in Rome, where Gregory the Great was pope, we have seen that a different understanding was planted and grew for a thousand years. In the *Dialogues* this more famous Gregory makes clear that he also personally knew the experience of healing. He tells of a severe illness and of begging one of the monks to pray for him; it is one of the many examples of healing he mentions. Some are plausible, while others stretch the imagination.[31] Healing, according to this Gregory, came from a power given directly by God to certain individuals. But he did not see restoring a sick person to health as very different from any other extraordinary happening, such as the miraculous replenishing of a supply of grain or oil. Either power, he concluded, was obviously a sign of God's personal favor and an indication of *moral perfection*. To claim such power was dangerous for ordinary people, even popes, with moral imperfections. This thinking is found all through the *Dialogues* and is implied elsewhere. Informed that his special emissary to England, Augustine, Archbishop of Canterbury, had healed a blind man by his prayers in the presence of a large assembly, he wrote a special letter to warn him of the need to temper such miraculous gifts with fear: "Rejoice that the souls of the English are, by the means of outward miracles brought to a participation of inward grace. But fear, lest amidst the wonders that are wrought, the mind, which is but weak, should be puffed up to presumption, and incur the inward guilt of vain glory, on account of that exterior honor."[32] Gregory the Great appears to be the last major writer in the church until modern times to describe a personal healing by God's power. Apparently it was not quite cricket to be touched by divine power; it is not consistent with proper humility. But at the same time as Gregory, others in the West were writing of healing: John of Bobbio and Bishop Ouen among them.[33]

Two of England's bishops at the end of the seventh century were known for their healing powers. The Venerable Bede described these miraculous gifts first in his *Life and Miracles of Saint Cuthbert*, the Bishop of Lindisfarne, at that time a center of Christian vitality and now a fascinating ruin. Then in his *Ecclesiastical History of the English Nation*,

---

[31] These stories are found in Saint Gregory the Great, *Dialogues* (1959) I.2, 4, 10, 12; II.11, 16, 26, 27, 30, 32, 38; III.2, 3, 5, 6, 14, 17, 21, 22, 25, 33 (including his own healing); IV.6, 11, 40 and 42.

[32] Sancti Gregorii Magni, *Epistolarum*, Lib.XI.28, Ad Augustinum Anglorum Episcopum, in *Patrologiae Latinae* 77 (1896), col. 1139.

[33] Ionas, *Vitae Sanctorum Columbani* II.24, Scriptores Rerum Germanicarum (1905), pp. 286 ff. S. Eligii Episcopi Noviomensis, *Vita*, in *Patrologiae Latinae* 87 (1863), cols. 482–594.

he recounts two incidents that occurred after Cuthbert's death.[34] Bede also gives a number of eyewitness accounts of healings by the saintly John of Beverley, who was Bishop of York until he retired to found a monastery. John healed the wife of an earl, as well as a man dying after a fall from his horse.

Another account shows John's love and compassion and his healing power. He took a mute boy, whose head was covered with scabs, to live with him during Lent. In the second week he called the boy and told him to put out his tongue. Making the sign of the cross on it, he asked him to say the word *yea*. The boy's tongue was immediately loosed, and the bishop had him repeat letters, then syllables and words. For the rest of the day, the boy hardly stopped speaking. Rejoicing, John ordered the physician to take care of his scurvied head, and with the help of the bishop's blessing and prayers a good head of hair grew as the flesh healed. Instead of a deformed beggar, a handsome, articulate boy was returned to his family.[35] These stories set down by the "father of English history" are examples of Christian love and concern, rather than of the magic and superstition usually associated with most medieval miracles and miracle workers.

At almost the same time another English Christian was becoming known for his healings among the Frisians in the Low Countries. This was the missionary Willibrord, who became Archbishop of Utrecht and whose miracles were later celebrated by Alcuin. In Alcuin's life of Willibrord, the great scholar of the Dark Ages tells of many wonderful works that were still being done in his time (about 800) through the relics of the saint. Alcuin describes particularly how people were healed by anointing themselves with oil from the lamps kept burning at his shrine. The equally famous Boniface, who spent three years with Willibrord, was also known for the miracles he performed by means of relics he had obtained from Rome. He was likewise renowned for arranging the condemnation of Adelbert, a Frankish bishop, for the sale of fraudulent relics, which he claimed to have received direct from the angels.[36]

[34] *Bede's Ecclesiastical History of the English People*, IV.30 (1969), pp. 444–49.

[35] *Ibid.*, V.2, pp. 456–69.

[36] *The Life of St. Willibrord* by Alcuin, *The LIfe of St. Boniface* by Willibald, and *Acts of the Synod of 25 October 745, Condemning Adelbert and Clemens*, in *The Anglo-Saxon Missionaries in German* (1954), pp. 19–21, 60, and 107–10.

A Change in Healing Experiences

The church in western Europe changed a great deal between the time of Augustine and Aquinas. In the chaos that followed the collapse of the western Roman Empire and the development of medieval Europe, the church became an authoritative institution regulating both religious and secular life. Sometimes one feels as though it proclaimed a God more like the vengeful Teutonic ones than the merciful healing one portrayed by Jesus of Nazareth.

God became more abstract and further removed from ordinary people. It apparently became easier to see the divine in special individuals: the saints, who received almost magical power to heal because the perfection of their lives was pleasing to God. Some of their healings were probably genuine. People generally do not become saints without evincing a good measure of divine love and care, and these qualities, which exemplify the nature of God, are usually healing in themselves. Meanwhile the whole idea of healing became more restricted to special instances, more superstitiously regarded, and further from the center of officially accepted Christian life. Records from this period, which are numerous, describe healing almost entirely in connection with saints or the relics of saints.[37]

About the year 1100 several of the most illustrious saints of the Middle Ages made their appearance. Around each of these, and around the other notable saints who were to follow, appeared the same kind of miraculous events, usually healings. In Lyons people took the leavings from Anselm's plate to heal their sick, and some attested to healing simply by hearing him bless the sacrament at the altar. Innumerable people were cured by eating bread blessed by Bernard of Clairvaux. Around 1200, many healings were attributed to Dominic, founder of the Dominican order, and St. Francis of Assisi. Indeed, St. Francis had

---

[37] Often, as with the miracles of Saint Benedict, there were various reports by different writers from several different shrines. For instance, *Les Miracles de Saint Benoit*, écrits par Adrevald, Aimoin, André, Raoul Tortaire et Hugues de Sainte Marie (1858) covers only the miracles associated with Benedict that happened in France from about 825 to 1100.

See also *Vita Sancti Anselmi*, Auctore Eadmero I.6, II.5 and 7 in, *Patrologiae Latinae* 158 (1864), cols. 76–80, 104–06, and 114–16; *Sancti Bernardi, Abbatis Clarae-Vallensis, Vita et Res Gestae*, bk I, Auctore Guillelmo IX.44, X.46, XI.53–54, XII.57 ff; bk VI, Auctore Philippo I–V, in *Patrologiae Latinae* 185 (1879), cols. 253–54, 256–60, and 373–86; *The Miraculous Powers of the Church of Christ Asserted Through each Successive Century from the Apostles down to the Present Time* (1756), pp. 250 ff.; Thomas of Celano, *Tractatus de miraculis S. Francisci Assisiensis* (1928); also Paul Sabatier, *Life of St. Francis of Assisi* (1938), pp. 192 ff.

to be buried hurriedly to keep his body from being dismembered by people who wanted even the smallest relic which still carried the healing power he had in life. Many accounts of these healings are available in the numerous lives of this incredibly saintly person.

Each of these saints apparently healed many persons individually by touch or prayer and the sign of the cross, and these incidents, well attested by eye witnesses, often occurred in the presence of numbers of people. Bernard, for instance, wrote the life of Malachy, the primate of Ireland, and recounted not only the acts of his life, but told of the crowded funeral where Bernard himself, noticing a boy with a withered hand, placed it on the dead saint's hand and saw it healed.[38] Other saints were not quite so famous, such as Antony of Padua, disciple of St. Francis, and in England Thomas of Hereford, Edmund of Canterbury, and Richard of Chichester, whose miraculous powers were also renowned.

Healing in a Divided Church

The gift of healing has continued to be given to those who have been most dedicated in the service of God, particularly people working to comfort the sick and poor. Those who are genuinely and deeply interested in caring for the misery of their fellow humans seem to have less resistance to healing them through spiritual means. St. Francis Xavier, for instance, had studied medicine and put it to good use in the Far East, yet his letters give clear details of several miraculous healings, while others have been related directly by eye witnesses. St. Vincent of Paul, who was able to heal by the power of God, is better known for his practical labors as founder of a hospital and orders to care for the sick. The healings of St. Catherine of Siena, somewhat earlier, are not more amazing than her life or service to the sick, combined with political service to the church. Yet she was slandered again and again because she followed God as an individual, rather than keeping to her

---

[38] S. Bernardi Abbatis Clarae-Vallensis, *De Vita et Rebus Gestis S. Malachiae* XVII.40–41, XX.45–46, XXII.49–50., XXIV.53, XXXI.75, in *Patrologiae Latinae* 182 (1879), cols. 1095–96, 1099–1100, 1101–04, and 1117–18; also James Cotter Morison, *The Life and Times of Saint Bernard, Abbot of Clairvaux* (1901), pp. 56 ff., where some of the miracles are described with the comment that, "No expression of disgust or of contempt is required now with reference to such a stage of human belief. The great majority of mankind have even held opinions similar to or identical with the above. The exception is to hold the reverse, and to substitute for Miracle a reliance on Law. Intrinsically, then, these groundless beliefs are nothing but silly tales, with little merit of either variety or invention. But, regarded historically, as stages in man's development, they assume quite a philosophic importance."

place within her order.[39] John Wesley, who later told of healings through prayer, also wrote an enormously popular book on practical medicine which helped many, many people in England.[40]

Luther, who had denied the gift of healing for his time, lived to see his friend Melanchthon visibly brought from the point of death through his own prayers. Five years later in 1545, the year before he died, when asked what to do for a man who was mentally ill, Luther wrote instructions for a healing service based on the New Testament letter of James, adding, "This is what we do, and that we have been accustomed to do, for a cabinetmaker here was similarly afflicted with madness and we cured him by prayer in Christ's name."[41] Like the two great saints of the church before him, Augustine and Aquinas, he seems to have learned in his mellower years to value, rather than to disregard, this gift from God.

About this time, too, there were St. Philip Neri, St. Francis de Sales, and St. Jean Francois Regis, whose healings by prayer or touch and the sign of the cross were widely known. One of the most famous of the many cures by means of relics also occurred in this period. Pascal's niece was healed at the dedication of a shrine, when the nun who was her teacher was inspired to touch her with the relic of our Savior. Pascal added to his crest the symbols of this healing with the words "*scio cui credidi*" ("what I once believed, I now know").[42]

George Fox, founder of the Society of Friends, knew the power of God to heal and recorded its use. Fox set down straightforward, concrete facts all through his *Journal*, and he also left a "Book of Miracles" in bound manuscript form, which was never published. All that remains of it today are the title and an index of brief notes about the experiences. Not even the record of the Society's discussion about publishing was kept, as with other works.[43] Apparently the Quakers had had their fill of ridicule and painful accusations of demonism, blasphe-

[39] Henry James Coleridge, *The Life and Letters of St. Francis Xavier* (1881), I:65–66, 147, and 215–16; *The Miraculous Powers of the Church of Christ*, pp. 266–67; Josephine Butler, *Catharine of Siena: A Biography* (1878), pp. 96–98 and 191; Margaret Roberts, *Saint Catherine of Siena and Her Times* (1906), pp. 51–52

[40] *Primitive Physick, or an Easy and Natural Method of Curing Most Diseases*, published in 1747, went into nearly fifty editions and reprints by 1850.

[41] W. J. Kooiman, *By Faith Alone: The Life of Martin Luther* (1954), p. 192; letter to Pastor Severin Schulze, June 1, 1545, in *Luther: Letters of Spiritual Counsel* (1955), pp. 51–52.

[42] Marcel Jouhandeau, *St. Philip Neri* (1960), pp. 55–60; *Miraculous Powers*, pp. 268–70. Pascal quoted by Dearmer, *op. cit.*, pp. 359–60, from a contemporary source published in Paris in 1656.

[43] Henry J. Cadbury, ed., *George Fox's 'Book of Miracles'* (1948), pp. 65–66 and 39–40. The editor has reconstructed parts of the "Book of Miracles" from the *Journal*, letters, and other sources. Healings are recorded in *The Journal of George Fox* (1911), 1:58, 61, 140–41, 199, 201; 2:22, 226–27, 229, 234, 243, 310, 437–38, and 466–67.

my, and glorifying Fox as a magic worker. The English generally were interested in any kind of miracle worked by spirits, "touch doctors," and even angels, but not in the direct power of God working through human beings.

Yet the king's touch was sought for healing in England, so much that tickets had to be issued for the ceremony. By anointing he was given divine power, and until 1715 the Prayer Book ordered a special prayer for his healing power. The early Baptists in England and America practiced anointing for healing and recorded their success, particularly with mental illness.[44] John Wesley described numerous miracles of God's healing, many of them through his own prayers and also told one of the most delightful and down-to-earth stories of the time. He was on his way to an important preaching mission when his horse suddenly became lame. Quite naturally he placed his hand on the horse and prayed that he might be well. When it was time to go on, the animal had recovered, and both arrived in good spirits.[45]

In 1815 Prince Alexander of Hohenlohe began his priesthood during an epidemic in Germany and only later found that something happened to sick people if he touched them with faith, asking God for healing. Father Matthew in Ireland was bringing thousands into the temperance movement when his healing powers were discovered by a sick woman who begged only for his blessing and a prayer. Dorothea Trudel, who ran a home factory in Zürich, was worried when four of her workers became ill and medical treatment did not help; as she asked God what to do, the prayer of faith came into her mind, and she was startled to find that it worked.[46]

In 1842 another amazing story of healings began in a village at the edge of the Black Forest, where Johann Christoph Blumhardt had come

[44] *The Records of a Church of Christ Meeting at Broadmead, Bristol 1640–1687*, quoted by Cadbury, *op. cit.*, pp. 2–3.
[45] Again and again in his *Journal* Wesley described experiences of healing. See *The Journal of the Rev. John Wesley*, Vol. 1, Feb. 21, 1736; May 19, 1738; Feb. 9, Sept. 3, 28, and Oct. 13, 1739; Nov. 16, 1740; Feb. 15, 19, 21, May 8, Nov. 20, 1741; Mar. 31, Dec. 20, 1742; Nov. 2, 1745; Mar. 17, Oct. 12, 1746 Vol. 2, May 24, 1749; Apr. 8, Sept. 19, 1750; Apr. 27, 1752; Sept. 7-11, 1755; Apr. 6, June 22, Sept. 22, 1756; May 5, 1757; Feb. 23, 1758; May 12, July 1, 1759 Vol. 3, Dec. 26, 1761; Oct. 19, 1762; Oct. 1, 1763; Mar. 19, 1766; June 21, Oct. 30, 1767; May 2, 1768; May 18, June 26, 1772 Vol. 4, Oct. 16, 1778; Sept. 5, 1781; Apr. 24, Sept. 3, 1782; May 23, 1783; Apr. 12, 1784; May 31, 1785; Oct. 24, 1787; Oct. 7, 1790.
[46] Dearmer, *op. cit.*, pp. 363–66, cites the original German, Austrian, and English sources for Prince Hohenlohe; John Francis Maguire, *Father Mathew* (1864), pp. 529–31, *Dorothea Trudel, or the Prayer of Faith* (1865), pp. 10 and 52–55.

as pastor. The clergyman needed to help a girl in his church who was seriously disturbed and whose illness was accompanied by unexplained and frightening psychic phenomena. He found himself face to face with a power that was working to split one personality and destroy others both physically and mentally. With every tactic of the Spirit, he was able in the end to help her regain mental and physical health and won her lifelong loyalty to the church. But this was only one of the results. Blumhardt himself found the power of the Spirit through this confrontation, and both he and his parish were changed by it.

People began coming to him to confess things they had done. Because he knew the satanic forces that were pitted against God, he could offer forgiveness in a way unorthodox for Lutherans. He also had to meet the same satanic forces in himself and ask God to hold off judgment for a while. His parish came alive; people flocked to church, looking and acting younger, and suddenly healing was occurring. A physician who came to investigate recognized one healthy woman as a patient who had been declared incurable at the clinic at Tübingen. As Blumhardt's church became crowded with people from other parishes, the church also came to investigate. In 1846 he was forbidden to make physical healing a part of his spiritual ministry. His reply, however, made it clear that he could not stop healings from happening if he continued this ministry, and he was allowed to go on within his own parish. Six years later he left the church to work fulltime with the sick at Bad Boll.[47]

This ministry did not escape notice by the theologians. When Karl Barth came to write about the gift of healing, he criticized Bultmann for remarking, "The stories of Blumhardt are an abomination to me!" Barth accepted Blumhardt's idea that a struggle with the devil offered "new light" on healing in the New Testament. But he did not have any more to say. Instead, he went right on to consider how the genuine struggle against sickness reveals a final kernel of truth: "that it is good for man to live a limited and impeded life."[48]

In the late years of the nineteenth century a new interest in religious healing began to take place in Europe and America. It bypassed most of the established churches, but has touched a great many people all over the world.

---

[47] Friedrich Zündel, *Johann Christoph Blumhardt* (1967); also *Pioneer of Divine Healing: Jon. Chr. Blumhardt,* author and date unknown, published by the Order of St. Luke the Physician.
[48] Karl Barth, *Church Dogmatics* 3, *The Doctrine of Creation* (1961), pt. 4:371 and 374.

CHAPTER 10

A New Understanding of Healing Emerges

During the first years of the nineteenth century the separation between medical healing and religious healing was nearly complete. The idea that the religious or emotional attitudes of people could affect the body was considered absurd in most quarters, both secular and religious. And then from many different sources evidence began to emerge that healing could take place through other than purely physical means. When the same insight emerges from very different sources it is usually an indication that some important aspect of life has been ignored. Seven different streams have contributed to the recent flood of interest in nonmedical methods of healing.

Hypnotism.

In the early years of the last century the discovery of hypnotism demonstrated that one person using suggestion could control the minds and bodies of others. Mesmerism, another word for hypnotism, derives its name from Franz Mesmer who demonstrated this practice all over Europe. Jean Charcot and Sigmund Freud used hypnotism as a therapeutic tool, and it has continued to have medical applications up to the present time. At the same time, New Thought and Science of Mind began to use the power of suggestion for purely religious applications.

The Unconscious Mind.

Although the idea of an unconscious part of the human psyche had been discussed widely during the nineteenth century, Freud brilliantly demonstrated in his clinical practice the reality of the unconscious in each of us and showed how it influences our behaviour, thoughts, emotions, and bodies. Freud waited until 1900 to publish *The Interpretation of Dreams*, because he considered his findings a monumental new discovery worthy of a new century.

Psychosomatic medicine.

The case studies of Freud and other depth psychologists led to the development of psychosomatic medicine, the study of how emotions affect the body and how bodies affect emotions. This in turn has led to psychoneurological immunology, the study of how emotions, and the brain chemicals released by them, affect our ability to fight disease.

New Scientific Evidence.

A new worldview began to develop among physicists beginning with Mme. Curie's evidence that atoms consisted of smaller parts. Mathematicians, anthropologists, medical doctors, psychiatrists, parapsychologists, and students of the history and philosophy of science contributed evidence that we live in a much more open and mysterious universe than we once believed, a universe in which mind influences matter as well as being influenced by it.

Pentecostal Christianity.

The pentecostal movement started some four centuries ago in the Cevenne mountains of southern France. It emphasized the gifts of speaking in tongues as well as all the other gifts of the Spirit, including healing. This movement poured over into mainline churches in England in the middle of the nineteenth century and had a new birth all over the world in the first years of the twentieth century. The Pentecostal churches attracted great numbers and became the fastest growing Christian denominations. The experience that started these churches then began to be experienced in the mainline Protestant churches and finally had a profound effect upon the Roman Catholic Church. Along with an emphasis on healing and the other gifts of the Spirit, the vision of a loving God reaching out to human beings no matter what their condition became an essential part of this movement.

Individual Experience.

Individuals from all walks of life have felt the healing touch of this loving God and written of their experiences, including Glenn Clark, Agnes Sanford, Starr Daily, John and Ethel Banks, and many others. It has been my privilege to know most of these leaders in the growing healing movement. During my years as rector of St. Luke's Church in

Monrovia, California, a lively healing ministry developed among four clergy, each of whom conducted a healing service. With the publication of *Healing and Christianity* I found myself more involved in the healing ministry throughout the country and abroad and have come to know a large number of those who have written on the subject or who have centers where vital Christianity and healing are encouraged.

Spiritual Non-Christian Healing.

On the whole, the healing movement has existed outside the confines of the traditional churches. In addition to Christian interest in healing, the New Age movement has emphasized healing and provided places where mental and physical healing are taught without reference to Christianity. Marilyn Ferguson's *Aquarian Conspiracy* gives an excellent statement of this movement. Carlos Castenada's books have led many people to take an interest in the healing practices of Indian shamans. Edgar Cayce's healing power has received wide attention and continues in the Association for Research and Enlightenment in Virginia Beach, Virginia.

This chapter traces the development of the religious and Christian interest in healing in our time. We begin with the healing work of Phineas Quimby and then look at the individuals who wrote, lectured, and organized groups to encourage this healing interest. I shall then examine the effects of the charismatic movement on the healing movement and finally look at the place of healing in the church in the late 1980s. The two following chapters survey the medical findings concerning the interrelationship of emotions, mind, and body and address the complex subject of clinical psychology that is involved in healing our emotional lives.

The Healing Sects Influence the Church

Around the middle of the nineteenth century in Boston, a remarkable man began to show notable ability to heal by religious means. Phineas Quimby taught and practiced a method of healing using mesmerism, clairvoyance, and the New Testament. As *The Quimby Manuscripts* show, his knowledge of the power of the mind came from his experiences with hypnotism. He also found how easily a clairvoyant, using hypnotism, could pick up what sick people had been told about their condition and then offer simple remedies that often produced cures.[1] He came to believe that disease resulted only from mental error and all healing from right belief or wisdom. He found that he was able to reach the need of many individuals below the surface of the mind and suggest wisdom based on the New Testament and his own practical good sense, but he could see no good in organized Christianity, which only perpetuated error.

Mary Baker Eddy came to him as a patient in 1862 and was soon well enough to begin treating other people by his methods. The inspiration of Christian Science came to her after his death. She experienced healing, while reading the New Testament. Mrs. Eddy tried to introduce healing into the traditional churches in Boston, but was so ridiculed that in 1879 she founded her own church. Eventually she determined to found a new church that would reject illness and even the reality of the body entirely. In 1879 she organized the Christian Science church, which has grown rapidly all over the world. Next came Unity, with its ministry of *Silent Unity*, and then Religious Science, and Science of Mind. Other New Thought groups were founded following Quimby's ideas. In spite of their sometimes naive philosophic approach, these sects have had a real insight into the historic ministry of Christianity to the emotions and the bodies of human beings and numbers of healings have unquestionably occurred in these groups, healings that were not happening in the traditional churches of the time.

A. J. Gordon, an outstanding Baptist minister in Boston, knew that his book, *Ministry of Healing*, published in 1882 would not be popular with theologians or with most Christians, who were obviously embarrassed if someone spoke of God's answering prayer. Yet Dr. Gordon took the trouble to describe the history of healing and even mentioned examples in his own ministry, remarking, "So far as our observation goes, the most powerful effect of such experiences is upon the subjects themselves, in the marked consecration and extraordinary spiritual anointing which almost invariably attend them. We can bear unqualified testimony on this point."[2]

Indeed, as others have realized, conservative Christianity has reason to thank these new groups for opening a door which its own philosophic approach had closed. Had the mainstream churches been more

---

[1] *The Quimby Manuscripts*, ed. Horatio W. Dresser (1961), pp. 29–36; also a section on Mrs. Eddy up to her publication of *Science and Health* in 1875, pp. 152–54. The 1921 edition contains a number of her letters to Quimby.

[2] A. J. Gordon, *The Ministry of Healing* (1961), p. 206. In his remarkable ministry Dr. Gordon brought to reality the dream he had had of Christ coming unknown into his church; see my book *God, Dreams, and Revelation*, pp. 186–88.

open theologically, the healing movement might have been integrated in them. But in view of their hostility toward the subject, the movement had to go forward on its own or come to an end. In a sense the theological rigidity of the established churches was directly responsible for the development of these sects. They will continue to grow until the seminaries and official bodies develop a theology with a place for the continuing action of God in the physical world.

Since the nineteenth century, a new spirit has been moving, both in some churches and in medicine. One pioneer movement began in Boston in 1905 with Dr. Elwood Worcester, his colleagues at Emmanuel Church, and several physicians and psychiatrists in his congregation. It brought results for many persons who had not been helped by either the medical or spiritual approach alone. At St. Mark's-in-the-Bowery Dr. Loring W. Batten, who also taught Old Testament literature at General Theological Seminary, carried on the same work and helped to spread the ideas of Emmanuel Church. At the same time the still active Guild of Health was organized in England, to practice and encourage Christian healing in cooperation with medicine. A few years later the Order of the Nazarene was formed in this country.

Percy Dearmer, an Anglican priest whose writings on liturgy had a profound effect on the Church of England, also became interested in Christian healing. His scholarship was impeccable. The publication in 1909 of his book, *Body and Soul*, made a great impact on the English church. His work was to a large degree responsible for the resolution in favor of healing by the assembled Bishops of the Anglican Communion in 1930. Many retreat centers and groups in Great Britain emphasize a ministry of healing to body, mind, and soul. Secularism has had less influence in the Anglican Church in England, and so the church has been more open to the healing movement.

With a gradual growth in medical understanding, two of the most influential groups in this country were started in the 1930s. Camps Farthest Out, established by Glenn Clark, have introduced a great many lay people and clergy to the reality of transforming religious experiences and of mental and physical healings. These camps have continued to grow in popularity and in numbers and are now to be found all over the world. During the 1960s I was a leader at several of these camps and met many of the leaders of this movement. When I came to Monrovia I found that Starr Daily, author of *Release* and a leader of Camps Farthest Out, lived in town. He led a retreat to initiate our ministry of healing there.

My wife Barbara and I first met Agnes Sanford at a Camps Farthest Out meeting in Estes Park in 1949. We were deeply impressed by her and invited her to speak at the Episcopal Cathedral in Phoenix, where I was a canon. While there she visited some of the sick unable to come to the healing services. On that occasion and several times later we saw remarkable physical healings take place when she laid her hands on people. She came many times to give healing missions at St. Luke's Church. Because of our friendship I came to know her son John, also an Episcopal priest. In 1955 he joined me at St. Luke's Church.

Agnes Sanford's husband, Edgar Sanford, was an Episcopal priest who realized that clergy had little or no exposure to the healing ministry in seminary. He and his wife organized the Schools of Pastoral Care, in which this ministry was taught to clergy and lay people. For many years I lectured at these schools and came to know Agnes very well, especially after she moved to Monrovia, where she was a member of St. Luke's church until her death. Because of her book, *The Healing Light*, I began to take the healing ministry seriously. Several of her books are still in print and widely appreciated. The number of people that she influenced and led into a *sane* healing ministry would be difficult to estimate.

During my first years at St. Luke's I came to know Ethel Tullock Banks and John Gaynor Banks, founders of the Order of St. Luke. I was with Dr. Banks when he died suddenly while speaking, and I will never forget being with Ethel immediately after his death, as she raised the glass of water that had been given her and said, "The water of life to John Gaynor." The Order to St. Luke has grown through the years and has spread all over the world. It emphasizes the need for lay people and clergy to practice a discipline of prayer and a healing ministry. Its monthly magazine, *Sharing*, reaches many thousands of people. Dr. Banks was the first leader of the healing movement I knew who was well versed in the history of the early church and taught that the healing ministry continued as a common practice for many centuries. He also directed me to Evelyn Frost's groundbreaking work, *Christian Healing*.

One of the most spectacular ministries of healing in the 1960s was that of Kathryn Kuhlman. At the suggestion of Agnes Sanford, I attended one of her healing services at the Shrine Auditorium in Los Angeles. Every one of the twelve thousand seats were taken. Buses brought people from hundreds of miles away. It was the first time I had experienced slaying-in-the-Spirit. As people came forward, Kathryn

Kuhlman reached out to touch them and they fell semi-conscious into the arms of those who assisted her. Many people claimed to be healed at the service. She seemed able to discern the condition of people far from her in the highest balcony. Her book, *I Believe in Miracles*, was enormously popular for many years.

During the 1930s another remarkable healer received acclaim throughout the United States and in Europe. Edgar Cayce appeared to be an ordinary person when you met him. He taught the adult Bible class in the Baptist Church in Virginia Beach every Sunday for over thirty years. During those years he went into trance twice a day, and a different personality with remarkable abilities emerged. Presented with the name of a sick person, Cayce would locate the person geographically, diagnose the disease and offer suggestions for treatment that were effective in a high percentage of cases. For many years I lectured regularly at the Association for Research and Enlightenment, which Cayce founded, and came to know the secretary who took down the messages that he gave in trance. I also knew his sons, Hugh Lynn and Charles Thomas Cayce. When asked by some conservative Christians why I lectured in a place that they believed had its source of power in questionable entities, I replied, "At least they believed that the power of God is still operating today and that is more than we find in many traditional and fundamentalistic churches." Cayce is probably the best recorded and one of the most remarkable psychic healers of all time. Hugh Lynn Cayce's book, *The Outer Limits of Edgar Cayce's Power*, gives a fine analysis of his father's healing ministry. At one time a hospital was conceived as a part of this compassionate ministry. Edgar Cayce never charged any money for his services. Although I cannot agree with all that came through him in his trances, particularly his teaching on reincarnation, there is little question that many people who had lost all hope found healing of body and mind through this ministry.

Pentecostal Healing

I have described the history of the Pentecostal movement in detail in my book, *Tongue Speaking*. Let me simply say here that the gift of healing went hand-in-hand with the ability to speak in tongues. As the Spirit moved through people, healings often occurred when they laid hands on others or anointed them. This came as a surprise to many leaders of the movement, since few of them knew about the long and continuous ministry of healing of the early church. The early leaders of the Pentecostal movement did not have a theology to oppose to the

secularism of their age and of most of the traditional churches. Therefore they withdrew from the world and developed their own religious
counterculture. Healing came to be an expected part of their religious
life, as in the apostolic church. As the Pentecostal churches grew, many
people were transformed and renewed. Few people in the traditional
churches knew the quality and power in these new churches. David
Wilkerson's book, *The Cross and the Switchblade*, was one of the first
books about Pentecostal life that reached the general reader, and, as
John Sherril remarked to me, it had to be translated from "pentecos-
talese" into ordinary English so that it might reach those readers.

Human beings in pain want more than ideas about salvation on the
other side of death. They want transformation now, and many of the
Pentecostal churches provided just that. I became acutely aware of the
power of the Pentecostal movement in a graduate seminar I conducted
at San Francisco Theological Seminary. Four of the students had been
born in Korea, and three of them were renounced by their families
when they joined the Christian church. But they found their charismatic Christian experience life-transforming. Pastor Paul Cho in his
book, *Successful Home Cell Groups*, tells of the vital life and growth of
his charismatic church in Seoul, which has hundreds of thousand members. Each member belongs to a cell group which meets weekly for
prayer and praise, for mutual support and healings, which do occur.

The television ministry of Oral Roberts is too well known to be
discussed at length. It has, however, attracted the interest and money
of millions, and thousands of people say that they have been healed
through Roberts's ministry. Two people who have been intimately associated with Oral Roberts tell me that amazing healings and transformations take place around him. He has established a university and a
large hospital as well. Many people question his methods, but many
others seem to have been helped by this ministry.

Finally, the vision and enthusiasm of the Pentecostal churches
spilled over into mainline Protestantism. Dennis Bennet and I were
closely associated when he found opposition to speaking in tongues
within his Episcopal church in Van Nuys, California. I also came to
know Jean Willans, who was active in the church at Van Nuys. Later I
visited her as she continued her ministry in Hong Kong. For a while
our staff at St. Luke's considered inviting Father Bennet to join us. We
already had three clergy who were involved in tongue speaking, and
we had conducted a healing ministry there for fifteen years. I was rector
of the parish and not a tongue speaker, but we sheltered many charis-
matics of whom the Episcopal church disapproved. In some ways self-

supporting Episcopal churches are as autonomous as Congregational ones.

Through Agnes Sanford and the Schools of Pastoral Care I came to know many of the leaders of the charismatic movement within the Baptist, Congregational, Methodist, Presbyterian, and Lutheran churches. I soon discovered that when one of the gifts of the Spirit is accepted, the others usually follow.

About the same time I became involved in Jungian analysis and studied at the Jung Institute in Switzerland. I found that my Jungian analyst friends were not scornful of tongue speaking or the gifts of the Spirit. Hilde Kirsch once said to me, "There's no reason that there can't be healing in the church as well as in the psychologist's office." These well-educated analysts, men and women, most of them Jewish, took the New Testament more seriously than had my professors at seminary. Through the wisdom of James Kirsch I came to see that Jung provided a worldview in which the physical and nonphysical (the spiritual or psychoid, as Jung called it) were real and interacted with one another. At this time, from four to eight each morning, I wrote *Tongue Speaking*. Jung provided a framework in which the gifts of the Spirit made sense. I then began to work in the same early morning hours on a book now entitled *God, Dreams, and Revelation*, which shows that God still speaks in dreams, as the spirit has spoken to people in the Bible and throughout the history of the church. I also began to realize that healing was no more miraculous than God's communicating with human beings in dreams, visions, meditation, and prayer. If we are entirely material beings and we get divine messages, then something nonmaterial has to move the cogs in the space-time box so the message gets through. All the gifts of the Spirit began to make sense once I had a theology that had a place for human contact with both the material realm and the spiritual one.

Healing in the Roman Catholic Church

In 1969 I was asked to come to the University of Notre Dame to teach in the Department of Graduate Studies in Education. I suddenly found myself in the center of the charismatic movement in the Catholic Church. The Second Vatican Council had just concluded; a fresh new spirit of openness and expectation filled the air. Pope John XXIII had called for a fresh outpouring of the Holy Spirit on the church, and something had happened. Protestants who have never read the Documents of Vatican II do not realize that this is one of the most unique religious documents of all times. A nearly totally authoritarian church gave back to the individuals the authority of their own conscience. In a few years the charismatic movement swept through the worldwide Roman Catholic Church and with it an emphasis on healing.

Vatican II made it quite clear to Catholics that healing is to be expected in the church. The Decree on the Apostolate of the Laity (I.3 f) not only directs the use of gifts received from the Holy Spirit, including the special gifts outlined by Paul in 1 Corinthians 12. And the constitution on the Sacred Liturgy (III.73 ff.) specifies that

"Extreme Unction," which may also and more fittingly be called "anointing of the sick," is not a sacrament for those only who are at the point of death. Hence, as soon as any one of the faithful begins to be in danger of death from sickness or old age, the appropriate time for him to receive this sacrament has certainly already arrived.

In addition to the separate rites for anointing of sick and for Viaticum [the last communion given to the dying], a continuous rite shall be prepared according to which the sick man is anointed after he has made his confession and before he receives Viaticum.

The number of the anointings is to be adapted to the occasion, and the prayers accompanying the rite of anointing are to be revised so as to correspond with the varying conditions of the sick who receive the sacrament.[3]

Healing had not ceased in the Catholic Church, although there was little place in Scholastic theology for it. When the crypt was built in Chartres Cathedral in the twelfth century, it was so constructed that it could easily be washed down after the sick pilgrims had left. This tradition of coming to sleep at a shrine, or at least to visit it, was common throughout Europe. In the eighteenth century the practice received new attention. From Lourdes and Fatima to Ste. Anne de Beaupré in Canada, new shrines have sprung up where people have experienced spontaneous contact with the Spirit. From 1860 on, the number of pilgrims has increased until more than two million people go to Lourdes alone each year. In 1882 a medical bureau was set up at which close to 100,000 persons now register annually, with well over a thousand nonmedical cures carefully examined since 1918. To recognize a genuine cure, standard procedures now require a full preceding medical record, as well as follow-up information at stated intervals. By 1957, fifty-four specific healings had been accepted as miracles—(i.e., as impossible by any natural means).[4]

---

[3] *The Documents of Vatican II* (1966), pp. 492–93, and 161. Italics mine.
[4] François Leuret and Henri Bon, *Modern Miraculous Cures: A Documented Account of Mir-*

Francis Thompson, a Catholic, wrote *The Hound of Heaven*, one of the finest religious poems of the twentieth century. Thompson, a morphine addict, was taken into the home of two devout Roman Catholics who saw the religious genius beneath his sickness. In 1905 he wrote his little book, *Health and Holiness* as a plea for understanding that "we can no longer set body against spirit and let them come to grips after the lighthearted fashion of our ancestors."[5] In the Catholic Church, to which he was speaking, one way was still open for a direct healing relation between body and spirit. This was the healing shrine, as we have described it.

Individuals with remarkable healing gifts have continued to appear. Neil G. McCluskey, a very careful and perceptive writer, has described the ministry of Theresa Neumann, whose spiritual gifts have been examined from all sides, particularly the visions she had so frequently, her fasts, and the stigmata she bore at special times. McCluskey's study, written after two visits to her, brings out her effect on the life of the parish, pointing to just the kind of situation in which such gifts as healing occur.[6] Dorothy Kerin in England was another such gifted person.

While at Notre Dame I was fortunate to make the acquaintance of Cardinal Suenens, Archbishop of Belgium. He had been touched by the charismatic renewal and spoke in tongues. This remarkable scholar and leader in Vatican II once remarked that the experience of tongues made him feel very much the little child that Jesus commends. He believed that healing was a much more important gift than tongues. Cardinal Suenens was concerned that emphasis on slaying-in-the-Spirit might be greater than interest in healing. I wrote the first part of my book, *Discernment*, for him as a study of that dramatic psycho-spiritual phenomenon. I traveled with him from a large charismatic meeting in St. Louis to Ann Arbor, where an influential charismatic Catholic group was based. At Notre Dame at that time the entire football stadium was filled during charismatic rallies, with tens of thousands of worshippers and hundreds of priests leading the procession to Eucharist. Barbara and I were invited by Cardinal Suenens to visit his charismatic community in Brussels and to stay with him at Malines and to speak on the impor-

---

acles and Medicine in the Twentieth Century (1957), pp. 107–15 and 205; see also Monden, *op. cit.*, pp. 194–99, for information from various sources and an excellent presentation of selected cases.

[5] P. 48.

[6] Neil G. McCluskey, S.J., "Darkness and Light over Konnersreuth," *The Priest* 10 (September 1954): 765–74.

tance of providing an adequate worldview in order for the charismatic movement to touch people on all educational levels. He was appointed by John Paul II to supervise and advise the Catholic charismatic movement throughout the world. We shall soon see that many of the leading writers on the subject of healing have been influenced by the charismatic thrust in the Catholic Church. It is also interesting to note that *Our Sunday Visitor,* hardly a radical Catholic publication, published an article on January 25, 1987, by Fr. Champlin entitled, "The Traditional Understanding of Healing." The Catholic parish in Coronado, California where I've spent a part of the winter introduced a healing service in March of 1988 as a regular part of its ministry. Few major Christian groups are more open to this ministry than the Catholic Church.

During a charismatic conference in Los Angeles in 1972 I had the good fortune of coming to know Abbot David Geraets of the Benedictine Monastery in Pecos, New Mexico. For the last fourteen years I have returned nearly every year to meet with the community and lecture on various aspects of the Christian life. I know of no other group that integrates the gifts of the Spirit more adequately into the traditional life and practice of the Christian church. Through their publishing house, Dove Publications, they have brought wisdom and depth to those seeking the gifts of the Spirit. In few places have I found a saner and wiser healing ministry. People are healed in mind, soul, and body as they come to the monastery to share in the community life, to make personal retreats, or to take part in the annual healing missions. In the fall of 1986 over six hundred people from all over the United States gathered at the Southern Baptist Conference grounds at Glorietta under the monastery's direction for a conference on psychology and religion. John Sanford and I led these people to consider how these sometimes hostile disciplines can work together to bring healing of soul, mind, and body.

During my first years at Notre Dame, I met Dr. Arnold Bittlinger, who was studying at the John XXIII Ecumenical Institute at St. John's College in Collegeville, Minnesota. He was a leader of the charismatic movement among the Lutherans and other protestants in Germany and Europe. For many summers I lectured at Schloss Craheim in Bavaria. Dr. Bittlinger was instrumental in organizing an ecumenical center there that was much involved in encouraging all the gifts of the Spirit. In 1982 Dr. Bittlinger, in conjunction with Stuart Kingma, M.D., of the Christian Medical Commission of the World Council of Churches, organized a conference on healing and loneliness in Zurich, Switzerland, in which Barbara and I participated. In Germany the charismatic movement had touched the upper and middle classes even more than the less-educated classes. (The movement had begun among the less-educated classes in the United States.) I had already met Larry Christianson, who was a Lutheran minister in the Los Angeles area when I was at St. Luke's Church. He has written several books and emphasized the healing and charismatic experience in that church.

Through a School of Pastoral Care organized by Dr. Francis Whiting for Baptist ministers I first met the Methodist evangelist Tommy Tyson. We complemented each other and soon became good friends. In 1965 I was invited to his hometown of Goldsboro, North Carolina, to develop the theological framework for a healing ministry and the gifts of the Spirit. For the last seven years I have worked with Tommy and his family at their healing retreat center, Aqueduct, near Chapel Hill, North Carolina. Many of the church leaders interested in reactivating healing have spoken there. President Carter's sister, Ruth Carter Stapleton, often spoke there before her untimely death. Her book, *The Gift of Inner Healing*, spurred many people on to fuller lives. Many people have found refreshment, renewal, friendship, warmth, and healing at this retreat center, one of the finest in the country.

Kirkridge is one of the finest retreat centers in the country. It sits high on the Blue Ridge Mountain equidistant from Philadelphia and New York. Over ten years ago Robert Raines, the director of Kirkridge, asked Barbara and me to select a group of leaders and lead a conference on training in the art of healing. Our goal was to provide an understanding of healing that included its physical, emotional, liturgical, and spiritual aspects. The conference drew people from many helping professions, including clergy, social workers, psychologists, nurses, and medical doctors. We have never been able to accommodate all those who wished to attend when we have repeated the conference. We developed a program to effect our goal that we shall describe in detail later. This same basic method has been used with the same effectiveness for the last five years at San Francisco Theological Seminary at San Anselmo, California. The conference there is entitled "Companions on the Inner Way." We believe that we act as true healers for others only as we become their companions and thus enter their conflicts and troubles.

Through the Upper Room Program of the Methodist Church, schools in spiritual disciplines are reaching many clergy and lay people. The Upper Room emphasizes healing and has published James Wagner's excellent book on healing, *Blessed to Be a Blessing*. It also maintains a phone prayer ministry. Hundreds of people call into the Upper Room prayer center for prayers for every human need, including healing of body, mind, and soul.

In the years after *Healing and Christianity* appeared, many books on healing began to be published. One of the most influential was written by Francis MacNutt, a former Dominican priest, entitled *Healing*. An editor at Notre Dame's Ave Maria Press asked me if I would read a manuscript that they were considering, but felt incompetent to judge. It was MacNutt's first book. As I read his book I was reminded of the early church writers on the subject. I encouraged the book's publication. The book was published just before the huge charismatic conference at Notre Dame in 1974, and the entire first printing was sold out. Frank MacNutt later thanked me for having researched the history of healing in the church, for he said it gave him a foundation from which he could write and confirmed his experience.

I met Dennis and Matthew Linn, both Jesuit priests, at a conference. Their ministry and writing have touched the lives of many people. One of their important books, *Healing Life's Hurts: Healing Memories Through Five Stages of Forgiveness*, uses the five stages of transformation that Elisabeth Kübler-Ross observed in dying people. The Linns' books give practical methods of opening ourselves to God's healing power.

Theodore Dobson, also a Catholic priest with whom I have been well acquainted, has emphasized the healing ministry in his excellent book, *Inner Healing, God's Great Assurance*. He now runs a healing and renewal center in Denver. Dobson is one of many Roman Catholic priests who have been awakened through the charismatic movement to the reality of God's loving and healing presence and is communicating the vital message of the early church to hungry and hurting men and women in our time.

One of the most significant developments for the acceptance of the healing ministry in the more conservative side of protestantism occurred at Fuller Seminary in Pasadena, California. Despite the continuous historical record describing a healing ministry in the early church and despite the recognition by many medical professionals of the importance of faith and meaning in the healing process, the academic side of Christianity has shown little interest in the Christian healing ministry. Almost all seminaries have ignored the subject. Barbara and I both spoke in 1982 at my own seminary, the Episcopal Divinity School in Cambridge, Massachusetts, on the importance of the devotional life. I also addressed a class taught by Don Colenback on Christian healing. The class, however, did not survive his demise. It would be difficult to find five seminaries, Catholic and Protestant together, where the subject is taught and the data from the Bible and church history are presented. As I have already indicated, the problem is basically theological.

For this reason the popular course at Fuller Seminary on signs and wonders was a most noteworthy event. This course and the reaction to it is described in *Signs and Wonders Today. Healing and Christianity* was used as a basic text in that course. John Wimber and Kevin Springer's book, *Power Healing,* is a fine statement of the healing movement in that branch of the church.

In 1955 the dean of the Church Divinity School of the Pacific invited me to speak on healing. The invitation was withdrawn, however, because the faculty felt that this was entirely too dangerous a subject for seminary students to consider. Later a limited program was presented because a wealthy patron interested in healing paid all expenses.

A lecturing tour in late 1987 took my wife and me through South Africa. We found an incredibly vital church. As so often in history when the church suffers persecution, it becomes vital again. We found an active healing ministry in the Methodist Church, the Anglican Church, and the Roman Catholic Church. In addition we visited the Zionist churches in Transkei and talked with three of the leaders of the Zionist movement. These churches combine much of traditional African culture with Christianity. One estimate places the number of those active in the Zionist movement at four and one half million people, the largest group in any of the black churches. In his book *Sound the Trumpet of Zion,* Professor H. L. Pretorius makes a careful analysis of this movement in the controversial homeland of Transkei. A large majority of the leaders have been called into the church because they were healed in a Zionist church. Several leaders tell of visions through which they were transformed and called into ministry and into the founding of new Zionist churches. Healing and the valuing of the dream-vision are as common there as in the early church. The Zionist leaders have introduced into their congregations the practice of healing common among the medicine people of African culture, an interest, as we have seen earlier, that was an essential practice of the first five centuries of Christian life.

When I gave the Finch Lectures in 1985 at Fuller Seminary I found a growing awareness that open-minded clinical psychological practice and transforming Christian spiritual practices need to befriend one another. I also learned that the School of Missions at Fuller had come to realize that much of Christian missionary work in Third World countries had resulted in secularizing these people rather than Christianizing them. Dispensationalism was seen as a form of secularism. Indeed the worldview of many of these non-Western people is actually closer to the point of view of the New Testament than was that of the missionaries who were trying to bring Christianity to these people. No wonder that John Wimber and Peter Wagner had developed a course of healing in such an atmosphere.

What happens when the various different Christian churches do not continue the church's healing ministry? The vacuum is filled by groups that introduce healing through Eastern religious points of view or through psycho-religious practices. There are many places where one can go to study healing within this context. In February 1987 on a plane to Denver, I began to talk with a senior vice president of a major national brokerage company. He was going to a seminar at one of the numerous places near Denver that teaches self-fulfillment, healing, and transformation without reference to Christianity. As we talked he was surprised to find that I had an interest in the same goals within the Christian perspective. He didn't even realize that Christianity had anything to offer in healing and transformation. He had no idea that there was Christian meditation such as I describe in *The Other Side of Silence*.

In the last fifteen years more books may well have been written from a psychological or medical point of view on the subject of healing through healthy emotional development and creative meditative practices than by church people. We turn now to a new understanding of the importance of meaning, faith, and meditation—within the medical world, to the influence of emotions, social relationships and personal attitudes—on the healing process.

CHAPTER 11

Body, Emotions, and Healing

In the middle years of the twentieth century, many people in the medical profession felt confident that the nature of disease would soon be fully understood. Within scarcely a hundred years, some of the most dangerous diseases had been almost eliminated. Physicians had even found ways to repair the human heart, and organ transplants had become possible. We had gained an understanding of the human body, including the enormously complex brain, the immune system, and blood chemistry, that could hardly have been dreamed of a century before. However, in the process a mechanistic approach to the human body had been growing among medical professionals.

All these advances were realized as medicine took the one-way approach to disease discussed in Chapter Two. This approach was needed, but gradually physicians came to view the human body merely as a complex aggregation of atoms reacting to physical laws, like any other aggregation of matter. Hospitals treated sick people as if they were mere chemical reactions in a sterile test tube. But as one friend in the medical profession—a person whose quiet concern and humor have helped bring many to health—recently remarked to a group of students, "You cannot cure an ulcer patient merely by performing a partial gastrectomy, or an asthmatic patient with an injection of aminophylin, or even an ulcerated colitis victim with a removal of the sigmoid colon. The separation of the psyche and the soma can only be effected by a removal of the cerebrum, and that has not been medically accepted."

Even mental illness came to be considered the result of some damage to, or deficiency in, the brain or nervous system. In 1913 hopes were high for finding a concrete cause of all emotional disturbances. But neurologists were able to account for only a few, like those of speech or body movements. As a matter of fact, in an autopsy under the microscope, a psychotic brain could not be distinguished from a normal brain. However, with the discovery of endorphins and the many drugs that helped to control anxiety, depression, and even some forms of psychosis, a great optimism grew. Many mental hospitals closed and turned their inmates out onto the street, to make up at least half of the homeless people in the United States.

An autonomous and nonphysical soul or psyche could not be a part of this closed mechanical system and neither could such a psyche—or even God—affect it. Mind and body together, the human being, was only one part of a vast system of matter, a machine which had been programmed and sealed. There was no room for argument. This basic assumption was accepted, not only by physicians, but by philosophers, theologians, and ordinary Christians. But Einstein, the Curies, Kurt Godel, Heisenberg, Freud, Jung, Mircea Eliade, and Teilhard de Chardin, among others, began to uncover a very different structure in the actualities they worked with. As new facts poured in from all sides, the assumption of the mechanistic naturalism of the universe began to shift. Paul Davies in *God and the New Physical* points up the anomalies and confusion reigning in the theoretical physics. If we cannot be sure about matter, how can we be sure of a body made of it?

Medical practitioners began to question basic assumptions, as they realized that certain psychoneuroses were simply being "talked away." The brain was still the same cellular organism, but the mind could be freed from sickness by understanding itself in a new light. Not only that, physical conditions such as hysterical blindness and paralysis— conditions that could closely simulate almost any organic malady— were cured at the same time, as were functional diseases of the intestines, heart, and other organs. Most of these conditions could be imitated by the person under posthypnotic suggestion.

Freud made a public address on psychoanalysis in 1909, at Clark University in Worcester, Massachusetts. To his great surprise, he found the audience interested in discussing freely and scientifically theories that medical circles in Vienna, had rejected, and he gained important backing at Harvard. Within twenty-five years clinical psychiatry had accepted a psychosomatic view, agreeing that the *psyche*, or mind, and the *soma*, or body, could really influence each other. In 1935 Dr. Flanders Dunbar, a young woman teaching in the medical school of Columbia University, published an exhaustive survey of all the research on psychosomatic interrelationships up to that time. Dr. Dunbar's book, *Emotions and Bodily Changes*, laid a firm base for further study. Four years later the journal *Psychosomatic Medicine* was founded. It has remained an important source of information and communication for those on this growing edge of knowledge.

Meanwhile World War I had introduced the concept of psychoneurosis into the headlines and polite conversation with the colorful term *shell shock*. The first textbook on psychosomatic medicine, published in 1943, pointed out that this country had already spent a billion dollars for physical care of veterans with neuropsychiatric disorders—that is, physical problems with a psychological base.[1] The authors quoted from several sources to make a strong plea for psychotherapy, so that these veterans and their families could return to normal life. They made clear that the neurosis is a general problem and that war merely offers a wider opportunity for its expression.

World War II showed the importance of psychiatry as a general medical tool. W. C. Menninger, then chief of the Army Division of Psychiatry, explained that "every army physician was confronted with a far greater number of patients having physical complaints in which no organic pathology could be found, than he saw in civilian life."[2] In the medical and surgical wards up to one fourth of the soldiers suffered from purely functional disturbances, particularly among the heart and gastrointestinal cases, while two-thirds of the psychiatric patients had physical complaints. The neurotic or emotionally disturbed organ was a startling reality.

The medical profession is divided in its theory and practice. On one side we find those who cling to the materialistic view. No one summarizes that point of view with greater perception and clarity than Melvin Konner in his book, *The Tangled Wing: Biological Constraints on the Human Spirit* (1982). He is violently opposed to B. F. Skinner's materialism because he doubts the effect of conditioning. Konner believes that human behavior is conditioned by the very structure of the genes. He states that human beings, both as personalities and as mechanisms, are merely the means through which genes reproduce themselves. This attitude pervades most medical schools in theory and practice and is the basic framework of many physicians, particularly of specialists, who do not have to deal with the entire person. Recently a gastrointestinal specialist told a close friend of mine that his ulcerated colitis was a purely physical problem and had no emotional involvement. When I related this comment to a newly graduated medical doctor, he laughed

---

[1] Edward Weiss and O. Spurgeon English,*Psychosomatic Medicine: The Clinical Application of Psychopathology to General Medical Problems* (1943).
[2] *Ibid.*, 2d ed. (1949), p. 54.

and pulled out his recent text on that specialty and showed me a passage stating that ulcerated colitis was one of the physical diseases most likely to be the result of psychological stress.

I could cite many examples of medical literature cast in this mold, but shall focus instead on the growing number of physicians who take another tack. I shall discuss some specific diseases where the evidence is quite conclusive and then describe the sympathetic nervous system, which serves as a bridge between emotions and body. I will conclude this chapter by discussing the emotions and attitudes that seem to have the most potent influence on the body.

A New Attitude Emerges

For many years, while rector of St. Luke's Church, I had lunch every other week with Dr. Leo Froke, a psychiatrist who had left the practice of internal medicine when he realized that he was treating the symptoms rather than the causes of disease. One of the most provocative books that he lent me was William Sargant's *Battle for the Mind*.[3] Sargent had investigated faith healing and had discovered how frequently it worked. A decade later, in his book *Persuasion and Healing*, Dr. Jerome Frank, a professor of psychiatry at Johns Hopkins wrote that today's medical evidence emphasizes the profound influence of emotions on health and suggests that anxiety and despair can be lethal, while confidence and hope are life-giving. The assumptions of modern Western society, which include mind-body dualism, has had difficulty incorporating this obvious fact and has therefore tended to underemphasize it. In concluding his study he wrote,

The question of how far a physician should go to meet a patient's expectations is a thorny one. Obviously he cannot use methods in which he himself does not believe. Moreover, reliance on the healing powers of faith, if it led to neglect of proper diagnostic or treatment procedures, would clearly be irresponsible. On the other hand, faith may be a specific antidote for certain emotions such as fear or discouragement, which may constitute the essence of a patient's illness. For such patients, the mobilization of expectant trust by whatever means may be as much an etiological remedy as penicillin for pneumonia.[4]

A delightful discussion of faith and healing is written by Harley Street British psychiatrist, Alan McGlashan, and entitled *Gravity and Levity*. In a chapter entitled "Concerning Humbug," he writes,

---

[3] William Sargant, *Battle for the Mind* (1961).
[4] Jerome D. Frank, *Persuasion and Healing* (1969), pp. 61 and 233–34. This understanding has spread widely in recent years.

It is in fact very difficult to cure anybody of anything by means of a remedy in which you yourself have no faith. The successful doctor, no less than the successful "quack," is the man who is really convinced he has got something. Every medical man has had experiences of achieving impressive results with a certain drug, so long as he believes in it himself. As soon as he has some failures and begins to doubt its remedial powers, the results on patients tail off, and in a few months the "wonder drug" is, as far as that practitioner is concerned, discarded and forgotten.

He goes on to say that the efficacy of the treatment applies not only to drugs,

but also more alarmingly, to surgical operations. It is written in the memory of many of us that a child who had several attacks of sore throat would almost automatically have its tonsils and adenoids removed. Statistics and authoritative textbooks of the period "proved" how correct and beneficial this procedure was. Now when belief in this particular measure has dwindled, statistics and authoritative textbooks of today "prove" precisely the opposite. This is not due to deliberate manipulation of the statistics. The procedure is no longer believed in: so it no longer works. The thing which was officially approved of by one medical generation is then scornfully condemned by the next.

McGlashan then speaks about some of the remedies which have had enthusiastic support in past generations—remedies such as usnea, shoe leather, and urine.[5] He also calls attention to the importance of the doctor's attitude, noting that before antibiotics few medicines actually had much healing influence.

During the same period that McGlashan was coming to his conclusions, a young oncologist (a medical doctor whose speciality is the treatment of cancer) and his psychologist wife had found that the use of imagery lengthened the lives of some of their cancer patients and brought remission of the disease to a significant number of them. Carl and Stephany Simonton presented their views before the Assembly of Episcopal Hospitals and Chaplains in 1975.[6] In 1978 they presented their conclusions in their controversial book, *Getting Well Again: A Step by Step Self-Help Guide to Overcoming Cancer for Patients and Their Families.*

---

[5] R. Alan McGlashan, *Gravity and Levity* (1976), pp. 37–38. Dr. McGlashan also mentions healing which seems to flow from the individual with no desire on the part of the healer, a kind of natural healer. In 1960 a British physician wrote a book entitled *The Nature of Healing*, anonymously, on this subject. Another such book was called to my attention by C. G. Jung: *The Reluctant Healer: A Remarkable Autobiography* by William J. MacMillan (New York: Thomas Crowell, 1952).

[6] The Institute of Religion and Medicine, Bishop Anderson House, 1743 W. Harrison Street, Chicago, IL 60612.

They show the strong correlation between cumulative stressful events and the onset of serious illness, including cancer. I had found the use of imagery essential in dealing with depression. When they spoke at a conference on healing organized by a group of professors at Notre Dame, I talked at length with Carl Simonton. He told me that he had first come upon the idea of using imagery in dealing with his facial skin cancer. He felt that he had to deal with his own fear of "losing face." One of Simonton's techniques is to have the patient imagine the body's T-cells (cells in the body that fight disease and cancerous cells) attacking and devouring the cancer cells. Earlier I mentioned the lapsed-time three-thousand-magnification movies of living lung tissue which show lymphocytes attacking cancer cells. It is much easier to use the imagination when one has seen these actual battles taking place.

Many physicians recommend meditation and guided imagery as an aid in the treatment of disease. Images and emotions may well be different aspects of one reality, as James Hillman suggests in his excellent book, *Emotions: A Comprehensive Phenomenology of Theories and Their Meaning for Therapy*. Herbert Benson, M.D., found that Transcendental Meditation had observable physiological effects on the human body, lowering blood pressure and altering blood chemistry. When the sponsors of Transcendental Meditation used his evidence for promotion, Dr. Benson continued his studies and showed that the same effect could be obtained using the word "one" in meditation and dispensing with the religious trappings of Hindu mantras. He published his conclusions in *The Relaxation Response*. In his 1984 book, *Beyond the Relaxation Response*, he advocates prayer and meditation to release the powerful effects of faith. When interviewed for the May 1984 issue of *American Health*, he stated that only 25 percent of the patients in a doctor's office can be helped by medicine. Another article in the same issue, "Healers in the Mainstream," tells of cardiologist William Haynes who prays for his patients using the laying-on-of-hands. A group of like-minded doctors have formed the Christian Medical Foundation. A questionnaire sent to doctors reveals that a large percentage of those responding pray for patients. Dr. Kenneth Bakken, who has attended and also lectured at the Kirkridge healing conference, combined his Christian faith and his medical knowledge in St. Luke's Health Ministries and has described his theory and practice in his book, *The Call to Wholeness*. Jeanne Achterberg's *Imagery in Healing* is one of the most recent and comprehensive treatments of the enormous effect of emotions and images on mental and physical health. Some of this enthusiasm has trickled down to our family practitioner in our rural town on the northern coast of California. A friend went to him for high blood pressure: part of his treatment plan included a time of meditation daily.

Few people have had a greater influence on popular interest in nonmedical healing than Norman Cousins, former editor of the *Saturday Review of Literature*. Cousins wrote an article for *Saturday Review* entitled "The Mysterious Placebo—How Mind Helps Medicine Work." He also wrote an account of his unexpected recovery from a serious illness for the *New England Journal of Medicine*. He later wrote several books on the importance of the patient's attitudes in recovering from disease. He has lectured on this subject at the medical school of the University of California, Los Angeles.

While Cousins was editor of Saturday Review he published an amazing article on healing entitled, "The Miracle of Regeneration: Can Human Limbs Grow Back?" by Susan Scheifelbein. She noted that salamanders naturally grow back a tail when it is cut off and described experiments showing that when a frog's leg is amputated, it can grow back as long as it is kept irritated and not allowed to heal over. Most of a rat's leg has been regrown through a similar procedure. Each cell seemed to have the wisdom to know what kind of cell needed to be produced next to it. This knowledge was the basis for cell cloning. Much of plastic surgery depends upon this principle.

In his book *The Body is the Hero* Dr. Ronald J. Glasser suggests that the human body is like an enormous movable city populated by many trillion individuals. Like any city that can only survive because of the different skills of its citizens, so the body is made up of cells with very different functions. The body has a communication system for dealing with the outer world and the inner one as well. The city-body has a ventilation system, sewage system as well as a communication system. The body has a billion miles of freeways, roads and alleys, stores and factories producing everything the body needs: food, light, heating and disposal of wastes. To keep the body-city functioning all it needs is a steady stream of essential raw materials and a method of disposing of waste. Dr. Glasser suggests that the body, like a city, is subject to disasters. It may be invaded by hostile creatures or smashed by outer injury. On the inside roads can be blocked, electrical systems can break down, ventilation can fail and communication systems can get mixed up. And even more important some of the cell-individuals may go wild and there can be insurrection or crime; these conditions are called diseases in the body. Dr. Paul Brand and Phillip Yancey describe some of the astounding wisdom built into the human body in their book, *Fear-*

fully and Wonderfully Made. David Black's article, "Medicine and the Body" is one of the finest articles on the interrelationship of mind and body.

Robert John, dean of the School of Engineering at Princeton University, has done some careful work on the capacities of the human mind. His article, "Psychic Process, Energy Transfer, and Things That Go Bump in the Night," classifies Psi phenomena and includes healing under the category of psychokinesis, the power of mind over matter. If our human caring and faith do have an observable effect upon physical reality, how can we doubt that the reality that created the human mind has an infinitely greater power?

Lawrence LeShan has been much interested in human experience of a nonphysical world. In his book, *The Medium, The Mystic and The Physicist*, he showed that the language of the theoretical physicist can hardly be distinguished from that of the religious mystic. His book, *You Can Fight For Your Life: Emotional Factors in the Causation of Cancer*, covers much the same ground as the Simontons. At one time he studied many religious healers. He found that some of them were genuine and really did effect remarkable cures. In analyzing his data he discovered that these healers had one characteristic in common: genuine love for others and a belief that they were channels of a greater love than their own.[7] An excellent and recent testimony by a physician on the importance of caring, courage, and religious faith is Bernie Siegel's *Love, Medicine and Miracles*. The evidence continues to increase.

Dolores Krieger, a registered nurse with a doctorate in nursing, showed that training nurses in therapeutic touch produced a statistically significant rise in hemoglobin in those so treated. Her findings were reported in *The American Journal of Nursing* and later in her book *The Therapeutic Touch*. Christianity has departed so far from its roots that she asked a Christian minister why he had come to a conference on healing that she was leading. Confirmation of some exchange of energy in the laying-on-of-hands appears in Kirilian photography. Pictures taken of healers and patients before and after therapeutic touch show greater energy fields around the healers' hands than before the experience and a diminished field in the healer afterward; at the same time the patient shows an increase in energy after the laying-on-of-hands.[8]

---

[7] *Prevention*, March 1977.

[8] The data for this is found in Charles Panati's book, *Supersenses* (1974) and in Kendall Johnson's *Photographing the Non-material World* (1975).

We human beings apparently are far more than purely material beings and can be carriers of infinitely more spiritual and healing power than most of us imagine.

The most impressive medical evidence on the effect of touch and human caring that I have found is that of James Lynch of the University of Maryland, a psychologist teaching psychiatry in the medical school there. In his first book, *The Broken Heart: The Medical Consequences of Loneliness*, he reviewed the work of Rene Spitz showing that babies in orphanages who are not touched and foundled often die of *mirasmus*. Lynch goes on to provide statistics showing that single people have higher death rates in nearly all major disease categories, particularly heart disease. And yet in the most important long-term study of heart disease, the Framingham study, marital status was not even recorded for each patient. He then demonstrates the quieting effect of human touch on the severely diseased human heart, even the touch of a nurse merely taking the pulse.

In *The Language of the Heart*, published in 1985, Lynch offers a new model for medicine, claiming that most medicine has viewed each human "body-person" as autonomous and separate. He was drawn to his subject by his own problem with blushing. His studies of the effect of talking on blood pressure and the catastrophic results of feeling alienated and alone on blood pressure, show that we are part of an invisible social milieu and this milieu has a profound effect upon people's bodily health. Once we believe, along with Teilhard de Chardin, that we are a part of divine milieu as well as a social one, we can understand why being out of touch with this divine reality can cause emotional and physical disease. Among the avant garde in medicine I find more belief in love and faith as healing agents than I find among most Christian clergy. Lynch deplores the fact that the church has to a large extent accepted the outmoded rational materialism of medicine. Dr. Provonsha points out that the real spirit behind modern medicine is not Hippocrates, but Jesus of Nazareth (see Appendix A).

One of the most impressive statements about the effect of our psyche on our bodies and their diseases is by the neurologist Oliver Sacks in his scholarly, yet delightfully readable, case studies of neurological disease, entitled *The Man Who Mistook His Wife for a Hat*.[9] He pleads for an understanding that mind or psyche is more than just neurology and

---

[9] Oliver Sacks, *The Man Who Mistook His Wife for a Hat* (1987), p. 97. For the importance of the placebo effect that relies upon the influence of our mental attitude see *Mayo Clinic Health Letter*, July 1987, pp. 5–7.

writes: "Complementary to any purely medicinal or medical approach there must also be an 'existential' approach: in particular, a sensitive understanding of action, art and play as being in essence healthy and free, and thus antagonistic to crude drives and impulsions, to the 'blind force of the subcortex' from which these patients suffer." In a sensitive and moving way he writes of a man who had lost all memory from 1945 until the present and who couldn't relate to other human beings. However, at the Catholic Eucharist in the hospital in which he was cared for he was totally engaged and quite clearly in touch with some reality.

The most comprehensive survey of the various ways in which our mental attitude can effect our dreaming, our intelligence, and our ability to overcome the effects of disease is found in the July 1987 issue of *American Health*. A series of articles details the most important scientific work in this increasingly accepted field and reviews the books relating to this subject. Many of these writers suggest methods of tapping the power of the imagination. I have suggested similar methods of using imagination to come into contact with religious reality in *The Other Side of Silence*.

Physicians Kenneth Bakken and Kathleen Hofeller have written a fine study of the relationship of emotions and healing in *The Journey Towards Wholeness: A Christ-Centered Approach to Health and Healing*. The authors summarize another line of investigation described by Blair Justice in his book *Who Gets Sick—Thinking and Health*. Both conscious and unconscious mental events affect the brain's incredibly intricate chemical balance and play an important part in both sickness and health.

Research psychologist Albert Rossi and renowned biochemist Candace Pert, chief of brain biochemistry at the National Institute of Mental Health, have hypothesized that the brain is an incredible apothecary that controls the health of the body through chemical transmitters, messenger molecules, which use either nerve fibers or the bloodstream to reach target sites. The brain can act directly and quickly through neurotransmitters such as norephinephrine or dopamine, or indirectly and more slowly (minutes to hours) through a cortex-hypothalamus-pituitary-gland-adrenal sequence. The signals that the brain/mind sends are profoundly influenced by the emotional, physical—and, we would submit, spiritual—environment of the individual. For example, PET [positron emission tomography] scanning of the brain shows that levels of norepinephrine, dopamine, and serotonin, chemicals associated with feelings of reward or pleasure, tend to decline when an individual is depressed. Excessive amounts of norepinephrine have been found in persons who tend to exhibit hostile attitudes. The presence of this chemical, associated with arousal of the sympathetic nervous system, has been linked to damage of the lining of the coronary arteries and elevated blood pressure. Over time, these conditions may lead to myocardial infarction or other heart disease.[10]

Perhaps the best way to illustrate the changing medical attitude is to look at the thinking in certain specific medical areas: for instance, tuberculosis. This is a physically communicated disease, caused without exception by the presence of *bacillus tuberculosis* in the affected area. It has been controlled by antibiotics and is a comparatively negligible cause of death today in this country, whereas in 1900 it was the leading cause. In short, it is a specifically physical disease about which medicine has a great store of knowledge, and yet, as with every other disease of every kind, in its etiology and pathology there is still a blank page.

In a time when one-seventh of the world's population was dying of tuberculosis, Sir William Osler, the greatest medical teacher of his day, warned his profession that the fate of tuberculosis patients depended more on what they had in their heads that on what was in their chests. It was known then that 90 percent of the world's city dwellers who died from other causes had small tuberculous lesions in their bodies. Today's wide use of X-ray has shown that few people in the past escaped infection at some time in their lives.

Allen K. Krause, who was probably the leading writer on tuberculosis in this country, noted that the bacillus lives and breeds persistently in the dirt and darkness found in tenements. In his book *Environment and Resistance in Tuberculosis*, he pointed out that tenement dwellers nearly all had live tubercule bacilli in them. However, by far the greater number of these refractory subjects never developed a symptom, and they lived to die of other diseases. Dr. Krause gave a real place to personality disturbance in the environment (much as James Lynch is now proposing) that either nourishes or retards disease. He wrote:

When, sick with angina pectoris and aware of the influence of psychic disturbance upon his physical condition, John Hunter said that his life was in the hands of any rascal in London who chose to take it, he simply indicated the possibly more disastrous effects of an environment about which our books on general medicine are strangely or perversely silent, yet which drives thousands of us mortals to our practitioners. This is the environment of personal association—of antagonistic personal association, in particular. . . . Until recently, when psychiatrists again brought this type of environment into prominence and coined a new nomenclature to speak intelligibly to one another of "repressions" and "conflicts," and the morbid results of these, formal medical instruc-

---

[10] Kenneth Bakken and Kathleen Hoffeller, *The Journey Towards Wholeness: A Christ-Centered Approach to Health and Healing* (1988).

tion, given to more material and mechanical views of disease, was apparently oblivious to its existence and influence.[11]

How unfortunate that sixty-two years later many people are surprised at James Lynch's evidence and theories.

Another leading permanent destroyer of health among communicable diseases is syphilis. But in spite of all that has been learned, the unexplained fact remains that over half the cases of untreated syphilis are spontaneously cured and show no sign of a third stage except for a positive blood reaction. The recent epidemic of acquired immune deficiency syndrome (AIDS) is another example of the different ways in which our bodies react to this virus. Probably a million people in the United States have been infected. Less than ten percent develop the deadly disease. Another twenty percent or so develop AIDS-related conditions, and the other roughly seventy percent appear to have no effects from the virus except the presence of the AIDS antibody in their blood.[12]

A wound that heals slowly, or is infected and fails to respond to treatment, poses direct questions about varying recuperative power. As physicians have reminded me on several occasions, it is not what they do that actually heals. Without the body's recuperative power they could do next to nothing—no surgery or suturing, for instance, would be possible. What the physician does is to remove the roadblocks so that the forces within the individual are free to work for healing and restoration. Yet these forces that heal may be slow to respond in one individual, or fail entirely in another.

These are questions raised by physicians themselves in the areas of medicine's greatest successes. They come up precisely because of those successes. No one any longer has to touch and bury the victims of black smallpox, or fear having a baby in the hospital because of puerperal fever, or see a child die of diphtheria. Since so many external and tangible causes of disease have been met and prevented, many physicians have turned to inner questions. Endocrinology has revealed the indispensable functions of the internal secretions; work on allergy has shown the body's own production of indisposing histamines; various fields are studying the maze of complex chemicals produced to keep

---

[11] Allen K. Krause, *Environment and Resistance in Tuberculosis* (1923), p. 11. Thomas Mann's novel *The Magic Mountain* is set in a tuberculosis sanitarium and is a fictional description of this reality.

[12] *Psychology Today*, March 1987, p. 18. However, the disease is so new that all the data about it is questionable. Some researchers believe a much larger percentage will come down with AIDS.

the body's economy going; while psychiatry, finally, is glimpsing how the mind relates to the whole.

Still both doctor and patient have time today to worry about illness that disables or incapacitates, and there is enough to worry over. Public health surveys show that nearly two-thirds of the adults outside of institutions in this country suffer from one or more chronic conditions.[13] These are mainly diseases whose causes are unknown, or which arise within the body itself. It is recognized today that emotional factors play a large part in them. While we may prefer to believe that the doctor can prescribe just the right pill or that the surgeon can simply remove the source of our pain, physicians have had to face the results of such practices. Adolf Meyer, who became world-famous in psychiatry during his many years of teaching at Johns Hopkins Medical School, once reminded the medical profession, "It is sad that we still do get patients who arrive practically eviscerated, for a last trial, which very often ought to have been the first—namely, that of getting the life adjustment within the range of socialized health offered while it can be fully used."[14]

It is odd how often commonly used folk sayings speak of emotions in terms of physical symptoms. Without stopping to think, one says, "I can't stomach it!" "It took my breath away!" "I was scared stiff." Or one speaks truthfully of an "angry throat," or tells someone, "You give me a pain in the neck!" When we stop to think (and perhaps we should do so more often), we see how common the knowledge is that emotions and feelings have a real physical effect. Stagefright, or blushing, or waking up afraid in the night bring actual physiological changes in the body, only a part of which are sensed by the mind. The same kinds of changes in muscular tension, blood pressure, and glandular secretion going on inside sick people's bodies can have a decisive influence on how they react to an illness.

Sociological studies have shown clearly that when white people have brought their cultural patterns to primitive areas, deaths among the natives have been due not only to the new diseases the whites brought, but also to the disruption of social life that occurred. Robbed of their culture and deprived of meaningful existence, native people have died like flies. As John Cowper Powys shows in *The Meaning of Culture*, life

---

[13] *Limitation of Activity and Mobility Due to Chronic Conditions: United States, July 1965–June 1966* (May 1968).

[14] Adolf Meyer, "The Psychiatric Aspects of Gastroenterology," *American Journal of Surgery* 15 (March 1932): 508–09.

can seldom exist without the matrix of culture. It must be remembered, however, that those who profess to have no purpose in life often have an unconscious will to live, while others who say they want to live may be unaware of their deep meaninglessness. Still, it is a safe conclusion that life unsupported by meaning seldom lasts long; it is terminated in one way or another.

A dramatic experience brought this home to me many years ago. It happened in a small hospital where my mother had been confined off and on for months with a heart condition. As usual, one gets to know a great deal about other patients and their troubles. When we were visiting one day, we heard that a woman with a condition similar to my mother's had just been admitted. Later in the week I was surprised to learn that she had died. The physician commented to us that she had not been particularly sick, but had no desire to live. Then he told me, "If your mother had as sound a heart as the dead woman had, she would be out playing golf right now."

The studies of taboo deaths among primitive peoples, and also of certain deaths in prisoner-of-war camps, indicate a close parallel. Dr. Jerome Frank has surveyed this material as well as relevant research on animals, showing that when terror or despair strikes either humans or animals, deaths can occur from this alone.[15] Recently I was told much the same thing by a surgeon to whom I happened to mention these studies. He said that he tried never to initiate surgery when a patient was extremely fearful. If he could postpone it, he did so, because he had seen so many unfortunate deaths from operating under those conditions.

Granting that these things are true, how can something as intangible as emotion have such effect on the physical body?

A Bridge Between Mind and Body

One of the principal ways that emotions produce direct physical changes in the body is through the autonomic nervous system. This remarkable mechanism, which actually consists of two systems, enables the human body to respond effectively to many situations without conscious direction. The parasympathetic part builds up the body and stores energy. It stimulates the organs that digest and assimilate food by dilating the blood vessels that supply them and at the same time

---

[15] Frank, *op. cit.*, pp. 38–43; also Herman Feifel, ed., *The Meaning of Death* (1959), pp. 302–12.

slowing down the heart and lowering blood pressure. It also has protective functions, such as contracting the pupils of the eyes against light or the bronchial tubes against foreign matter.

The sympathetic system, on the other hand, prepares for a quick release of energy, organizing the whole body to meet an emergency. It works mostly in opposition to the parasympathetic system and countermands its directions. The impulses are sent out all at once, changing the blood supply and ordering new secretions and chemicals needed for exertion.[16]

Both these parts of the nervous system originate in the hypothalamus, a part of the midbrain near the head of the spinal column which evolved early in vertebrate life. Unlike the cortex, which can be consciously activated, it is not under ordinary conscious control. Once an impression is received in the hypothalamus and the autonomic nervous system is set in action, one can rarely if ever just switch it off.[17]

For example, suppose that we are driving a car at a reasonable rate in a thoroughly law-abiding manner. Suddenly there is a siren or flashing red light in the rearview mirror. As we come to a stop we find our breathing heavy, our hearts pounding, our bodies tense. It makes no difference whether we want to have these reactions or not; we may not feel any conscious fear of authority figures at all. But when the officer looms up, these reactions occur. Once we perceive something that is alarming, the body is activated by the sympathetic nervous system. It can seldom be controlled by logical thinking. We may be quite unaware that anything is frightening us, but our unconscious fear still triggers this system. In fact, if we constantly react from sympathetic stimulation without seeing a reason, we may be quite sure that an unknown fear is affecting us. There is no point in telling people to "snap out of it"; most people who have such reactions cannot do so. Only as our fear is removed can our reactions be controlled.

The sympathetic system organizes a fight or flight response to danger. Aggressive emotions—resentment, hostility, or hatred—set the sympathetic nervous system in motion. Active emotional withdrawal—

---

[16] We are describing the principal and general function of the sympathetic system; these nerve pathways also carry specific messages to individual organs—for instance, to dilate the pupils of the eyes to adjust to darkness.

[17] James Hillman has made an excellent study of the whole subject of emotion from a phenomenological point of view. In his book, *Emotion* (1964), pp. 214–18, he calls attention to the studies by M. Choisy of a group of rigorously disciplined yogis who were able to resist physiological reaction when presented with cobras and scorpions. This is extremely rare, however. Whereas logical thinking seldom blocks or changes autonomic reactions, the use of images can sometimes do so.

concern, apprehension, or anxiety—sets the sympathetic system in action. Anger and fear are strangely similar; indeed they are opposite sides of the same coin. Both are reactions to a threatening situation. In anger we feel that we can meet the threat by attack, while in fear we feel that we are inadequate to deal with it and must run away or freeze, but the physiological response is almost identical.

A complex chain reaction begins with a chemical discharge into the pituitary, which then alerts the adrenals and other glands to start the chain of commands. Immediately the blood vessels to the stomach and intestinal areas are shut down. Digestion, assimilation, and elimination all nearly halt, and blood driven away from these areas is sent to the brain, lungs, and external muscles, where energy is suddenly required. A flow of adrenalin speeds the tempo. Both heart and lungs are stimulated to move fuel and oxygen faster. The bronchial tubes relax, admitting more oxygen. The liver and other storage depots are directed to release carbohydrates as quickly utilizable blood sugar. Blood pressure rises; the clotting time of the blood decreases as the body prepares itself for a possible wound.

What an admirable system this is for the primitive human being suddenly confronted by a bear or an attacking enemy. Immediately the whole body is mobilized for action. Energy is concentrated for release. The vegetative tendencies are inhibited, and a spurt of adrenalin spurs the person under attack to instant decision and action. Without any conscious thought the individual is ready to put maximum energy into a fight, or to turn and run faster than normal and climb trees unclimbable before. The sympathetic system works magnificently in the face of real physical danger. But it is a bit superfluous if the anger, resentment, or fear is directed toward the stock market or one's mother-in-law, toward government spending, or the IRS, the inefficiency of an airline or a threatening world, or just a meaningless existence. Yet these threats can produce the same physical reactions produced by a charging bear, or a berserk cave person.

These fears or resentments have the same effect on our bodies even when we are unaware of being afraid or angry. They may be attitudes tucked away in an overlooked corner of the psyche, and yet they may still touch off the entire reaction, just as if we were constantly confronted by a raging beast. But if the "beast" is an unconscious worry, our energy is not directed or utilized. Instead, the entire body is constantly ordered to prepare for what does not happen. The parasympathetic impulses, directing our organs to return to their natural functions, are constantly contradicted. Unconscious fear simply defeats the autonomic system search for balance between hunger and exertion.[18] Indeed, the threats and fears of which we are not conscious cannot be dealt with.

It may seem implausible that people who appear calm and controlled may be undergoing these pronounced physical reactions in their bodies, produced by fears they are unaware of or by anger they do not know they harbor. Aldous Huxley has called people who cannot hold their temper "adrenalin addicts." How they hurt themselves, and others when that anger suddenly emerges and strikes another! But *unconscious* fear and anger can react incessantly on our hearts and kidneys, our stomachs, the circulatory system, or the immune system, without our knowing it, until the structure of one organ or another has been changed enough to cause pain. The lie detector functions on exactly this principle, recording physical reactions to memories a person wants to conceal. A medical "lie detector" has shown clearly that the same reactions occur in patients who may not know they are angry or afraid.

This technique was used to study hypertension or high blood pressure, the greatest health problem of adult middle life.[19] In one study the physician talked with patients about everyday things, while the the patients' blood pressure and flow of blood in the kidneys were recorded. When the patients discussed very personal matters, their blood pressure rose even though they showed little or no emotion outwardly. At the same time the blood vessels in the kidneys were constricted

---

[18] There may also be a withdrawal reaction that results in constant overstimulation of the parasympathetic system, as we shall see.

[19] The deadly effects of hypertension on the eyes, brain, heart, and kidneys are caused by constriction of the peripheral arteries, which cuts down the blood supply to certain areas. Nearly a fourth of all deaths after fifty are still due to this disorder, most of them resulting from stroke, heart failure, or kidney failure.

A great deal has been learned about its cause. While a tendency seems to be inherited, in practically every case there is also a direct relation to emotional tensions. It is generally associated with damage to the kidneys from severe limitation of the blood supply caused by the sympathetic nervous system. This first began to be understood about 1933, when an ingenious silver clamp was applied to a dog's renal arteries; the kidneys deteriorated, and the dog developed persistent high blood pressure. He then remained diseased even though the nerves were severed so that the sympathetic nervous system no longer functioned. The researchers suggested that the starved kidney releases a chemical into the blood stream that continues to constrict feeder arteries all through the body, further damaging the kidneys so that the hypertensive reaction thus becomes self-perpetuating. The later work of Hans Selye at Montreal University has shown that this may well be the case. See "The General Adaptation Syndrome and Diseases of Adaptation," *Journal of Clinical Endocrinology* 6 (February 1946): 217 ff.

In addition, hypertension is almost entirely a disease of Western civilization. American blacks have no racial inheritance of it. Yet black people in this country have a tendency to develop this disorder two and a half to three times as great as the white American, and statistics show that it generally runs a severer course in blacks than in white people. Weiss and English, *op. cit.*, 2d ed. (1949), pp. 303–07.

enough to account for the increased blood pressure throughout their bodies: renal blood flow fell off by as much as 25 percent. When the patients then talked about things that made them feel secure, their blood pressure went down and kidney circulation returned to a more normal level. (James Lynch discusses this research in *The Language of the Heart* (1985) and draws important conclusions from it.)

If such reactions occur every day, with emotional pressure continually producing physical pressures, what happens? Platelets begin to appear in the bloodstream and attach themselves to the arterial walls, restricting blood flow to the various organs. If they clog the coronary arteries, a heart attack occurs. Unless the cycle is interrupted, any of the blood vessels can become clogged with fatty platelets; functional high blood pressure becomes organic high blood pressure, with irreversible damage to heart and kidneys and brain. A hard-hitting article in *Fortune* magazine described these physical changes, to show business executives the imperative need to deal with stress before anything else.[20]

Any organ can become the target of the autonomic system when the body is continuously misused as an emotional outlet. If the blood vessels in the stomach keep being overconstricted and then dilated, a pocket can form in the lining and burst. And if this is followed by overstimulation of the parasympathetic system, with plenty of acid and no food, the stomach may go to work on itself, and an ulcer results.

In much the same way, high blood pressure over a long period can cause a stroke or heart failure. As the body responds to continuous threat with new secretions, the artery walls thicken and pressure builds up until a weakened spot in the system gives way. Or fear and anger can simply start a clot moving toward a constricted artery in the brain and suddenly cause the whole body to die, or destroy a bit of brain tissue. It is fine for people faced with wild beasts to have their blood-clotting time decreased and the pressure raised. But for people on Wall Street, faced instead with a ticker tape, this physical response to anxiety increases the possibility of angina, or of a break or a clot causing all sorts of physical effects from coronary thrombosis to cerebral accidents. As one New York physician remarked to a friend, the cardiologists made their money on Wall Street when the ticker tape went down and heart disease increased.

---

[20] Walter McQuade, "What Stress Can Do To You," *Fortune* (January 1972), pp. 102–07, 134–41. People with a family history of stroke and heart failure, need to make a special effort to avoid stress. Heredity does play a part.

John Hunter, the famous English surgeon, used to say that his life was in the hands of any rascal who chose to worry him. He was right: he died of angina pectoris, and his fatal attack happened during a fit of anger. To put over the same point Dr. A. M. Master, consulting cardiologist at Mt. Sinai Hospital in New York, some years ago told a postgraduate group of heart specialists that angina patients must learn not to get angry at a nagging wife, or worry about unimportant things like being overcharged or shortchanged.[21] If they learn this essential lesson they not only stay alive, but longer and more happily than if they had never had a chest pain. "But," Masters added, "only 25 percent of the people with angina are able to avoid emotional stress and keep calm in the face of aggravation and frustration." It is all too clear that nothing more than emotion, uncontrolled and ill-used, can simply destroy the human body. Yet how can it be otherwise in the face of life as it is?

The Body Taking the Brunt

Physicians have known for a long time that illness can be a means of escape from anxiety or other emotional upset. There are many reports of cases in which a physical disorder appears to be a psychological necessity for some patients, and they react to physical cure by developing another, more serious, ailment. This is known as a conversion reaction: emotional distress is converted into a bodily disorder. For example, when a young man who came from South America to study in New York, he found the wild life of the great city far more interesting than his studies. At examination time he was unprepared and developed stomach trouble so severe that he had to be sent back to his own country under medical care. He was not malingering: his illness was genuine, but he recovered quickly when he was safe at home. One cannot tell people with this kind of illness just to snap out of it, however, and expect them to get well. This is just what they cannot do. If people have no way of resolving an emotional conflict except by neurotic illness, treatments may differ, but the patients are just as sick as if they had measles.

---

[21] Dr. Masters's comment was part of a lecture in the American College of Cardiology, held at Scripps Clinic and Research Foundation in La Jolla, California, in December 1965.

This kind of illness may also serve as a means of controlling other people. In the textbook *Psychosomatic Medicine*, one of the authors recounts such an instance to show how he learned early in practice that "treating sick people consists of something more than a knowledge of disease."[22] A young woman under his care for headaches grew steadily worse instead of getting well. When she finally had to be hospitalized with intestinal complications, an old physician was called who quickly put his finger on the problem. The girl's only brother, for whom she cared deeply and who carried family responsibility, was planning to marry. The patient's illness expressed her opposition, and when she understood its meaning she promptly recovered.

Most of us know at least a little about such illness. Most of us have known some person who never married because mama's heart invariably went bad at the sight of an eligible partner. Or if we have had any real neurotic trouble ourselves—and my experience is that most people fall into this class—we have probably thought at some time or another, "If only I could be just sick enough to get off the hook!" And perhaps our body has in fact granted our wish. Then we usually wish that we had only to deal with our neurosis, once we discover how difficult it can be to change these ways in which our body has learned to express emotional distress.

A great deal of evidence exists to show that diabetes, a disease that produces many physical complications, can be triggered by an emotional crisis. In one study, twenty-five new cases of full-blown diabetes were investigated. None of the patients had shown any previous sign of the disease. Twenty of these persons had either lost someone close to them or suffered a severe personal setback shortly before their symptoms were diagnosed. Another study showed that, during personal crises, patients who had been doing well on insulin suddenly found their disease was out of control again.[23] At present all over the country research teams are working on problems like these, trying to learn how the mind and nervous system are linked.

They have discovered that sexual function (and dysfunction) is directly controlled by certain parts of the brain, which apparently keep a constant check on the body's need for particular hormones. When a need for ovarian hormone is determined, the hypothalamus puts out a

---

[22] Weiss and English, *op. cit.*, 2d ed. (1949), p. vii.
[23] Paul F. Slawson, *et al.*, "Psychological Factors Associated with the Onset of Diabetes Mellitus," *Journal of the American Medical Association* 185 (July 20, 1963): 166–71.

chemical message telling the pituitary to supply it. But if the experimenters interrupt the process in the brain, there is no message and no hormone is produced.[24] In a small animal, the ovaries simply wither away. In human beings, unconscious images, ideas, and emotions clearly affect the hypothalamus and can produce just as damaging an interruption in a bodily process. In this way emotions may well exert a very direct influence for sickness or for health in many parts of the body.

Various questions are being asked today about the body's immune system and how it is affected by the hypothalamus, which is sometimes called "the drugstore in the brain." The direct effect of mental distress on the body's defenses is known; an increase in the production of "stress" hormones can slow down the formation of antibodies to fight an invading organism. An increasing number of researchers believe the antibody system originally developed to dispose of cells altered by mutation, and suggests that cancer cells develop and are disposed of in this way every day in most human bodies. Yet the system can apparently be interrupted by stress. Still other doctors are studying the relation of certain allergies, ulcerated colitis, and rheumatoid arthritis to this whole question of immunity and emotions. Sometimes it seems that the immune system turns upon its own body and chews it up; sometimes the immune system does not realize that doctors are trying to help and rejects an organ transplant.

A great deal of research is being done on the chemicals produced by the hypothalamus during sleep. Scientists at Duke University have discovered that angina attacks frequently occur during dreaming.[25] Researchers are also studying the increased flow of body chemicals during dreaming periods. Dr. Arnold J. Mandell, at the University of California at Los Angeles, suggests that the emotional content of certain dreams may be responsible for many heart attacks that occur during the night. These dreams cause changes in the body's chemistry that can increase the direct and indirect load on a heart. Thus dreams—which at the very

---

[24] By implanting a solid piece of ovarian hormone in the hypothalamus, an impression of adequate supply is given to the brain, and the communication system breaks down. But the same implant made directly in the pituitary gland has no effect; the brain still senses the body's need, decides and sends a message, and the pituitary does as it is told. The hypothalamus appears to be a unique part of the brain; it not only senses, but also functions like a gland, secreting the chemical messengers that tell the system, through the pituitary gland, what to do next. This has emerged from research done under Dr. Charles H. Sawyer at the University of California at Los Angeles.

[25] Dr. J. B. Nowlin and his associates monitored several patients during sleep, by electroencephalograph recordings which show when dreams are occurring. Out of 39 attacks that occurred during the study, 32 coincided with periods of dreaming.

least are an expression in images of unconscious emotion—can have an effect on one's health.

The growth process of children can also apparently be interrupted by chemical changes initiated by the hypothalamus. This process is governed by hormones secreted by the pituitary gland. Its function can be essentially halted by conflict in the home. Children who seem dwarfed will often grow from five to ten inches in a single year if they are removed from unpredictable environments. If they are returned to the same unhappy home, the growth stops again.

This is only one of the ways that children, by reacting to the conflicts of their parents, can start life with emotionally inherited difficulties expressed as physical illness. Physicians' files are full of stories like one told me by the psychiatrist of a five-year-old, a child who developed ulcerated colitis when her goldfish bowl was upset and one of the fish died.[26] Often only a psychiatrist can pinpoint what aspect of a "normal" home has brought about a result like this.

There is a dramatic parallel in the work of experimental psychologists on animals. In Howard Liddell's neurotic sheep at Cornell University, the animals were given as fine a barn as the laboratory could arrange, and were disturbed only for short sessions in which they learned to stand quietly when a metronome began ticking, only flexing one leg that was given a mild electric shock. They adjusted quickly and went on with the placid life of normal sheep. Later, if they were given more frequent shocks or if the metronome was started repeatedly *without* a shock, the sheep suffered many of the symptoms of a human nervous breakdown—sleeplessness, rapid heart beat, and irritability. If the sheep were removed to pasture for a year or so, the heart rate quieted down and other symptoms improved. But when they were brought back to the laboratory, the first tick of the metronome, and even the smell of the laboratory barn, produced trembling, palpitation, and all the other functional disturbances.[27]

---

[26] After intensive medical care and then months of psychiatric help, the child's symptoms essentialy disappeared. But the physician who told me about the case commented on the mother's inability to adjust to the daily demands of life without guilt and apprehension; he remarked that she had had only superficial support for her own problems and had not changed very much.

[27] Howard S. Liddell, *Emotional Hazards in Animals and Man* (1956), pp. 61–72; also "Conditioning and Emotions," reprinted from *Scientific American*, January 1954. None of the studies was designed to produce neurosis. In the first instance the animal was learning a more difficult task, to flex its leg for a shock on the sixth click of the metronome, and the schedule was doubled to get the results in time for a scientific meeting. The second result occurred when the signal (in this case a buzzer) was given without the expected

Do we think that children are any less sensitive than sheep? When parents tick with unpredictable pressures, so that children are emotionally insecure and cannot depend on their environment, then the children may suffer just as the sheep, but with worse consequences. Put an adult or a child in a situation where expectations and the required responses keep shifting, and both emotional life and physical health can be permanently damaged. Medicine has made significant progress in understanding and treating the physiological response to such environments, but often people are nevertheless unable to recover until their confusing environment has been changed.

Deep emotional disturbances can bring about feelings of meaninglessness and lead to death. On the other hand an experience of meaning can restore a person to life. A brilliant young man came to see me when I taught at Notre Dame. His life had suddenly fallen apart, he could no longer function, and he thought he was going to die. I told him that it was not his body, but an old ego adaptation that was dying. I told him that I had been through a similar crisis and survived. I gave him concrete suggestions to open himself to meaning. It was a long struggle, but he has become one of the most gifted therapists I know in helping those who face similar crises. This story could be repeated in many variations.

Freud was one of the first to show the physical ramifications of our emotional states and to demonstrate that physical illness can disappear when the neuroses from which it springs are resolved. Dr. Flanders Dunbar related an interesting example from Freudian annals: a woman with an exophthalmic goiter consulted a surgeon, who recommended an operation. But when the surgeon realized how tense she was, he postponed the operation and sent her to a psychiatrist for help with her anxieties. Six months later she came back, minus the anxieties *and* the goiter.

Harold Wolff at Cornell has shown migraine patients their need for emotional insight by demonstrating to them the contrast between the physiological effect of their fears and that of faith. As they talked about their grievances and felt the abrupt onset of a headache, they saw the sharp pulsation waves of the distended temporal artery recorded in a mechanical tracing. With an injection of simple salt solution, which the patient believed to be a powerful constricting drug, the pulsation waves subsided as suddenly as they had magnified, and the headache was

---

shock in order to extinguish the animal's conditioned reflex; instead the flexing was intensified, along with varied signs of neurosis.

entirely gone. Faith in the power of the physician and his medication had constricted the arteries in the brain. James Lynch has described a far better way of healing migraine headaches in *The Language of the Heart*.

Many such startling changes in physical condition have been observed by psychologists and physicians, as patients have replaced their tensions, anxieties, fears, and feelings of anger, hopelessness, and guilt with confidence, hope, and faith, as they have *experienced* a loving reality in the very center of their being. If these results can be facilitated by a psychologist, is it too much to believe that a loving God can do as much to any person who allows God in? Certainly the sense of well-being and wholeness that comes from an experience of such a relationship with God might work the same way. Is it absurd to believe that God cannot have at least the same influence on the human body as the analyst, if we believe in God at all?

What Parts of the Body Can Be Affected?

No part of the body is immune to the possible ill effects of emotion. It is not clear why certain organs seem to become a target for emotional disturbances. Physical medicine has generally found most of the reason in the inherited structure. However, some illness seems to be symbolic of specific fears and concerns, and psychiatry and psychosomatic medicine have looked for the causes in personality structure, and in the emotional environment as well. New developments in psychology and in genetics point to the importance of the inherited psyche.[28] Most likely all of these factors play a part in determining why a person often has trouble in one part of his body and not in another.

At any rate, it is interesting to realize how much easier it is to admit simply that we have a poorly functioning heart or glands than to admit that our poorly directed emotions may be the cause. We prefer to see physical illness as the result of fate, whereas if it is the result of our emotions, then we feel responsible for it. Most of recent medical writers referred to earlier in this chapter believe that we need to take some responsibility for both our emotional and physical difficulties.

---

[28] Work with plants at the controlled environment laboratory at California Institute of Technology has produced a pea that "remembers" the environment in which the seed developed and under new conditions reproduces the growth patterns evoked by the old environment.

But a "weight on the chest" can mean that in reality one has a "load on the mind." Emphysema, asthma, and hay fever are often connected with emotional troubles, and it is becoming increasingly recognized that respiratory infections, the common cold, and tuberculosis in particular are related to emotional stress. When a throat culture is done on a large group, nearly all have streptocci bacilli in their throats. Why don't we all come down with a strep throat? Because our antibodies and T-cells are at work.

Both the skin and the eye have been thoroughly studied as organs of emotional expression. We know that the skin often expresses emotional conflict in blushing, pallor, and perspiration, while many allergies and skin eruptions have been traced to like causes, although the emotional basis is often very difficult to identify. The eye is especially sensitive to feelings; it has been called the window of the soul, and for medicine it is a diagnostic window. Glaucoma, among other eye conditions, is often tied to emotional shock or tension. In addition, our eyes may be partly responsible for individual immunity to airborne infection. When we release feelings through tears, we produce lysozyme, a powerful germ-killer contained in tears and in the nose. Lysozyme can inactivate even the polio virus on a few moment's contact.

There is no question about the response of the gastrointestinal system to conflict and fear. Digestive ailments all the way from cardiospasm (difficulty in swallowing) to simple constipation can represent the body's adjustment to tension, overwork, or anxiety. Many studies of this relationship are well known. We have shown some of the more critical ways in which the cardiovascular system responds directly to deeper emotions and how, especially in hypertensive conditions, other parts of the body are seriously affected.

Bedwetting in older children is one indication of the way the genitourinary tract is often affected by emotions. Feelings so naturally underlie all disturbances of sexual functioning that their psychic beginnings have been widely understood but seldom put into words. The studies of sexual infertility and impotence, pregnancy and childbirth difficulties, and menstrual and menopausal disorders clearly show emotional causes and a relation to other diseases.[29]

---

[29] Consider simply the fact of natural childbirth under hypnotic suggestion, and the effect of adopting a child on a couple who have thought one or the other of them to be sterile, and how often pregnancy comes as a surprise after they have become parents by adoption. It is also interesting that contraceptive pills act in the brain, working through the hypothalamus, or higher up, to give orders to the glandular system. My book, *Sacrament of Sexuality* deals at length with sexual malfunctioning.

The central nervous system and the entire glandular system are even more closely related to physical conditions. Insomnia, headaches, neurotic and psychotic disorders, and even certain tumors are warnings of nervous reaction to stress. They can also be symptoms of the distress of another part of the body. It is well established that the endocrine system often takes the brunt of emotional strain and distributes the effects like lesser shock waves. Carl Jung noted that he had seen the temperature of a patient rise two degrees purely as a result of emotional distress. This is one indication of how mental, psychic, and instinctive activity affects the glands, which in turn affect the body. Physical states like fatigue, hyperactivity, obesity, and emaciation are acknowledged as, at least in part, the effects of emotional stress on glandular function.

Whatever else is influenced by our emotions, it would seem that teeth should certainly stand as a sure rock of physicality. Yet dentists are busy developing their own theories of psychosomatic dentistry. The outline of a recent University of California extension course for dentists featured a prominent neuropsychiatrist as lecturer. The course put together facts that dentists see every day to show that diseases of the mouth have a clear correlation with emotions. Even tooth decay, erosion of the teeth, and difficulties in occlusion can be affected by anxiety. A dentist who treated students at Notre Dame once told me that trench mouth occurred among these patients only at exam time.

A study of cases in a hospital accident ward indicates that rebellious people may let off steam by having "accidents" instead of developing a neurosis or physical disease. When Flanders Dunbar and her associates were looking about for a group of normal, healthy people with whom to compare diabetic and heart patients, they chose as a control group those who had submitted to hospitalization "accidentally."[30] They were disconcerted to find that the fracture patients selected were not particularly normal at all. Their emotions were, on the whole, more obviously disturbed than other patients, but they expressed it by being accident-prone. What easier way to avoid meaninglessness than to let one's unconscious psyche produce an interesting or even fatal injury? As Carl Jung observed, frequent physical injury can reflect inner conflict just as much as frequently hurt feelings, and a broken leg may well be a signal of injury to one's psychic "standpoint."

---

[30] At about the same time, industry was beginning to take a serious look at the employee who is involved in more than one accident, and a number of psychiatrists were making a careful study of the emotional states that lead to particular accidents.

Is the fight for control never done? The body can expend tremendous physical energy in bypassing a clogged blood vessel or rebuilding damaged nerves. Or it may unconsciously choose another route for the same energy, misdirecting cells to produce the growth of cancer. It can turn creative force to recovery from tuberculosis or to resisting an invasion of polio or the common cold. Or the same force may direct harmful bacteria to fight back by breeding new and stronger strains. The body can secrete innumerable chemical compounds in order to digest food or fight poison, to stimulate its own reproduction or get the highest brain cells into action. Or it can secretly turn these secretions on itself, to digest or poison or overstimulate itself.

In some ways this seems to be a realm apart, a field where the material and the immaterial join, where good or evil are determined by an unknown force. There is ample room here for both scientific knowledge and religious wonder. For very possibly, answers to a number of questions about disease lie in the religious consideration of problems of the emotions and resistance, of destructive and creative realities affecting our psyches and bodies. We have seen that many scientists are looking at meditation, faith, and prayer as therapeutic tools. It is time for Christian theology to offer a worldview in which all this makes sense and for Christian practice to offer Christian healing as a normal church service.

The scientists who wrestle with these mysteries are now convinced that there is little fundamental difference between mental and physical illness, and that "all illness has both psychological and psychosomatic components."[31] Some of the recent psychiatric treatment of psychosomatic illness also sounds strangely more religious than medical. To the physician today our often unconscious feelings are of the utmost importance. Let us look at those that have the greatest negative influence on the body.

Emotions That Play a Part

Several destructive emotions arise when we human beings try to deal with a difficult, hostile, or meaningless world. We react in four

---

[31] C. P. Kimball, "Conceptual Developments in Psychosomatic Medicine: 1939–1969," *Annals of Internal Medicine* 73 (August 1970), p. 307. Dr. Kimball, who teaches at Yale, was writing for the American College of Physicians.

basically different ways to threat, helplessness, and powerlessness. One response is agitated fear, the flight response, which produces a pervasive sense of anxiety. The physiological and psychic damage produced by anxiety are legion, as we have already indicated. Or we may exhibit the fight response and turn against the world and those around us with anger, hostility, rage, and violence. Any human being under constant agitation will sustain physical damage, and other human beings are likely to suffer as well. A third response is the egocentric approach, in which people believe they are responsible for taking care of the problems of the whole world. This is a heavy burden and results in unbearable stress and ultimately in social, psychological, and physiological problems. The fourth response is simply collapse before the threat. There is neither fight nor flight, nor sustained stress, just hopelessness, depression, and loss of meaning. The individual sees no point in doing anything, and suicide becomes a real possibility. This hopelessness sometimes feels like an intolerable pain, almost like being tortured inwardly. It is no wonder that many cultures have described this as being under attack by demonic forces. Depression of this kind is the common cold of modern psychiatry and the physiological results are found in every doctor's office daily.

Negative emotions can sometimes be dealt with by comparatively simple means. One psychologist has remarked that many people practice excellent psychotherapy without knowing it simply by expressing friendly warmth and heartfelt encouragement. Bruno Klopfer, the authority on the Rorschach test, once told me that in his opinion 50 percent of all effective psychotherapy consists of warm, positive concern. James Lynch has shown the incredibly destructive results of loneliness, alienation, and isolation.

How very important it is to avoid negative suggestion in the course of a disease or, for that matter, in any crisis in one's life. One cannot estimate the amount of misery caused by unconscious negative suggestion. Probably each of us has had the experience of feeling quite well until several people casually remark that we are not looking at all well; it takes a very strong personality not to be influenced by such statements. When the suggestion comes from an authority, the effects may be tragic indeed. Bernie Siegel makes this point with great force in *Love, Medicine and Miracles*.

I once worked for many months with a young man who had had just this experience. He had been getting along remarkably well until he went to a physician for a routine checkup. In the ordinary exercise test his blood pressure rose a good bit more than the normal. The physician's voice registered shock that suggested terrible consequences. My parishioner reacted by going to pieces. Not until he was completely reassured of the hidden ways God has given the mind and body for healing was he able to get on with his normal work and life. It seems that he simply had a blood pressure mechanism that fluctuated easily. Forty years later he is healthy and busy doing the work of two people.

Most patients are quite capable of complicating their own illnesses without such medical suggestion—their need is for the powerful healing effect of positive but sensible confidence. The effectiveness of sugar pills (placebos), when given by a doctor who inspires faith, has long proved this. Double-blind experiments have made this even more clear. In a series of studies several years ago, tranquilizers were given to one group of psychoneurotic patients and placebos to a control group. Neither the patients nor their physicians knew which patients got tranquilizers and which patients got sugar pills. When the results were checked, it was found that as many as 35 percent of those receiving placebos had improved.[32] A number of tranquilizers advertised in medical journals claim to be effective for 17 percent of the patients who take them. Apparently a placebo can do twice as well!

Sometimes a straightforward discussion of the problems is all that is needed for a cure. A young woman was sent to me at Notre Dame because she was depressed. I listened to her story about the tragic death of two young men, one after the other, whom she had loved and planned to marry. When she was finished, I told her I was amazed that she could function at all and that with such pain and sorrow she ought to be depressed. No longer worried about her depression, she began to take life in stride. I only saw her twice more, once for more encouragement and a final time when she came to thank me for my support.

However, all emotional problems are not so easily solved. It is the unrecognized hostility, fear, sorrow, guilt, meaninglessness, and psychic pain that cause the most devastating physical reactions. Conscious knowledge at least provides a means to counteract the effect of known feelings. But when we are not conscious of these emotions, it is nearly

---

[32] Henry K. Beecher, "The Powerful Placebo," *Journal of the American Medical Association* 159 (December 24, 1955): 1602–09. See also Norman Cousins, "The Mysterious Placebo—How the Mind Helps Medicine Work," *Saturday Review* (October 1, 1977), pp. 9–16 and Frank, *op. cit.* (1969). In a 1987 TV show a doctor told of the practice of inserting a balloon in a patient's stomach and telling them that they would be less hungry and lose weight. They did. Some patients were told a balloon had been inserted when in fact nothing was inserted. They too felt less hungry and lost the same amount of weight.

impossible to deal with them, let alone resolve them. In such cases we often need help in understanding our own inner reactions if we are ever to be whole emotionally or physically. Such hidden emotions are far more common than we generally realize.

I know of no method of healing the illnesses that result from unconscious emotions except to dig into repressed fear, hatred, meaninglessness, and guilt. This is a dangerous process, but their damage to the body is equally dangerous, not to mention the psychological misery they can induce. It is always best of course to use the simplest and most direct method available to resolve the difficulty, and not go deeper than necessary. If physical remedies will work, then one should be grateful and let well enough alone. On the other hand, how much more effective the healing is when the emotional life can be dealt with consciously and creatively so that drugs are no longer needed to counterbalance the diseased physical system. Many people are able to abandon medication when the tensions causing their physical imbalance have been resolved. Most medications also have some unpleasant side effects.

These harmful emotions can be caused by a conflict within the individual, by a conflict between the individual and another person, and between the individual and the total world and its meaning. Within the individual, the conflict may be between two opposing attitudes, perhaps a sense of duty toward a parent and the desire to go out into the world. Or perhaps a conflict arising toward parental values that have never been examined and are unconsciously stumbled over with each step in the world, or between conflicting desires. Again, for an individual who finds relationships with others a source of irritation and pain, all sorts of psychological conflicts can arise. The most persistent, depression and misery, may be caused by a lack of feeling loved and cared for, or by feeling unable to love. Harry Stack Sullivan based a whole theory of psychological illness upon such effects of interpersonal relationships.

Finally, the conflict of individuals with their world, their total worldview, can cause unending difficulty. If the universe is viewed as basically meaningless or hostile, the whole emotional life of the individual may be greatly affected. How can one be free from fear, emptiness, and rebellion if one's life is seen as no more than a holding action against meaningless forces that will ultimately crush or snuff it out? Indeed, all the negative emotions are aroused when we see ourselves as mere atoms, moved about mechanically or by blind chance. With no relationship to any spiritual dimension that gives continuing meaning, there can be no forgiveness, no real way to cope with the deep sense of guilt that most of us bear, nor is there any way to stand against the condemnation of other people and society. How can we help but be egotistical if we are the only purposeful entities in the universe, if all is transitory, without ultimate value?

If we see only blind indeterminacy in the heart of being, our response is likely to be utter despair, abiding sorrow, and deep psychic pain, or at best an existential courage, anxious and stoic. Religion can provide an adequate worldview and a way of relating to transcendental reality. Real religion brings an experience of spiritual reality that can touch the psyche of the individual and transform the body as well. Sometimes spiritual reality touches and heals the body directly, and this transforms and heals our attitude towards ourselves and the world.

There is no sharp line of demarcation between the religious, spiritual, emotional, and physical—between the body and the psyche. If it can be shown that religious life has a vital effect upon the total emotional life of human beings, upon that which Christians are apt to call the soul, then it may be assumed that it can have a like effect upon the body of the believer. However, it must be clearly noted that just because psychic causes predominate in some illnesses, we must not jump to the conclusion that every illness is predominantly psychic in origin. Some illness are, as far as we know, almost entirely physical in origin—the mechanism has simply broken down. Also, the psychosomatic relation is a two-way street: profound and lasting sickness of the body can have a deep effect on the psyche, on the mental and emotional attitudes of sick people, and also on their religious life.

There is a great deal of profound literary support for the contention that our moral and religious life influences our bodies directly. One modern author has risked his life and reputation to propound this thesis from behind the Iron Curtain. Pasternak's witness is all the more impressive because he has known the experiences that undergird the rigid materialism and mechanical determinism that rule his country. In the conclusion to *Doctor Zhivago* he wrote:

Microscopic forms of cardiac hemorrhages have become very frequent in recent years. They are not always fatal. Some people get over them. It's a typical modern disease. I think its causes are of a moral order. The great majority of us are required to live a life of constant, systematic duplicity. Your health is bound to be affected if, day after day, you say the opposite of what you feel, if you grovel before what you dislike and rejoice at what brings you nothing but misfortune. Our nervous system isn't just a fiction, it's part of our physical body, and our soul exists in space and is inside us, like the teeth in our mouth. It can't be forever violated with impunity. I found it painful to listen to you,

Innokentii, when you told us how you were re-educated and became mature in jail. It was like listening to a horse describing how it broke itself in.[33]

Is there any psychological system that takes into account all aspects of the human psyche? During a crisis in my own life, I found a psychological understanding that actually reestablished and strengthened my religious experience and faith. Then I read a profound study of the history of psychology and its meaning that confirmed my own experience: Richard Coan's book *Hero, Artist, Sage or Saint?: A Survey of Views on What Is Variously Called Mental Health, Normality, Maturity, Self-Actualization, and Human Fulfillment*. Let us look at how our destructive emotions and attitudes can be healed.

---

[33] 1958, p. 483.

CHAPTER 12

Healing the Emotions

Clinical psychology and psychiatry form the youngest of the healing professions, one that did not even begin until long after religious healing had ceased to be an accepted part of Western culture. In fact, there was little interest in what was hidden in the souls and minds of troubled people almost until the century in which Freud made his original far-reaching discovery.[1] As we have already shown, the church, both Catholic and Protestant, had long since abandoned the religious ministry of healing to this tragic group of people so common in the first five or six centuries of its life. It is hard to realize that scarcely a hundred years before Freud's discovery, Westerners witnessed the last beheading of a witch on the continent of Europe.

It is also difficult to believe how the mentally ill were treated up until that time. Until almost into the nineteenth century, most "mad" people were kept in chains, often in dungeons. They were beaten, dosed with purgatives and emetics, and left to brutal keepers, because "the more painful the restraint, the better the results."[2] Humane treatment was first tried in Italy, at the Hospital of St. Boniface in Florence, beginning in 1789. Three years later in England, where the recurring insanity of George III aroused popular sentiment and questions, the Quaker William Tuke began the reform that finally changed hospitals in that country.

But ironically, it was in Paris during the reign of terror that medical psychiatry was born. In 1793 Philippe Pinel undertook his duties at the

---

[1] He made it jointly with Joseph Breuer and first published in 1893, followed in 1895 by their book, *Studies in Hysteria* (1961).

[2] Franz G. Alexander and Sheldon T. Selesnick, *The History of Psychiatry* (1966), p. 116. This book gives the best picture available of the development of the present understanding of mental illness.

Bicêtre, the institution for insane men, and he was thought mad himself when he removed the chains from his patients and gave them real medical care. But Pinel was a quiet thinker who intended to change the treatment. The results were so good that two years later he was asked to do the same thing for the women at the Salpêtrière. There in 1817 Esquirol, who succeeded Pinel, established the first psychiatric clinic, giving physicians a chance to look at the psychotic patient as a medical problem.

Twenty years after the death of Esquirol, Jean Martin Charcot came to the Salpêtrière as professor and chief physician. It was in a lecture hall of that hospital, under a painting of Pinel striking off the chains of inmates, that Charcot had among his students the young man from Vienna, Sigmund Freud. Here Freud found a neurologist—the leading neurologist of the time—who truly looked at and listened to his difficult patients.

Hysteria was one of the main problems, and it is no wonder that the first successes of psychotherapy were with these patients who showed physical symptoms where no physical cause could be discovered. Charcot saw this ailment as an illness to be studied and treated. He was not afraid to investigate hypnotism, or to recognize the psychic influences that affected so many people physically. Like Freud at that time, however, Charcot was interested in the physical causes of nervous diseases; he did not actually comprehend the psychological problems he was raising. It was Freud who later began to discover that his patients did not fit the ideas of personality he saw expressed around him.

Nineteenth-century Vienna, like the rest of the world at the time, considered human personality as relatively simple. Children were expected to listen to their elders, who would obviously feed them the right mixture of experience and teach them the right ideas to produce correct, law-abiding citizens. Everyone at this period believed that individuals came into the world like lumps of clay, and it was society's duty to mold them into reasonable adults.

Of course there were those who did not turn out that way, and imperial Vienna had its closets for family skeletons, as did Victorian England. But for the most part it was expected that the shaping could be corrected. Even if people had a perverse will and resisted, they could be remolded by punishment, or shown where they had to shape up and accept right ideas and habits of action. It was society's responsibility to provide the punishments and institutions of correction for those whose wills needed altering, such as criminals and the mentally ill. But if this failed to bring people in line, then the poor devils simply had to be removed from society so that they would not become rotten apples in the barrel.

These ideas were based, of course, on a very old theory of personality, a psychology which assumes that the psychic structure is built solely out of conscious rationality. Up to the time of Pinel there were almost no voices raised against it. It not only provided the rationale for a penal system from debtors' prisons to the guillotine, but also the only real basis for treating mental illness until almost the nineteenth century.[3] This psychology has bequeathed to us a punishment system which still does more to promote antisocial behavior than it does to keep people out of jail. Mental institutions have been changed only because of Freud and those who followed his ideas. These people were willing to risk reputation and livelihood to try something different.

This theory of personality which we have discussed at some length, in contrast to the attitude and psychology of Jesus of Nazareth,[4] was essentially implicit in the ideas of Aristotle. Because the medieval Scholastics adopted this idea in the name of all Christians, this view of human beings entered the modern world without being questioned. It was the basis of practically all legal codes in the West, including ecclesiastical censure, and once the Christian church accepted it, there were few who cared to question it. It was simply assumed that punishment was more effective in transforming personality than love and understanding.

Today a similar personality theory is still held by many people who would be quite indignant if it were suggested that they had any psychological viewpoint at all. It exerts such a tremendous hold on unreflective people that they meet any challenge of this assumption with determined resistance. In addition, it has recently been revived as a theory of personality and restated with sophistication by certain modern psychologists who rely largely on reward rather than on punishment.[5]

---

[3] For instance, irritants were even applied to the skin of insane persons to be sure they would feel the chains and carry the scars.

[4] See Chapter Four, pp. 47–51.

[5] A closely related point of view is presented by the behaviorist B. F. Skinner in *Science and Human Behavior* (1953), *Walden II* (1960), *Beyond Freedom and Dignity* (1971). Behaviorism denies the reality of both consciousness and the unconscious and sees treatment as a process of conditioning the individual through positive stimuli. Human behavior is reduced to conditioned physical responses which can be varied by appropriate stimuli to produce the desired results. As one student remarked to me, he did not discuss his real problems with the professors of behavioral psychology, because he did not want to be manipulated and treated as an object. This is not the place to discuss the history of psychological thought, which I have already done briefly in *Christianity as Psychology*

Freud, on the other hand, was trying to see what lay behind the illness and pain, to discover the psychic distress of his patients. His great contribution was to offer a theory of personality that takes these experiences into account and thus allows room for nonrational events in human consciousness. From the very first of his discoveries, Freud had to make room for healings that were anything but rational experiences.

Freud, the Great Innovator

Although Freud was by no means the first modern student to question whether there might be unconscious parts of the human mind, this was still a relative innovation in modern thinking. As L. L. Whyte pointed out, Western languages did not even speak of "unconscious" or "an unconscious mind" until after Descartes had arbitrarily defined mind and thought as solely a clear, conscious, rational process. Interestingly enough, Descartes did not seem to notice that he had left out something of importance for comprehending the human mind and personality, even though his own understanding had come through a process that was hardly clear, conscious, or rational. His inspiration came to him in dreams on the night of November 10, 1619, in one of those experiences of the unconscious which he eliminated so well that the modern world still has trouble grasping them, even after all Freud's careful evidence.[6]

Freud was the first to give careful, verifiable proof of the reality of the unconscious. Knowing that he had means to deal with the illnesses that came to him, that "symptoms vanish with the acquisition of knowledge of their meaning," he began to look at the ways people express an underlying conflict.[7] When patients' basic problems were revealed to them by their words and actions, they suddenly became aware of re-

---

(1986). We have already referred to the biomedical view of psychiatry so well detailed by Melvin Konner. Much of the material that follows, including diagrams, is taken from or is close to *Christianity as Psychology*.

[6] My book, *Dreams*, p. 194, contains a brief account of the development of interest in the unconscious. Lancelot Law Whyte's book, *The Unconscious Before Freud* (1960), offers the best general study of early thought on the subject and also some idea of the beginnings of modern psychological understanding.

In *Studies in Hysteria* (Breuer and Freud, p. 200), Freud has shown how his own ideas began to develop as he found that hypnosis could remove symptoms but often failed to cure the disease or stop the formation of new symptoms. Freud's *Interpretation of Dreams* and his lectures published as *A General Introduction of Psychoanalysis* contain the basis of his understanding and method.

[7] *General Introduction to Psychoanalysis* (1960), p. 292.

actions in themselves which had been kept under cover until then. With the right help to focus on them, they could understand and learn to handle these things. Freud therefore studied the mistakes of his patients, their slips of the tongue, free associations, and dreams.

He continued to build up evidence showing how the conflict between unconscious, autonomous contents and the conscious attitudes of people could keep them constantly upset without their knowing the reason. Simply because they were unconscious of these contents, they were powerless against the conflict, and this, Freud concluded, was responsible for neurosis and even the more serious psychological disorders.

His descriptions of the results of inner tension have stood the test of medical practice. This conflict causes both compulsive actions and phobias, subjecting persons to fetishes or to extremes of behavior, such as stealing, fighting, or emotional rage. Such conflicts may lead to phobias, which prevent people from doing things they want to do because they are afraid, for example, of studying, or crowds, or high places, or closed-in ones. The tension may manifest itself in free-floating anxiety, depression, and despair, the very emotions that have the most devastating physiological response. Finally, if the unconscious conflict becomes intolerable, the individual ego may be fragmented or dissolved, and the result is schizophrenia, the most tragic of mental illnesses.

As Freud realized that patients were driven by ideas, feelings, and emotions that had been repressed and buried since childhood, and that much of this conflict related to sexuality, it became clear why the resulting disturbances could so often be "talked away." When a patient became aware of these drives and learned to deal with them consciously, the psyche no longer automatically compensated for ignorance and innocence by destructive tension or neurotic physical illness. As is even better understood today, once a conflict becomes conscious, there are other channels of discharge than through the autonomic or other central systems of the body.

Freud would have been quite happy if he could have accounted for all mental illness on the basis of physical causes, but he could not, and so he provided a theory very much at odds with the materialistic ones. He did not deny that there are physical causes for mental illness, but he proposed that in addition to the brain and the conscious attitude, which he called the *ego*, there is in each of us a deep and hidden part of our personality that he called the *unconscious*, borrowing this term from popular thinking of his day. The nonphysical contents of the unconscious, such as wishes, fantasies, buried memories, and desires could result in irrational actions, painful physical and mental symptoms.

According to Freud, the ego enables us to manage our lives in relation to the outer world and other people. It also keeps us from being overwhelmed by our inner world. The unconscious contains our personal unconscious and also the pleasure-seeking principle, the *id*, which seeks pleasure indiscriminately. An inner censor, or *superego*, Freud claimed, keeps us from remembering the contents of the personal unconscious and from becoming aware of the id; we would find facing the desires of the id intolerable. Freud maintained that the censor even scrambles our dreams, which can reveal the real nature of the depth of ourselves. In his later years, Freud also came to believe that there is a death wish in each of us that is opposed to the life force of the id. The death wish seeks to drag us back into the deathlike immobility of inorganic reality. If we do not honestly face those horrors within ourselves and learn to deal with them, we may develop mental illness, or perhaps commit suicide, or get physically ill, or we may project them out onto other people. Such projections, according to Freud, are the source of human aggression and war.

Freud's thought can easily be diagrammed. The two triangles pictured in figure 1 represent two total human psyches, conscious and unconscious. The box represents the outer, material world with its physical limitations on the psyche. The small triangle tip stands for the

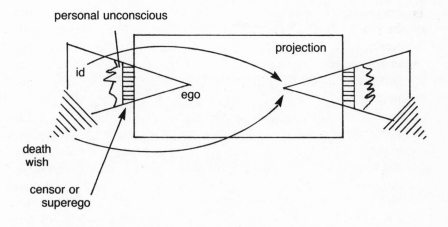

Figure 1

ego, the center of consciousness that enables us to get around in the world. The unconscious is divided between the personal unconscious and the id. The censor stands between the total unconscious and the ego, protecting the ego from objectionable contents in the unconscious. The death wish is represented by the diagonal lines at the lower left of the id. Projections of the contents of the unconscious are represented by lines reaching out to other people, the other triangle. Although this theory does not explain all human behavior, it certainly has helped many people get a better handle on why they act as they do, and it has also enabled many to gain better control of their lives.

According to Freud, the conscious, disciplined human ego holding its rational own against the id, the death wish, the superego, and an often hostile world is the highest development in the universe. There is no religious help available from beyond the human ego. Indeed, in his book *The Future of an Illusion* (1949), Freud describes religion as a regressive return to the womb, to dependence on something that does not exist. Religion was for him an avoidance of the cold, hard, bitter reality of life. For Freud, religious belief is detrimental to mental health; it is a reliance on illusion. In other words, Freud was very pessimistic about life, feeling that most of us are determined by subhuman forces. In a letter to Einstein he wrote that human beings will always go to war; if people don't project out the death wishes in aggression and war, Freud thought, they are likely to commit suicide.[8] In the light of this point of view we can admire even more Freud's courageous struggle against cancer during his last years.

A Place for the Spirit in Modern Psychology

There were many reactions to both the mechanistic view of behaviorism, to biomedical psychology and to the pessimistic dynamic attitude of Freud. Existentialist psychologists felt that these disciplines did not adequately emphasize the value of the human person. Some of these thinkers—Victor Frankl, for example—had a deeply religious point of view. Others, such as Sartre, saw nothing beyond the human being. Cognitive therapy assumes meaning and tries to show people how they can be in touch with it through erasing old tapes and learning new ones.[9]

---

[8] These letters are found in the appendix of Karl Menninger's *Man Against Himself* (1938).
[9] See Chapters One and Two of my *Christianity as Psychology* (1986).

Another school of psychological thought has developed in which religious experience and faith *and* the unconscious are vitally important. Indeed, religious experience is seen as mediated largely through the unconscious. In his Gifford Lectures of 1901–1902, William James, one of the founders of modern psychology, set the stage for this development. James described many examples of religious experience, often of the Christ, that brought people from miserable, ineffective agony to creativity and effectiveness. He wrote that the inability of many people to believe and be transformed by religious experience and faith "may in some cases be intellectual in its origin. Their religious faculties may be checked in their natural tendency to expand by beliefs about the world that are inhibitive, the pessimistic and materialistic beliefs, for example, within which so many good souls, who in former times would have freely indulged their religious propensities, find themselves nowadays, as it were, frozen; or the agnostic vetoes upon faith as something weak and shameful, under which so many of us today lie cowering, afraid to use our instincts."[10] James's point is that beliefs about the world can have a profound effect on our psychological and physical health.

Still other followers and associates of Freud accepted Freud's view of the dynamic unconscious, with its stress on the unconscious elements in the personality, but broke with his determinism, his pessimism, and his atheism. Roberto Assagioli, an Italian psychotherapist, who founded an institute of psychosynthesis in Rome, wrote a book entitled *Psychosynthesis*, in which he stated his belief that human beings cannot be whole unless they relate to the transpersonal spirit. Assagioli even provided methods to achieve this end. And in their later writings both Otto Rank and Alfred Adler came to many of the same conclusions, but the death of Rank at 52 and Adler at 62 kept them from fully developing this aspect of their thought.

It was Carl Jung who integrated religious experience into psychological thought more fully than any other psychologist. Jung lived to be almost 86 and wrote until three weeks before his death; during the final 15 years of his life—from the time of a nearly fatal illness until his death—Jung's main preoccupation was the significance of religious experience for psychiatry and psychology.

However, Jung's interest in religion and its importance in facilitating wholeness had come to him much earlier as a result of his own inner struggle and experience. In 1932 Jung gave a talk to the Alsatian Pas-

---

[10] William James, *Varieties of Religious Experience* (1920), p. 204.

toral Conference entitled "Psychotherapists or the Clergy." In it he said that for more than thirty years people had been coming to him from all the civilized countries of the world. "Among all my patients in the second half of life—that is to say, over thirty-five—there has not been one whose problem in the last resort was not that of finding a religious outlook on life. It is safe to say that every one of them fell ill because he had lost what the living religions of every age have given to their followers, and none of them has been really healed who did not regain his religious outlook."[11]

Jung also had an excellent philosophical background. He had read Kant's *Critique of Pure Reason* at age 18. He was well acquainted with the philosophical and scientific developments of the first part of the twentieth century. Some of his patients and collaborators were those on the forefront of scientific thought, people like Wolfgang Pauli, Mircea Eliade, and Heinrich Zimmer. Leaders in many fields of thought met each year at Eranos, the home of a friend of Jung's in southern Switzerland, to share their latest thinking. The papers presented there have been published. In constant dialogue with the leaders in many fields, Jung developed a carefully worked out philosophical framework in which God and the experience of God were integrated into a sophisticated worldview and psychological theory.

This theory has clear, specific, practical applications. For example, in *Let Go, Let God,* an excellent study of the spiritual significance of Alcoholics Anonymous, John Keller shows that before psychiatrists began to take seriously the spiritual dimension of alcoholism and addiction, they were unable to bring healing to people with this affliction. He draws on the work of Dr. Harry Tiebout, a psychiatrist who worked with alcoholics. Keller, a Lutheran pastor who has spent more than thirty years in ministry with alcoholics, calls on the secular healing profession to look at the religious dimension in healing addiction and other mental illness. On the other hand, he asks the Christian community to hear the words of Dr. Fulton Outler of Perkins School of Theology: the church, Outler argued, will never have an adequate doctrine of the human person without the insights of psychiatry. Jung knew the founder of Alcoholics Anonymous and wrote to him, calling alcoholism a "spiritual disease."

Richard Coan, a professor of psychology at the University of Arizona, has spend a large part of his professional career seeking to determine the nature of the optimal human personality; he has provided a

---

[11] *Collected Works,* Vol. 11 (1958), p. 334.

survey of his findings in his book *Hero, Artist, Sage or Saint? A Survey of Views on What Is Variously Called Mental Health, Normality, Maturity, Self-Actualization, and Human Fulfillment.* Coan began by showing that psychology as a science cannot provide the goals for human life. He claimed that if any goals *are* provided by psychology, the psychologists must either introduce them surreptitiously or openly acknowledge the need for religion and transpersonal meaning.

Coan concluded that there are five elements that characterize the fully developed human person: efficiency, creativity, inner harmony, relatedness, and transcendence. (Most thinkers and many societies, he pointed out, emphasize one or two of these to the neglect of others.) As Coan described these elements, efficiency is the heroic quality. Heroes accomplish things with effectiveness, have strong egos, and are able to focus the direction of their lives. Freud demonstrated the necessity of a strong ego and his psychological method helps develop one. Jung remarked that psychotics may have great religious experiences, but they are unable to do anything with them; the truly religious person, however, not only needs experiences of the risen Christ but also needs to be an effective instrument of that power in the world. This heroism can be embodied in outer actions, in thinking, in scientific discovery, in religious practice, or in theological study.

The second element, creativity, is often represented by artists, who are able to present images, poetry, or ideas in a new way so that they touch others with a dimension beyond the physical. Of course, there is little real art without discipline, and the greatest art (as found in Dante's *Divine Comedy*, for example) usually touches the transcendent and transpersonal.

The third element is embodied by the sage, the person who has achieved inner harmony. According to Coan, one goal of life is to reduce the tension and fear and conflict within us, and to come to harmony. This harmony can be found either by obliterating upsetting emotions or by finding a reality that gives inner peace even amid the pain and brokenness of this life.

The fourth element, relatedness, is manifested by the saint, the person who treats others with understanding, caring, love, empathy, social sensitivity, compassion. Saints make other people feel loved and help them love. Christian sainthood is certainly characterized by Jesus' command to "love one another as I have loved you." Coan quotes James Baldwin's statement of the world's need for such saintliness: "The moment we cease to hold each other, the moment we break faith with one another, the sea engulfs us and the light goes out."

The fifth element is transcendence. This is the vertical aspect of saintliness. (Relatedness may be considered its horizontal dimension.) Relatedness becomes intolerable unless we are empowered from above. Clergy burnout occurs when religious professionals try to live the Christian life without the empowerment supplied by prayer and meditation that leads to an experience of divine Love. In its hunger for true caring, the world engulfs and destroys us if we are not given constant divine support. Life burns out, falls apart, and loses its meaning if we have no experience of a God who reaches down, touches us, and draws us into the transcendental dimension both now and at death; indeed, sometimes our experience of transcendence is actually a sense of being saved from the forces of evil within and around us.

Coan suggested that Jung, as thoroughly as any modern psychologist, gave consideration to each of these elements of human wholeness and developed a framework in which they all have a place. This has also been my experience, after reading psychology for thirty years. And as I listen to the message of Jesus of Nazareth and the church built on his resurrection, I hear the affirmation of these elements as essential features of the full Christian life.

Dr. Roger Walsh, who earned a doctorate in psychology as well as a medical degree, wrote an article published in the June 1980 issue of the *American Journal of Psychiatry*. Entitled "The Consciousness Disciplines and the Behavioral Sciences: Questions of Comparison and Assessment," this careful, sophisticated statement, shows that much of modern psychiatry has ignored human experiences of the transpersonal. In doing so, Walsh says, psychiatry has failed in its task of dealing with the *whole human being*. It is notable that a September 1984 television program on depression presented by the American Medical Association did not mention lack of meaning as a factor in depression or mention the value of transpersonal experience in treating depression. And yet depression is one affliction in which loss of ultimate meaning, lack of being in contact with God, certainly is a contributive factor.

Walsh quoted with approval a letter that Carl Jung wrote to P. W. Martin in August 1945. Martin was a Quaker whose book, *Experiment in Depth*, was one of the first religious books to acknowledge the religious significance of Jung. "You are quite right," Jung wrote. "The main interest of my work is not concerned with the treatment of neuroses but rather with the approach to the numinous. But the fact is that the approach to the numinous is the real therapy and inasmuch as you attain to the numinous experiences you are released from the curse of pathology. Even the very disease takes on a numinous character."[12] Jung borrowed *numinous* from Rudolf Otto's *The Idea of the Holy;* the "numinous" is what human beings experience when in contact with God. After Jung's break with Freud he was thrown into unconscious turmoil. He wrote that he survived because "I had an unswerving conviction that I was obeying a higher will." In later life Jung had a numinous near-death experience that he describes in a chapter entitled "Visions" in his autobiography, *Memories, Dreams, Reflections.*

Let us look at the philosophical and psychological framework that Jung proposed. Jung built on the work and ideas of those before and around him. He was knowledgeable in all areas of psychology and psychiatry, and he recognized the value of using a wide variety of techniques for healing patients. He saw the place for behavioral, cognitive, existential, and Freudian therapeutic methods, and he accepted the use of therapeutic drugs. He was critical of these methods only when they claimed to offer exhaustive accounts of the human psyche and when they neglected important data found in the religious search of humankind from the beginning of human consciousness.

The serious problem in reading Jung is that he assumes that the reader knows Freud and knows that Jung agrees with Freud when he does not explicitly disagree with him. It is difficult to understand Jung without a Freudian background. This is one reason I have explained Freud's thinking in some depth. Matters that Freud covered adequately, such as strength of the ego, Jung does not discuss at length or at all.

The diagram in figure 2 may help us understand Jung's thought.[13] As we compare this diagram with that representing Freud's view, we see that Jung started with the Freudian model, but changed it in four major ways. These changes make a crucial difference. The triangle in the center represents one human being, and the whole diagram depicts the experiences that converge upon this individual. In a sense, the diagram depicts the entire universe as one coherent whole. The Self is the creative principle at the heart of all reality, psychoid (spiritual) and physical. These two aspects of reality can be distinguished, although they interpenetrate one another. Jung usually referred to the spiritual realm as the *psychoid:* it is like the human psyche—conscious, knowing, willing, etc. (In his autobiography, *Memories, Dreams, Reflections,* and in

---

[12] *Jung's Letters,* Vol. 1 (1973) p. 377.
[13] In the former edition of this book the diagram could have been interpreted dualistically. This diagram avoids that implication.

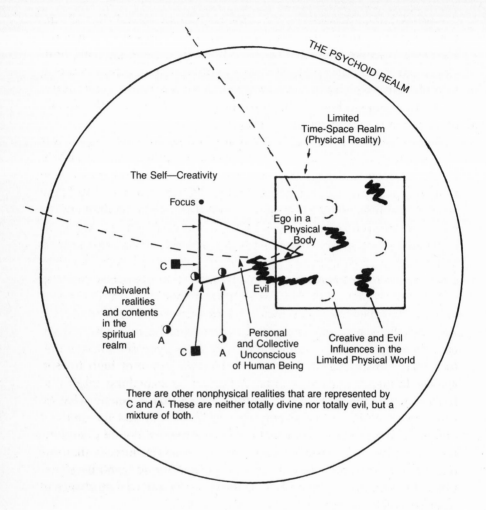

Figure 2

his letters, Jung spoke directly about God, but in most of his other writings he used less religious terminology, hoping to reach the scientific communities.) Within and surrounded by the limited spiritual realm is the limited, physical, space-time, energy-mass world. Human beings in their essential nature are related to and embedded in both these worlds. Through the five senses we receive knowledge of the physical dimension of reality; most of the data accepted by psychology and psychiatry is limited to that which is given by the physical world through the five senses. But in the Jungian schema there is also the mysterious presence of evil, which has a spiritual origin through which it touches human beings directly. It is also found spread through the physical world, just as we find evidence of God's presence throughout the physical world. Jung also suggested that there are organizing principles within the psychoid realm—both within human beings and outside of them—which he calls *archetypes*. These can have a great impact upon those human beings who are energized by them. Archetypes are often revealed in dreams and visions.[14]

Jung's first and most important change in the Freudian system was to claim that while we are indeed physical creatures, we are also in touch with, surrounded by, and a part of a meaningful, more than human, nonphysical dimension of reality. He wrote to me: "We know as little of supreme being as of matter. But there is as little doubt of the existence of supreme being as of matter. *The world beyond is a reality*, an experiential fact."[15] And this nonphysical world is not meaningless or subhuman, as Freud believed; rather, it contains an advocate, a helper who wishes to bring human beings to wholeness, to salvation. Jung called this *das Selbst*, which translates literally as "the itself," a reality superior to and independent of the human being. In *Psychology and Alchemy* (1968), his study of *das Selbst*, Jung stated that no one is bothered by the idea that the human psyche contains layers *below* and *inferior* to human consciousness, but we consider it a crime of high treason against human nature to suggest there can be something *superior* to human beings that is trying to help them. Yet that is exactly what he experienced as he looked deeply into his own soul and the souls of others. Jung also pointed out that it is only a tiny fraction of humanity, those who live in the heavily populated peninsula of Eurasia that juts out into the Atlantic and think that they are "cultured" who have proposed the idea that "religion is a peculiar kind of mental disturbance of undiscoverable purport."[16]

Jung felt that religion was necessary for human development, and he could not imagine why people could not understand that he was speaking of a real, nonphysical dimension of reality when he spoke of the human psyche and the spiritual realm from which it issued. He wrote in a letter: "I did not create the psyche. If we speak of God as an archetype, we say nothing about His real nature, but are letting it be known that God already has a place in that part of the psyche which is

---

[14] I have described Jung's hypothetical system and its relation to Christianity in detail in *Christo-Psychology* (1982) and also in *Prophetic Ministry* (1982).

[15] *Jung's Letters* Vol. 2 (1975), p. 435.

[16] *Two Essays in Analytical Psychology* (1956) pp. 215–16.

pre-existent to consciousness, and that therefore He cannot be considered an invention of consciousness. We neither make Him nor remove or eliminate him but, bring Him closer to the possibility of being experienced."[17] God's Spirit has its foothold in the human soul, and so the psalmist cries out to God not to take away his Holy Spirit. Knowledge is not confined to the five senses; we human beings can experience a psychoid reality, and we can have direct experience of God and other spiritual realities. It took me nearly ten years of working with some of Jung's followers to break out of my materialism and understand what Jung was saying, and to realize that Jung's view on this subject was similar to that of Jesus of Nazareth.

The second major change that Jung made in Freud's schema was to suggest that the psyche is not an organized system of self-deception, but that through revelations, visions, intuitions, dreams, gifts of healing, knowledge, wisdom, and other experiences we are given genuine knowledge of this other dimension of reality. Modern neurophysiology of dreaming supports Jung in his contention that the space-time distortion in dreams is not created by a psychic process. We are also given the gifts of discernment to help decide what is of God and what is not. Along with most of the church fathers, Jung believed that something wiser than ourselves speaks through our dreams. Unlike Freud, Jung did not believe that the messages of the unconscious had been scrambled by a censor; he claimed rather, that we have forgotten how to understand the language of symbolism. As we learn the meaning of symbols in the Bible, in the parables of Jesus, in art and literature and drama, we can begin to understand our dreams.[18]

In addition, Jung became convinced that the human psyche contains many more drives than those for sex and power. So he made a third change in Freud's system. He believed that unless we come into touch with God, we are likely to become neurotic. We have already quoted Jung's statement that neurosis is a religious matter and that the church as well as psychiatrists and psychologists should be helping people with their psychological problems. Jung also believed that the full dogma and practice of the Christian church was the best therapeutic system ever given to human beings. He maintained that real Christianity deals with whole people and that through its dogmatic beliefs and religious

---

[17] Quoted by Vera van der Heydt, *Jung and Religion*, pp. 9–12.
[18] John Sanford shows in *The Kingdom Within* (1987) that understanding the symbols of dreams is similar to truly understanding the symbols of Jesus' parables.

rituals and practices it enables us to experience the Holy and avoid the "curse of pathology."

In his book *Psychotherapy and the Cure of Souls in Jung's Psychology*, Hans Schaer provided an excellent analysis of Jung's attitude toward Christianity, both Catholic and Protestant. Schaer was a close friend of Jung's and a minister of the Swiss Reformed Church. In the chapter entitled "Man and Religion," he sketched out Jung's deep admiration of Catholicism and then Jung's attitude toward Protestantism. Jung believed that the Catholicism of his time provided human beings the best objectification of the total unconscious (and therefore the greatest psychotherapeutic help) of any religious system. He believed it superior to Eastern religions because these symbols were seen as part of the objective, outer world. He also believed that Protestantism stripped Westerners of their symbols and forced many of them into a confrontation with the unconscious for which they were not ready.

Jung's thinking about symbol systems contains one major flaw. He assumed that an individual is either inside the dogmatic system where the symbols have meaning and saving power, or outside of it and unable ever to reenter. My experience is that we can be outside the naive acceptance of dogma and still find that the symbols have saving power. Paul Ricoeur calls this "the second naïveté." Jung seldom acknowledged this possibility.

A fourth change that Jung made in Freud's thought was to give an alternative to the notion of an innate death wish. Jung proposed that just as there is a healing reality that seeks to bring us to wholeness (what Christians call God or the risen Christ or the Holy Spirit), there is also a destructive force that tries to pull us down into its own destructiveness.[19] Jung saw evil as a reality both within and beyond the human psyche, a reality that tries to cripple us. Radical evil needs to be distinguished from our personal human shadow, which may consist of good parts of ourselves that we have repressed and that often appear as hostile parts of ourselves. These we need to face and deal with.

Essential evil cannot be handled by human beings alone, but only with the intervention of God or, as Christians would say, by the risen

---

[19] Jung's writing about evil is ambiguous. At times, as in *The Answer to Job*, he portrayed evil as a part of God, while in *Aion* (1968) he made no reference to this idea. John Sanford has pointed out to me passages in the second volume of his *Letters* (pp. 120, 134, 494–95) supporting the former idea. However, there is no suggestion of this idea in the passage equating God with love that we will quote in a few pages. In *Aion* and other places, evil is seen as a radical and destructive force apart from God.

Christ who has already defeated evil. One part of Jung's thought therefore came close to the early church's idea of evil. We have already shown that the church fathers called evil *death* and believed that it affected human beings in four ways: morally in sin, psychologically in demonic possession and mental illness, physically in sickness and disability, and finally in physical death itself.

We have already looked at the numerous references to Jesus' healing of the demonized and to the many other statements about demons in the New Testament. I have dealt with that matter in depth in *Discernment: A Study in Ecstasy and Evil*. In it I quote several passages from Jung showing how seriously he viewed the subject. Indeed he saw Nazism as the powers of Evil demonizing a whole nation. When I am asked what I think about evil I paraphrase Jung's statement when he was asked if he believed in God. I reply: I do not believe in evil, I know it. From the diagram above it would appear that all of us are infected with Evil to some degree. Jesus alone faced it and rejected it and knew himself well enough so that he could be totally rid of it. Those human beings who think that they are entirely devoid of evil (and then in the position to judge others) are like the scribes and pharisees and are the ones most likely to be unconsciously caught in it.

We need to steer a course between rejecting all substantial evil (and the demonic) on one hand and seeing it under every bed and in every neurosis on the other hand, between ignoring it and exorcizing it in nearly every situation. One of the most sensible treatments of dealing with demons is found in Chapter 6 of John Wimber's *Power Healing*. He rejects the idea of possession as either/or and suggests that some of us are more severely demonized (attacked by the demonic) than others. Even the best of committed Christians can have their lives infiltrated with the destructive influence of the demonic. I would prefer to say that all of us are unconscious to some degree and through our unconsciousness Evil and his/her minions gets access to our lives. Our very unconsciousness of who and what we are contributes to our evil. Jung has written that our willingness to remain unconscious is the very essence of evil. Unfortunately it is often the case that the further we progress on the Christian way, the more we can be especially prized targets for Evil's attack. I have listed ten distinguishing marks of Evil in *Discernment*.[20]

At least one essential aspect of reality appears to be ultimately destructive, driving us to physical and mental illness. It is represented in

---

[20] Pp. 78–85, 100–105.

the New Testament and depicted, for instance, by the witches in *Macbeth* and Mephistopheles in *Faust*, and also by the Evil One and the demonic so accurately portrayed in Dante's *Divine Comedy*. Jung has described his own personal encounter with this destructive element with terrifying reality in the sixth chapter of his autobiography, *Memories, Dreams, Reflections*.

He has also made important contributions to the problem of dealing with evil, and one of the most significant of these is found in his outburst of poetic active imagination, *The Answer to Job*. As he was recovering from what had been an excruciatingly painful and nearly fatal illness, he dealt with his own agony by identifying in feeling with Job. Toward the end of this book he wrote, "Everything now depends on man: immense power of destruction is given into his hand, and the question is whether he can resist the will to use it, and can temper his will with the spirit of love and wisdom. He will hardly be capable of doing so on his own unaided resources. He needs the help of an 'advocate' in heaven, that is, of the child who was caught up to God and who brings the 'healing' and making whole of the hitherto fragmentary man."[21]

Jung remonstrated with those who see evil only as the absence or deprivation of good (the *privatio boni*). He was convinced that evil is a reality of experience with which we are required to deal. We cannot philosophize it out of existence. Indeed he saw this tendency as a dangerous one because it made people unconscious of the evil within them, so that instead of dealing with it they projected it out onto others. In the midst of a long discussion of the *privatio boni* in *Aion*, Jung remarked with some exasperation, "One could hardly call the things that have happened, and still do happen, in the concentration camps of the dictator states an 'accidental lack of perfection'—it would sound like mockery."[22]

People who venture into the depths of the unconscious confront the source of such evil, and they are helpless against it unless they are guided and guarded by a power greater than their own. But at the same time, in the real experience of these depths, the very meaning of religion is revealed in its essence when they call upon a creative reality that lifts them out of the power of darkness and leads them on. Jung devoted most of the last part of his life to understanding and describing the creative, restoring aspect of the unconscious, and this integrative

---

[21] *Collected Works*, Vol. 11, p. 450.
[22] *Ibid.*, vol. 9, pt. 2:53.

saving reality which he called "the Self" is detailed in works like *Psychology and Alchemy, Aion,* and others. So important were these religious and numinous contents that unless patients began to find relationship to them, they did not come to a full use of their capacities or recover fully from their neurosis and its physical complications.

Jung was primarily a physician, and sickness was an evil to him. He believed that psychological (emotional) healing and physical healing went hand in hand. Discussing the effects of the unconscious upon the physical world and particularly upon the human body, he wrote, "The same relationship of complementarity can be observed just as easily in all those extremely common medical cases in which certain clinical symptoms disappear when the corresponding unconscious contents are made conscious. We also know that a number of psychosomatic phenomena which are otherwise outside the control of the will can be induced by hypnosis, that is, by this same restriction of consciousness."[23]

To show the reality of the psyche, in the first part of *Psychology and Religion* he gave example of these physical effects that he had seen in his own practice:

Since my readers may not be familiar with these medical facts I may instance a case of hysterical fever, with a temperature of 102 degrees, which was cured in a few minutes through confession of the psychological cause. A patient with psoriasis extending over practically the whole body was told that I did not feel competent to treat his skin trouble, but that I should concentrate on his psychological conflicts, which were numerous. After six weeks of intense analysis and discussion of his purely psychological difficulties, there came about as an unexpected by-product, the almost complete disappearance of the skin disease. In another case, the patient had recently undergone an operation for distention of the colon. Forty centimetres of it had been removed, but this was followed by another extraordinary distention. The patient was desperate and refused to permit a second operation, though the surgeon thought it vital. As soon as certain intimate psychological facts were discovered, the colon began to function normally again.[24]

In discussing dreams he wrote that they often show "a remarkable inner symbolical connection between an undoubted physical illness and a definite psychic problem," so that in many cases it looks as if the physical disorder were directly mimicking the psychic condition. Jung did not stress this problem because, as he pointed out elsewhere in relation to glandular disorders, it is hard to know which is cause and

---

[23] *Ibid.,* 8:232.
[24] *Ibid.,* 11:11–12. From the Terry Lectures, given at Yale University in 1937.

which effect. He went on to say, "It seems to me, however, that a definite connection does exist between physical and psychic disturbances and that its significance is generally underrated, though on the other hand it is boundlessly exaggerated owing to certain tendencies to regard physical disturbances merely as an expression of psychic disturbances, as is particularly the case with Christian Science."[25] Thus Jung found that when human beings try to live as if they could simply break all connection with the unconscious and avoid inner evil as well as the Savior available to them by dealing only with the physical world, they often got sick. And very frequently, as psychologists everywhere have found, the symptoms they develop look like a mock-up of what is going on in their unconscious. When Jung broke his foot, the beginning of his nearly fatal illness, he realized that something was wrong with his "standpoint." He wrote this to a friend who suffered a similar accident.

All in all, Jung's framework is quite similar to that of the New Testament and the teachings and practice of Jesus and to the teachings and practice of the early church. I am deeply grateful to Jung and his followers. Years ago I found myself a Christian minister still caught in an unconscious materialistic worldview with no place for the world of spirit. What I professed consciously as a Christian I denied unconsciously. When I listened carefully in the middle of the night, I heard the dark voice telling me that I didn't really believe what I was saying, that I was split in two, that I was a fraud. Sometimes as I was preaching I heard the same voice whispering into my left ear, "You don't really believe any of that claptrap." Such an attitude is very uncomfortable; it is the stuff of which neurosis is made.

When I found myself in this condition, none of my Christian colleagues were in a position to help. It was Jung who provided me with a reasonable worldview in which the reality of Jesus' incarnation, life, death, resurrection, and ascension, and the giving of the Holy Spirit made sense. *Jung was not the Savior, but he released me from the materialistic box in which I had been imprisoned; he gave me the freedom to let the full saving power of the risen Jesus begin a process of transformation in me.* During my visit with Jung, I asked him which psychological approach was closest to his own method. Instead of naming a psychologist, he replied, "The spiritual directors in France in the late nineteenth century—people like Abbé Huvelin."

---

[25] *Ibid.*, 8:261.

I want to make myself perfectly clear. I am not a Jungian, but a Christian for whom Jung opened the door out of the materialistic prison of which William James spoke. Even Jung himself, by the way, once remarked that he was glad that he was Jung and not a Jungian. I am deeply grateful for Jung's help, but at the same time I want to make my belief clear: *Jung is not the whole answer.* He can only open the door; he does not bring us into the presence of the Saviour. When I visited with Jung, he told me that both theologians and medical doctors misunderstood him. He said that he was simply a psychiatrist, a doctor of the soul, who had found that both the spiritual domain and the saving power available there were real, and that we human beings could not live truly satisfactory lives and come to our full potential if we did not take these realities into consideration. It was not his task, Jung said, to be a minister or priest. He once begged the great Anglican theologian, Archbishop William Temple, to send him clergy to train so that they could bring about this integration of theology and psychology.

When Jung himself theologized, however, as he did in several books, he sometimes showed a lack of good historical understanding of theology and Christianity. He also never told readers when he was discussing an issue about which he had changed his mind, so readers have to know when a given book was written in order to understand whether it represents Jung's mature and final understanding of a subject. His books, furthermore, are often difficult, because Jung had a wide European education, read both Greek and Latin fluently, knew most of modern psychological and scientific thought, and expected his readers to know just as much. I have already noted that he also expected readers to know their Freud, and to know that—except in regard to certain specific issues—he accepted the Freudian framework. In addition, Jung was not a systematic thinker. We have already indicated his ambiguity about evil. He gave his deepest and best understanding of a subject at the time of writing. Sometimes his interpretations of a subject are at variance with one another. Like the Bible, Jung must be interpreted, and there are differing interpretations. You have received mine in these pages.

But the greatest problem that Christians have in reading Jung is that Jung is ambivalent about institutional Christianity and about its belief in the resurrection of Jesus and its saving power. He was raised by a father who was a minister in the Swiss Reformed Church. His father's intellectual faith was not based in experience and was different from his unconscious belief. Jung believed that his father's inner split led to his early death. Jung's father expected his son to accept faith on authority, without discussion. Jung was a deeply religious boy and young man, but he was scarred by this relationship. So even though Jung thought of himself as a Christian, he did not see the importance for himself of the saving action of Jesus's death and resurrection. In *Christianity as Psychology* I have sketched out some of the reasons for Jung's resistance to this central part of the Christian message.

In spite of all this, Jung's last written statement about religion is found in his autobiography: "Man can try to name love, showering upon it all the names at his command, but still he will involve himself in endless self-deceptions. If he possesses a grain of wisdom, he will lay down his arms and name the unknown by the more unknown, *ignotum per ignotius*—that is, by the name of God. That is a confession of his subjection, his imperfection, and his dependence; but at the same time a testimony to his freedom to choose between truth and error."[26] This is the same conclusion reached by some of the greatest Christian saints. I think that Jung was far more Christian than he himself knew. I wish more Christian theologians were as clear about the nature of God as Jung is in this passage.

The Process of Healing

Jung stressed again and again that it was not the psychiatrist's task to heal the sick person, but rather to guide people to the source of healing within, a source that seemed to come from beyond and outside of them, like a spring bubbling up into a small pond. The psychiatrist was a midwife, encouraging and aiding natural processes. These several different processes are not totally separate; they merge into one another, and they do not necessarily take place in the order that I suggest. As we grow out of our problems and neuroses, we pass often through each of these stages. Climbing a circular staircase we pass the same point again and again, but each time at a higher level.

Exploration of the inner world

Jung brought a conviction to his patients that the inner world of images, fantasy, visions, and dreams was as real as the physical world,

---

[26] *Memories, Dreams, Reflections* (1963), p. 354.

but more enduring. When I visited with Jung, he reminded me that the word "convince" means to be conquered by. He told me the story of the schizophrenic patient who presented him with a strange fantasy of the source of the wind being a tube that hung from the sun. Later he discovered an almost identical formula in some ancient mystical papyri dug up out of the sands of Egypt. This experience broke him out of his materialism and enabled him to realize that we are in touch with a real psychoid (spiritual) world that exists in its own right. Still later he discovered a saving figure that led him through the agony of his break with Freud and on to his greater confidence in the meaningfulness of existence and the primacy of love.

The five Jungian therapists with whom I have worked shared this same basic conviction. Someone who has not *experienced* the reality and saving power available in this psychoid realm can hardly lead another in and through the darkness of the unconscious. Jung wrote that psychiatrists are surgeons whose only scalpels are their own personalities. Jung then went on to hypothesize the basic schema that I diagrammed a few pages back. Jung was the first modern thinker to offer me an acceptable view of the universe with a place for both a spiritual reality and a saving power as well as a real physical world always in process. Without this alternative to my materialism I doubt if I could have taken seriously this method that was offered for dealing with my confrontation with the unconscious. Reading *Modern Man In Search of a Soul* opened me to a way of dealing with the spiritual dimension of reality. In the question and answer appendix to *Analytical Psychology in Theory and Practice,* Jung tells of a young artist who could not get well until he realized from experience that the psychoid realm was real and learned to take it seriously—not just as "art."

To what extent therapists should provide worldviews for their clients is a sticky problem. On the one hand, therapists cannot proselyte for their own saving figure; on the other hand, it seems immoral to me to leave people in a vacuum of meaning when loss of meaning is what is making them sick and we have found a way of dealing with it. I know of no better description of therapeutic intervention with meaning than Andrew Canale's book, *The Healing Image: From Depression to Meaning* (manuscript as yet unpublished). Is this more questionable than intervening with drugs? The analysts with whom I worked opened the door so that meaning was a possibility for me. I had a good theological background and could provide my own saving images— and they worked. But what about those without this theological background? Would it be immoral to offer these as well? Cannot clergy provide the same healing worldview to confused and struggling human beings?

Helps in confronting inner chaos

As Jung worked through his own confrontation with the unconscious he discovered methods that helped him deal with these onslaughts of chaos, and he passed these on to his patients. Books have been written on each of the processes, which include journal writing, dreams, imaginative meditation, and companions for the inner journey.

Jung found journal writing almost essential in his own healing. What is written has greater concreteness and brings about more changes within us than images merely thought about. In addition what is written can be read later and criticized by one's ego consciousness. Our task is not to be overwhelmed and swallowed by either the unconscious or the ego, but to bring these into confrontation. We need to know as much about ourselves as possible and then bring this knowledge to our experience of the Holy. This is not far from Dr. Roy Fairchild's description of prayer: "to bring all we know of ourselves to all of God that we know." I have provided an introduction to Christian journal writing in my book *Adventure Inward*.

The simplest kind of journal writing is merely recollection and reflection. To stop, be quiet, and take note of who and what we are. To look at our foibles and desires, our angers and fears, our failures and successes, our relations with others, our goals, our use of time. How few people ever stop to reflect, and yet when our emotions are out of control or when life does not seem satisfying, it is nearly impossible to move ahead psychologically or spiritually without this kind of reflection. Nearly all of the great religions of the world advise this kind of reflection as necessary for genuine spiritual growth. When this kind of reflection is not recorded in some permanent way it cannot have its full influence upon us, nor can it form a foundation upon which we can build.

And then there are dreams. Freud called them the royal road to the unconscious. Jung pointed out that dreams can reveal the turmoil within the unconscious and can give us spiritual visions of the greatest significance. Jung also showed how we have forgotten to think symbolically and so need to learn to interpret dreams, for they are messages in symbols. In *God, Dreams and Revelation*, I have shown how central the interpretation of dreams is to the whole Biblical tradition and to the life and practice of the Christian church throughout the ages—with the exception of Western Christianity since the Enlightenment. In *Dreams,*

A Way to Listen to God, I offer a simple way to listen to the religious messages of the dream. Dreams can tell us where our lives are off the path, how to get back on our way, where we are going, and how to get there. Jung's understanding of dreams is similar to what has been our Christian heritage.

In fantasy, imagination, contemplation, meditation we can turn inward consciously and awake; we can enter into the same realm that the dream reveals in sleep. Few modern people have offered more wisdom and guidance in the use of imagination than Jung and his followers. Jung rediscovered the power of the imagination in the crisis that overwhelmed him following his break with Freud. He discovered that hidden in the depth of each emotion is an image. As destructive images are revealed, we can bring more creative images to counter them and these images can displace the destructive ones. He called this process active imagination. This practice is not a matter of just revealing the images or letting fantasy flow, but is hard work, work that can bring transformation. In *The Other Side of Silence* I have described this process in detail and given several examples of it. There are two quite different kinds of meditation within the Christian tradition of prayer: the apophatic, in which images are banished and one finds God in imagelessness; and the kataphatic, in which the image is used as a mediator of the Divine. The very idea of the incarnation is quite kataphatic: God is presented to us in a human being. When I read Ignatius of Loyola's *Spiritual Exercises* at Notre Dame in preparation for a seminar on religious experience, I realized that I was much at home. I had been trained by my Jungian analyst friends in the very same kind of process, and I *knew* the transforming power of the process that Ignatius was using. Some scholars believe that Ignatius's work was a brilliant summary of what had been the best Christian practice for centuries. However, some people do not find image prayer congenial; for them, imageless prayer contributes more to their spiritual growth.

Jung survived the onslaught of the unconscious alone, and so did Ignatius of Loyola and Teresa of Avila. All three were people of incredible psychic strength and courage. One of the finest descriptions of Jung's way and at the same time a comparison of his way with that of Teresa of Avila is John Welch's *Spiritual Pilgrims: Carl Jung and Teresa of Avila*. These two describe the same inner realities and a similar process for dealing with them. It should be noted that this kind of inner journey is a dangerous process and is not for everyone; one needs to be called to it.

However, this is a dangerous way to travel alone and all those who go deeply into the inner world are urged to find someone who has already gone that way to be one's companion and friend. Finding a Jungian analyst is not essential, but finding someone who has been and is still on that way is nearly essential, so that one doesn't get lost in the complex and dangerous inner world. Finding a spiritual guide or companion is not easy, but people are available if we persistently look and pray for them. Jung once said that we get the analyst that we deserve. The important thing is to keep searching until one finds a companion on the way.

Importance of self-acceptance and love

Seldom does transformation take place except within the context of human interaction, love, caring. Unless we know how to be loved and to love, we seldom step into the flame of divine transformation. We have already noted how Jung in one of his last written statements equated "love" and God. My own experience with Jung is the same as that of hundreds of other people. He had an enormous ability to care for others—sometimes so much that he has been criticized for it. The best description of the importance of transference (the psychological term for deep, positive emotional involvement with another person) is found in Murray Stein's *Jung's Treatment of Christianity*. It is dangerous to love and to be loved, but without stepping courageously into such relationships, we stunt not only our psychological growth, but our spiritual growth as well. Jung did not believe that remaining objective and aloof often resulted in healing. Jung also wrote that some of his patients became his best friends.

One of my most important spiritual experiences brought me to the realization that unconditional love was not only necessary in order to be a successful pastor, but was essential for the health of my family relationships and for my own psychological growth. It is also essential in order to follow Jesus Christ: we are told that we are following him only as we love one another as he loved us.

In *Caring: How Do We Love One Another?*, I have sketched both the centrality of loving and caring and how we can learn to love creatively. We human beings seem to have as many if not more inclinations toward selfishness, revenge, and hostility as we do toward unconditional love. It is no easy matter to seek more to be consoling than to be consoled, more to be understanding than to be understood, more to be loving than to be loved.

In order to start on this way we need first of all to learn to listen. Until we listen to other people we are treating them more as things than as fellow human beings (or as a "thou"—to use Buber's phrase). And then we need to cease our judging. Jung has pointed out that we never help another by condemnation. God sends the rain upon the just as well as the unjust. God has created many strange situations and quite different people and to accept them as they are is the beginning of relationship and transforming love. As Jesus often said, "Judge not lest you be judged." Most condemnation and judgment come from projecting our own darkness onto other people. We seldom come close to people when we judge. Instead we isolate already alienated people, alienated from themselves and others. The third step in the process may be necessary before we are able to accomplish the other two fully: we need to accept and love ourselves as we are. Only so can we begin to allow the love of God to change us and use us. To hate ourselves is to deny the love of the crucified and risen Jesus who underwent all this for broken, lost, and depraved human beings. This is the nearly unbelievable message of Jesus of Nazareth. To hate ourselves is a refusal to accept God's love and usually a first step toward hating others.

Self-discipline and education

The next stage is that of education. As we try to grow more conscious and loving, we come to the realization "that no confession and no amount of explaining will make the ill-formed tree grow straight, but that it must be trained with the gardener's art upon the trellis before normal adaptation can be attained."[27] The healing of personality from which emotional and physical healing flow is not an automatic process. Training and discipline are required to bring the conscious will into harmonious teamwork with unconscious contents.

One must learn, on one hand, that there are many different ways of relating to the world and other people. We need to understand human differences and honor them. It is also essential to learn how to keep a relation going with the unconscious so that the widening of one's consciousness will not come to a halt. And often as we come to greater harmony within, our physical sicknesses disappear, but sometimes they don't. This relation of the physical, emotional, and spiritual is a great mystery.

How long does this process take? When do we arrive? When do we become fulfilled? The answer is that the further we go, the more we

---

[27] *Modern Man in Search of a Soul* (1933), p. 46.

realize how far we have to go. The people who have thought of themselves as the most wretched of human beings (without hating themselves) have often been the saints. As we learn more about ourselves
and try harder and harder to love, we are often given glimpses of God's
unconditional love. As we try to bring all these elements of our experience into an integrated whole, we often have fresh revelations about
ourselves and our failures to love and our lack of discipline and lack of
faithfulness to God. And then we start the whole process all over again.
As we look back over twenty or thirty years we can sometimes see some
progress, but we also see more clearly how much more growing is
possible for us. We read the lives of the saints; we try to understand
scripture; we listen to the best reflections of psychologists and keep
courageously on the path toward love, wholeness, integration, and still
there is always further to go. I am so grateful for the vision of Jesus
and of those who have lived the Christian life most deeply. They speak
of life beyond this one, eternal life in which we can grow eternally and
come into the fullness of the sons and daughters of God, in a place
larger than earth, kinder than home.

Experiencing God's unconditional love

Every now and then, as we pursue this path, and sometimes out of
the blue, we have a sense of God's presence, of being totally and un-
conditionally forgiven, cared for, and loved, of being whole. We have
experiences in which all the pieces fit together. We are lifted to a new
level and get intimations of our eternal value and worth, of the ultimate
nature of reality. We have already given some of the data regarding
such experiences. As I have shown in *Christianity as Psychology*, a large
percentage of people have such experiences, such encounters with transcendence.

Important as our effort and discipline are, however, they do not
actually resolve our basic inner conflict. Our situation at this point is
paradoxical. All we can do to develop understanding and will and consciousness does not constellate the Self or God, and yet, without our
conscious hard work, usually nothing happens. It reminds one of the
dilemma of orthodox Christianity. Salvation is not achieved by our own
efforts; the church had to consider this idea very carefully in order to
avoid the heresy of Pelagianism. Yet neither are we saved entirely by
the action of God unrelated to our own efforts, as the predestinarian
holds. We must try as hard as we can, knowing that it is not enough,
that God gives salvation as his own free gift. What Jung has described

as a psychological process has essentially the same quality as the finest Christian religious way.

In fact, in this final development, religious virtues of the highest nature are needed if one is to continue seeking growth and integration in the face of one's own inability to pull together the fragments of one's human personality. When we are doing the best we know how, and still nothing happens, we need patience, persistence, courage, and faith. We need to be able to bear the tension of unresolved opposites within ourselves, and also within those around us, until the solution is *given*. We generally find an analyst or companion on the inner way to be a source of great help and strength at this time. In *Companions on the Inner Way*, I have described the great need for Christians trained both religiously and psychologically who can act as companions to the large number of people hungry for inner growth. I also suggest a program by which such companions might be trained.

The saints have described this situation as the dark night of the soul. It is often described as midlife crisis: old adaptations have worn out, but no new ones have appeared. Jung also noted that this crisis often comes midway in life, between thirty-five and forty-five. Saints are the women and men who, doubting their own courage, give others the courage to bear on through the darkness until light appears. Without courage we cannot hope for success; after doing all we can, we often find it is not enough. Our statement is like that of Job and his friends. They had argued through three rounds of discourse with no solution; instead the conflict only became more violent and bitter. But Job persisted and God appeared.

The individuals who persist on, neither backing down nor giving up, often find the conflict solved for them on a higher level. As with Job, God appears in a whirlwind to set things right and resolve the stalemate. In fact, several cases have been reported of a solution coming to people as they dreamed of a whirlwind. What people could not do for themselves was done for them and they were raised to a new level, where conflict loses its bitterness. This experience is called by Jung the constellation of the Self, in which an unknown arises in the life of individuals to bring order out of chaos—to integrate the conflicting tendencies and parts of their personalities. Theologically this is known as religious experience. Jung speaks of a transforming symbol by which the difficulties are resolved irrationally. In the religious experience, the fragmented and warring parts are united by common meaning and values; a satisfying sense of wholeness and value is given by God. There is a real similarity to the experience of Christians in former times who stood before a martyr's shrine in need of healing and found themselves healed and their lives changed as well.

Jung observed an instinctual drive toward wholeness within the psyche. In his words, "To strive after τελέωσις—completion—in this sense is not only legitimate but is inborn in man as a peculiarity which provides civilization with one of its strongest roots. This striving is so powerful, even, that it can turn into a passion that draws everything into its service."[28] Very much as nature abhors a vacuum, the psyche abhors separation and division. One example of this instinctual drive is transference, in which we find wholeness symbolically through another person, who carries an essential part of the psyche for us. And if this instinctual drive is followed through to its own conclusion, it leads to a wholeness such as is experienced in religious life. Thus it may be said that human beings are instinctively religious and that they cannot often be whole in soul, mind, and body until they have come to this experience, or—to use religious terms—until they have been touched by the reality of God and try to live in this presence. We are welded into a whole and given meaning. In the last analysis, health of body and mind often depends upon our religious life.

Experiences of wholeness, however, do not eliminate human problems. Even while we are living as fully and consciously as possible, new conflicts and problems arise, and so there must be new experiences of the Divine, a new integration and transformation. In other words, the task of achieving consciousness goes on and on. On the one hand, contact with the unconscious, which gives power, can almost imperceptibly swallow us. On the other hand, we become egocentric when our own egos are out of relation with the unconscious depth. So we remain between the danger of being swallowed and inflated or of being spiritually dehydrated. Hence the religious quest goes on in this positive and creative tension.

Indeed, this process is limitless; we have far greater capacity for growth than we ordinarily realize. In Christian thinking, the religious experience was not understood as a final encounter which ended the need for further growth. It was seen rather as an initiation into the religious way, which leads us ever further and deeper into the mysteries of reality. Real psychological integration and real religious life are both growth *processes*, equally seeking the goal of life without bounds. While ultimate goals, of course, are not for this life, one does obtain many

---

[28] *Collected Works* Vol. 9, pt. 2:69.

intimations of these and the confidence that the process needs to go on in the life beyond death.

If we are to stay well, emotionally as well as physically, we need to keep on a path of growth both psychologically and religiously, not so much in order to reach a destination as to remain on a religious journey.[29] Indeed, Jung saw the analytical process as no longer bound only to the consulting room of the doctor. He said very specifically of analytical psychology: "We might say that it transcends itself, and now advances to fill that void which hitherto has marked the psychic insufficiency of Western culture as compared with that of the East."[30]

If Jung and his followers are right about the nature of the psyche and its relation to a nonphysical world, they have something very important to say about our physical and mental health. They have something to say to us very close to the original message of Christianity. How then does it fit with our present scientific knowledge of the world?

Unless we have a place in our worldview for such transcendent experiences, we do not give them the weight that they deserve. One friend said to me, "Morton, I have had many deeply powerful religious experiences. If I believed them I would have to take up the religious way." He was a confirmed materialist, and so he dismissed them out of hand and did nothing. We have diagrammed the worldview that Jung proposed. Let us look at this worldview and see if it is one that can be used by open-minded and conscious women and men. As we move into the twenty-first century let us also evaluate the relevance of an experiential Christianity that has brought many people to health of soul, mind, and body.

---

[29] One of the most interesting studies of the correspondences between the Christian way and depth psychology at its most comprehensive may be found in an anthology, *The Choice Is Always Ours* (1960), compiled by Dorothy Phillips and others. Here great passages of Christian devotion are placed side by side with passages from depth psychology and deep human experience. It often becomes clear that each discipline is expressing, in different words, the same essential experiences and insights.

[30] *Modern Man in Search of a Soul*, p. 53.

CHAPTER 13

A Place for Religious Healing in the Modern World

Either there is a place for religious healing in today's world or there is not, and this can only be decided on facts. But Christian theology does not seem to be looking at the facts—although, as we have seen, these are certainly not lacking. Instead, one has the distinct impression of a foregone conclusion. The most comprehensive survey of recent theology, John Macquarrie's *Twentieth Century Religious Thought*, makes this quite clear. Healing is simply overlooked. Of the 150 theologians discussed in that book, *not one* emphasizes the effect of our religious life on our mental and physical health, as do the more perceptive psychiatrists and students of psychosomatic medicine. Few of these religious thinkers, in fact, even bother with the arguments against healing.

Of course there are some who, on the side, poke fun at the theological vagaries of Mary Baker Eddy and others, or decry the extravagances of "faith healers." But the real reasons for ignoring the possibility of healing are much deeper than this. Our culture has no place for such experiences. Most people feel helpless when confronting them, and Christian theology offers no answers. Indeed, Christian thinkers cannot consider experiences of healing today because of the tacit acceptance, philosophically and theologically, of a worldview which allows no place for active presence of divine power operating in the world. Divine interference in our world, such as healing, is simply considered an impossibility.

Both theology and philosophy attempt to put experience into a meaningful and consistent framework. When the world is seen as a closed mechanical system, (as in most modern thought), consistency requires that human beings be understood within the system and that all human experiences be explained by it. But it is difficult to explain incidents of religious healing within a system which admits only the reality of the material realm and human consciousness. The only choice is to ignore a supposed healing—or rationalize it, say, as coincidence or the result of some natural force not yet understood. One cannot, with logical consistency, withhold judgment and see whether the experience implies other, perhaps more desirable, alternatives.

This point of view can be diagrammed very simply. It consists of the central square in the diagram on page 246. All is ignored except the data given by sense experience refined through scientific methods and reason.

This, as current studies show, is the framework within which most of the influential modern theologians operate, whether they realize it or not. If religious healing is to have a hearing, it will be necessary for Christian theologians to take off these philosophical blinders and consider facts which our modern worldview shuts out entirely. To do this, we must first understand the present outlook quite clearly. While it is not possible to go into this fascinating story in detail, we shall look briefly at how it started and how it was later adopted into Christianity in preference to the alternative and, in fact, original point of view. This will give some idea of how important one's outlook is in determining the facts one is able to accept.

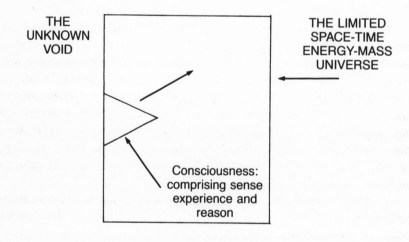

Figure 3

A fascinating experiment was devised by Postman and Bruner in the cognitive learning laboratories at Harvard. They took a black six of spades from a deck of playing cards and had it painted red. The card was reinserted in the deck and shown to a large number of subjects. Practically none of them reported the card as a red six of spades. They reported seeing either a black six of spades or the six of diamonds or hearts. What they had no place for in their belief system they actually did not see. This failure to perceive is called cognitive dissonance.

We shall then look at some facts that make necessary a different point of view, one that takes healing into account. As we shall see, one cannot isolate the physical world from a nonphysical or psychic realm as most modern philosophers do. Perhaps the separation is obvious to them, but the "obvious" is usually what one has not fully examined.

The task of providing a new point of view, of taking a new theological stance, is a difficult one. We must consider where we have been and where we are going. Let us look together at this ancient and modern history, trying to open up a new conscious understanding for a better tomorrow. The following sketch is brief and technical, but necessary to understand the rejection of religious healing among most modern theologians. I have provided a more detailed account of this development in my book, *Encounter With God: A Theology of Christian Experience*.

A Closed System

The idea that we human beings live within a closed rational and physical system, receiving information only by our sense experience and our reason, was first worked out in detail by Aristotle in the fourth century B.C. Other philosophers had suggested that we might be only material beings, but Aristotle was the first to develop the full implications of this idea. In opposition to both the philosophy of Plato and the popular view of his time, he maintained that there is no reality apart from the known world of sense experience and reason. Forms or ideas, he held, have no separate existence and become real only as they are expressed in material substance.

It was incongruous to Aristotle to believe that human beings might be influenced by a reality independent of the physical world. For one thing, he believed that human beings could have no freedom or morality if something other than our moral choice could influence our lives, so he ignored or denied the significance of visions, dreams, prophecy, and other nonrational aspects of human experience. They certainly had nothing to do with God. Aristotle was so afraid of the power of these experiences that he denied them or explained them as irrelevant by-products of the physical mechanism.

Although Aristotle was not very popular in the ancient world, his thinking was later seized by Islam and became the basis for the brilliant Arab civilization of the Middle Ages. And at length his influence was felt in Western Europe. Against his crisp and logical ideas, the thinking of the church, based on a misunderstood and otherworldly Platonism, did not stand a chance. A new worldview emerged, which represented an attempt to synthesize the Christian and Aristotelian points of view.

The most careful and sophisticated representative of this school was Thomas Aquinas, whose Scholasticism was head and shoulders above most of the thought of his time. On the basis of his work, the church erected a system in which the certainties of Aristotle's logic and metaphysics were applied to teachings and ideas of Christianity. What resulted was a final and logical theological system. There was no need for further *experience* of God. Human beings were saved, not through contact with God, but by accepting the total system. In the thinking of Aquinas, little room was left for the gifts of the Spirit that Paul enumerates in his first letter to the Corinthians.

Aquinas, as we have seen, quite naturally had difficulty with healing. Unless one believes in a very actual spiritual reality, which not only exists apart from the material world but interpenetrates it, sacramental healing *is* a logical absurdity. In other books I have shown also the trouble Aquinas had with dreams, tongue speaking, and the other spiritual gifts. Angels and demons got into the act as rational creatures by a feat of logic—as Father White has shown in his book, *God and the Unconscious*. Scholastic and Aristotelian thought has had a pervasive and lasting influence upon both Catholic and Protestant ideas as well as upon Western civilization. It was not seriously questioned by the church--largely because until quite recently secular thinking followed the same track.

So pervasive is this influence that it seldom occurs to us that there is another traditional outlook which gives an entirely plausible view of religious healing. This other tradition is stated with clarity and profundity by Plato. It was also the basic point of view of Jesus, the Fathers of the church, and the whole of Eastern Christianity. This viewpoint finds human beings interacting not only with a real physical world, but with a real nonphysical one as well. From this stance, healing is one of the direct ways in which the spirit and nonphysical reality make their impact on us. It is one of five such ways described at length and thoroughly discussed in the New Testament.[1] Indeed, nearly half the verses of the New Testament deal in one way or another with these direct experiences of nonphysical reality.

Yet modern Christians very rarely wonder about these things, even though an understanding and acceptance of them would make it possible to comprehend the facts about religious healing which are accumulating more and more rapidly today. Instead of trying out this line of understanding, most of us allow a view of life and reality based on logical certainty and sense experience to determine unconsciously which facts we will seriously entertain and which we do not see at all. A *worldview* has this power, the capacity to actually screen the data that get into our consciousness. It would be wise for us to know how our present outlook came to prevail so universally and who have been its most influential supporters. As briefly as possible, hitting only the high spots, let us glance at the main developments of modern philosophy and theology.

Modern thinking takes off from the Aristotelian-Scholastic base in a quest for certainty about external reality, as well as about logical ideas. It was inaugurated by Descartes when he tried to find solid ground for what we know by fitting all experience into the model of analytical geometry, which he had discovered. In the Cartesian system all unclear or shadowy ideas and beliefs were eliminated, and all else was to be doubted until proven true. Objects were stripped of qualities and seen only quantitatively, while the subject was seen as separate from the object, with no mathematical way to prove the existence of the object from thought alone.

In addition—and quite different from Aristotle—the subject (or thinking person) was viewed as pure consciousness—although, as we have seen, Descartes did not operate on this basis even in developing his method. But his thinking still has a profound influence on modern science, philosophy, and theology.

In England this was followed by the great deductive system of Thomas Hobbes, who anticipated many of the rationalistic conclusions of modern thinking, including disbelief in the healing miracles of the New Testament, which did not fit into his system. Hobbes was suc-

---

[1] They are: 1) revelations, dreams and visions, 2) special divine knowledge and wisdom, 3) prophecy and tongue speaking, 4) experiences of angels and demons, and 5) healing.

ceeded in turn by the empiricists, led by John Locke, who held that the only sure knowledge is mathematical, all else being derived from sense experience.

The dangers of this view were sensed by the brilliant and graceful Bishop Berkeley. Proposing the first Western idealism, Berkeley made a competent rescue of the material world—as ideas held in the mind of God—thus bridging the gulf in Cartesian dualism that extended to skepticism about matter itself. He remained an influence until most Western philosophy ruled out metaphysics in the 1930s. But meanwhile David Hume carried the ideas of the empiricists to their logical conclusion in a total skepticism in which individuals know only the stream of impressions that come before them, nothing more—not even their own identity.

Kant, however, soon reestablished dualism, maintaining that human beings can never know either the object in itself or the subject in itself. For him, experience was the product of the interaction of these two unknown realities, with only the conscious aspects of the subject considered. He left human beings with real phenomenal knowledge, but with final doubt as to whether we will ever know reality in itself. Kant defined the limits of human knowing, and some thinkers believe that his critical conclusions have yet to be overridden. He also cast doubt on all the customary Scholastic arguments for God and tried to base his belief in God on entirely different grounds, on the human moral sense. It never occurred to him, in the closed system of sense experience, that the divine had any way to touch and influence us.

At the same time practical philosophers were gradually coming to have great confidence in human reason and in our knowledge of the world around us. The confidence of Descartes in his skepticism was backed up by the Enlightenment, and then given further support by the work of Newton and Darwin. By the late nineteenth century this view was solidifying into dogma: *the material alone was real, and evolved according to rational and mechanical laws which would eventually be understood in toto.* Human beings were prisoners in this closed and unalterable system, since the psyche was merely an epiphenomenal by-product, "nothing but" an insignificant chance result of this material process.

Since then most philosophy has been occupied in trying to support or deny the results of this dogma. Popular thinkers from Comte and Spencer to Mach and Skinner have developed its implications. The behaviorist utopia is even provided in Skinner's novel *Walden II.* Hegel, on the other hand, tried to escape the uncertainty of Kant and support the autonomy of "mind" and "idea" by proving dialectically, with logical certainty, that the entire experienced world is a manifestation of "mind." But with no place for the individual, Hegel's "ideal" system left human beings as much prisoners of an unvarying order as they had been in the materialistic system. It was on the basis of Hegel's dialectic, of course, combined with the materialism of the current science, that Karl Marx gave the modern communist movement its philosophic base, thus providing a materialistic dogma for large sections of the modern world, an incredibly important influence to say the least.

Kierkegaard and the existentialists who followed him reacted violently to Hegel's magnificent dialectic. Realizing that the unique individuality of each person was lost in it, they turned their attention to the individual, yet did not question the idea that each of us is utterly caught in a closed physical system. It was as impossible for Kierkegaard as for the naturalists to believe that God could be interacting with us in the here and now in history.[2] Since they saw no way for nonrational or nonsensory meaning to come in, or for human beings to reach out to it, all they could offer was a blind jump of faith into an unknown through the tension of anxiety and dread.

The lead of Hegel was picked up again in phenomenology by Edmund Husserl. In an attempt to arrive at the same certainty as the natural sciences had apparently achieved, he based an entire philosophy on the logical presuppositions of the human's conscious, intentional act. He saw no way by which we could reach meaning except through intellectual analysis. He dismissed the unconscious as a meaningless concept, assuming that nothing breaks through into the closed system of our consciously understood space-time world.

Strangely enough, the strongest influence on theology today still comes from a synthesis of the thinking of these two men. Working from the ideas of Kierkegaard and Husserl, a group of Europeans, notably Heidegger, Jaspers, Sartre, Marcel, and Merleau-Ponty, have produced the significant movement of existentialism. Although there are many differences between these thinkers, philosophically they are all existentialists. They all hold that we can know only our own conscious existence—perhaps best known through contemplation of death and dread, and understood through ontological analysis. None of them suggests any experience of a transpersonal realm or of any reality other than the personal, and thus the idea of religious healing for these men is simply absurd.[3]

---

[2] See particularly Kierkegaard's *Training in Christianity* (1944).
[3] For a more detailed treatment of this school, see my article, "Is the World View of Jesus

The influence of this philosophy on modern theology—through Barth, Bultmann, Bonhoeffer, Tillich, and their popularizer John A. T. Robinson—has been enormous. While Barth actively denies any influence, he still goes along with their assumption that God does not naturally interact with the space-time world, finding various reasons for seeing the Biblical period as the one exception. Bultmann and Bonhoeffer frankly acknowledge their dependence on these philosophers, and the Tillich of the *Systematic Theology* is clearly related to them. None of these theologians can conceive of any possibility but a closed logical and materialistic system in which we live and die, and they do not consider any evidence that might indicate any other possibility. To them, the idea of a transpersonal reality influencing the human psyche or body for sickness or health is not worth discussing seriously. No wonder we found their ideas on the subject so negative in Chapter Two. They reject a healing ministry on philosophical grounds. If they rejected the evidence, that would at least make more sense in today's science-oriented world. I have already referred the reader to the works where such evidence can be found.

Another approach in current philosophy, the British school of empiricism, built on the genius of Wittgenstein, Russell, and others, has taken a different tack. These philosophers see logic as tautological and not productive of any new knowledge. In their view, all knowledge is derived from empirical observation, from experience. Since one cannot know with logical certainty what new experiences will bring, all knowledge is then only probable and hypothetical. As A. J. Ayer shows in his brilliant exposition of these ideas in *Language, Truth and Logic*, this school has not denied that human beings could have other levels of experience than that of the senses, or that another realm of reality might not break in and affect human life. But by pushing aside other possibilities, they have gone along with the assumption that humankind is contained in a closed physical system, and so they write off metaphysics, theology, and moral theory with a stroke of the pen.

One need not look far to find the connection between the religious ideas of our time and these concepts of philosophy. In modern studies of how we know God, the present understanding of philosophy is accepted, almost assumed, with the conclusion that we must infer our

---

Outmoded?" *Christian Century* 86 (January 22, 1969): 112–16. In some of Heidegger's most recent thought, however, there are new insights into the importance of intuition, suggesting a somewhat broader view. See also my *Companions on the Inner Way*, Chapter Five.

knowledge of God from events of this world and not from any direct or immediate experience of the divine.[4]

Only as we begin to understand human life and all aspects of reality (the true task of philosophy) in terms of a viable meaning, only then can we explore and elaborate the possibility that we can find relationship to this meaning (which, overall, is *theology*) in such experiences as revelation and healing. It would seem obvious that the two go hand in hand. If our understanding of life excludes belief in any possible relationship to a meaning that could be called God except through inference from the organizational principles which can be seen in matter and in history, then we can learn very little from theology. We would do better to study evolution, or law, or politics, and compare notes with scientists in other fields, if we would learn how God works.

There are indications, however, that a new understanding of the world is growing, involving quite a different view of its meaning and of the place of human beings in it. This is occurring in two different but related areas: one is in the scientific world as a whole, and the other is psychology.

New Facts

Early in the twentieth century awareness was growing that the nineteenth-century outlook—the rational materialism which saw humankind within a closed naturalistic system—was too narrow to take in the data now becoming known about our world. Through the work of Becquerel and the Curies, of Planck, Heisenberg, and others, the substantial atom exploded into an increasing number of particles which could not be understood on a basis of Newtonian mechanics. Einstein, in one of the greatest intuitions of this age, came to the conclusion that space might not be Euclidean and common sense in nature, and his studies of the speed of light brought a new concept of time.

Our whole conception of time and matter and scientific truth were undergoing a traumatic change. The scientific method has not produced

---

[4] For instance, see F. R. Tennant, *Philosophical Theology* (1956); Douglas Clyde MacIntosh, *The Problem of Religious Knowledge* (1940); John Baillie, *The Idea of Revelation in Recent Thought* (1956) and *The Sense of the Presence of God* (1962); John H. Hick, *Faith and Knowledge* (1966); and Bernard J. F. Lonergan, S.J., *Insight: A Study of Human Understanding* (1957). None of the standard works of systematic theology by Gordon Kaufman, John Macquarrie or Paul Tillich suggest such a possibility. Thomas Bokekotter in *Essential Catholicism: Dynamics of Faith and Belief* (1986), shows that neither Hans Kung, E. Schillebeck nor Karl Rahner have any place for such experience. *Process Theology*, ed. Evert Cousins (1971), has no place for the divine-human encounter for obvious reasons.

final and certain truths after all, but only hypotheses which could be overturned by new research and replaced with new understanding. Scientific "laws" could no longer by seen as ultimate truths; they were like maps, increasingly accurate but still only maps of a territory that could never be fully known.

In biology and paleontology it was found that the idea of survival of the fittest does not always fit the facts, that the relation between genetic factors and what Darwin observed appears to be directed in far too complex a way to be expressed without some idea of purpose. Thus, through thinking about evolution, the idea of teleology was reintroduced into the study of humankind. Pierre Teilhard de Chardin has stated these facts with brilliance and clarity in his books. We have already shown some of the evidence adduced by psychosomatic medicine in this area.

But this thinking has not taken hold in the popular mind. Although it is making a deep impression on the philosophy of science, the idea has not occurred to many philosophers and theologians that these new conceptions may have a relation to our own humanity, to our search for meaning in this universe.

One great theological mind, Baron Friedrich von Hügel, grasped the significance of the scientific method for theology and philosophy. His greatest work, *The Mystical Element of Religion as Studied in Saint Catherine of Genoa and her Friends*, sketches out a theory of religious knowledge similar to what we provide. Indeed, it was von Hügel who first opened my eyes to the possibility of the divine-human encounter. It was Jung who provided me a way to participate in that encounter and a schema or model of reality that makes sense of the New Testament experience of God and the mystical tradition in the Christian church.[5]

Jung was grounded as few other scientists in the history of philosophy. He developed this background because of his interest in healing, rather than for theoretical reasons. He found that his patients usually had a variety of physical symptoms, which could arise simply from loss of meaning. Being a committed physician, he did whatever he could to help them recover, even turning to philosophy and theology to fill the gap left in their lives by the loss of a traditional approach to religion.

Jung was trained in rigorous scientific method; he also had a wealth of empirical data available to him about human beings and their ways

---

[5] Other significant books by von Hügel are: *Eternal Life* (1929), *The Reality of God and Religion and Agnosticism* (1931), *Essays and Addresses on the Philosophy of Religion* (1931, 1939).

of finding meaning.[6] Through experience with hundreds of patients, he was able to describe from their direct inner experience the processes which Teilhard de Chardin and others described from the outside. Building on this evidence, he carefully sketched out an empirical framework in which our psychic, unconscious experiences were given the same value as our experiences of the physical world. At the same time Jung was participating in the growth of a new attitude within the scientific community itself.

He realized that theories of the unconscious were as difficult to understand or accept from the nineteenth-century point of view as theories of quantum mechanics. In fact Jung often drew attention to the analogy between quantum mechanics and depth psychology. He saw that in taking the unconscious seriously as an operative part of the human personality, he was breaking with philosophic tradition from Kant on, and also with the popular psychological ideas of Wundt on which today's experimental psychology is based. He was prepared to support his position; while he did not write a great deal about his methodology and philosophical presuppositions, he was well aware of them, and they were clearly formulated in passages scattered throughout his writings.[7]

Jung and Modern Thought

Jung frankly accepted the philosophic realism of modern science and its organic and empirical emphasis. But he did not limit his empiricism only to facts that can be verified in a physical sense. He applied the method of the physical sciences to personal encounters with the unconscious, testing them with basically the same questions: How does it work? Is it repeated? What is the result in the individual? As Raymond Hostie put it in describing Jung's work at some length in *Religion and the Psychology of Jung,* his method was actually a "non-experimental empiricism."[8] Jung was fond of remarking that in experimental research the scientist asks the questions, while in clinical practice the patient and nature ask it, and that it is not hard to see which asks the more

---

[6] I have suggested the nature of the evidence in the discussion on pp. 238–253.

[7] Jung was quite close to the physicists Wolfgang Pauli and Max Knoll. He collaborated with the Nobel prize winner Pauli in one publication, while Knoll (one of the inventors of the electron microscope) supplemented and amplified some of Jung's ideas, particularly in "Transformations of Science in Our Age," *Papers from the Eranos Yearbooks* Vol. 3, *Man and Time* (1957): 264–76.

[8] 1957, pp. 9–14.

difficult questions. Scientific experiment gives carefully defined data about a small area of nature. Jung's method gives less defined data about the nature of human beings, data which can direct the next step and even be roughly verified.

Philosophically, Jung started from the base of Kant's critical study of human knowledge but extended the subjective component of *the experiencing act* to include unconscious contents and processes. This part of the subjective component—perhaps the major part—was made up of contents not always as personally subjective as they might appear. They were experienced subjectively, but this is also the way we experience the physical world, and there were many psychic contents that seemed to come into the individual psyche from outside itself and to have the same givenness as sense experience.[9]

Thus Jung maintained that we have contact with an objectively real physical world, which of necessity is experienced subjectively, and that we have contact with an equally real world of collective or autonomous psychic contents, also experienced only subjectively by necessity. In addition we have contact with an equally real world of personal psychic contents, which are experienced directly, inwardly, and of course also subjectively. All these experiences give only phenomenal knowledge. None gives final or certain knowledge of "the thing-in-itself," but only what can become known through its reaction with the subject. The experience of the subject tells us all we can know about either the physical object or the psychic content, although this knowledge can be made more certain as more attention is directed to the phenomena themselves.

What Jung wrote to me in 1958 summarizes this understanding especially well: "The real nature of the objects of human experience is still shrouded in darkness. The scientist cannot concede a higher intelligence to theology than to any other branch of human cognition. We know as little of a supreme being as of matter. But there is as little doubt of the existence of a supreme being as of matter. *The world beyond is a reality,* an experiential fact. We only don't understand it."[10] He stressed that "natural science is not a science of words and ideas, but of facts," found through or within human beings where two different kinds of reality meet and interact in a special way.

---

[9] I have discussed this view at length in *Companions on the Inner Way: The Art of Spiritual Guidance,* Chapter Five, "Atheism, Agnosticism and Spiritual Guidance."
[10] *Jung's Letters* (1975), Vol. 2, p. 435.

Let us look for a moment at how physical scientists handle the facts of experience. First of all, scientific method consists in slow, tedious, painstaking observation and in comparisons of the data observed. Then comes a second step, by which one comes to an hypothesis as to how these data are related. This is not done by reason but by intuition and imagination. Once the hypothesis is framed, we use our best powers of rational analysis and deduction to sketch out the implications of our theory. We continue the process of observation to see how the data compare with the implications we have drawn from our theory. Each new experience that does not fit this hypothesis requires an expanded or often entirely new hypothesis. One inconsistent fact, small enough to be overlooked by most observers, may even require a whole new worldview. It is at this point that logical thought, right down to mathematical relationships, is most needed to work out the implications and details of new hypothesis and a new theory.

For instance, one such fact, which literally started a chain reaction in science, was Becquerel's experience in 1896 of finding his sealed photographic plates mysteriously exposed by a supposedly inert metallic salt. Once Marie Curie became interested in this experience, it was no longer an isolated phenomenon. The properties of uranium, thorium, and radium were discovered, followed by work with neutrons, protons, "heavy" atoms, and finally nuclear fission. And it struck home, even to unsophisticated people, that matter is not very dead or inert. A new understanding was needed, which, as we have seen, began to develop in various parts of the scientific world.

Jung, who began his work a few years after Becquerel and the Curies, came upon his evidence just as unexpectedly. Listening to the people who came to him for healing, he found they were experiencing strange images and other contents thrusting into consciousness. Many of these patients were practical scientists, schooled in scientific certainty, who had neglected the whole area of feeling and unconscious experience, since it had no conceivable place in that framework. As they encountered and dealt consciously with these unconscious contents, these people not only found healing but often experienced strange elements of mythology and extrasensory perception. In many instances it was through an experience of just this nature that patients began to find meaning and new energy and recovered their health. To help understand this, Jung began an intensive study of mythology and dream symbols, and also of experiences synchronized with similar or identical events in the outer world.

Thus he came to new and detailed knowledge of the unconscious, which—coming from the most complex aggregations of matter, human beings—showed that a new hypothesis was needed to understand both consciousness and the unconscious and their relation to the material world. The older theories were no longer adequate. Jung suggested a new hypothesis which stepped beyond the deterministic naturalism of the nineteenth century and therefore offered meaning for wide areas of our human experience. The implications of his theory are both philosophical and theological.

This direction was supported by a strong pragmatic bent. Jung believed that a course of action that results in permanent healing—in human wholeness—comes closest to living with reality as it is. He was much influenced by the pragmatism of William James, whose writings he knew well and often quoted. Like James, he expressed the assumption that runs unexpressed through much of modern science: what works in practical life is closely correlated with what is real.

In pragmatism there is a further hypothesis which Jung accepted: that life is more than just a chance and meaningless epiphenomenon. If there is ultimate meaning in the universe, and if humankind expresses a high level or stage of that meaning, then what furthers and develops human life is likely to correspond to that same meaning in the universe. And alternately, what blocks or destroys human life—including neurotic and physical illness—is alien to that meaning, just as living life fully and completely is likely to express it. Jung offered the theory that nature is meaningful in itself, and then adduced volumes of evidence from our inner life to corroborate this thesis.

This approach was reinforced by Jung's realization, discussed above, that there are experiences of unconscious contents which are not merely primitive and atavistic. The unconscious can produce understanding which is often superior to the reasoning of consciousness, although it usually presents these understandings in images rather than as abstract concepts. But, as Jung carefully demonstrated in his introduction to *Symbols of Transformation*, we are quite capable of thinking in this way, as well as of using the directed, conceptual reasoning of practical science and Aristotelian logic. We use the intuitive, symbolic "thinking" that comes in images from the unconscious to convey our deepest insights and our emotional meaning. Art, drama, liturgy, folktales, mythology, and scientific intuition all make use of archetypal images, and each night the dream also presents its significance in similar symbols and pictures.

It is important that our logic be broad enough to deal with these aspects of experience. When we lose touch with our capacity to think symbolically, as most of us have today, we are no longer able to understand either our own myth and dreams and sickness or our relationship to the world around us. This is one fact which scientific thinkers are beginning to appreciate today.[11]

Mapping a New Understanding

If Jung's evidence from the unconscious is taken seriously, then we clearly need a new understanding of the total world of experience and of our place within that world. The hypothesis that Jung offers is very different from the materialistic rationalism that has swept the house bare for most of us. Jung's hypothesis finds human beings faced with two quite different kinds of experience. We are influenced not only by the objective reality of a physical world, but also by experience relating to the objective, autonomous reality of the psychic world. These worlds interact; Jung's studies of synchronicity described these interactions. Aniela Jaffe has discussed these in her little book, *From the Life and Work of C. G. Jung*. It is, however, within human beings that these come to the most profound and meaningful interplay. We humans are a very significant bridge between these two worlds.

The vast psychic world with which we are presented through unconscious contents and meanings, Jung found, is as objectively real, and as meaningful and possible to experience, as the physical world. In our present state of knowledge we cannot, for the sake of logical tidiness, reduce either one of these realms of experience to the other. In his comprehension of this Jung came very close to Plato's understanding of "Ideas," which Jung saw as the philosophical version of his "psychically concrete" archetypes, rather than as eternal concepts.[12] He

---

[11] Evidence of the transformation in scientific thinking is found in Max Knoll's article mentioned in the footnote on p. 273, and also in Friedrich Dessauer's "Galileo and Newton: The Turning Point in Western Thought," in *Papers from the Eranos Yearbooks Vol. 1, Spirit and Nature* (1954): 288–309. Two other leading scientific thinkers who profess the same Platonic point of view are Werner Heisenberg, who speaks for himself in *Physics and Philosophy: The Revolution in Modern Science* (1962), and Kurt Godel, whose complex presentation is discussed by Ernest Nagel and James R. Newman in *Godel's Proof* (1964). See also Stephen Toulmin's excellent summary of recent thought, *The Philosophy of Science: An Introduction* (1960), and Mary Hesse, *Models and Analogies in Science* (1966). See also the latest evidence that we introduced in Chapter Eleven.

[12] *Collected Works*, Vol. 8, p. 191.

also agreed in principle with Plato that we do not come to experience and know the realm of "Ideas" through the exercise of reason, but only through just the kind of irrational means Plato described as prophecy, dreams, healing, art, and love. As we have already seen, Jung stresses each of these areas and shows particularly his appreciation of love and its cognitive value.

Let us look again at the diagram of this point of view, considering it philosophically and theologically, rather than only psychologically. This diagram, Figure 4, is the same as that on page 244 except that we have different names for the realities involved. The human being is comprised of both an ego and an unconscious knower. We are bombarded from the physical world with sensations that do not reveal the full nature of that reality. We are bombarded from the spiritual realm with all sorts of contents that have been described as the angelic and demonic by most of the major religions of humankind. These experiences often can also be misleading and need critical evaluation. Not only are we able to come into a genuine experience of the divine, but the Holy Spirit dwells within our psyche and can lead us into that encounter if we will allow it to happen. From a Christian point of view this unlimited divinity is the ultimate creator of all reality and is best characterized by Jesus of Nazareth, because of the incarnation of God in Jesus. Evil, a part of the spiritual realm that rebelled against God, is very real and very much at work both in the physical and spiritual realms.

If this religious and philosophical interpretation of Jung is correct, we can see that it is very similar to that of Jesus of Nazareth and the thinkers of the early church and to the continuing view of reality expressed in the Orthodox churches up to the present day. We human beings are in touch with complex realities of at least two kinds. There are those that we can handle physically using our knowledge, skill, and ego strength; and there are others that we cannot deal with in this way—realities that can be known only as men and women have the courage to encounter this other realm, try to understand it and relate to it. The key to wise relationship to this realm is knowing the reality of the God who wishes to be known, who comes to us as the resurrected Jesus or the Holy Spirit to guide us through danger and difficulty to fullness of life. In fact, Jung's thinking can provide a philosophical base for a modern experiential theology with an approach to healing—just as Plato's worldview provided such a framework for the church fathers to express their experiences of Christ and Christian healing in the first vital centuries of the church's life.

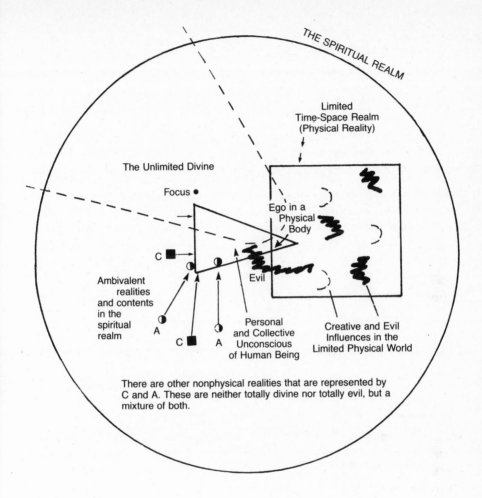

Figure 4

Religious people in all ages and among all peoples have spoken of a spiritual world apart from the physical world. As one of the greatest modern physicists, Werner Heisenberg, has reminded us, words like these which come from the natural language express a more direct connection with reality than even the most precise abstractions of science.[13] Since Jung's evidence shows that there is a realm in which we can come into contact with a healing function superior to human consciousness, the idea of a healing God appears not to be mere metaphysical specu-

---

[13] *Op. cit.*, pp. 200–01.

lation after all, but rather the name which religious people have applied to their experience of such a healing reality. In Jung's worldview the religious undertaking and the religious object are not only potentially meaningful, they are necessary if we are to survive as whole, healthy individuals. Jung has laid the foundation, and empirical theology can build upon that base. Jung told me in a visit with him that he was just a country physician and that it was not his task to work out the theological implications of his point of view.

Two of Jung's own statements, late in his work, clearly point out what we have sketched. In the first he wrote:

I have, therefore, even hazarded the postulate that the phenomenon of archetypal configurations—which are psychic events *par excellence*—may be founded upon a *psychoid* base, that is, upon an only partially psychic and possibly altogether different form of being. For lack of empirical data I have neither knowledge nor understanding of such forms of being, which are commonly called spiritual. From the point of view of science, it is immaterial what I may *believe* on that score, and I must accept my ignorance . . . Nevertheless, we have good reason to suppose that behind this veil there exists the uncomprehended absolute object which affects and influences us—and to suppose it even, or particularly, in the case of psychic phenomena about which no verifiable statements can be made.[14]

The other remark, which Jung made in his British Broadcasting Company interview, is almost too well known to be repeated, but it crystallizes all the other ways he tried to put this over: "Suddenly I understood that God was, for me at least, one of the most certain and immediate experiences . . . I do not believe; I know. I *know*."

In addition, Jung's understanding of the problem of evil has almost equally important implications for healing. For sickness of body and mind was viewed by Jesus and the early church as evil, something alien to God. Jung suggested that theologians take the reality of evil more seriously. His experience made him balk at the Aristotelian position that evil is only the absence or deprivation of good, the accidental lack of perfection in creation—the *privatio boni*. Jung would have agreed with the author of Ephesians that "our fight is not against human foes, but . . . against the superhuman forces of evil in the heavens." We have to wrestle with darkness to find out its nature, and then either integrate or reject it. Jung believed that the doctrine of the *privatio boni*, first laid down for the church by Augustine and later developed by Aquinas,

---

[14] *Memories, Dreams, Reflections* (1963), pp. 351–52.

crippled us in our struggle with evil. It deceives us about the seriousness of our struggle. "The growing awareness of the inferior part of the
personality," Jung wrote, "should not be twisted into an intellectual
activity, for it has far more the meaning of a suffering and a passion
that implicate the whole man."[15] Dealing with unconscious contents or
with God can be a painful process, a *via crucis* which most people avoid
at any cost. This emphasis on creative suffering has much in common
with the teaching of the New Testament and the church fathers.

The destructiveness—the very reality that we call evil—results in
separation and disintegration within the psyche, which leads in turn to
emotional ill health and to physical illness. Healing of either mind,
emotions, soul, or body involves throwing back the forces of evil. But
when evil is seen as merely an accidental lack of perfection, we are left
with no approach to the psychic forces of destructiveness in which most
sickness is at least partially rooted. To see evil as nothing but the absence of good leaves us with no ground to stand on for a fair fight
against these forces. Instead they are able to operate in the unconscious
autonomously and without interference. Unrecognized, evil is then giv-
en free rein to take control of the psyche.[16]

Thus when the reality of evil is ignored it either causes destruction
within the psyche and the body or uses the individual psyche to promote destruction in the outer world. In one case we have emotional
and physical ills, in the other social ills. Religiously the results are no
better. If evil has no reality, then either our ills come from the direct
action of God or we end in denying that God has power to act. Either
God becomes a monstrous being—somewhat less moral than human
beings, as Jung suggested in his imaginative statement *The Answer to
Job*—or else we find ourselves in a meaningless world, with no real
answer for human sickness, physical or spiritual. Life becomes as absurd as portrayed by Sartre and Camus. In the long run there seems to
be no alternative when people are unable to see the reality of evil.
Making human beings the original source of evil destroys any hope of
healing and wholeness—which is the view of Sartre and some existentialists.

To admit the reality of evil, however, puts a different kind of responsibility on human beings. It is then up to us to deal with the

---

[15] *Collected Works*, Vol. 8, p. 208.

[16] This is an obviously complex problem which cannot be completely discussed here. A
fuller treatment is offered in my book, *Discernment: A Study in Ecstasy and Evil*. I have
already noted that Jung is ambiguous on the subject, and I give my interpretation of
his data (see *Christianity as Psychology*, pp. 41 and 81–85).

unconscious or spiritual forces of evil, and this involves the whole person. We then need to learn a process of finding creative relationship with the unconscious so as to turn back the dark, destructive side of it. For most individuals this process involves learning to care or love. Jung saw this very clearly, as did Plato. Evil, he found, is seldom overcome or forced to withdraw until, through human love, we have opened ourselves to the power of divine love, which then forces the destructive powers into retreat. Indeed the process of healing requires and results in deepened caring human relationships. Most of us will not make this effort unless we make the wager that acting according to love is the way of the universe and God; this attitude is called faith.

Christian Theology and Healing

The worldview we have sketched opens up a way for new appreciation of the vital experiences of Christianity and the theological ideas that formerly kept them alive and meaningful. One of the most central and living of these was the idea that the Christian became a source of healing, essentially and simply as a continuation of Christ's life through the church. The church was seen as the body of Christ. As Irenaeus and Justin Martyr both stated, Jesus became what we are in order that we might become what He is. Healing was a basic part of early Christian thought and experience as it had been in the life of Jesus. Thus the continuation of healing in the church's ministry can best be understood in its integral relation to the other fundamental ideas of Christianity. Let us look at these ideas about the incarnation, the atonement, the sacraments, and the church as they relate to healing.[17]

Once the *natural* interpenetration of the spiritual and physical worlds is understood, we are no longer startled or offended by the idea of the incarnation. In a very real sense every human being is spirit incarnate. Difficult as this is to describe in terms of Aristotelian categories, the data accumulating today show that we are just such a hybrid of flesh commingled with what can only be called spirit. Ordinary people today, when they encounter the spiritual realm have uncanny experiences quite different from sense experience. Is it then difficult to imagine that the Spirit of God could become incarnate in one human being, first received in the womb of a woman and then born as a human

---

[17] The material of this section is found in similar form in my *Encounter With God: A Theology of Christian Experience,* Chapter Seven.

infant, or to accept that at such a time there might have been the star, the visions of angels, the dreams of Joseph, the Wise Men, the fore-warning, and the flight into Egypt? These things are scarcely incredible; rather they show the incarnation actually to be the ultimate extension of the action of God in human life.

But for the early Christians there was something even more behind this doctrine. The apostles who had lived and suffered with Jesus were awed by what they met. They knew that something beyond the ordinary had occurred before their eyes. There was an unearthly wholeness and power in the one they saw as the messiah, the Christ. Through Jesus they were touched by the numinous, the transcendent—the same experience they had had in their most profound religious encounters as good Jews. In the healing of the sick and demon-possessed, a degree of love and harmony and wholeness was manifested that left them thunderstruck.

Then in the resurrection came the confirmation of all their deepest intuitions about Jesus. The person they had followed was not conquered by the actions of unconscious human beings under the influence of the Evil One. They hung him to a cross, and the God wrote, in actual fact, into history—into the fabric of the physical world—the mythical dream which had beaten in upon the intuition of human beings from the dawn of time. Jesus rose from the dead and appeared to them. What had touched them in dream and vision and myth they now saw actualized. With this experience they realized that the realm of the Spirit ruled over all reality and that in the end there was nothing to fear. Through the master who had led them until his death, and then returned, they could still find the same new quality of life which he had imparted as a living human being.

Unquestionably this experience is difficult to describe. But experiences of individuals returning to someone they cared for are reported so often that this evidence is denied only by those who are unable to consider such facts. In ancient times Ambrose told of consoling encounters in his dreams with his deceased brother Satyrus. Sulpitius Severus carefully described his vision of Martin of Tours almost at the time Martin, unknown to him, was dying. I have several modern accounts describing similar experiences. In May 1970 an incident near Gary, Indiana, was in the news all over the country: a father was guided by the voice of his murdered son, step by step, to the killer. Particularly at the time of a death, living women and men seem to have the capacity to experience the psyches of the departed directly and not through ordinary sense experience. If this can happen when ordinary men and women die, how much more likely it was for this person who carried the very Spirit of God in a human body.

There is also evidence that several people sometimes experience the same vision at the same time, and the resurrection appearances are easily understood as *at least* a numinous breakthrough of such a collective vision. Jung has described this phenomenon, and sees the flying saucer as a more mundane example of it.[18] Various instances have been reported of different individuals having the same dream. This does not, however, in any way detract from the possibility of an objective physical appearance. If Jesus was the incarnation of the very force that created this incredibly complex world, then what could prevent this objective spiritual reality from taking to itself the dead and torn body of Jesus, and any other physical material at hand, and giving it new form and new splendor. Those who know anything of the "emptiness" and energetic quality of matter will certainly not dismiss it as implausible. Experience of a resurrected body, of sudden appearance and disappearance, and of passing through doors, are only incomprehensible in terms of nineteenth-century physics.[19]

In the ascension this particular manifestation of matter returned in a blaze of glory to the Creator. This experience will not overwhelm thinking people who understand the moment-by-moment destruction and creation of atoms in a star, and who have seen human beings create new atoms and turn carefully selected ones into a blaze of power in the atomic bomb. If human beings can collect just the right particles to do these things, it is not hard to believe that God was able to do something similar in the resurrection and ascension of Jesus, rounding out divine creativity by the salvation of human beings sought out by divine Love.

After the ascension the followers of Jesus were given a new awareness of the Spirit along with the almost tangible manifestation of an ecstatic speech. These women and men had lost everything but the hope of new life. As I have written elsewhere:

The Jews indeed carried a burden, a crushing burden. Their task was to make God's righteousness manifest in their external lives. They carried it through suffering and exile; political subjection only intensified it. They yearned for some direct manifestation of God. While Jesus was with the group, he appeared

---

[18] *Collected Works*, Vol. 10, pp. 307–35.
[19] I have described this point of view at length in my book *Resurrection: Release from Oppression* (1985). See also the remarkable book of a Jew, Pinchas Lapide, *The Resurrection of Jesus* (1983).

to meet and satisfy their Jewish thirsting. But after the crucifixion and the ascension they were alone again. The only stability these men and women had was to sit still and wait as they had been told, both by Jesus and in a vision; being human beings who had known suffering and hope, they did just that. They stayed together and prayed, not knowing what might come. It was then that the experience of glossolalia first occurred. This experience was evidence to them that God's spirit was with them. It helped give them the conviction which sent them courageously into a hostile world.[20]

The encounter with the Self, described by Jung, is just such a central and vital experience. Again and again he observed that an objective, nonphysical reality like this could bring wholeness—indeed, health and harmony—to individuals, if they could allow it to operate. If ordinary people, then, have experiences of a power like this, one would expect it even more for the followers of Jesus, after all they had experienced and suffered. When the Spirit did break through, it came not only with the evidence of speaking in tongues, but with the power to heal, which continued and was passed on to other converts. When speaking in tongues broke out again in the Pentecostal revival in the twentieth century, it was again accompanied by gifts of healing.

These common experiences made the church, the fellowship, necessary. People found that they were more open to the transforming power of the Spirit as they met together in one spirit. Their worship experiences even had the flavor of Pentecost itself and were anything but sedate experiences. Out of this common worship grew a fellowship of love and caring which was the most remarkable characteristic of the early church. Ecstatic worship, individual experience, a fellowship of concern reaching out to those in need, and the healing ministry—all were parts of one complex whole.

The experience of being filled with the Holy Spirit is a kind of mysticism usually found only in Christian thought. In it, ultimate religious experience does not annihilate the ego. In Plato's thinking there was a foretaste of this; he saw the ultimate experience as a love relationship between the psyche and the divine which ceases to be meaningful if the ego is dissolved. Christian thinking, in terms of the schema we have presented, sees the Holy Spirit infilling the psyche (covering it), bringing harmony out of the tension of discordant contents (and spirits), integrating as much of human unconsciousness (which often appears as evil darkness) as possible, and forming a shield against irreconcilable evil. The psyche is brought to an entirely new level of

---

[20] *Tongue Speaking: An Experiment in Spiritual Experience* (1981), pp. 18–19.

reality. Far from entering the void of nirvana, or losing itself by seeking to be transcended as in the later Neoplatonism, the ego is transformed.[21] It is made a harmonious part of a total human psyche, which now has a new center and focus. The old center and the new remain in relation, a new relationship of wholeness.

This experience is one of the most moving we can sustain, but our human condition does not allow it to remain fixed. Wholeness is tasted for a moment and then becomes a goal, the end to be sought in life and finally found in the next life. After such an experience we can even completely turn our backs to it and reject it at any time, because there is no static end to this process. It is a way, not a safe harbor at the end of a journey.

Those who enter this way are faced with ever greater consciousness and the task of integrating more and more of their own unconsciousness, which so often appears as destructive darkness. Each such experience brings new harmony of purpose, often with a sense of creative peace, as well as physical healing, because the conscious stress that produces so much disease is relieved. Each experience opens us further to intrusions of the Spirit in dreams and visions. It also brings greater understanding and compassion for others, changing the destructive critical nature in each of us: we are more kind, or more firm when necessary. In fact the surest way to tell whether the Spirit has had a hand in such an experience is to see whether the person has become more forgiving, charitable, and loving. If not, we may be possessed by some archetypal power, partial and ambivalent, rather than by the Spirit of God, of wholeness.

The Spirit that broke through in such a dramatic way on Pentecost resulted almost immediately in the healing of a crippled beggar. As the Spirit continued to show in the lives of Christians by such actions, it also brought understanding of these experiences. A sophisticated doctrine developed of the soul as mediator of the spiritual world. In discussing these beliefs about how the Spirit speaks to humans, John Sanford has shown how close a parallel there is between the thinking of Jung and the ideas of the early theologians of the church.[22] These

---

[21] In the Neoplatonism of Plotinus, for instance, the final aim was to allow the divine content to take over entirely, reducing the ego to next to nothing. This was very similar to the nirvana of Oriental religious thought, and it became the ideal of such Christian mysticism as Hesychasm in the Eastern church. Plato's understanding was quite different. For a further discussion of his thought on this subject, see Paul Friedländer's *Plato: An Introduction* (1964), Chapters 1–3. Christian tradition provides both ways to God.

[22] In an unpublished manuscript on the epistemology of the church and presented partially in his book *The Kingdom Within* (1987).

early Christians saw clearly that God and the world of spirit made a direct impression on the human soul. A new imprint, they saw, sprang from the fact that God had been revealed in Jesus. The same power and revelation continued with speaking in tongues, healings, visions, dreams, intuitions, and prophecies.

There was nothing unusual about revelation. God had been reaching out to touch women and men through all ages. Once the divine became incarnate in historical time and space, and meaning had been unveiled, the way was open, and human beings were in a better position to appreciate the experiences God could give them. Thus the experiences of individuals, shared and tested by the fellowship, gave personal guidance and understanding as well as direction to the struggling church. Knowing as they did that God loved humanity enough to become embodied in the physical world and to die and rise again, it was not hard to believe that divine love would continue to break through to them in visions and dreams, in prophecies and healing. It would have been surprising if this had not happened.

The early church apparently held little of the idea that human brokenness and sin are so repellent that God will have nothing to do with them. The apostles told of God touching their lives, not only in clear messages, but also in images on which they had to meditate as Peter did after his dream-ecstasy in Joppa. The same tradition continued, for instance, in the *Shepherd of Hermas* and the account of St. Perpetua's martyrdom, among the ante-Nicene writers, and then in all the doctors of the church.[23] We have sketched the experiences of healing that the church has set down from the earliest days to the present. With their understanding that the soul participates in the spiritual world, these Christians did not question the need to listen to these experiences. If God or the Holy Spirit was available at any time, it was up to the individual to be open to the spiritual world and whatever it brought in dream and vision—in intuition or spiritual and psychological transformation. It was also their job to pass on to other human beings whatever a person was able to receive in understanding and healing experiences.

There was one danger in this. Being so open to the spiritual world, the Christian was open to evil as well. Indeed, it was expected that the more Christians were committed to the Christian community and its life and the greater their influence in the world, the more they would be selected as a target by the Evil One. Christians would be tested again

---

[23] In Chapters Four, Five, and Six of my book *God, Dreams and Revelation*, most of these materials from the New Testament and the important early leaders of the church up through the fifth century are discussed in some detail.

and again. As Tertullian remarked with characteristic exaggeration, the devil was fully known only to Christians. But they also had the experience of being able to withstand these attacks through keeping alive and vivid the experience of the cross and resurrection and being open to the power of the Holy Spirit.

Through the fellowship of the church, its sacraments and symbols, through experiences of healing—particularly in laying on of hands, anointing, and exorcism—Christians were able to meet evil, much of it incredibly destructive, and not go to pieces in one way or another. From such experience the doctrine of the atonement developed. Somehow through the cross and resurrection, it was found, the forces of evil had been turned back. The crucifixion and resurrection of Jesus seem to have wrought a change in the objective nature of the spiritual world. Those who were close to him were given protection and saved from evil. At present this was partial, but in the last days his kingdom would come fully, and evil would be cast out or transformed.

The atonement in terms of the worldview we have presented is the spiritual result of a victory worked out by Christ, as Spirit, in the physical world through Jesus, as human being. If, as it appears, the actions of ordinary women and men can influence events in the psychic, nonphysical world—if, through active imagination, they can even change both psychic and physical circumstances—then the atonement is the supreme example of such action. What happened in Judea when Pontius Pilate was procurator there was a spiritual drama made concrete in that time and place, with eternal consequences in a world that is not subject to time and space as are our five senses. Christ's struggle with Evil was fought out in both outer and inner worlds, and thus his victory was fixed in the eternal spiritual world.

But this doctrine of the atonement was not conceived just intellectually. In the early church it was the hypothesis developed to account for the experience of freedom and power Christians knew as they came into the Christian fellowship, often finding themselves no longer subject to mental and physical illness, to demons, or simply to giving up in the face of persecution. Indeed, as Christians took part in the Eucharist, joining in the celebration of the Last Supper, they found themselves transformed by the Spirit. The living presence of the risen Christ, it was seen, was present, infusing the bread and wine and the worshippers who gathered to make the sacrifice. This sacrament became the experience, par excellence, in which Christians could be touched and transformed, and sometimes physically healed, by the Spirit.

This and the other sacraments of the church, in the framework of our model, are events in the physical world through which we can come into contact, touching and participating, with realities at work in the spiritual world that seek healing and other such effects. In other words, they are an outward and visible sign of an inner and spiritual grace. As Jung has written in regard to one sacrament, "Baptism endows the individual with a living soul. I do not mean that the baptismal rite in itself does this, by a unique and magical act. I mean that the idea of baptism lifts man out of his archaic identification with the world and transforms him into a being who stands above it. The fact that mankind has risen to the level of this idea is baptism in the deepest sense, for it means the birth of the spiritual man who transcends nature."[24] It was just *this experience*, this sense of transformation, that led to the doctrines surrounding this sacrament and helped to perpetuate it.

The Eucharist is a rite through which the individual participates in the death and resurrection of the Lord. Just as it was believed that the spirit is carried in the human body and that Christ was incarnated in a human body, so this rite is, basically, a structured situation in which it is possible for the individual to find contact with realities in the spiritual world that have moved Christians since the first century. Of this Jung has written in "Transformation Symbolism in the Mass," "If the inner transformation enters more or less completely into consciousness, it becomes one of the vividest and most decisive experiences a man can have of his individual fate."[25] Through the centuries this experience has kept the living mystery of the Mass alive, and from this the church developed its teaching and dogma of the Eucharist.

Once the possibility is considered seriously that a spiritual world does exist alongside of the physical world, independently and interpenetrating it, then the idea of life after death became quite natural. There are many occurrences which people have described as coming from beyond the borders of this life, including Jung's examples in *Memories, Dreams, Reflections*,[26] but the resurrection itself stands for the permanence of the human soul as no other event in history.

When human beings are conceived of as a physical structure housing a psyche that is integrated into matter but still able to relate to an

---

[24] *Collected Works* Vol. 10, p. 67.
[25] *Papers from the Eranos Yearbooks* 2, *The Mysteries* (1955), p. 335 I cannot find this statement in Jung's revision of this work in *Collected Works*, Vol. 11.
[26] Chapter Six.

independent nonphysical world, then it is not reasonable to insist that the whole psyche—which has already reached out beyond the body—must dissolve with the dissolution of the body. The idea of a destiny beyond this life puts human life in quite a different perspective, giving us a very different picture of how we want to live it. It also has decided effects upon our mental and physical health.[27]

The early church was specifically a healing community. Men and women came to the church as they had to the temples of Aesculapius, and often they were healed. As early as Plato, the ancient world recognized that psychic disorder would cause sickness and infirmity in the body. It was only natural that a fellowship whose experiences brought wholeness and salvation to the individual psyche would bring healing to sick bodies and minds as well, and this was the experience of the followers of Jesus and the early church.

These people saw sickness, not as the result of God's disfavor, but as the result of the actions of the Evil One and its minions. Just as the church had been given power over Evil through the victory of Jesus on Golgotha, it had also received healing power over mental and physical illness. The experiences of healing, which are found everywhere in the church's history, thus were interpreted within a framework essentially in agreement with the worldview we have presented. Christian healing was one of the natural results of God's particular influence in the space-time world in this special way. But this view, quite obviously, leaves some fairly difficult questions hanging fire.

Some Unanswered Questions

Strangely enough, the question that seems the hardest on the surface is actually the easiest to approach. How can a miracle happen? As we have seen, the most intelligent minds today find that human beings so far have not achieved any final knowledge of the world around them. Since most "laws" are actually only statistical averages—road maps as it were—there is not much meaning, scientifically or theologically, in the idea that a miracle is some event which is clearly an impossibility. The world is more fluid than nineteenth-century science could comprehend, and miracles seem to be those unusual occurrences which tell us something about its movement and direction. They help us to understand the teleological, "spiritual" aspect of reality which seems to be

---

[27] In *Afterlife: The Other Side of Dying*, I have looked at the evidence and meaning of life after death.

moving in and through physical reality. This irregular movement in human evolutionary history has been charted with remarkable success by Teilhard de Chardin in his many works. In the case of religious healing, the unusual or miraculous quality most often has to do with the time factor, and this offers little difficulty when one views time in the relative manner of modern thought. Instantaneous healing is no more a breach of natural law than air-lifting a fifty-ton cargo.

Whether or not we believe that God can influence this world will depend upon our worldview and our openness to the facts of experience. For this reason we sketched an alternative view of reality earlier in this chapter. Jung and the Nobel Prize-winning physicist Wolfgang Pauli devised a theory they called synchronicity, in which both ordinary causality and noncausal influences have an effect upon the courses of events in this world or ours. This can be illustrated in a diagram. In this diagram ordinary causal influences operate from A to B to C . . . and on indefinitely. In addition, each event is related to every other event at each moment and to the flow of meaning or spirit represented by wavy bands at the top. Thus A, A', A'', A''' . . . represent the innumerable discrete events related in a noncausal way to each other. Healing miracles are those events where the influence of spirit is stronger or greater than those of ordinary causality.[28]

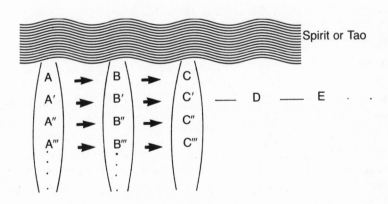

Figure 5

[28] I have discussed this theory of miracles in *Christo-Psychology* (1982) pp. 128–30. I de-

We have already seen that physicists investigating the ultimate nature of matter find paradoxes and conflicting, irreconcilable theories, rather than a simple easily understood, rational theory of simple particles of matter. We live in a mysterious world. When we do not know what matter is or how it is constituted, we cannot say what spirit isn't. Is the world of Spirit likely to be any less complex or mysterious than matter? Investigating the unusual events that do not fit into the causal pattern is one way of learning something of the world of Spirit and God. Bergson has reminded us that no amount of logic can disprove a fact of experience. Indeed, unusual religious healing as well as religious experience, religious dream interpretation, and other similar phenomena are evidence that this is God's world after all—a dangerous and vital world of unlimited, living possibilities in which no open-minded person can be bored. People whose minds have no place for these strange happenings are caught in a rigid worldview with no place for what they cannot understand, a view quite at variance with modern theoretical physics. The final question is whether we know exactly how God and our world works, or whether God is still influencing this world of ours today according to ways as incomprehensible as the nature of the physical world. Religious healing may, indeed, tell us something about the love of God that we can learn in no other way.

In his book *In Mathematical Circles* (1969), Howard Eves suggests a mathematical origin for the miracle.[29] He gives an equation that produces a regular pattern and one point totally apart from that pattern. He quotes the great mathematician Babbage, who suggests that God is the master programmer who can produce regularity and exceptions to that regularity at the same time. God is certainly as capable of that as a mathematician working with equations.

A second question is a good deal more difficult. Why are some persons healed when others are not? This is a problem for which there are some partial explanations, but no satisfactory answer. It can really be considered only in connection with the problem of evil. But the fact that we cannot answer the question is no reason to doubt the actuality of religious healing. It does not upset the evidence of healing any more than the inability of nuclear physicists to pinpoint the movement of particular electrons disproves the fact of atomic radiation. That we do

veloped this diagram (Figure 5) for that publication. I have also discussed this theory in an article, "Modern Perspectives in Miracles," *The Encyclopedia of Religion* (1987), Vol. 9, pp. 548–51.

[29] Vol. 2, p. 74.

not understand why one person is healed and another is not, is a reflection on our imperfect human knowledge, and on our inability to become channels of the power of the Spirit. Our inability to understand the Spirit and use it perfectly does not mean it does not work.

Why then is there evil, and what is its source? Again, there is no final answer. As Jakob Boehme and others have defined it, evil is a partial good that takes over the whole by pretending to be the total good. Or, as Whitehead so beautifully says, "Evil is the brute motive force of fragmentary purpose, disregarding the eternal visions.[30] This is true of a psychic complex that rises up and runs the whole personality. In a way it applies to an invading organism or cancer cell which takes over and makes the human body a factory for its own uses. But this does not tell us very much about the forces that cause such things to happen. We cannot even foresee how a particular evil will affect us, and there is certainly no easy way to deal with it. Even Jesus was able to deal with evil only by the drastic action of being born among human beings and being crucified and resurrected. Christians, it seems clear, cannot expect final answers to these questions.

One of the evils associated with healing is the inflation of the healers, who come to believe that they are special agents of God or better than their fellows. This attitude is common for many gifts. Even singers have been known to display it, and all church choirs are not noted for their humility and perspective. This does not mean, however, that singing is not a gift and cannot be used to touch people religiously. With all its profound significance, the same surely applies to healing.

Christians are faced with enough physical illness and misery as it is. Obviously people who are tied up in knots, whether by physical illness or neurosis or psychosis, are not as free to find full relationship with God. If Christians are to help, they must of course have all the knowledge they can to deal with human collective and social problems,

---

[30] *Science and the Modern Man* (1948), p. 192. See also my discussion of evil in *Discernment, A Study in Ecstasy and Evil* (1978). The finest historical study of evil is the four volume work of Jeffrey Burton Russell, *The Devil: Perceptions of Evil from Antiquity to Primitive Christianity, Satan: The Early Christian Tradition, Lucifer: The Devil in the Middle Ages, Mephistopheles: The Devil in the Modern World.* Walter Wink has provided the definitive study of evil in the New Testament and the implications of this study for today in two books, *Naming the Powers: The Language of Power in the New Testament* (1985), *Unmasking the Powers: The Invisible Forces That Determine Human Existence* (1986). The consensus of humankind is that there is a destructive dimension of reality as well as a creative one. Christianity deals with this by stating that Jesus was God's answer to evil and that in the resurrection of Jesus we are given evidence that God is more powerful than evil and that in the end all will be well. Evil is a temporary rebellion against the love of God.

human unconsciousness, and even our sometimes willful estrangement from God. But human reconciliation with God does not, in the end, depend upon final answers, scientific or metaphysical. It depends upon our experience, and perhaps in the last analysis on that particular experience of love which Paul described in his letter to the Ephesians, when he spoke of what had been revealed to him, and asked for the churches "that he would grant you, according to the riches of his glory, to be strengthened with might by his Spirit in the inner person; that Christ may dwell in your hearts by faith; that ye, being rooted and grounded in love, may be able to comprehend with all saints what is the breadth, and length, and depth, and height; and to know the love of Christ, which passeth knowledge, that ye might be filled with all fullness of God."[31]

Healing, however sporadic in effect and however incompletely understood, is an important evidence of that love. To offer religious healing is one way in which Christians can express that love which is so much needed by people today.

---

[31] Ephesians 3:16 (KJV).

CHAPTER 14

Implementing the Healing Ministry in the Church Today

The case for spiritual healing rests. If we are convinced that the ministry of Christian healing has a place in the life of the church of our day, what are we going to do about it? If we continue to ignore this aspect of the church's ministry we are not following the practice of Jesus of Nazareth, the apostles and the early church. We are probably caught in a worldview that truly doubts any continuing transforming effect of the spiritual dimension of reality upon the material world in which we live. We are also ignorant of the newest data in modern physics, anthropology, mathematics, psychology, and parapsychology—all of which suggest that this physical world does not stand alone.

Most of the clergy trained in our seminaries have been given no suggestion that a healing ministry has a place in today's ministry and certainly no instructions on how to undertake such a ministry. Lay people in most mainline churches, whether conservative or liberal, have been taught that there is no reason to expect such a healing ministry today. This presents a formidable obstacle for those who have studied the subject. Many of us have come to the conclusion that Christian healing was an integral part of Christian practice and evangelism in its most vital period of growth and is still an integral part of ministry today.

But how does one begin a healing ministry either as an official part of the church's ministry when the church cannot accept such a ministry, even as an action of dedicated laypeople? If one begins, how does one avoid the absurdities that are often seen in healing sects? Healing is one part of the Christian witness; when it becomes the main emphasis, then something often goes wrong. As I have pondered the subject I have come to see three different levels of learning and training if the ministry of healing is to be integrated once more into the normal life of the Western Christian church.

First of all are those aspects of Christian life that lay a sound foundation for a ministry of healing for both clergy and laypeople. Then there are the actual practices one undertakes to start and carry out a healing ministry as laypeople or clergy. Along with these suggestions we will offer some very definite guidelines. Finally, we will provide a method that a group of us devised for training ministers, those in the helping professions, and interested lay Christians in the healing ministry. We discuss each of these suggestions below.

Vital Christianity

Christian healing is an integral part of vital Christianity, but has little to do with conventional Christianity where people are Christians merely by conditioning or by acceptance of faith as a part of the social group of which they wish to be a part. In *Companions on the Inner Way,* I examine five qualities of vital Christianity, building upon three elements of vital religion described by Baron von Hügel: an institution, religious experience, and sound critical thinking. The healing ministry is evidence that human beings can be channels for the power of the Spirit of God. Healing is one facet of religious experience. But even religious experience can go astray unless it is based on some well-tested, historical, religious tradition and is supported by our best understanding of reality and is consistent with our view of the world as a whole. In addition to von Hügel's three elements, in order to understand and facilitate religious experience, we need to know something about the depth and capacities of the human psyche. We need to have a psychology that deals with the depth of human beings and has a place for our human experience of transcendence. Since the Christian religious tradition tells us that God is love and that the life of Jesus as well as his death and resurrection demonstrate that love, religious experience and activity that do not express love may be inspired by some other aspect of the spiritual domain than God. The fifth element of vital Christianity is love.

In earlier chapters we have shown how the healing ministry is an integral part of Christian tradition, both in its canonical scripture, the New Testament, and also in the continuing history of its life. There is a ticklish problem here, however. The healing ministry is not integral to the Old Testament. Indeed, a God who punishes for sin is found in many places there. This is embarrassing when people wish to view all passages of the Bible as equally inspired. One of the finest statements about biblical inspiration was adopted by the Mennonite Church General Assembly in June 1977. This statement is found in Willard Swartley's book *Slavery, Sabbath, Women and War,* a remarkable study of the difficulties of a literal and flat interpretation of the Old and New Testaments. This document states that the entire Bible needs to be read through the eyes of Jesus who is the incarnation of God. What agrees with Jesus' teaching, practice, death, and resurrection is of the highest order of inspiration and what does not is less inspired on the many-pointed scale from 0 to 100 percent. Because so many Christians, influenced by some passages in the Old Testament, still view God as wrathful and the giver of illness, disaster, and death, they do not see the centrality of the healing ministry in the incarnate son of God, Jesus of Nazareth. Without a clear view of biblical revelation and inspiration and a knowledge of the love and healing mercy of God, Jesus, and the Holy Spirit, the healing ministry cannot be a normal, essential part of Christian ministry.

The basic idea upon which the Christian healing ministry is founded is that the healer is the instrument and carrier of the healing love of God transmitted through the Holy Spirit. Along with this is the conviction that the power of this creative love is greater than any obstacles. The healing power that operated through Jesus and raised Jesus from the dead is now operating in and through the church of which we are members. Some nonmedical healers use suggestion (where suggestion leaves off and hypnotism begins is difficult to define), and their own psychic energy. They may teach methods of thought control and self-suggestion, but this is *not* Christian healing. Christian healers may have psychic gifts which are enhanced and empowered by the Holy Spirit that can make them a more effective instrument of the creative and healing love of God. Other healers from other religious traditions, including Shamanism and Buddhism, may also bring sick people into touch with the loving creative power at the heart of things. I am much more comfortable with healers who represent a historic religion than with those who come from recently developed cults. No other major religion of humankind, however, provides a founder like Jesus of Nazareth, who spoke so clearly about the love of God and who made healing a central part of his public ministry and then went on to teach and empower disciples to carry on that ministry. Jesus also did not claim to heal with his own power, but rather because of his unique relationship with God. What his disciples experienced at Pentecost was a share in that unique relationship with God.

Many people in most of the major religions are afraid of God or fear that the demonic realm has as much or more power than the divine. Jesus and vital Christianity state that, in spite of all the evidence to the contrary, the loving God is the ultimate core of the universe and that healing and transformation of mind, body, and soul will ultimately come about here or in the world beyond for those open to it. Paul expresses this essential idea magnificently in his letter to the Romans: "For I am convinced that there is nothing in death or life, in the realm of spirits or superhuman power, in the world as it is or in the world as it shall be, in the forces of the universe, in heights or depths—nothing in all creation that can separate us from the love of God in Christ Jesus our Lord." When Jesus states that we need faith, he is speaking of this kind of conviction, that the ultimate ground of the universe is *for* us, not against us, and wishes us to be healed and whole.

Separating love and faith is nearly impossible for followers of Christ. Faith is the conviction that the love manifested in Jesus is at the heart of being and expresses the essential nature of God. When we do not try to live in accordance with this love we are out of synch with God, the nature of the universe, our neighbors, and ourselves. Jesus said, "You are my followers as you love one another as I have loved you." Jesus gives us a clear picture of the nature of love in his teaching and life. Christian love is seldom complete until those we love feel loved by us. The healing ministry flowed naturally from Jesus' love of human beings.

What we do is a better indication of what we believe than what we think. Our true belief in the healing ministry is what we do about it. Do we stay in close communion with the loving, healing God in prayer, meditation, Bible reading, and Eucharist? Do we reach out to others with consolation, love, understanding, touch, prayer, anointing? True belief involves obedient response and action.

Before a significant, normal, and continuous practice of healing returns to the church, we need to have people who truly believe that a loving God reaches into and can change our minds and bodies. And we need to take time to remain in constant communion with that divine love. We need to know that Jesus and his followers practiced a ministry of healing because they wanted to express God's love. And then we need to reach out in every way possible to broken, fragile, hurting human beings, well aware that followers of Jesus obediently loved, preached, taught, and healed. Let us take a deeper look at these two essential ingredients of a healing ministry: faith and love.

The Importance of Faith

One of the problems with the word *faith* is that it means so many different things to different people. For many people the word stands for "the faith," the detailed propositions of a belief system. It is also understood by some as belief in that for which there is no evidence, as in the persistent belief in unicorns. Here faith depends simply upon authority. To believe by faith in this framework means to make a jump of belief that cannot be examined critically and rationally. Still others use the word *faith* when it is not appropriate. They use it to describe experiences of a nonphysical dimension of reality. Because they are so convinced that only the material world is real, they cannot believe that any other dimension of reality can be real. Still others see faith as wishful thinking, believing what we wish.

Faith describes none of these. It is rather the basic conviction that the world around us, both physical and spiritual, is essentially kindly intentioned toward us, *in spite of the evidence to the contrary*. Faith says that the power of good and love are infinitely more powerful than the power of destruction and alienation.

This attitude springs most naturally from a childhood in which the child is valued, cared for, and loved and is treated with the same kind of concern when difficult, in pain, angry, or disobedient. This kind of treatment fosters an attitude that our total environment is supporting and caring at the core, and that not only those close to us, but our body, our community, the physical and even spiritual reality can be counted on. What a difference it makes whether children learn to suspect and doubt the concern and caring of those around them because of parental blunders and lack of consistency, or whether children learn to expect concern and care. One's attitude acts as a filter, selecting and interpreting the data of life. When children learn that life is uncaring in the home and family, it takes either the careful attention of a trusted person or some breakthrough such as a dramatic religious experience to turn around their basic attitude toward life. Sometimes it takes both.

As a child's horizon expands, the attitudes acquired in childhood are widened to take in the whole world. Those with faith see the universe as essentially friendly and caring, accepting the evidence to the contrary as one of the necessary problems of life. Those who find it difficult to trust and have confidence in the universe, see the difficulties and pains as normative and moments of caring as chance occurrences. To such persons the universe is either essentially meaningless or hostile.

A great percentage of people raised in the Western world, whether capitalist or Marxist, have been solidly indoctrinated in the dominant materialism of our culture. Inevitably they see human beings as essentially irrelevant, purely chance products of a meaningless universe. There is nothing to have faith in. Reality is an inexorable, blind, mechanical process. If it goes wrong and one cannot right it mechanically, there is no changing it. Life ends at the grave, and there is no continuing life to look forward to. What we do not get now, we never obtain. For such people to have faith, they must be shown that some of the most creative modern scientists no longer think they know enough to believe in such mathematical materialism. If physicians, psychologists, or clergy are to facilitate the faith process in a person without faith they must certainly have some alternative to that materialistic and mechanistic conviction. An alternative view can be learned and taught.[1]

Many primitive peoples believe that the universe is hostile, with demonic and destructive tendencies predominating. They see the universe as essentially capricious, or else as a punitive and demanding parent, punishing us when we do not live up to impossible standards. Since this is the way many parents do, in fact, treat their children, it is easy to see how many of us are prepared for such an attitude. This point of view is even more difficult to turn around than the former one.

Faith, then, is an attitude that is a part of our central frame of reference. It views the world and its inhabitants as essentially friendly and concerned. God is seen as equally well-intentioned toward the individual and the physical world. In the last analysis, the realities and powers of the universe are supportive of the one who has faith; they can be reached out to and depended upon. People without faith are on their own.

This does not mean that there will be no fear or anger or striving for success in those with faith. To have faith does not mean that we are carried about in an eternal womb. However, the fear and anger will be appropriate to each situation in which we find ourselves. The person with faith is convinced that life and reality can be managed and diffi-

---

[1] We have already presented this evidence in earlier chapters.

culties can be overcome because the core of reality is kindly disposed toward human beings. In addition the loving God we have known on this side will provide for our continued growth in the kingdom of heaven on the other side.[2] When death leads to such a kingdom as Jesus portrays, it loses its horror. Death is not evil in itself. Evil is, instead, premature death and the sickness and agony that so often surround dying. These tragedies are the work of Evil, not of God, and there is hope even here if these can be redeemed on the other side.

Destructive emotions arise when we are without faith and are faced with a meaningless or hostile world. There is usually a sense of helplessness, powerlessness, and threat to which human beings react in four basically different ways. Let us review what we described earlier. We can react to this threat with agitated fear, the *flight* response, which creates a life covered with a pall of anxiety and terror. The physiological and psychic damages resulting from this attitude are legion. On the other hand, one can react with the *fight* response, turning against the world and other people with anger, hostility, rage, and violence. Any human being under this kind of constant pressure will also sustain physical or psychological damage and may inflict this on others as well. Similar to the fight response is the egocentric approach, in which individuals take on the problems of the whole world. This impossible burden results in unbearable stress, with all its psychological and physiological complications. The fourth response is simple collapse before the threat. There is neither fight nor flight, just hopelessness, depression, loss of meaning. The individual gives up, since there is no point in doing anything. Simple depression of this kind is the common cold of modern psychiatry in spite of drug therapy. The physiological results of this kind of giving up are found in every doctor's office; the emotional ones are a pastoral problem in every church.

John Sanford has written of the importance of faith in his recent book, *The Strange Trial of Mr. Hyde—A New Look at the Nature of Human Evil*. He concludes that Jung is ambiguous about faith in his *Answer to Job*. He goes on to say that faith is essential to the healing process, for without faith the soul despairs and gives up the struggle of life. He then says that the Gospels, as well as other religious classics, do not give all the answers, but they do give faith and that although it is hard to live in uncertainty, it can be creative "as long as the door is left open

---

[2] In *Afterlife: The Other Side of Dying* (1982), I have presented the full evidence for such a life and a picture of the Kingdom of Heaven drawn from The Beatitudes.

for the soul to exercise the faith and hope it needs in order to make its way through the perils of this earthly existence."[3]

How do we facilitate this faith in ourselves and in others? One of the greatest comforts to me is that God does not require total certainty or perfect people before we human beings can be instruments of the Holy Spirit. Nor does divine love require perfect faith on the part of those who are to heal or to be healed. As I stated in the Preface, I found myself used the moment I was obedient, and then when I gained a little knowledge through Agnes Sanford's *The Healing Light* I found myself drawn deeper and deeper into relationship with God and the healing ministry. The healing ministry needs at least some tentative (hypothetical) faith and then reinforces it. I know of no other traditional religion that offers such a ground for faith and healing as that given by God through Jesus of Nazareth.[4]

I can only facilitate this kind of faith in others as I keep in living communion with the loving God, the Holy Spirit and the risen Jesus. I find that in addition to having a worldview that makes such a communion reasonable I need time to spend time with the God who would use me to minister to and to be a channel of healing for other people. I need at least five different kinds of time. First, I need at least half an hour to an hour daily to rest quietly in God's presence, listen, reflect on scripture, disentangle my life, and receive again the assurance of God's love. Second, I find a daily Eucharist centers me in the fullness of the Christian faith. It is a time of corporate prayer with my wife or the gathered church. Third, at least once a year I need one and sometimes many days of quiet, light fasting, and reviewing where I have been on my journey with God and where I have gone wrong, where I need to change and what my priorities and direction are to be. Fourth, whenever I sit down to my typewriter or get up to speak, or when I am facing a difficult situation in counseling or healing, I need to stop and ask with the psalmist that the spirit may not be taken from me and that what I say or write or do may be according to God's will and in God's power. Finally, at least every three or four weeks *or whenever the darkness* seems to engulf me in hopelessness and saps my faith, I need to set aside at least three hours either to do some spiritual house cleaning or to bring my fears and doubts and darkness before the One who

---

[3] John A. Sanford, *The Strange Trial of Mr. Hyde—A New Look at the Nature of Human Evil* (1987), p. 161.

[4] Much of this material on the meaning of faith has been drawn from Chapter Four, "Faith and the Healing Ministry," of my book *Prophetic Ministry, The Psychology and Spirituality of Pastoral Care* (1982). The material was originally written for a book entitled *Dimensions in Wholistic Healing, New Frontiers in the Treatment of the Whole Person* (1979).

defeated evil on the cross by rising again and is still available to defeat the evil that threatens me. Since this last process in a sense includes the others, I will give an example of such an encounter with darkness that occurred a few years ago.[5]

Me: I am not sure why I am here, Lord. As I awoke I felt heavy and as though there were little or no hope. Some post partum darkness having finished the lectures and reading the proofs from the publishers—fear of not sleeping, fear of exposure, fear for my children . . . how much I care about them . . . fear of being a fraud and not believing what I write.

Then the whole money problem . . . Lord, you seem so far off—heaven such an impossibility, death so final. The evil all around—Shirley and Ruth so sick . . . seemingly overwhelming passions . . . fear of being rejected by you for not doing enough or being a bad person. This morning I am not as down as during the night, and even then not the horrible darkness and pain, but still defeating.

Voice: Yes, what is it like?

Me: The image of the edge of the abyss giving away. But I do not fall into a deep pit—rather onto a vast and waterless desert, uninhabited except by the voices of the gusts of wind that torment me. No human habitation . . . alone, alone. Nothing but the flat featureless desert—behind me the cliffs from which I fell. I turn around and look at it. How did I fall from it without being smashed to pieces? But perhaps I am dead and this is sheol with whining voices laughing, taunting . . . nothing to confront—the furies of the Greeks always out of grasp. The darkness has assumed a new form. The sun is scorching and no tree or bush or rock under which to find shade . . . baked and parched and alone. It seems that I should be more down than I am—

Dark Voice 1: Fraud and deceiver, giving hope where there is no hope—only meaningless material reality and then this meaningless kingdom of hell . . . alone in the scorching desert—

Me: Strange, dark one, you only half frighten me.

Dark Voice 2: The one you love is going under, and he will drag you with him, and you will feel the pain that he can't bear.

Me: You touch a tender cord, but I don't believe it, and I have enough resources to stand within the gap. And God has protected me before and will again.

---

[5] Obviously this is only a brief summary of the method of prayer that begins in silence and moves into relationship with God. I have treated this subject at length in *The Other Side of Silence, A Guide to Christian Meditation* (1978) and in *Companions on the Inner Way, The Art of Spiritual Guidance* (1984).

Dark Voice 3: What a vile despicable creature you are, no control of your inner feelings and attitudes. Only hell would want you, vomit of the earth, excrement, mold on the earth's dying surface . . . wandering, wandering and wandering . . . getting nowhere because there is no place to go—no end, no meaning, no hope. What an ugly misshapen creature you are, a monstrosity. Your time in Malaysia showed how none of your friends care about you—only want what you can give.

Dark Voice 4: And look at the ravages of hell around you: sickness, disease, misery. Where is the joy, the love, the concern you write about? Only misery and pain and ugliness. Even the faultless typewriter fails (I have to stop and find a new ribbon). Typical. Earth and sea are but the rotting remains of dying matter and human beings the rot. And you expect some meaning from this meaningless rot. . . . fool.

[Swirling around, the voices keep up this litany and continue as I stumble through the desert trying to get away from them. It seems I should be more despairing.]

Me: I do not understand where I am at present. A new ribbon—perhaps a new way . . . Lord, speak to me out of the whirlwind and silence these sand devils. . . .

Dark Voices [in chorus]: You think that there is hope . . . look at your world about to explode with nuclear war, people killing one another in war and bigotry or crime, concentration camps and torture, all the poverty, misery, and oppression—How could there be any meaning in this? Face the reality of endless hell, oh rot and scum of the earth.

[Their voices rise in pitch and intensity, buzzing around me and within me.]

Dark Voices: All is lost and hopeless, lost and hopeless. Give up and die.
Only pain and ugliness and vile passion.
No meaning, no end, a slow dribble of life running out
until the skin is empty and the wind carries it away.

Me: Lord, I have heard another voice. Speak, Lord, come.

[I have not looked up into the sky, but I realize that my head is not aching and my skin is not burning. Great masses of clouds cover the sky. The thunder crashes and bolts of lightening streak across the sky. A mighty wind rises from the East and sweeps away the sand devils and then the rain, first gentle and then a torrent. I lift my face to it. The sky is alive with jagged streaks of fire. It is a warm rain, a comforting rain. Then out of the great mass of clouds piled one on top of another the black funnel spins forth. The electric flashes cease, the wind abates . . . the whirlwind, the tornado comes toward me. I fall prostrate upon my face, the earth around me is sucked up into the twisting cone. Then I am in the eye of the storm and a voice speaks out.]

Voice: Never forget that I am power as well as love. I laid out the foundations of the heavens, made this mysterious earth in all its complexity, the physical heavens and the spiritual heavens as well. The lost angels that were just tormenting you . . . trying to forget their misery and draw you into their agony . . . poor pitiful creatures.

[I am prostrate on the ground. Then in the midst of the darkness a great light that I can feel through my skin—penetrating, searching out, probing—but not hot, not burning, just light, ineffable light, the source of light. All my guilt and ugliness are laid bare, but instead of salt to make them smart, a soothing balm is applied by a loving hand. Then the voice—no longer like thunder, but human, caring, loving—]

Voice: And I am Love, Love, also. Open your eyes and see me. The one who created green things in the willing of it—that One has recreated your earth and you.

[I open my eyes. Beside me is the loving One, the light made human, now substantial and now spiritual glory—both at the same time—the resurrected One. His arms are outstretched and he smiles at me. He is seated beside me on a little mound. The eye of the storm . . . the earth around us has been sucked away. Back of us are the cliffs from which I fell. A stream of water has broken forth from the rocks and falls laughing down the multicolored cliffs from ledge to ledge. The sun has come out, and it makes rainbows in the spray. And the earth is green, the green of heaven, and around the falling water there is a garden, exquisite with blooming flowers, trailing vines, dark and light trees, a tapestry of life. The earth around us is covered with flowers, carpeted with them, flowers of every color, every shape, a tumultuous riot of shape and hue. Then my ears are opened and I hear the songs of birds and then I see them hiding in the trees, courting one another. It is the garden of heaven and through the trees I see a castlelike place built against the cliffs, and I hear the sound of joyous voices . . . men and women, or are they both at the same time? . . . laughing and playing . . . a new heaven and a new earth.]

Me: Lord, how can this be? It is almost too wonderful to bear. And I feel so unworthy, so out of place. Here I am in my ragged clothes covering a ragged body containing a ragged soul.

Voice: Look at yourself.

[Up to that moment I had only seen the cliffs, the soft sunshine, the trees laden with fruit and water droplets, seen the flowers and heard the water mingling with bird songs and behind that the laughing children and rich songs of joyful adults. Now I looked at myself. My hands and arms were clean, just as if they had never been soiled. Covering my body was a robe of such beautifully woven cloth and superb design that I was lost in wonder. On my feet were sandals of leather and gold and on my hand a ruby ring engraved with the face of the One who sat beside me. Inside I felt clean . . . a little fear, but even that was not raging, and I barely heard the murmur of the furies, the lost voices, at the edge of the garden fearing to enter and seeking to keep others out.]

Me: Lord, why all this?

Voice: Because Love is also Joy and Light, and it seeks to share its being with its creation if only people will stop and let us give them.

Me: But Lord, we have messed up things so horribly.

Voice: Only those who feel so, know so, realize their unworthiness and can be given the simultaneous fruition of life without bounds. Come, let us go toward the Holy City where they are waiting for us.

[He helps me to my feet and embraces me and then with an arm around my shoulder, we walk over a little bridge that crosses the shining water to a path through the towering trees to the City that shines as if made of every precious stone. And as we come, people run out to meet us and I see many familiar faces. One of them cries out that we are just in time for the banquet and the throng escorts us back through the gates of the City to the great banquet room and great tables laden with food and other tables set with our names upon them, near fountains that laugh when the other laughter ceases. My Lord stays with me and eats with me and us. I am weary and he takes me through long corridors painted with stories that I know and recognize and then to my room where a bed is laid out in which I can rest and sleep. My Lord lies down beside me and holds me as a loving parent does a frightened child and I sleep.]

Within an hour or so after this time of meditation and communion, the darkness lifted, hope and faith returned, and I could go on. I could again reach out to people with hope and the love that I had experienced in this time of prayer. This kind of experience makes faith possible, opens us to knowledge that the God of conquering love is real. Overcoming darkness in this way is one way to God. Quietly resting and centering in light and love is another way.

The Necessity of Love in Christian Healing

One of the most characteristic aspects of true Christian healers is their capacity to love, to be channels of divine love. Many social-action oriented ministers have come to me burned out because they were trying to love from the standpoint of their own ego, their own will. We can be continuously healing to others in soul, mind, and body, in their social oppression and poverty, only as we remain in touch with divine Love and let it move in and through us to others. God wants us to be ambassadors of the good news of God's love and healing presence. I am an ambassador when I know the message of the country that I represent and try to present it in terms that are understandable to those to whom I am sent. My task is to be a messenger of the kingdom of heaven, appropriating it to myself and my situation and then adapting it to the unique situation of the person to whom I am reaching out.

The Christian healing ministry that is not rooted and grounded in love seldom achieves lasting results or brings people to the full potential of which they are capable. Most of the people who are called saints are those who loved God and their fellow humans so much that healing flowed from them as naturally as it did from the apostles and from Jesus. A brash reporter once asked Mother Teresa, "Are you a saint?" She replied by poking her finger into the other's chest and saying, "Yes, and so are you." We all have the potential of saintliness when we know God's love and share it with others. Ministry, whether clerical or lay, is knowing and accepting the love of God in Jesus and sharing it with other people.

If we are to be full instruments of God's healing power, our activity will be based in loving concern for all people. Love opens the door so that people can come to us to receive what gifts of the spirit we have. Only love opens another's heart. The fortress, the citadel of another human being, is opened only by love. When I truly love another human being and the other is open to that love, the divine communes within itself, using two human beings as instruments. Out of such an experience of God's love moving through us is the healing ministry born and empowered. There is a great difference between the love that is seeking another only for ourselves and the divine love that gives expecting nothing in return. We need to learn to love in God's way, and this is not an easy task. How can we begin to love as Jesus did?[6] I offer several suggestions.

First of all I need *faith* to wager my life on the idea that love is the essential nature of God and the universe. I simply will not put my best effort into the pursuit of love until I make that step.

---

[6] My book, *Caring: How Can We Love One Another?* (1982), gives a full treatment of this all important aspect of the healing ministry. We cannot, however, avoid offering some hints about it at this point.

And then I need *discipline*. Until I begin to take responsibility for my life and try to control it, I will love when I feel like it and hate when I feel like it. Love requires that unpleasant effort known as discipline. Love that comes and goes like the wind is worse than no love at all. God's kind of love is action springing from the hidden depths of us and acting with kindness and caring *even when we don't feel like it*. I repeat: love is not just our feeling of love, but the movement of my entire being toward others so that they feel loved. Love is transitive, not intransitive. The love of God in Jesus Christ means little until I feel it in my heart so that it increases my light or lifts me out of the darkness. Jesus went to the extreme of dying on the cross to get that message across to us, and he would have died for each of us if we had been the only one.

If we do not *love ourselves* as Jesus loved us, we reject the saving grace he offers to us. Often I find it harder to love myself than to love others. The only way that I personally can love myself is to come back to the source of Love in my times of quiet communion with God and find that the risen Jesus is always there waiting to pick up my wounded, fragile, erring soul and body and heal them. How can we hate or ignore ourselves when God loves each of us so much?

I can learn to love only as I spend time in *prayer and meditation* with the divine Lover, the risen Christ, the Holy Spirit. In my times of communion with God I ask God to show me what needs to be changed within me and to help me change what I can and to transform what I cannot change. When I am praying for others, I try to bring them into the presence of God and let that healing presence touch and transform them. This seems impossible only when we forget that time and space are very relative. When I lay hands upon another, however, I find it even easier to know God's presence with us, but more about that later.

It is impossible to love others until we *listen* to them. Ollie Backus used to say in her classes, "Without listening, there is no love, whether we are dealing with friends, family, or children. When we do not listen to others, we don't know what there is within the other person that needs our love and so we cannot convey it. Love without listening is merely projecting, seeing in others hidden aspects of ourselves. We cannot love those who are capable of responding to us unless we can listen to them without judging them."

We cannot love other people until we realize the *uniqueness* of other people. Each of us is unique, and we have many different ways of acting and valuing. Until we realize that it is natural for others to be different from us, it is very difficult to love them, particularly those whose point of view seems almost opposite to our own.

Any time that we think that we have conquered all our *hostility* and have no more anger in us, we are deluding ourselves. We are likely to become one of those people with the never-failing sugary smile who make most of us want to run in the opposite direction. When people bury and deny their hostility, their anger owns them. Rather than being under their control, their anger may burst out at the most inappropriate and destructive moments. We need to recognize our hostilities and the hurts that lie beneath them, so that we can deal with them in ways that do not hurt other people.

Those who love other people and do not love their own *families*, come close to hypocrisy. God gave us our families in order that we might grow in love. I can love anyone for an hour in my office, but my family is the crucible in which my love is refined.

When two people are married and living together and there is no touching, caring, tenderness, or sexuality, something has gone wrong. Real *sexuality* is the enclosed, long-term committed relationship and communication in which love reaches ecstasy. For this reason sexuality apart from love degrades sexuality. Sexuality can be the capstone of love.[7]

We need to love our *acquaintances*: the clerk in the store, the people for whom we work and those who work for us, the people in the bridge club or the P.T.A., those in the Altar Guild, the minister, and his wife and children.

Jesus made it perfectly clear that we are not only expected to love our families and neighbors, but even our *enemies*. As long as we harbor hatred in us for others, we restrict the flow of love in and through us and we tie ourselves to those people we like the least. We need to remember that the enemy is not only the person we do not like, but those who do not like us. Sometimes we find that as we go further on the spiritual way, many more people are annoyed and disturbed by us. Starr Daily used to say that we grow spiritually as we take our enemies into the sphere of God's love with us.

And then Jesus tells us to reach out to *the prisoners, the homeless, the shut-ins, the dying*. We have three terribly black spots on our American conscience. First of all, there are the homeless. Contemplate the horror of at least two million of them in the wealthiest country on earth! How little most of us know about our prisons. Most prisons are the most degrading places imaginable, the most efficient schools of crime avail-

---

[7] In *Sacrament of Sexuality*, Barbara and I described the relation of sexuality and love and see sexuality as one sacramental action of love.

able. Take fairly innocent or confused people (and most "criminals" are disturbed people), put them in the average prison, and in a few years we have produced skilled criminals.

Have you recently visited what are euphemistically called "rest homes?" These are the institutions where we place our elderly when they are too much trouble for us to care for. So often these people are forgotten. Yet they need to be ministered to, they need love and healing. Our culture has forgotten what most of the other great cultures have known: the aged and feeble need to be honored, not rejected. If we ever visited a "rest home," we might find how lonely and needy these people are and how healing and comforting a friendly visit can be. There are few such places that will not welcome visitors who come to sit and listen and hold another's hand. Among the patients are those who are the dying, who are so often avoided, and who face a lonely transition to another dimension of reality. Our own fear of death often keeps us away from them. If we know the God of the living and the dead and have some measure of faith that something better than this life awaits the dying, we can bring incredible healing consolation to dying people.

Ministry to the increasing number of *depressed people* is another way of showing love. If we cannot cope with these people who have given up, then we need to find someone who can cope and who can bring these people together. Reaching out to the depressed can also be a special Christian healing ministry.

In order to help the enslaved, the oppressed, the poor, and the rejected, more is needed than merely ministering to their immediate situation. *Social action* that changes the structures (social, economic, and political) that cause these miseries is needed as well. Each of us needs to have some project in which we reach out to these people, a project that we support by our own work and money. When Evelyn Underhill came to Baron von Hügel for spiritual direction, the first thing that he suggested for the development of her *spiritual* life was to go down into the slums of London and work in the soup kitchen one day a week, and she went and grew in a new way.

The world gets better not so much because people make major impacts or write books but because we listen to the depth of the voice of God within us and respond as we are best we can. Somebody asked Mother Teresa, "How do you stand it? There you are in Calcutta. You probably don't touch more than one percent of the suffering and dying in that city." And Mother Teresa answered, "I was not called to be successful; I was called to be faithful." A recent trip to South Africa showed me a church struggling with love to overcome tyranny and oppression.

All we can do is to be faithful. We can't take on all needy and broken people all over the world, but we need to have some vision of the people who need our love all over the world and listen to the voice of God's love that tells us which of the world's hurting, miserable, sick, and broken people belong to us and to which of them we are called to minister.

When we look at what it means to love, we are often frightened at the immensity of the task. One of the best answers to our fear are the words of Father Zossima in Dostoevsky's *Brothers Karamazov*:

Never be frightened at your own faint-heartedness in attaining love. Don't be too frightened even at your evil actions. I'm sorry I can say nothing more consoling to you, for love in action is a harsh and dreadful thing compared with love in dreams.

Love in dreams is greedy for immediate action, rapidly performed and in the sight of all. Men will even give their lives, if only the ordeal doesn't last too long. But it's soon over, with all looking on and applauding as though on stage.

But active love is labor and fortitude and for some people, too, perhaps a complete science. But I predict just when you see with horror, that in spite of all your efforts, you are getting further from your goal instead of nearer to it— at that very moment—I predict that you will reach it and behold clearly the miraculous power of the Lord who has been all the time loving you and mysteriously guiding you.

Some people who are striving to love as God does will find that their particular calling is the *healing ministry*. When love becomes central to our lives, then our very presence becomes healing and our touch empowered. When Lawrence LeShan studied a group of effective religious healers, he found certain similarities. He found that they were empowered by an intense feeling of love and caring. "One successful healer has said, 'Only love can generate the healing fire.' Another has explained: 'We must care. We must care for others deeply and urgently, wholly and immediately; our minds, our spirits must reach out to them.'"[8] Our potential to heal is closely related to our capacity to love, and that is closely related to our openness and experience of the continuing love of God seeking to flow into and through us.

Our capacity to heal through spiritual means is generated by love and is at the same time an expression of that love. A healing ministry is one way to love other people. How do we go about this ministry?

---

[8] "The Therapeutic Touch," by Emrika Padus. *Prevention* (March 1977), pp. 94–100.

Beginning the Healing Ministry

There are several different levels of the healing ministry. First of all is the loving parent, mother or father, tending to their own family. Mothers usually know instinctively that loving touch heals. This natural healing touch can be enhanced when parents are taught that God wants to heal through them. When they take time to be open to God's love and when they pray for God's love to move through them their touch can be healing for their children or spouses. Families in Chrysostom's time stole oil from the church lamps to anoint the sick within the family. How helpful if would be if churches provided classes in the healing touch, replacing the false image of a vengeful god with the image of a loving god and showing how central the healing ministry was to Jesus and the early church. For many people it would be helpful to see that nurses, doctors, psychologists, and other professionals acknowledge the reality of touch empowered by faith and prayer. People who are laying hands upon another may or may not mention that they are praying. It depends upon the openness and responsiveness of the others to the idea of healing prayer.

The next level of healing ministry is the layperson or minister who feels called to this particular ministry personally but is not in a position to introduce it into the regular life of a church or prayer group. Agnes Sanford started in this way. She found that when she laid her hands on people in her husband's parish, many of them recovered. She recorded her experience in *The Healing Light*. She had experienced healing through a minister who became convinced that this practice was a part of normal Christian ministry. She tells the story of her entering the healing ministry in her book *Sealed Orders: The Autobiography of a Christian Mystic*. Her novels, *Oh, Watchman* and *Lost Shepherd*, describe more of her healing practice, as I heard her speak of it in the Schools of Pastoral Care, than her specifically religious works. We worked together for over 15 years. For several years she was a member of the church of which I was rector. When she spoke of her ministry, she mentioned several essential elements. I have found them right on the mark and have summarized them below.

1. She found a Christian minister who believed that spiritual healing was possible. With the laying on of hands he healed her of a depression that had lasted several years. First of all we need someone with experience and background in the healing ministry to introduce us to its reality.

2. The minister did not pray for her healing and then end the prayer, "if it be thy will." The minister believed that it was God's will to heal and that sickness was not sent by God. She said that had he added, "if thy will be done," she would never have been healed.

3. She studied the Bible, Christian history, and books on Christian healing. She realized more and more that healing was an essential part of the ministry of Jesus and the early church.

4. She began her ministry with those close to her in her own family.

5. When she had an opportunity to pray for others, she discovered that healings often took place. They happened again and again. She did not rush into a room and say: "Now I am going to lay hands on you and heal you." She came quietly and naturally touched the other and prayed.

   A young man without any religious background was brought to her with a serious eye injury. In a very natural way she talked to the thirteen-year-old boy until he was quite comfortable with her. Then she said, "Some people think that I am able to get in contact with a power out in the universe greater than my own and that it can move through me and help heal others. Do you mind if I lay my hands on you and pray that this power can come through me and heal you?" The boy assented and she laid her hands on him and prayed using words that he could understand. By the time the boy got home the eye had healed.

6. She saw this ministry as God using her as a channel and empowering and multiplying her natural gifts of healing touch. She believed that the essential aspect of her ministry was not her own giftedness but keeping in communion with God through prayer, so that God's power could flow through her. She also realized that certain people had special gifts in the healing ministry.

7. Wherever she lived she was part of a prayer group in which she could share her experiences with Christian peers who could interact with her and keep her grounded. She also always belonged to a church and received Eucharist regularly. All people involved in any kind of healing, particularly spiritual healing, need peer support and review.

8. She never promised anyone that she would heal them. If the person did not get well, she never blamed the sick person but concluded that she had not been an adequate channel of God's

love. She did not let failures discourage her. She also asked in prayer if the person who asked for healing was one she should continue to work with.

9. Once her experiences of healing were published, she was in demand at conferences all over this country and in many places in the world. Her attitude never changed. She considered herself an inadequate but sometimes effective instrument of God's grace.

10. She believed confidently in a life beyond this one. There was a time for death and entrance into a place "more kind than home, more large than earth." She believed, however, that this passage need not be premature or fraught with pain and agony.

11. She was paid for her lecturing, but she never asked anything of those who came for healing. In Edgar Cayce's remarkable healing ministry it is noteworthy that he lost his power when he asked for a fee or used his power for gain.

12. When she held healing services in churches or conferences she wanted people other than herself to lay hands on people or anoint them. She taught and believed that this was a ministry for which some have special gifts, but one in which all Christians can participate.

13. She told the story about a long train journey she made after a healing conference, when she was very tired. A person next to her noted her fatigue, handed her a copy of The Healing Light and told her that it might help her.

14. She never claimed to be a completely healthy person, never got over all of her minor ailments. She did, however, emerge from her depression and conducted healing conferences all over the world well into her eighties. She found that such conferences were often draining. She viewed herself as a wounded healer.

15. At one point she and a group of friends were introduced to the charismatic experience of tongue speaking. She told me how this experience had infused her with new energy and new insights into healing.

16. Agnes believed that fasting often enhanced one's spiritual gifts, including the healing gift. Her fasts were not dramatic; she would do little things like giving up the sugar in her tea to remind her of the power of Jesus' passion. She knew, however, that no one should ever fast when depressed, because fasting depletes our energy when we need it most.

17. In *The Healing Light* she wrote of the tremendous value of sacramental confession in speeding the healing process and in enabling her to become a more effective healer. She believed that confession removed blocks within individuals that might hinder the flow of the Holy Spirit.

18. In addition to the genuine caring that flowed from her when she was ministering by laying hands upon those who came to her, she used to imagine seeing the diseased part of the person as whole, well, and shining with health. She would often speak the images of wholeness that she saw in her mind's eye. Nearly all effective healers use some kind of positive imagining while they are ministering to people. She describes this process in her novel, *Oh, Watchman*.

19. She worked with psychologists and psychiatrists and taught that the more we know in these areas, the more able we are to remove the resistances that some people have to being healed.

20. When medical help was required, she suggested that it be obtained. She believed in cooperating with doctors and psychologists. What she offered was above and beyond what they could give, not instead of it. Again and again she said, "God also works through doctors and psychologists." She said that sometimes when she was taking medicine she would ask in prayer that the pill would do its work and this gave a faith boost to her medication.

    In some instances spiritual healing opens people to the use of proper medical methods or makes them realize that they need spiritual guidance or psychological counseling. Those involved in the healing ministry need to find medical doctors and psychologists who are congenial to the Christian healing ministry and can work with people in that context. One warden of the Order of St. Luke (an organization dedicated to Christian healing) was both a medical doctor and a minister involved in Christian healing.

    When the healing ministry was active in St. Luke's Church, I kept a list of the names of well-trained and trustworthy psychologists, psychiatrists, and practitioners of many specialties to whom I could refer people. What can be taken care of easily in a medical way is not something that we need to use our prayer energy upon. We had a psychological clinic at our church as well as four healing services. The well-known television healer,

Oral Roberts, has founded a model hospital as well as a college in Tulsa, Oklahoma, in addition to his emphasis on Christian healing.

21. I have found that healing services that take place along with the other sacraments are often more effective than when the healing services stand alone. Both baptism and Eucharist have a healing intent. They often bring about transformation of the total person. When combined with the laying-on-of-hands or anointing, healing is more likely to occur.

   When a sick person comes for forgiveness, wishing to confess and be forgiven sacramentally (the sacrament of absolution), often the person is open to healing, and I have found remarkable results take place. The forgiveness is not the cause of the healing, but rather the opening of the person to the full influx of God's grace. Agnes Sanford speaks of this in the second part of *The Healing Light*.

22. We have already noted that tongue speaking has often been associated with healing. For many people for whom tongue speaking is a meaningful prayer form, praying in tongues with the laying-on-of-hands is effective.

23. Some of my most startling experiences of healing, as I have already mentioned, occurred when I was acting out of pure obedience. Jesus told us to preach, teach, and heal. If I am to be a follower of Jesus in line with the apostles, then it is my task to follow their example. I *would never refuse the laying-on-of-hands or anointing to anyone who asked for it*. In the final analysis this is God's work, and I am only a fragile and inadequate instrument of that grace.

24. When people seek to grow spiritually and seek out spiritual directors, they are often opened to healing and wish to seek it. When they are more open to the Spirit they find, like Agnes Sanford, that they can not only be healed, but that they can heal as well.

25. What about death? If there were no life beyond this one, the healing ministry would be meaningless indeed. However, as we have already pointed out, this ministry is seen as evidence that the Kingdom of Heaven is breaking through into this world and healing the souls, minds, and bodies of suffering human beings. Jesus, the apostles, and the early church are of one voice in this understanding of healing. As we are touched by the love, mercy, and compassion of the Kingdom and healed, often we experi-

ence the Kingdom now and are given increased confidence in the reality of the Kingdom in which we can grow eternally and so are enabled to come to our full potential as children of God.

I have described Jesus' understanding of the beyond in my book *Afterlife*. This is not the place to do more than point out that life in the Kingdom is one of being filled, comforted, healed, strengthened, transformed, given mercy, and made children of God and coworkers in the Kingdom. Paul writes to the Philippians that he does not know whether it would be better to die and be with Christ or continue his work among the churches. One of the finest modern visions of the Kingdom was given by Thomas Wolfe in his last book, *You Can't Go Home Again*. It came to him before he knew of his fatal illness.

Dear Fox, old friend, thus have we come to the end of the road that we were to go together . . . and so farewell.

But before I go, I have just one more thing to tell you.

Something has spoken to me in the night, burning the tapers of the waning year; something has spoken in the night, and told me I shall die. I know not where. Saying:

"To lose the earth you know, for greater knowing; to lose the life you have, for greater life; to leave the friends you loved, for greater loving; to find a land more kind than home, more large than earth—

—Whereon the pillars of this earth are founded, toward which the conscience of the world is tending—a wind is rising, and the rivers flow."[9]

The final and total healing is living eternally in that Kingdom. Healing of body and mind and soul now can give us a foretaste of that Kingdom and help us turn our lives in that direction. Like any other ministry or action in life, this involves risks. At the conclusion of a conference on healing someone handed me the following words. She did not know the author and I have not been able to discover who is or was the author of them.

To laugh is to risk appearing the fool.
To weep is to risk appearing sentimental.
To reach out for another is to risk involvement.
To expose feelings is to risk exposing your true self.
To place your ideas, your dreams, before a crowd is to risk their loss.
To love is to risk not being loved in return.
To live is to risk dying.
To hope is to risk despair.

---

[9] Thomas Wolfe, *You Can't Go Home Again* (1940), p. 743.

To try to heal is to risk failure.

But risks must be taken, because the greatest hazard in life is to risk nothing.

The person who risks nothing, does nothing, has nothing, and is nothing.

They may avoid suffering and sorrow, but they cannot learn, feel, change, grow, love, live.

Chained by their attitudes, they are a slave, they have forfeited their freedom.

Only a person who risks is free.

Beginning a Healing Ministry in a Church

Most people in most of the mainline conservative and liberal churches know little or nothing about the healing ministry. If a minister or a group of lay people wishes to inaugurate services in a church, the worst way of approaching it is to spring it on the congregation without warning by announcing, "Next Sunday morning at the eleven o'clock service we will have a healing service." Several preparatory steps are advisable.

First of all, the people introducing the subject need to have done their homework. They need to know how central this ministry has been in the church and have a theological framework in which it makes sense. One way to accomplish this goal is to attend a conference on healing, where they can participate in a healing service after being provided with background material. A group of us have provided intensive workshops on healing and the spiritual life both at Kirkridge Retreat Center in Pennsylvania and at the San Francisco Theological Seminary in San Anselmo, California. John Wimber has conducted many retreats and conferences directed toward teaching the healing ministry, and we have referred to his book *Power Healing* many times.

Once those seeking to introduce healing are well grounded in a worldview that supports the healing ministry and the evidence of the Gospels and church history, then the leaders of the church need to be shown that this is not only a legitimate, but an essential, part of Christian ministry. This book in its former edition served this purpose for many congregations. For those of a more conservative persuasion, John Wimber and Kevin Springer's book, *Power Healing,* can serve this purpose.

There are many off-beat and far out healing ministries, and unfortunately they have received most of the media's attention. Often they are on television, are sensational, and emphasize healing at the expense of the rest of the Christian message. If a church is to undertake a solid, continuous, creative healing ministry, the leaders need to understand that this makes sense both as Christians and as people living in the twentieth century.

The next step is acquainting the congregation with Christian healing by inviting one of the well-known leaders in spiritual healing to conduct a healing mission at the church. As preparation for such a mission, a group of people who are convinced that healing is a part of authentic Christian witness can meet together to pray for the openness of the congregation to this aspect of ministry. Personally I believe that a church that does not have a continuous prayer group led by the clergy or by a well-trained layperson is not providing the spiritual food that people are looking for in the church. Such prayer groups are needed to support any ministry and particularly the healing one.

The next step is setting up a service during the week or Sunday evening, *not* at the regular Sunday worship. Healing should not be forced on those who are uncomfortable with it, but rather provided for those drawn to this renewal of a neglected way of ministry. If these steps are taken few people will be upset or negative. The church should serve those that aren't comfortable with the healing ministry as well as those who are. The time to prepare for questions about the healing ministry is before the services begin, not afterward. As I have already noted, at St. Luke's Church in Monrovia, four different regular healing services connected with Eucharist and prayer groups took place each week. Few people would go to the hospital without coming to one of these healing services, and it became customary for people to call the church office and let us know when they were in the hospital. Our visits to those in hospitals were an expected and regular part of our healing ministry to the congregation. I had more problems with the vestry and the congregation trying to institute a modern educational program for children and adults than I did in providing a healing ministry and allowing tongue speaking groups in the church. The only time I ever had to lay my job on the line with my church board was to support Ollie Backus's truly innovative religious educational proposal.

A Program for Training In Christian Healing

For ten years a group of people interested in the total field of healing were gathered by the director of Kirkridge, Robert Raines, to provide seminars in the art of healing at the retreat center near Bangor, Pennsylvania. Many people attending have found these events life-changing, and through these eight-day conferences many clergy and lay people have begun active ministries in Christian healing. Doctors, nurses, psychologists, and social workers have been attracted to these events to round out their knowledge of healing. The people attending were required to remain for the entire conference. One of the first attempts was to get people out of their left-brain thinking and acting and to realize that they had other capacities as well. People learn more from what they do than from what they hear. The whole matter of Christian education is not an easy one, as I have detailed in my book *Can Christians Be Educated?* Experiential learning is important in becoming effective in the art of Christian healing.

The Kirkridge conferences opened with a meeting for people to introduce themselves. A brief overview of the nature of the week was offered and then some noncognitive ways of breaking through our reserve and learning to mingle with one another was provided. A conference on Christian healing that does not provide those who attend it with a sense of being cared for is neither healing nor Christian. Indeed any Christian gathering in which people feel lost and unwanted is hardly Christian. Sometimes people who are emotionally ill come to such conferences. They need to be singled out and cared for. It is important at any in-depth conference to have professional people present who can pick out the emotionally ill and give them support and direction while they are present and then refer them to counselors or psychologists or healing ministers after they get home.

Caring for all different kinds of people is very difficult for any honest person. In order to show how different we are, the Myers-Briggs Personality Type Indicator was administered the first evening.[10] Later several teaching sessions were held on the interpretation of this instrument. Most people like to learn about themselves and want to understand why other people rub them the wrong way. One of the most creative experiences in Barbara's and my marriage was taking this indicator and finding that we were very different people and that we were not trying to annoy each other; we were just different and had different ways of experiencing life, responding and valuing.

Each morning people were led first into quiet and then in meditative movement exercises. It is difficult to allow God's spirit to come into our bodies when we dislike them or are uncomfortable with them. June Keener Wink led people in this kind of meditation, helping them to realize that we are a unique combination of body, mind, and spirit. Religious dance has been part of most religious traditions, and church processionals can be a form of dance.

---

[10] Those who are unable to obtain the Myers-Briggs Type Indicator will find an excellent substitute in the Keirsey Temperament Sorter, contained in *Please Understand Me*, by David Keirsey and Marilyn Bates (1984).

After breakfast there was time for cognitive input. As we have emphasized, we need to have a worldview in which healing makes sense. We need to know how much both the latest modern medicine and psychology support a healing ministry. We need to see the centrality of Christian healing throughout the most vital periods of the church's life. We need some suggestions on how to start a healing ministry. We need to know how to deepen our communion with the risen Jesus. We need to understand the centrality of love in Christian fellowship. These aspects of Christian life seldom become central in our lives until we have considered them. Following these presentations, written questions were answered. We found that writing questions provided anonymity for people, helped introverts express themselves, helped people clarify their questions, and limited the lectures from the floor. Unless there was such feedback in questions and answers, the materials presented cognitively seldom had much effect.

After a refreshment break the seventy to eighty people divided into groups of no more than eleven, each group with a *trained* leader. It is impossible to get to know seventy other people well in a few days, but we can get acquainted and listen to each other in smaller groups. People told why they were there: their life stories, their fears and angers, their hopes, their frustrations. Unless there is some structured time for group sharing, people get lost and Christian love is not expressed. These are not therapy groups, but they provide something of the same kind of support that Wesley's early Methodist group meetings offered, or the intimacy that is provided in Paul Cho's enormously vital and growing church in Seoul. Jesus also gathered twelve unlikely people around him and was with them intimately throughout his ministry. These unlikely people went out and conquered the ancient world.

Few people acknowledge or realize how lonely and alienated most of us are from one another; how few of us have or can share all of us with other people. It is difficult to find a group that is confidential and accepts all of us, where pain and alienation are not avoided, a group that provides a loving, healing atmosphere that opens people to the sacramental ministry of healing. Clergy are particularly alone at the top and unable to share their brokenness, their fragility, their pain. Congregations so often expect them to be perfect. These small groups have provided experiences of Christian love, have united people in genuine Christian fellowship, given support and encouragement. Often during these groups there was spontaneous laying-on-of-hands and prayer. Fortunately or unfortunately, the group leader is tremendously important for the group members. The group will usually mirror the unconscious of the leader. It is crucial for the leader to be aware of his or her personal fears and angers and to be comfortable with the transcendental dimension of life and the healing ministry. Many people have been lifted out of the tormenting and destructive isolation (in which so many people live) by this group experience, and many of the people continued relationships with one another after the conference was over. Some people were encouraged to create such groups within their churches or outside of them when they returned to their homes.

Some problems are so delicate and painful that people are not ready to bring them up within the group. Indeed the group experience brought them into touch with areas of life that they had been repressing. The leaders of the groups were then available for one-to-one conferences with the members of their own groups or of other groups if advisable. Again it was crucial to have well-trained people present, professionals who could deal with deep depression, overwhelming anxiety, unresolved grief, or the tension so often created by sexual conflict. Once people had talked these problems over privately, it was sometimes possible for them to share these burdens with the group, and they were able to enter once again into the human race. Many of the people who came to the conferences had never before found this kind of caring, supporting, unjudging fellowship in religious groups, seminaries, or within the official hierarchy of the church.

The afternoons offered a variety of activities and time that was free for meditation, assimilation of their experiences, and quiet walking on the mountain on which Kirkridge is situated. People were also given the opportunity to draw, to work individually on sand trays, work with pottery—whatever the spirit directed them to do.

Walter Wink provided in-depth Bible study of the passages relating to Christian healing. His Socratic method of teaching involved participants intensely and drew the meaning of the biblical text from the group. Walter led people into the New Testament experience of healing. We were encouraged to use pottery, poetry, and drawing to find the voice of the pharisee within us who says that we cannot be forgiven or healed. We were led to experience the feelings of the woman in the Bible who broke into *a men's party, an unthinkable action at that time,* poured ointment over Jesus, washed his feet with her tears, and wiped them with her hair. Walter's method is described in his book *Transforming Bible Study.*

And just before dinner we gathered for informal Eucharist. Various traditions of Eucharist were represented. How often we forget that both Calvin and Luther were daily communicants. Eucharist is perfect prayer. We moved through space and time and entered the upper room with Jesus and his disciples. We reenacted the crucifixion and resurrection and experienced the risen One in our midst seeking to feed us with himself and to heal our minds, bodies, and souls. People who have not been used to the tradition of daily Eucharist often find these times of meditative sharing and partaking of the life of the risen One both healing and transforming. In the evaluations received many spoke of the build-up that occurred, starting with the movement-meditation of the morning, the answering of questions provided by the lectures and responses to people, the fellowship of the small groups, experiencing the healing events of the Gospel, and climaxing in the Lord's Supper.

The evenings provided different types of experiences. The theory and practicality of personality types was explained. Specific problems of interest to the groups were discussed. Several evenings were spent in leading people into different kinds of prayer experiences, and just before the end of the conference a healing service was provided. This and the final Eucharist, just before we left each other, were often the most moving experiences of this intensive time together. Many laypeople and ministers had never experienced a healing service and had never taken part in one. Teams of the group leaders or some of the attending group who had had experience with this kind of ministry offered the laying-on-of-hands to those present. For most people this service was an incredibly deep and moving experience. Often the leaders without any prior knowledge found themselves praying for the very problems that had plagued those who had come forward for prayer.

Most of the people who have attended these conferences have found them life-changing and many have been led to go into one aspect or another of the healing ministry. People, even skeptical ones, can be opened to the importance of the healing aspect of Christian ministry and trained for it.

As We Conclude

Healing of the body, mind, and soul is a living process and an inner mystery. In the end this process is known only to the body and to the psyche, the whole psyche—conscious and unconscious—and to the One who created both body and psyche, who dwells in the psyche and draws it to the Kingdom. It is a process about which we need to keep learning as much as we can, both spiritually, psychologically, and physically. In the end healing is given by God, the creative center of things, who is not only loving, but who has given us many ways of facilitating healing.

With knowledge and preparation, adequate education, and experience, we can offer sick people the help that they need, physically through medicine, emotionally through psychotherapy and counseling, and spiritually through the ministry of providing touching and healing, caring, sacramental action, and spiritual direction. In particular, healing occurs when the conditions are right. There are physical conditions that the physician is most qualified to know and prepare. And sometimes God acts without this preparation. There are also emotional conditions that can be made ready by those trained in psychotherapy. Again God sometimes breaks through and acts when those conditions are not prepared. And finally, healing requires conditions of a spiritual nature that can best be seen and helped along by those trained and practiced in the unique traditions of vital Christian life and in the ministry of healing. Together these different instruments of the loving God can give healing now and prepare us for eternal life.

APPENDIX A
The Healing Christ*

Christianity has traditionally considered physical healing as somehow related to its primary concerns. This is no mere accident. Always there has been before it the figure of the Master who, as portrayed by those who knew Him best, was more often engaged in acts of healing than in almost anything else. Despite the major inroads of a Hellenistic soul-body dichotomy, and the Gnostic and Manichean down-grading of matter which so profoundly influenced early Christian thought, despite a later monastic tendency to confuse sickness with saintliness, over the centuries the healing Jesus remained a figure to be reckoned with. Although the true meaning of His Ministry may often have been obscured by attempts to reconcile it with the Church's overt hostility toward undue concern for the "body," it was impossible to deny that the "body" had been an important object of His concern.

The actual life of Jesus was spent in a cultural milieu which knew little of sharp Hellenistic soul-body distinctions. Surprisingly, only in recent years have Christian theologians begun to note this fundamental difference between the Hebrew (and consequently primitive Christian) conception of man, and that of the Greeks with which Christianity eventually came to terms.

The Hebrew conception of man, as the late Dr. Wheeler Robinson reminded us in a now famous sentence, "is an animated body, not an incarnated soul." Or, as John A. T. Robinson has phrased it in his monograph on the body in Biblical thought: "Man does not have a body, he *is* a body. He is flesh-animated-by-soul, the whole conceived as a psychophysical unity." On the other hand, in the dominant Greek view the soul was regarded as the essential personality, imprisoned in a body that was non-essential. Indeed, as expressed later in Gnosticism and Manicheanism, the body was positively evil and ultimately to be

* Quoted in full from the *Current Medical Digest*, for December 1959.

eliminated. This view was basically incompatible with the Hebrew conception of the resurrection of the body, an idea that dominated the New Testament. (It will be recalled that it was while discussing the resurrection that St. Paul met his rebuff at the hands of the Athenian philosophers.)

The healing ministry of Christ can be accurately understood only against this backdrop. Jesus thought not simply of "saving souls," to use a familiar Christian cliché. His redemptive concern necessarily encompassed the whole of man, including his body. For example, in His mind there was no sharp cleavage between sickness and sin—the former belonging to the body and the latter to the soul—in the classical sense. Concerning the man "sick of the palsy," He could ask, "Which is easier, to say, Thy sins be forgiven thee; or to say, Arise, and walk?" (Matt. 9:5). His ministry was directed to a total need.

How strangely congenial this aspect of Jesus sounds to our modern ears. Once again we are beginning to consider man not in terms of a division of soul and body or a trichotomy of soul and body and world, but as a psychosomatic or psychosoma-world unity in which whatever affects him in one area has implications for the whole of him. We have come to think of disease not only in isolated terms of organ pathology or disturbed physiological processes, but also in terms of disrupted interpersonal relations-of guilt and the need for love.

Although greatly influenced by non-Christian interpretations of man's nature, the Post-Apostolic Church often saw the healing ministry of Jesus, and that committed to the Church, as radically opposed to the methodology of "pagan" physicians of the period. It was miracle against scientific method—Christ's healings were miraculous, not scientific! But the early Church often failed to distinguish between "miracle" and "magic." Healing is always miracle—and never more so than when at its center is the greatest of all miracles—love.

Tragically, the Church generally tended to make magic the normative element of healing; thus the later scientific investigator with his dissecting tables, his microscopes, and his pharmaceuticals was left to feel that the Great Healer, as healer, did not truly belong to him. This was to miss the central significance of Jesus. Not method but redemptive concern lay at the heart of His ministry—concern that encompassed the whole man—the making of the whole man, whole. The physician, if informed and alert to the modern implications of his vocation, cannot miss this real point of identity with Christianity's real figure. Insofar as he is aware of the total need of his patients, insofar as his ultimate concern transcends mere objective method, and insofar as he as a physician is characterized by agape, to use the New Testament word for Godly love, he walks today in the steps of the Master.

It has become traditional to identify modern doctors in spirit with a long line of historic greats reaching back to the impressive Hippocrates. This notable Greek, a veritable pinnacle in ancient medicine, often called the "Father of Medicine," largely set the pattern for current professional attitudes and relationships. But sometimes it is forgotten that medicine owes its greatest debt not to Hippocrates, but to Jesus. It was the humble Galilean who more than any other figure in history bequeathed to the healing arts their essential meaning and spirit. During this Christmas season physicians would do well to remind themselves that without His spirit, medicine degenerates into depersonalized methodology, and its ethical code becomes a mere legal system. Jesus brings to methods and codes the corrective of love without which true healing is rarely actually possible. The spiritual "Father of Medicine" was not Hippocrates of the island of Cos, but Jesus of the town of Nazareth!

JACK W. PROVONSHA, M.D.,*
Contributing Editor

---

* Dr. Provonsha is Professor of the Philosophy of Religion and Christian Ethics, Loma Linda University, Loma Linda, California.

APPENDIX B
Biblical Criticism and Healing

Some of the most careful and critical recent studies of Jesus' life and teachings affirm the necessity of recognizing the reality of his healing ministry.

Günther Bornkamm in *Jesus of Nazareth* (1960) points to the relation between faith and miracle. "At the same time," he writes, "there can be no doubt that the faith which Jesus demands, and which alone he recognizes as such, has to do with power and with miracle. And this not in the general sense, that God is all-powerful and can work miracles, but in a very concrete sense: faith as very definitely counting on and trusting in God's power, that it is not at an end at the point where human possibilities are exhausted" (p. 131).

Norman Perrin, in *Rediscovering the Teaching of Jesus* (1967), discusses the history of Biblical criticism and points out that modern prejudice should not blind us to the reality of the healing aspect of Jesus' ministry. He then goes on to compare this ministry of Jesus to pagan parallels, suggesting that

A further problem is that many of the most characteristic sayings about faith in the gospels are associated with miracles, especially healing miracles, and critical scholarship has found this aspect of the tradition very difficult. Liberal scholars tended either to rationalize the stories, or to speak movingly of "the supreme meaning of Jesus' wonders: God's will of mercy and salvation was expressing itself through him," and then move quickly to a more congenial subject! Form criticism, building on the foundations of the immense comparative studies of the *religionsgeschichtliche Schule*, dismissed the stories as typical products of the legend-making propensities of ancient religious movements, to be paralleled in both Jewish and Hellenistic religious literature. In either case, there was no desire to discuss the concept of faith involved in these stories as an aspect of the teaching of Jesus. . . .

Today, however, it is being increasingly recognized that the tradition of miracle stories in the gospels deserves much more serious attention than either the older liberal or the earlier form-critical scholarship gave it. . . .

The view of the miracles held by critical scholarship has, then, changed, and for this there are a number of reasons. One is that parallels quoted from Jewish and Hellenistic literature have been more carefully examined, and they turn out to be not completely convincing as sources for all that we find in the synoptic accounts (pp. 15 ff. and 131 ff.).

Appendix C

Overture

Healing, a Valid Ministry of the Church

Submitted by the 1978 Annual Meeting of the Vermont Conference of the United Church of Christ.

Purpose

The 183rd Annual Meeting of the Vermont Conference of the United Church of Christ overtures the Twelfth General Synod to recognize healing as a valid ministry in the United Church of Christ and to adopt implementing actions to promote an environment in which the healing of the whole person through prayer, touch, and the Sacraments is accepted and encouraged; and to acknowledge the place of healing alongside of preaching and teaching as ministries commissioned by Jesus Christ (Matt. 10:5–8a; Luke 9:2, 10:9).

Background

The Vermont Conference submits that members of the United Church of Christ are seeking healing through prayer, touch, and the Sacraments from their churches. No instrumentality of the United Church of Christ provides resources for help in meeting these needs. Many people have not been helped to find Christ's healing in churches of the United Church of Christ and have become susceptible to spurious healers. Because people are hungering for deeper experience of the power of God which is at work bringing healing and new life, we believe the United Church of Christ is called to obedience to God through the ministry of healing, as well as through the ministries of providing food for the hungry, clothes for the naked, and justice for the oppressed.

Theological and Biblical Rationale

Matthew says of Jesus, "And He went about all Galilee, teaching in their synagogues and preaching the Gospel of the Kingdom and healing every disease and every infirmity among the people. So His fame spread throughout all Syria, and they brought Him all the sick . . . and He healed them" (Matt. 4:23–24). George Buttrick, in *The Interpreter's Bible* commentary on this passage in Matthew notes:

Teaching, preaching, healing . . . Note these three cardinal words and methods . . . As for healing, that function has been almost entirely surrendered to medicine and psychiatry, despite the fact that both these endeavors are largely robbed of meaning unless they have the right spirit and are directed to the true end of life . . . Christ was concerned for the health of both body and soul. To Him pain was not in itself a blessing even though it could be turned to noble ends. Body and soul were "fitted neatly together and compacted" (Eph. 4:16), and He came to give abundant life.

Jesus' evidence to John of His Messiahship: "Go back and tell John what you have seen and heard; the blind see again, the Good News is proclaimed to the poor" (Matt. 11:5). Luke records, "After this the Lord appointed seventy others, and sent them on ahead of Him, two by two, into every town and place where He Himself was about to come . . . and He said to them . . . "Whenever you enter a town and they receive you, eat what is set before you; heal the sick in it and say to them, 'the Kingdom of God has come near to you!'" (Luke 10:1–2a, 8–10). In John our Lord says, "he who believes in Me will also do the works that I do; and greater works than these will he do because I go to the Father" (John 14:12).

Paul himself refers to healing as a sign of his authenticity as an apostle (II Cor. 12:12), and the Pastoral Epistles do not fail to mention the importance of healing. "Is any one among you sick? Let him call for the elders of the church, and let them pray for him, anointing him with oil in the name of the Lord" (James 5:14). For further reference see Psalm 103:2–3; Jer. 30:17; Mark 6:56; John 10:10.

As healing had an integral, accepted, and expected role in the Early Church, it is attested to in the writings of the Church Fathers. In Clement's First Letter healing the sick is included in Christian responsibility. In our Reformation tradition Martin Luther wrote to a fellow pastor in 1545 giving specific and practical advice on ministering to the sick through prayer and laying-on-of-hands.

In our day we believe we must reclaim the role of faith in healing, a role which has been largely surrendered to medicine and psychiatry. All healing is of God, regardless of the means. Healing through prayer, touch, and the Sacraments complements medicine and counseling but *is not* a replacement for them. As Paul Tillich remarks in his *Systematic Theology* (Vol. III) in speaking of the relationship between medicine and psychiatry and faith, "the other ways of healing cannot replace the healing power of the Spirit."

In our own time and place the Eleventh General Synod of the United Church of Christ spoke with eloquence on the centrality of the healing ministry. In its resolution on "The Church and Persons with Handicaps" we are called upon to continue the ministry of Jesus:

who healed the sick and told His followers that their ministry to the sick was a ministry to Him (Matt. 25:31–46) . . . The Christian Church is a community of Faith responding to God's healing, reconciling, and empowering work in Christ. The mission of Jesus meant good news for the poor, release for captives, recovering of sight for the blind, and freedom for the oppressed (Luke 4:18). As signs of His ministry Jesus points to its gifts for the blind and lame, lepers, the deaf, even the dead (Matt. 11:4–6). Christ's followers are called to continue the ministry of reconciliation that God carried out in Him" (II Cor. 5:18).

Implications

The adoption of this proposal will open the way for

1. Seminary courses on healing through prayer, touch and the sacraments.
2. Conference-sponsored workshops on healing through prayer, touch, and the Sacraments.
3. The affirmation of churches and ministers now involved in the healing ministry as well as the encouragement of others to begin such ministry.
4. The growth of expectant communities where people come together to seek God's help in the healing of hurting people.

The Action

THEREFORE, BE IT RESOLVED that the Twelfth General Synod of the United Church of Christ

Reclaims healing through prayer, touch, and the Sacraments as a valid ministry of the church.

BE IT FURTHER RESOLVED that the Twelfth General Synod of the United Church of Christ

1. Encourages seminaries to provide instruction and resources in the ministry of healing through prayer, touch, and the Sacraments.
2. Directs the Office for Church Life and Leadership to include in the forthcoming United Church of Christ book of worship prayers for the sick, healing services, and other appropriate resources, and
3. Directs the Office for Church Life and Leadership to provide an annotated bibliography on the healing ministry.

Approved by the Board of Directors, December 2, 1978.

BIBLIOGRAPHY TO 1970

Alexander, Franz G., and Sheldon T. Selesnick. *The History of Psychiatry*. New York: Harper & Row, 1966.

Ambrose, Saint. *Theological and Dogmatic Works*. Translated by Roy J. Deferrari. Washington, D.C.: Catholic University of America Press, 1963.

American Handbook of Psychiatry. Edited by Silvano Arieti. vol. 1. New York: Basic Books, 1959.

Anderson, Odin W., and Monroe Lerner. *Measuring Health Levels in the United States, 1900–1958*. Research Series no. 11. New York: Health Information Foundation, 1960. (Pamphlet)

Anderson, Sir Robert. *The Silence of God*. Grand Rapids, MI: Kregel Publications, 1952.

Andrieu, Michel. *Les Ordines Romani du Haut Moyen Âge*. Louvain: Spicilegium Sacrum Lovaniense, 1931–1948.

Anglo-Saxon Missionaries in Germany, The. Translated and edited by C. H. Talbot. London: Sheed & Ward, 1954.

Anointing and Healing: Statement. Adopted by the adjourned meeting of the 1960 convention of the United Lutheran Church in America, June 25–27, 1962, Detroit, MI. (Pamphlet)

Anson, Harold. *Spiritual Healing: A Discussion of the Religious Element in Physical Health*. London: University of London Press, 1924.

Ante-Nicene Fathers, The. Grand Rapids, MI: Wm. B. Eerdmans, various dates.

Apostolic Fathers, The. Translated by Archbishop William Wake. Vol. 1. Edinburgh: John Grant, 1909.

Aquinas, Saint Thomas. *The "Summa Theologica."* Literally translated by the Fathers of the English Dominican Province. London: Burns, Oates & Washbourne, various dates.

Auden, W. H. *The Age of Anxiety: A Baroque Eclogue*. New York: Random House, 1946.

———. *For the Time Being*. London: Faber & Faber, 1946.

Augustine, Saint. *The City of God*. Translated by Gerald G. Walsh, S.J., and Daniel J. Honan. New York: Fathers of the Church, 1954. Books 17–22.

———. *Letters (204–270)*. Translated by Wilfrid Parsons. New York: Fathers of the Church, 1956.

Aulén, Gustav. *Christus Victor: An Historical Study of the Three Main Types of the Idea of the Atonement*. New York: Macmillan, 1951.

Authorized Daily Prayer Book of the United Hebrew Congregations of the British Empire, The. With a new translation by S. Singer. London, 1912.

Ayer, Alfred Jules. *Language, Truth and Logic.* 2d ed. New York: Dover Publications, 1946.

Babylonian Talmud, The. Edited by I. Epstein. London: Soncino Press, vols. 23 and 24, *Sanhedrin,* I and II, 1953; vol. 32, *Seder, Kodashim, Bekoroth, 'Arakin,* 1948.

Baillie, John. *The Idea of Revelation in Recent Thought.* New York: Columbia University Press, 1956.

———. *The Sense of the Presence of God.* London: Oxford University Press, 1962.

Banks, Ethel Tulloch. *The Great Physician Calling.* San Diego, CA: St. Luke's Press, n.d. (Pamphlet)

Banks, John Gayner. *Healing Everywhere: A Book of Healing Mission Talks,* San Diego, CA: St. Luke's Press, 1953.

Baragar, C. A. "John Wesley and Medicine." *Annals of Medical History* 10:1 (March 1928), 59 ff.

Barth, Karl. *Church Dogmatics.* Edited and translated by G. W. Bromiley, T. F. Torrance, and others. Edinburgh: T. & T. Clark, 1936–1969.

———. *Epistle to the Romans.* Translated by E. C. Hoskyns. London: Oxford University Press, 1963.

Basil, Saint. *Ascetical Works.* Translated by M. Monica Wagner. New York: Fathers of the Church, 1950.

Batten, Loring W. *The Relief of Pain by Mental Suggestion: A Study of the Moral and Religious Forces in Healing.* New York: Moffat, Yard & Co., 1917.

Beard, Rebecca. *Everyman's Goal: The Expanded Consciousness.* Wells, VT: Merrybrook Press, 1951.

———. *Everyman's Mission: The Development of the Christ-Self.* Evesham, Eng.: Arthur James, 1952.

———. *Everyman's Search.* New York: Harper & Brothers, 1950.

Bede's Ecclesiastical History of the English People. Edited by Bertram Colgrave and R. A. B. Mynors. Oxford: Clarendon Press, 1969.

Beecher, Henry K. "The Powerful Placebo." *Journal of the American Medical Association,* 159:17 (December 24, 1955), 1602–1606.

Berry, George Ricker, ed. *The Interlinear Literal Translation of the Greek New Testament.* Chicago: Follett, 1960.

Bishop Sarapion's Prayer-Book. Edited by John Wordsworth, Bishop of Salisbury. London: Society for Promoting Christian Knowledge (hereafter S.P.C.K.), 1923.

Blatty, William P. *The Exorcist.* New York: Bantam Books, Harper & Row, 1971.

Blum, Richard and Eva Blum. *Health and Healing in Rural Greece.* Stanford, CA: Stanford University Press, 1965.

Boggs, Wade H., Jr. *Faith Healing and the Christian Faith.* Richmond, VA: John Knox Press, 1956.

Bonhoeffer, Dietrich. *Letters and Papers from Prison.* New York: Macmillan, 1953.

Bonnell, John Sutherland. *Do You Want to be Healed?* New York: Harper & Row, 1968.

Book of Common Prayer, The. According to the Use of the Anglican Church of Canada. Toronto: Anglican Book Centre, General Synod of the Anglican Church of Canada, 1962.

Book of Common Prayer, The. According to the Use of the Church of England. Oxford: The University Press, 1970.

Book of Common Prayer, The. According to the Use of the Protestant Episcopal Church in the United States of America. New York: Church Pension Fund, 1945.

Bornkamm, Günther. *Jesus of Nazareth.* New York: Harper & Row, 1960.

Botte, Bernard, ed. *La Tradition Apostolique* [Hippolytus of Rome]: *D'Après Les Anciennes Versions.* 2d ed. Paris: Éditions du Cerf, 1968.

Breuer, Joseph, and Sigmund Freud. *Studies in Hysteria.* Boston: Beacon Press, 1961.

Brewer, E. Cobham. *A Dictionary of Miracles, Imaginitive, Realistic and Dogmatic,* 1885, republished in 1901.

Bultmann, Rudolf. *Existence and Faith: Shorter Writings of Rudolf Bultmann.* Translated by Schubert M. Ogden. New York: Meridian Books, 1960.

————. *Jesus Christ and Mythology.* New York: Charles Scribner's Sons, 1958.

————. "The New Testament and Mythology." In *Kerygma and Myth: A Theological Debate.* Edited by Hans-Werner Bartsch. New York: Harper & Row, 1961.

Butler, Cuthbert. *The Lausiac History of Palladius.* Hildesheim: Georg Olms, 1967.

Butler, Josephine. *Catharine of Siena: A Biography.* London: Dyer Bros., 1878.

Cadbury, Henry J., ed. *George Fox's 'Book of Miracles.'* Cambridge, Eng.: The University Press, 1948.

Caesarius of Heisterberg. *The Dialogues on Miracles.* Translated by H. von E. Scott and C. S. Swinton Bland, 1929.

Calvin, John. *Institutes of the Christian Religion.* Translated by Henry Beveridge. Grand Rapids, MI: Wm. B. Eerdmans, 1953.

Castaneda, Carlos. *The Teachings of Don Juan: A Yaqui Way of Knowledge.* Berkeley, CA: University of California Press, 1968.

Charisma in Hong Kong. Hong Kong: Society of Stephen, n.d. (Pamphlet)

Chertok, L. "Psychosomatic Medicine in the West and in Eastern European Countries." *Psychosomatic Medicine* 31:6 (November-December 1969), 510–21.

Christian Faith and the Ministry of Healing. Approved by the Church Council of the American Lutheran Church, Minneapolis, July 1965. (Pamphlet)

Christiani, Leon. *Evidences of Satan in the Modern World.* New York: Macmillan, 1962.

Christmann, Harold L. *A Pattern for Healing in the Church.* San Diego, CA: St. Luke's Press, 1959. (Pamphlet)

Chrysostom, Saint John. *Baptismal Instructions.* Translated by Paul W. Harkins. Westminster, MD: Newman Press, 1963.

Church's Ministry of Healing, The. Report of the Archbishop's Commission. Westminster, Eng.: Church Information Board, 1958. (Pamphlet)

Clark, Glenn. *How to Find Health Through Prayer.* New York: Harper & Brothers, 1940.

Clarke, W. K. Lowther, ed. *Liturgy and Worship.* London: S.P.C.K., 1954.

Coleridge, Henry James. *The Life and Letters of St. Francis Xavier.* London: Burns & Oates, 1881.

Cullman, Oscar. *Immortality of the Soul or Resurrection of the Dead? The Witness of the New Testament.* New York: Macmillan, 1959.

Daily, Starr. *Recovery.* St. Paul, MN: Macalester Park Publishing Co., 1948.

———. *Release,* New York: Harper & Brothers, 1942.

Dalmais, Irenée Henri. *Eastern Liturgies.* New York: Hawthorn Books, 1960.

Daniélou, Jean. *The Bible and Liturgy.* Notre Dame, IN: University of Notre Dame Press, 1956.

Dearmer, Percy. *Body and Soul.* London: Sir Isaac Pitman & Sons, 1909.

Desert Fathers, The. Translated by Helen Waddell. London: Constable & Co., 1936.

Dessauer, Friedrich. See *Papers from the Eranos Yearbooks.*

De Stoeckl, Agnes. *Not All Vanity.* London: John Murray, 1950.

Dix, Gregory, ed. *The Treatise on the Apostolic Tradition of St. Hippolytus of Rome.* Rev. by H. Chadwick. London: S.P.C.K., 1968.

Documents of Vatican II, The. New York: America Press, 1966.

Dodds, E. R. *The Greeks and the Irrational.* Boston: Beacon Press, 1957.

———. *Pagan and Christian in an Age of Anxiety.* Cambridge, Eng.: The University Press, 1965.

Dorothea Trüdel, or the Prayer of Faith: With some particulars of the remarkable manner in which large numbers of sick persons were healed in answer to special prayer. London: Morgan & Chase, 1865.

Dresser, Horatio W. *The Quimby Manuscripts.* New York: University Books, 1961.

Duchesne, Louis. *Christian Worship: Its Origin and Evolution.* 5th ed. London: S.P.C.K., 1919.

Dunbar, Flanders. *Emotions and Bodily Changes.* 4th ed. New York: Columbia University Press, 1954.

Dwyer, Walter W. *The Churches' Handbook for Spiritual Healing.* New York: Ascension Press, 1960. (Pamphlet)

Early Christian Biographies. Edited by Roy J. Deferrari. Various translators. New York: Fathers of the Church, 1952.

Easton, Burton Scott. *The Apostolic Tradition of Hippolytus.* Ann Arbor, MI: Archon Books, 1962.

Eliade, Mircea. *Shamanism: Archaic Techniques of Ecstasy.* Princeton, N.J.: Princeton University Press, 1970.

Eliot, T. S. *The Cocktail Party.* New York: Harcourt, Brace & World, 1950.

———. *Four Quartets.* New York: Harcourt, Brace & World, 1968.

Evans, Lester J. *The Crisis in Medical Education.* Ann Arbor, Mich.: University of Michigan Press, 1965.

Feifel, Herman, ed. *The Meaning of Death.* New York: McGraw-Hill Book Co., 1959.

Ford, Peter S. *The Healing Trinity.* New York: Harper & Row, 1971.

Fox, George. *The Journal of George Fox.* Edited by Norman Penney. Cambridge, Eng.: The University Press, 1911.

Frank, Jerome D. *Persuasion and Healing.* New York: Schocken Books, 1969.

Freud, Sigmund. *Beyond the Pleasure Principle.* Translated by James Strachey. New York: Liveright, 1961.

———. *Civilization and Its Discontents.* Translated by Joan Riviere. Garden City, NY: Doubleday, n.d.

————. *Collected Papers*. New York: Basic Books, 1955.

————. *The Future of an Illusion*. Translated by W. D. Robson-Scott. London: Hogarth Press, 1949.

————. *A General Introduction to Pyschoanalysis*. New York: Washington Square Press, 1960.

————. *The Interpretation of Dreams*. New York: Basic Books, 1955.

————. See Breuer, Joseph, and Sigmund Freud.

Friedländer, Paul. *Plato: An Introduction*. Translated by Hans Meyerhoff. New York: Harper & Row for the Bollingen Foundation, 1964.

Friedman, D. B., and S. T. Selesnick. "Clinical Notes on the Management of Asthma and Eczema: When to Call the Psychiatrist." *Clinical Pediatrics* 4:12 (December 1965), 735–38.

Frost, Evelyn. *Christian Healing: A Consideration of the Place of Spiritual Healing in the Church of Today in the Light of the Doctrine and Practice of the Ante-Nicene Church*. London: A. R. Mowbray, 1940.

Garrison, Fielding H. *An Introduction to the History of Medicine*. 4th ed. Philadelphia: W. B. Saunders, 1929.

Glasser, William. *Reality Therapy*. New York: Harper & Row, 1965.

Good Angel of Stamford, The: Or an Extraordinary Cure of An Extraordinary Consumption, In a true and Faithful Narrative of Samuel Wallas *Recovered By the Power of God, and Prescription of an Angel*. Reprints of English Books 1475–1700, edited by Joseph Arnold Foster, no. 17. London: Ingram, 1939. Originally printed in London, 1659.

Goodspeed, Edgar J. *The Story of Eugenia and Philip*. Chicago: University of Chicago Press, 1931.

Gordon, A. J. *The Ministry of Healing*. 2d ed. Harrisburg, PA: Christian Publications, 1961.

Graham, David T. "Health, Disease, and the Mind-Body Problem: Linguistic Parallelism." *Psychosomatic Medicine* 29:1 (January-February 1967), 52–71.

Grégoire, Georges Florent [Gregory of Tours]. *Les Livres des Miracles et Autres Opuscules*. Translated by H. L. Bordier. 2 vols. Paris: Jules Renouard, 1860.

————. *Sélections from the Minor Works*. Translated by William C. McDermott. Philadelphia: University of Pennsylvania Press, 1949.

Gregory the Great, Saint. *Dialogues*. Translated by Odo John Zimmerman. New York: Fathers of the Church, 1959.

Gregory of Nyssa, Saint. *Ascetical Works*. Translated by Virginia Woods Callahan. Washington, D.C.: Catholic University of America Press, 1967.

Gross, Don H. *The Case for Spiritual Healing*. New York: Thomas Nelson & Sons, 1958.

Guggenbühl-Craig, Adolf. *Power in the Helping Professions*. New York, Spring Publications, 1971.

Gusmer, Charles W. "Anointing of the Sick in the Church of England." *Worship* 45:5 (May 1971), 262–72.

Guze, Samuel B. "Hysteria and the GP's Role," *Psychiatry 1970*, edited by Eli Robins. New York: *Medical World News* publication, 1970, p. 11.

Hamilton, Mary. *Incubation (or the Cure of Disease in Pagan Temples and Christian Churches)*. London: Simpkin, Marshall, Hamilton, Kent & Co., 1906.

Handbook on the Healing Ministry of the Church. Toronto: The Bishop's Committee, n.d. (Pamphlet)

Harding, Esther. *Journey into Self*. New York: David McKay Co., 1956.

Hastings, James, ed. *Encyclopedia of Religion and Ethics*. New York: Charles Scribner's Sons, n.d.

Hatch, Alden. *Le Miracle de la Montagne: L'Histoire de Frère André et de L'Oratoire Saint-Joseph à Montreal*. Paris: Librairie Arthème Fayard, 1959.

Healing Church, The: The Tübingen Consultation 1964. World Council Series no. 3. Geneva: World Council of Churches, 1965. (Pamphlet)

Heisenberg, Werner. *Physics and Philosophy: The Revolution in Modern Science*. New York: Harper & Brothers, 1962.

Herolt, Johannes [Discipulus, ca. 1440]. *Miracles of the Blessed Virgin Mary*. Translated by C. C. Swinton Bland. London: George Routledge & Sons, 1928.

Hesse, Mary. *Models and Analogies in Science*. Notre Dame, IN: University of Notre Dame Press, 1966.

Hick, John H. *Faith and Knowledge: A Modern Introduction to the Problem of Religious Knowledge*. Ithaca, NY: Cornell University Press, 1966.

———, ed. *Faith and the Philosophers*. New York: St. Martin's Press, 1964.

Hillman, James. *Emotion: A Comprehensive Phenomenology of Theories and Their Meanings for Therapy*. 2d ed. Evanston, IL: Northwestern University Press, 1964.

Hippocrates. *Works*. Vol. 4, *Regimen*. Translated by W. H. S. Jones. Cambridge, MA: Harvard University Press, 1957.

Hostie, Raymond. *Religion and the Psychology of Jung*. New York: Sheed & Ward, 1957.

Husserl, Edmund. *Phenomenology and the Crisis of Philosophy*. Translated by Quentin Lauer. New York: Harper & Row, 1965.

Ikin, A. Graham. *New Concepts of Healing: Medical, Psychological, and Religious*. New York: Association Press, 1956.

Interpreter's Bible, The. New York: Abingdon-Cokesbury Press, 1952–1965.

Ionas, *Vitae Sanctorum Columbani* (Scriptores Rerum Germanicarum). Edited by Bruno Krusch. Hanover: Impensis Bibliopolii Hahniani, 1905.

Jaffé, Aniela, *From the Life and Work of C. G. Jung*. New York: Harper & Row, 1971.

James, William. *The Varieties of Religious Experience*. New York: Longmans, Green & Co., 1925.

Jaspers, Karl, and Rudolf Bultmann. *Myth and Christianity: An Inquiry into the Possibility of Religion Without Myth*. New York: Noonday Press, 1958.

Johnson, Thomas W. "Japan's New Religions: A Search for Uniformities." *Kroeber Anthropological Society Papers* (University of California), no. 42 (Spring 1970), 112 ff.

Jouhandeau, Marcel. *St. Philip Neri*. New York: Harper & Brothers, 1960.

Juliani Imperatoris, *Quae Supersunt Praeter Reliquias apud Cyrillum: Omnia*. Edited by Friedericus Carolus Hertlein. Vol. 1. Lipsiae: B. G. Teubneri, 1875.

Jung, C. G. *Collected Works*. New York: Pantheon Books for the Bollingen Foundation,
  Vol. 5, *Symbols of Transformation*, 1956.
  Vol. 7, *Two Essays on Analytical Psychology*, 1953.
  Vol. 8, *The Structure and Dynamics of the Psyche*, 1960.
  Vol. 9, pt. 2, *Aion: Researches into the Phenomenology of the Self*, 1959.
  Vol. 10, *Civilization in Transition*, 1964.
  Vol. 11, *Psychology and Religion: West and East*, 1958.
  Vol. 12, *Psychology and Alchemy*, 1953.
  Vol. 16, *The Practice of Psychotherapy*, 1954.
———. *Memories, Dreams, Reflections*. Recorded and edited by Aniela Jaffé. New York: Random House, 1963.
———. *Modern Man in Search of a Soul*. New York: Harcourt, Brace & Co., 1933.
Kaplan, Melvin H., and J. Dermot Frengley. "Autoimmunity to the Heart in Cardiac Disease: Current Concepts of the Relation of Autoimmunity to Rheumatic Fever, Postcardiotomy and Postinfarction Syndromes and Cardiomyopathies." *American Journal of Cardiology* 24:4 (October 1969), 459–73.
Karagulla, Shafica. *Breakthrough to Creativity*, Los Angeles: De Vorss, 1968.
Kasturi, N. *The Life of Bhagavan Sri Sathya Sai Baba*. Prasanthi Nilayam, South India: Sanathana Sarathi, 1969.
Keenan, Mary Emily. "Augustine and the Medical Profession." *Transactions and Proceedings of the American Philosophical Association* (Haverford, PA) 67 (1936), 168–90.
———. "St. Gregory of Nazianzus and Early Byzantine Medicine." *Bulletin of the History of Medicine* 9:1 (January 1941), 8–30.
Kelly, Thomas R. *A Testament of Devotion*. New York: Harper & Brothers, 1941.
Kelsey, Morton T. *Dreams: The Dark Speech of the Spirit*. Garden City, NY: Doubleday, 1968.
———. *Encounter with God: A Theology of Christian Experience*. Minneapolis, MN: Bethany Fellowship, 1972.
———. "Is the World View of Jesus Outmoded?" *Christian Century* 86:4 (January 22, 1969), 112–15.
———. *Tongue Speaking: An Experiment in Spiritual Experience*. Garden City, NY: Doubleday, 1964.
Kemp, P. *Healing Ritual: Studies in the Technique and Tradition of the Southern Slavs*. London: Faber & Faber, 1953.
Kepler, Milton O. "The Importance of Religion in Medical Education." *Journal of Religion and Health* 7:4 (October 1968), 358 ff.
Kerényi, C. *Asklepios: Archetypal Image of the Physician's Existence*. New York: Pantheon Books for the Bollingen Foundation, 1959.
Kerin, Dorothy. *The Living Touch*. London: Hodder & Stoughton, 1965.
Kierkegaard, Søren. *Training in Christianity*. Translated by Walter Lowrie. Princeton, NJ: Princeton University Press, 1944.
Kimball, C. P. "Conceptual Developments in Psychosomatic Medicine: 1939–1969." *Annals of Internal Medicine* 73:2 (August 1970), 307 ff.
Klausner, Joseph. *Jesus of Nazareth: His Life, Times and Teaching*. Translated by Herbert Danby. New York: Macmillan, 1929.

Kluger, Rivkah Schärf. *Satan in the Old Testament*, Evanston, IL: Northwestern University Press, 1967.

Knoll, Max. See *Papers from the Eranos Yearbooks*.

Kooiman, W. J. *By Faith Alone: The Life of Martin Luther*. Translated by Bertram Lee Woolf. London: Lutterworth Press, 1954.

Krause, Allen K. *Environment and Resistance in Tuberculosis*. Baltimore: Williams & Wilkins, 1923.

Kuhlman, Kathryn. *I Believe in Miracles*. Englewood Cliffs, NJ: Prentice-Hall, 1962.

Kyle, William H., ed. *Healing Through Counselling: A Christian Counselling Centre*. London: Epworth Press, 1964.

Laing, R. D. *The Politics of Experience*. New York: Ballantine Books, 1968.

Lambeth Conference 1930, The: Encyclical Letter from the Bishops, with Resolutions and Reports. London: S.P.C.K., n.d.

Large, John Ellis. *God Is Able: How to Gain Wholeness of Life*. Englewood Cliffs, NJ: Prentice-Hall, 1963.

————. *The Ministry of Healing*. New York: Morehouse-Gorham, 1959.

Lesser, Graham. *Why? Divine Healing in Medicine and Theology*. New York: Pageant Press, 1960.

Leuret, Francois, and Henri Bon. *Modern Miraculous Cures: A Documented Account of Miracles and Medicine in the Twentieth Century*. Translated by A. T. Macqueen and John C. Barry. New York: Farrar Straus & Cudahy, 1957.

Lewis, C. S. *Christian Reflections*. Edited by Walter Hooper. Grand Rapids, MI: Wm. B. Eerdmans, 1968.

Liddell, Howard S. "Conditioning and Emotions: An account of a long-range study in which neuroses are induced to clarify how irrational emotional behavior originates and ultimately to indicate how it may be prevented." Reprinted from *Scientific American* for January 1954. San Francisco: W. H. Freeman.

————. *Emotional Hazards in Animals and Man*. Springfield, IL: Charles C. Thomas, 1956.

Lietzmann, Hans. *A History of the Early Church*. Cleveland, OH: World Publishing Co., 1961.

Limitation of Activity and Mobility Due to Chronic Conditions: United States—July 1965–June 1966. Public Health Service Series 10, no. 45. Washington, D.C.: U.S. Department of Health, Education, and Welfare, May 1968.

Lipowski, Z. J. "Psychosocial Aspects of Disease." *Annals of Internal Medicine* 71:6 (December 1969), 1197–1206.

Lonergan, Bernard J. F. *Insight: A Study of Human Understanding*. New York: Philosophical Library, 1957.

Luther: Letters of Spiritual Counsel. Edited and translated by Theodore J. Tappert. London: S. C. M. Press, 1955.

Luther's Works. Edited by Jaroslav Pelikan. St. Louis: Concordia Publishing House, 1955–

McCluskey, Neil G. "Darkness and Light over Konnersreuth." *The Priest* 10:9 (September 1954), 765–74.

MacIntosh, Douglas Clyde. *The Problem of Religious Knowledge*. New York: Harper & Brothers, 1940.

MacMillan, William J. *The Reluctant Healer: A Remarkable Autobiography*. New York: Thomas Y. Crowell, 1952.

Macquarrie, John. *Twentieth Century Religious Thought: The Frontiers of Philosophy and Theology, 1900–1960*. New York: Harper & Row, 1963.

Maguire, John Francis. *Father Mathew*. London: n.p., 1864.

Manual of Christian Healing: A Handbook for the International Order of Saint Luke the Physician, and for Other Clergy and Laity Engaged in the Work of Spiritual Therapy. Edited by John Gayner Banks. 11th ed. San Diego, CA: St. Luke's Press, 1960. (Pamphlet)

Martimort, Aimé Georges. *L'Église en Prière: Introduction à la Liturgie*. Paris: Desclée, 1961.

Martin, Bernard. *The Healing Ministry in the Church*. Richmond, VA: John Knox Press, 1960.

"Mass Hysteria." *Time* 95:4 (26 January 1970), 59 ff.

Meer, F. van der. *Augustine the Bishop: The Life and Work of a Father of the Church*. Translated by Brian Battershaw and G. R. Lamb. London: Sheed & Ward, 1961.

Mehta, Ved. *The New Theologian*. New York: Harper & Row, 1966.

Pieper, Josef. *Love and Inspiration: A Study of Plato's Phaedrus*. London: Faber & Faber, 1965.

Pioneer of Divine Healing: Jon. Chr. Blumhardt. London: Order of Saint Luke the Physician, n.d. (Pamphlet)

Plato. *Dialogues*. Translated by B. Jowett. New York: Random House, 1937.

Powys, John Cowper. *The Meaning of Culture*. New York: W. W. Norton, 1929.

Prayer Book Studies III: The Order for the Ministration to the Sick. The Standing Liturgical Commission of the Protestant Episcopal Church in the United States of America. New York: Church Pension Fund, 1951. (Pamphlet)

Provonsha, J. W. "The Healing Christ." *Current Medical Digest* (December 1959).

Puner, Helen Walker. *Freud: His Life and His Mind*, New York: Dell, 1959.

Quasten, Johannes. *Patrology*. Vol. 3, *The Golden Age of Greek Patristric Literature after Irenaeus, from the Council of Nicaea to the Council of Chalcedon*. Utrecht: Spectrum, 1960.

Ranaghan, Kevin and Dorothy Ranaghan. *Catholic Pentecostals*. New York: Paulist Press, 1969.

Reinhart, John B., and Allan L. Drash. "Psychosocial Dwarfism: Environmentally Induced Recovery." *Psychosomatic Medicine* 31:2 (March-April 1969), 165–72.

Relation of Christian Faith to Health, The. Adopted by the 172nd General Assembly of the United Presbyterian Church in the United States of America. Philadelphia, May 1960. (Pamphlet)

Report of the Bishop of Toronto's Commission on the Church's Ministry of Healing, The. Toronto, May 1968. (Pamphlet)

Roberts, Margaret. *Saint Catherine of Siena and Her Times*. London: Methuen, 1906.

Roman Ritual, The. Translated and edited by Philip Weller. Milwaukee, WI: Bruce, 1952.

Ross, James Davidson. *Dorothy: A Portrait.* London: Hodder & Stoughton, 1958.

Ryrie, Charles Caldwell. *Dispensationalism Today.* Chicago: Moody Press, 1965.

Sabatier, Paul. *Life of St. Francis of Assisi.* Translated by Louise Seymour Houghton. New York: Charles Scribner's Sons, 1938.

Sanford, Agnes. *Behold Your God.* St. Paul, MN: Macalester Park Publishing Co., 1958.

———. *Dreams Are for Tomorrow.* Philadelphia: J. B. Lippincott, 1963.

———. *The Healing Gifts of the Spirit.* Philadelphia: J. B. Lippincott, 1966.

———. *The Healing Light.* St. Paul, MN: Macalester Park Publishing Co., 1947.

———. *The Healing Power of the Bible.* Philadelphia: J. B. Lippincott, 1969.

———. *Lost Shepherd.* Plainfield, NJ: Logos International, 1971.

———. *Oh, Watchman!* Philadelphia: J. B. Lippincott, 1951.

Meier, C. A. *Ancient Incubation and Modern Psychotherapy.* Translated by Monica Curtis. Evanston, IL: Northwestern University Press, 1967.

Menninger, Karl A. *Man Against Himself.* New York: Harcourt, Brace & Co., 1938.

———, with the collaboration of Jeanetta Lyle Menninger. *Love Against Hate.* New York: Harcourt, Brace & Co., 1942.

Meyer, Adolf. "The Psychiatric Aspects of Gastroenterology." *American Journal of Surgery* 15:3 (March 1932), 504–09.

Ministry of Healing, The: Report of the Committee Appointed in Accordance with Resolution 63 of the Lambeth Conference, 1920. London: S.P.C.K., 1924.

Miracles de Saint Benoit, Les, écrits par Adrevald, Aimoin, André, Raoul Tortaire et Hugues de Sainte Mariê (Moines de Fleury). Librairie de la Société de L'Histoire de France. Paris: Mme. Ve. Jules Renouard, 1858.

Miraculous Powers of the Church of Christ, The, Asserted through each Successive Century from the Apostles down to the Present Time. England: n.p., 1756.

Monden, Louis. *Signs and Wonders: A Study of the Miraculous Element in Religion.* New York: Desclée, 1966.

Morison, James Cotter. *The Life and Times of Saint Bernard, Abbot of Clairvaux,* London: Macmillan, 1901.

Mowrer, O. Hobart. *The Crisis in Psychiatry and Religion.* Princeton, NJ: D. Van Nostrand, 1961.

Nagel, Ernest, and James R. Newman. *Gödel's Proof.* New York: New York University Press, 1964.

Neihardt, John G. *Black Elk Speaks: Being the Life Story of a Holy Man of the Oglala Sioux.* Lincoln, NB: University of Nebraska Press, 1961.

Nicodemus [Melville Salter Channing-Pearce]. *The Midnight Hour: A Journal from 1st May to 30th September 1941.* London: Faber & Faber, 1942.

Oursler, Will. *The Healing Power of Faith.* New York: Hawthorn Books, 1957.

Papers from the Eranos Yearbooks. Edited by Joseph Campbell. New York: Pantheon Books, 1954–. Vols. 1–3.

    Dessauer, Friedrich. "Galileo and Newton: The Turning Point in Western Thought." Vol. 1, *Spirit and Nature* (1954), pp. 288–321.

    Knoll, Max. "Transformations of Science in Our Age." Vol. 3, *Man and Time,* (1957), pp. 264–307.

Wili, Walter. "The Orphic Mysteries and the Greek Spirit." Vol. 2, *The Mysteries* (1955), pp. 64–92.

Pasternak, Boris. *Doctor Zhivago*. New York: Pantheon Books, 1958.

Patrologiae: Cursus Completus (Latinae et Graecae). Edited by J.P. Migne and successors. Paris: Garnier Frères, various dates.

Pedalion ["Rudder"], *The*. Translated by D. Cummings. Chicago: Orthodox Christian Educational Society, 1957.

Perrin, Norman. *Rediscovering the Teaching of Jesus*. New York: Harper & Row, 1967.

Phillips, Dorothy, *et al.*, eds. *The Choice Is Always Ours*. Rev. ed. New York: Harper & Row, 1960.

Sanford, Edgar L. *God's Healing Power*. Evesham, Eng.: Arthur James, 1962. Reprinted in 1971.

Sanford, John A. *The Kingdom Within: A Study of the Inner Meaning of Jesus' Sayings*. Philadelphia: J. B. Lippincott, 1970.

Sawyer, Charles H., M. Kawakami, and S. Kanematsu. "Neuro-endocrine Aspects of Reproduction." Chap. 4 in *Endocrines and the Central Nervous System*, edited by Rachmiel Levine. Association for Research in Nervous and Mental Disease, vol. 43. Baltimore: Williams & Wilkins, 1966.

Scherzer, Carl J. *The Church and Healing*. Philadelphia: Westminster Press, 1950.

Schlier, Heinrich. *Principalities and Powers in the New Testament*. New York: Herder & Herder, 1961.

Schroeder, H.J. *Disciplinary Decrees of the General Councils*. St. Louis, MO: B. Herder, 1937.

A Select Library of the Nicene and Post-Nicene Fathers of the Christian Church. 1st and 2d series. Grand Rapids, MI: Wm. B. Eerdmans, various dates.

Selesnick, Sheldon T., and Zanwil Sperber. "The Problem of the Eczema-Asthma Complex: A Developmental Approach." In *Psychoanalysis and Current Biological Thought*, edited by Norman S. Greenfield and William C. Lewis. Madison, WI: University of Wisconsin Press, 1965.

Selye, Hans. "The General Adaptation Syndrome and Diseases of Adaptation." *Journal of Clinical Endocrinology* 6:2 (February 1946), 217 ff.

Service Book of the Holy Orthodox-Catholic Apostolic Church [the Euchologion]: Compiled, translated, and arranged from the Old Church-Slavonic Service Books of the Russian Church and collated with the Service Books of the Greek Church by Isabel Florence Hapgood. Rev. ed., with endorsement by Patriarch Tikhon. New York: Association Press, 1922.

Services for Trial Use: Authorized Alternatives to Prayer Book Services. Protestant Episcopal Church in the U.S.A. New York: Church Pension Fund, 1971.

Sharing, journal of the International Order of Saint Luke.

Silverman, Samuel. *Psychobiological Aspects of Physical Symptoms*. New York: Appleton-Century-Crofts, 1968.

Skinner, B.F. *Science and Human Behavior*. New York: Macmillan, 1953.

———, *Walden II*. New York: Macmillan, 1960.

Slawson, Paul F., *et al.* "Psychological Factors Associated with the Onset of Diabetes Mellitus." *Journal of the American Medical Association* 185:3 (20 July 1963), 166 ff.

Swann, W.F.G. "The Living and the Dead." *Saturday Review* 43:23 (4 June 1960), 43–44.

Teilhard de Chardin, Pierre. *The Phenomenon of Man*. New York: Harper & Brothers, 1959.

Tennant, F.R. *Philosophical Theology*. Cambridge, Eng.: The University Press, 1956.

Thomas of Celano. *Tractatus de Miraculis S. Francisci Assisiensis*. Edited by the Fathers of the College of Saint Bonaventura. Rome, 1928.

Thompson, Francis. *Health and Holiness*. St. Louis, MI: B. Herder, 1905.

Toulmin, Stephen. *The Philosophy of Science: An Introduction*. New York: Harper & Brothers, 1960.

Unesco Courier, The, editorial feature, no. 3 (March 1960), p. 22.

Van Buskirk, James Dale. *Religion, Healing & Health*. New York: Macmillan, 1952.

Villasenor, David V. *Tapestries in Sand: The Spirit of Indian Sand Painting*. Healdsburg, CA: Naturegraph Co., 1966.

Visitatio Infirmorum: Or, Offices for the Clergy in Praying with, Directing, and Comforting the Sick, Infirm, and Afflicted. 3d ed. London: Joseph Masters, 1854.

Von Bertalanffy, Ludwig. "The Mind-Body Problem: A New View." *Psychosomatic Medicine* 26:1 (January-February 1964), 29–45.

Weatherhead, Leslie D. *Psychology, Religion and Healing*. New York: Abingdon-Cokesbury Press, 1951.

Weiss, Edward, and O. Spurgeon English. *Psychosomatic Medicine: The Clinical Application of Psychopathology to General Medical Problems*. Philadelphia: W.B. Saunders, 1943 (2d ed., 1949; 3d ed., 1957).

Wesley, John. *The Journal of the Rev. John Wesley*. Edited by Ernest Rhys. London: J.M. Dent, n.d.

Western Fathers, The. Translated and edited by F.R. Hoare. London: Sheed & Ward, 1954.

White, Hugh W. *Demonism Verified and Analyzed*. Ann Arbor, MI: University Microfilms, 1963.

White, Victor. *God and the Unconscious*. Cleveland, OH: World Publishing, 1961.

Whitehead, Alfred N., *Science and the Modern World*. New York: Mentor Books, 1948.

Whyte, Lancelot Law. *The Unconscious Before Freud*. New York: Basic Books, 1960.

Wili, Walter. See *Papers from the Eranos Yearbooks*.

Wittkower, E. D., J. M. Cleghorn, Z. J. Lipowski, G. Peterfy, and L. Solyom. "A Global Survey of Psychosomatic Medicine." *International Journal of Psychiatry*. 7:1 (January 1969), 499–516. Critical evaluations, pp. 516–24.

Wolf, Stewart, and Harold G. Wolff. *Headaches: Their Nature and Treatment*. Boston: Little, Brown & Co., 1953.

Worrall, Ambrose A. and N. Olga. *The Gift of Healing*. New York: Harper & Row, 1965.

Year Book of Neurology, Psychiatry and Neurosurgery, The. 1966–1967 Year Book Series. Edited by Roland P. MacKay, Sam Bernard Wortis, and Oscar Sugar. Chicago: Year Book Medical Publishers, 1967.

Young, Richard K., and Albert L. Meiburg. *Spiritual Therapy: Modern Medicine's Newest Ally*. New York: Harper & Brothers, 1960.

Zündel, Friedrich. *Johann Christoph Blumhardt*. A summarized translation by Art Rosenblum. Chicago: privately printed, 1967.

Additional Bibliography

Achterberg, Jeanne. *Imagery in Healing*. Boston: New Science Library, 1985.

Adams, Junius. "Psychic Healing—Does it Really Work?" *Cosmopolitan* (March 1984), p. 244.

Althouse, Lawrence W. *Rediscovering the Gift of Healing*. Nashville, TN: Abingdon, 1977.

Assagioli, Roberto. *Psychosynthesis*. Baltimore: Penguin, 1976.

Bakken, Kenneth L. *The Call to Wholeness: Health as a Spiritual Journey*. New York: Crossroad, 1985.

Bakken, Kenneth L., and Kathleen H. Hoffeller. *The Journey Towards Wholeness: A Christ-Centered Approach to Health and Healing*. New York: Crossroad, 1988.

Baldwin, Robert. "Healing of the Sick as a Catholic Tradition," *Our Sunday Visitor* (July 12, 1987), p. 9.

Banks, Ethel. *The Great Physician Calling*. San Diego, CA: St Luke's Press, n.d.

Benjamin, Walter W. "Sounding Board: Healing by the Fundamentals," *The New England Journal of Medicine*, Massachusetts Medical Society 311:9 (30 August 1984), 595–97.

Benson, Herbert. "The Faith Factor," *American Health* (May 1984), pp. 46–52.

———. *The Relaxation Response*. New York: Times Books, 1978.

———. *Beyond the Relaxation Response*. New York: Times Books, 1984.

Black, David. "Medicine and the Mind," *Playboy*. n.d.

Bokekotter, Thomas. *Essential Catholicism: Dynamics of Faith and Belief*. Garden City, NY: Image Books, 1986.

Brand, Dr. Paul, and Philip Yancey. *Fearfully and Wonderfully Made*. Grand Rapids, MI: Zondervan, 1980.

Brown, Michael. "The Psychic Search." *American Health* (November 1985), pp. 64–70.

Burnham, Sophy. "Healing Hands." *New Woman* (March 1986), pp. 72–78.

Burton, Jeffrey Russell. *The Devil: Perceptions of Evil from Antiquity to Primitive Christianity; Satan: The Early Christian Tradition; Lucifer: The Devil in the Middle Ages; Mephistopheles: The Devil in the Modern World*. Ithaca, NY: Cornell University Press, 1977, 1981, 1984, 1986.

Canale, Andrew. *The Healing Image: From Depression to Meaning* (manuscript as yet unpublished).

———. *Masters of the Heart: A Modern Spiritual Seeker Dialogues with the Great Sages of History*. New York: Paulist Press, 1978.

———. *Understanding the Human Jesus*. Mahwah, NJ Paulist Press, 1985.

Castaneda, Carlos. *A Separate Reality: Further Conversations with Don Juan*. New York: Simon and Schuster, 1971.

———. *Journey to Ixtlan: The Lessons of Don Juan*. New York: Simon and Schuster, 1972.

———. *Tales of Power*. New York: Simon and Schuster, 1974.

Cayce, Edgar Evan, and Hugh Lynn Cayce. *The Outer Limits of Edgar Cayce's Power*. New York: Harper & Row, 1971.

Champlin, Joseph. "The Traditional Understanding of Healing." *Our Sunday Visitor* (25 January 1987).

Chesanow, Neil. "Is It Time to Take Psychic Healing Seriously?" *Family Health* (January 1979), pp. 22–28.

Cho, Paul Yonggi, with Harold Hostetler. *Successful Home Cell Groups*. Plainfield, NJ: Logos International, 1981.

Coan, Richard W. *Hero, Artist, Sage, or Saint?* New York: Columbia University Press, 1977.

Colenback, Don F. "Matters of Living and Dying." *Episcopal Times* (January 1979).

Cousins, Evert. *Process Theology*. New York: Paulist Press, 1971.

Cousins, Norman. *The Healing Heart*. New York: Avon Books, 1983.

———. "The Mysterious Placebo—How Mind Helps Medicine Work." *Saturday Review* (1 October 1977), pp. 9–16.

Davies, Paul. *God and the New Physics*. New York: Simon and Schuster, 1983.

Day, Albert E. *Letters on the Healing Ministry*. Nashville, TN: The Upper Room, 1964.

The Dimensions of Healing: A Symposium (transcript). Sponsored by The Academy of Parapsychology and Medicine. Los Altos, CA, 1972.

Dobson, Theodore Elliott. *Inner Healing, God's Great Assurance*. New York: Paulist Press, 1978.

Dourley, John P. *The Illness that We Are*. Toronto: Inner City Books, 1984.

Droege, Thomas A. *Ministry to the Whole Person: Eight Models of Healing Ministry in Lutheran Congregations*. Valparaiso, IN: Valparaiso University, 1982.

Dubos, René. "Health and Creative Adaptation." *Human Nature* (January 1978), pp. 74–82.

Ellerbroek, W. C. "Language, Thought and Disease." *The CoEvolution Quarterly* no. 17 (Spring 1978).

The Encyclopedia of Religion. Edited by Mircea Eliade. New York: Macmillan, 1987.

Epstein, Gerald. "The Image in Medicine: Notes of a Clinician." *Advances* 3:1 (Winter 1986), 22–32.

Eves, Howard. *In Mathematical Circles*. Boston: Prindle, Weber and Schmidt, 1969.

Ferguson, Marilyn. *The Aquarian Conspiracy*. Los Angeles: J. P. Tarcher, 1980.

Fine, Carla. "New: Nurse Healers." *Woman's Day* (26 June 1979), pp. 40–44.

Fosshage, James L., and Olsen, Paul. *Healing: Implications for Psychotherapy*. New York: Human Sciences Press, 1978.

Frank, Jerome D. *Persuasion and Healing*. New York: Schocken Books, 1969.

Friedländer, Paul. *Plato, An Introduction*. New York: Harper & Row, 1958.

Fuller, John G. *Arigo: Surgeon of the Rusty Knife*. New York: Thomas Y. Cromwell, 1974.

Fuller, Reginald. *Interpreting the Miracles*. London: SCM Press, 1963.

Furness, George M. "Healing Prayer and Pastoral Care." *The Journal of Pastoral Care* 38:2 (June 1984), 107–19.

Gardner, Emily Neal. *The Healing Power of Christ*. New York: Dutton, 1972.

———. *A Reporter Finds God Through Spiritual Healing*. New York: Morehouse, 1965.

Gaydos, Michael. *Eyes to Behold Him*. Carol Stream, IL: Creation House, 1973.

Geddes, Francis. *Healing Training in the Church*. A dissertation project presented to The Committee for Advanced Pastoral Studies, San Francisco Theological Seminary, February 15, 1981.

Gelpi, Donald L. *Experiencing God: A Theology of Human Experience*. Mahwah, NJ: Paulist Press, 1977.

Glasser, Ronald J. *The Body Is This Hero*. New York: Random House, 1976.

Greeley, Andrew. "The Sociology of the Paranormal: A Reconnaissance." *Sage Research Papers in the Social Science*. Beverly Hills, CA: Sage Publications, 1975.

Grof, Stanislav. *Realms of the Human Unconscious, Observations from LSD Research*. New York: E. P. Dutton, 1976.

Health and Health Care. A Pastoral Letter of the American Catholic Bishops, USCC, 19 November 1981.

Heaney, John J. *The Sacred and the Psychic, Parapsychology and Christian Theology*. Ramsey, NJ: Paulist Press, 1984.

Hunt, Dave, and McMahon, T.A. *The Seduction of Christianity*. Eugene, OR: Harvest House, 1985.

"In Search of Wholeness . . . Healing and Caring," *Contact*, special series no. 2 (June 1979). Geneva, Switzerland: Christian Medical Commission.

Israel, Martin. *The Pain that Heals*. New York: Crossroad, 1981.

Jahn, Robert G. "Psychic Process, Energy Transfer, and Things That Go Bump in the Night." *Princeton Alumni Weekly* (4 December 1978).

James, William. *Varieties of Religious Experience*. New York: Longman, Green and Co., 1920.

Johnson, Kendall. *Photographing the Non-material World*. New York: Hawthorn Books, 1975.

Jones, Carol. "Photos Show How Faith Can Heal." *Prevention* (December 1973).

Journal of Holistic Health, vol. V. Del Mar, CA.: Mandala Open Circle, 1980.

Jung's Letters, vol. 1. Edited by Gerhard Adler and Aniela Jaffe. Princeton, NJ: Princeton University Press, 1973.

Jung's Letters, vol. 2. Edited by Gerhard Adler and Aniela Jaffe. Princeton, NJ: Princeton University Press, 1975.

Justice, Blair. *Who Gets Sick—Thinking and Health*. Houston: Peak Press, 1987.

Kaufman, Gordon D. *Systematic Theology: A Historical Perspective*. New York: Charles Scribner's Sons, 1968.

Keating, Charles J. *Anointing for Healing*. Mystic, CT: Twenty-third Publications, 1973.

Kee, Howard Clark, *Medicine, Miracle and Magic in New Testament Times*. Cambridge, MA: Cambridge University Press, 1987.

Keirsey, David, and Bates, Marilyn. *Please Understand Me.* Del Mar, CA: Prometheus Nemesis Book Co., 1984.

Keller, John. *Let Go, Let God.* Minneapolis, MN: Augsburg, 1985.

Kelsey, Morton T. *Afterlife: The Other Side of Dying.* New York: Paulist Press, 1979. In paperback: Crossroad, 1982.

———. *Can Christians Be Educated?* Birmingham, AL: Religious Education Press, 1977.

———. *Caring: How Do We Love One Another?* New York: Paulist Press, 1982.

———. *The Christian and the Supernatural.* Minneapolis, MN: Augsburg, 1976.

———. *Christianity as Psychology: The Healing Power of the Christian Message.* Minneapolis, MN: Augsburg, 1986.

———. *Christo-Psychology.* New York: Paulist Press, 1982.

———. *Companions on the Inner Way.* New York: Crossroad, 1983.

———. *Discernment: A Study in Ecstasy and Evil.* New York: Paulist Press, 1978.

———. *Dreams: A Way to Listen to God.* New York: Paulist Press, 1978.

———. *Encounter with God.* New York: Paulist Press, 1987.

———. *God, Dreams, and Revelation: A Christian Interpretation of Dreams.* Minneapolis, MN: Augsburg, 1974.

———. *Myth, History and Faith.* New York: Paulist Press, 1974.

———. *The Other Side of Silence: A Guide to Christian Meditation.* New York: Paulist Press, 1976.

———. *Prophetic Ministry.* New York: Crossroad, 1982.

———. *Resurrection.* New York: Paulist Press, 1985.

———. *Sacrament of Sexuality.* Warwick, NY: Amity House, 1986.

———. *Tongue Speaking: The History and Meaning of Charismatic Experience.* New York: Crossroad, 1982.

———. *Transcend.* New York: Crossroad, 1981.

Kingma, Stuart J. *A Unified View of Healing—The Centrality of Hope and Reconciliation.* Unpublished lecture given at a conference on healing and loneliness in Zurich, November 1982.

Kinlein, Lucille. "Pioneer Says Nurses Need to Escape Medical 'Yoke'." *Nursing Alternatives,* Washington edition (November 1983).

Konner, Melvin. *The Tangled Wing: Biological Constraints on the Human Spirit.* New York: Holt, Rinehart and Winston, 1982.

Koromvokis, Luggeri. "Faith Healers in the Laboratory." *Science Digest* 90:5 (May 1982).

Krieger, Dolores. *The Therapeutic Touch.* Englewood Cliffs, NJ: Prentice-Hall, 1979.

———, Erik Peper, and Sonice Ancoli. "Therapeutic Touch—Searching for Evidence of Psychological Change." *American Journal of Nursing* (April 1979).

Krippner, Stanley. *Song of the Siren, A Parapsychological Odyssey.* New York: Harper & Row, 1975.

Krippner, Stanley, and Alberto Villoldo. *The Realms of Healing.* Millbrae, CA: Celestial Arts, 1976.

Lapide, Pinchas. *The Resurrection of Jesus.* Minneapolis, MN: Augsburg, 1983.

LeShan, Lawrence. *Alternative Realities—The Search for the Full Human Being.* New York: M. Evans, 1976.

————. *The Medium, The Mystic and The Physicist.* New York: Viking Press, 1966.

————. *You Can Fight for Your Life, Emotional Factors in the Causation of Cancer.* New York: M. Evans, 1977.

Linn, Dennis, and Matthew Linn. *Healing Life's Hurts: Healing Memories Through the Five Stages of Forgiveness.* New York: Paulist Press, 1978.

————. *Healing of Memories.* New York: Paulist Press, 1974.

Linn, Dennis, Matthew Linn, and Sheila Fabricant. *At Peace with the Unborn: A Book for Healing.* Mahwah, NJ: Paulist Press, 1985.

Locke, Steven, and Douglas Colligan. *The Healer Within—The New Medicine of Mind and Body.* New York: E. P. Dutton, 1986.

Lynch, James J. *The Broken Heart: The Medical Consequences of Loneliness.* New York: Basic Books, 1977.

————. *The Language of the Heart: The Body's Response to Human Dialogue.* New York: Basic Books, 1986.

MacNutt, Francis. *Healing.* Notre Dame, IN: Ave Maria Press, 1974.

————. *The Power to Heal.* Notre Dame, IN: Ave Maria Press, 1977.

————. *The Prayer that Heals: Praying for Healing in the Family.* Notre Dame, IN: Ave Maria Press, 1981.

Macquarrie, John. *Principles of Christian Theology.* New York: Charles Scribner's Sons, 1966.

Madden, Daniel J., Jr. "A Theological Foundation for an Intentional Healing Ministry in the Church." Dissertation, St. Mary's Seminary and University.

Maddocks, Morris. *The Christian Healing Ministry.* London: S.P.C.K., 1981.

Martin, P. W. *Experiment in Depth.* Darby, 1982.

McAll, Kenneth. *Healing the Family Tree.* London: Sheldon Press, 1982.

McGarey, William, and Gladys McGarey. *There Will Your Heart Be Also: Edgar Cayce's Readings About Home and Marriage.* New York: Warner Books, 1975.

McGarey, William. "Healing Round the World." *Arizona Medicine* (October 1971).

McGilvray, J.C., ed. *The Quest for Health—An Interim Report of a Study Process.* Cleator Moor, Eng.: Bethwaites Printers, 1979.

McGlashan, R. Alan. *Gravity and Levity.* Boston: Houghton Mifflin, 1976.

McQuade, Walter. "What Stress Can Do to You." *Fortune* (January 1972).

Miller, Emmett E. "Patient, Heal Thyself." (Magazine unknown, n.d.)

Menninger, Karl. *Man Against Himself.* New York: Harcourt Brace, 1938.

Naranjo, Claudio. *The Healing Journey—New Approaches to Consciousness.* New York: Ballantine Books, 1973.

Native North American Spirituality of the Eastern Woodlands. In *The Classics of Western Spirituality.* Edited by Elisabeth Tooker. Ramsey, NJ: Paulist Press, 1979.

Newcomb, Franc Johnson. *Hosteen Klah—Navaho Medicine Man and Sand Painter.* Norman, OK: University of Oklahoma Press, 1964.

Nolen, William A. *Healing—A Doctor in Search of a Miracle.* New York: Random House, 1974.

Nouwen, Henri. *The Wounded Healer.* Garden City, NY: Image Books, 1972.

O'Connor, Edward D. *The Laying on of Hands*. Pecos, NM: Dove Publications, 1969.

Ostrander, Sheila, and Lynn Schroeder. *Psychic Discoveries Behind the Iron Curtain*. Englewood Cliffs, NJ: Prentice-Hall, 1970.

Otto, Herbert A., and James N. Knight, eds. *Dimensions in Wholistic Healing—New Frontiers in the Treatment of the Whole Person*. Chicago: Nelson-Hall, 1979.

Otto, Rudolf. *The Idea of the Holy*. Oxford: The University Press, 1958.

Paciorkowski, Richard. *Guérisons Paranormales dans le Christianisme Contemporain*. Varsovie: Academie de Théologie Catholique, 1976.

Padus, Emrika. "The Therapeutic Touch." *Prevention* (March 1977).

Panati, Charles. *Supersenses—Our Potential for Parasensory Experience*. New York: Quadrangle/New York Times Book Co., 1974.

Quindlen, Anna. "The Healing Touch." *McCalls* (May 1981).

Reed, William Standish. *Surgery of the Soul*. New York: Family Library, 1969.

Sacks, Oliver. *The Man Who Mistook His Wife for a Hat*. New York: Harper & Row, 1987.

Sandner, Donald. *Navaho—Symbols of Healing*. New York: Harvest/HBJ Book, 1979.

Sanford, Agnes. *Sealed Orders: The Autobiography of a Christian Mystic*. Plainfield, NJ: Logos International, 1972.

Sanford, John A. *Dreams and Healing, A Succinct Lively Interpretation of Dreams*. Ramsey, NJ: Paulist Press, 1978.

———. *Healing and Wholeness*. Ramsey, NJ: Paulist Press, 1977.

———. *Song of the Meadowlark*. New York: Harper & Row, 1986.

———. *The Strange Trial of Mr. Hyde—A New Look at the Nature of Human Evil*. San Francisco: Harper & Row, 1987.

Sargant, William. *Battle for the Mind*. Baltimore, MD: Penguin Books, 1961.

Scanlan, Michael. *Inner Healing*. Paramus, NJ: Paulist Press, 1974.

Scarf, Maggie. "Images that Heal—a Doubtful Idea Whose Time Has Come." *Psychology Today* (September 1980).

Schaer, Hans. *Psychotherapy and the Cure of Souls in Jung's Psychology*. New York: Pantheon, 1950.

Schiefelbein, Susan. "The Miracle of Regeneration: Can Human Limbs Grow Back?" *Saturday Review* (8 July 1978), pp. 8–11.

Schillebeeckx, E. *Revelation and Theology*. New York: Ward and Sheed, 1967.

Schmidt, Edward C. "The Sacrament of Healing," *The Lutheran*, n.d.

Shlemon, Barbara Leahy, Dennis Linn, and Matthew Linn. *To Heal as Jesus Healed*. Notre Dame, IN: Ave Maria Press, 1978.

Siegel, Bernie S. *Love, Medicine and Miracles*. New York: Harper & Row, 1986.

———. "Love is a Medical Miracle," *Redbook* (December 1986), p. 110.

Signs and Wonders Today. Compiled by the editors of *Christian Life Magazine*. Wheaton, IL: Christian Life Magazine, 1983.

Simonton, Carl and Stephanie Simonton. "The Cancer Personality and How to Modify It." Lecture given on March 10, 1975, and reported in *Chaplaire*, newsletter of the Assembly of Episcopal Hospitals and Chaplains, Naples, FL.

———. *Getting Well Again: A Step by Step Self-Help Guide to Overcoming Cancer for Patients and Their Families.* New York: J. B. Tarcher, 1978.

Skinner, B. F. *Beyond Freedom and Dignity.* New York: Alfred A. Knopf, 1971.

Sontag, Susan. *Illness as Metaphor.* New York: Farrar, Straus and Giroux, 1977.

Spraggett, Allen. *Kathryn Kuhlman—The Woman Who Believes in Miracles.* New York: World Publishing Co., 1970.

St. Luke Health Ministries. *Health Promoter Training: Awareness/Peptic Ulcer.* Baltimore, MD: privately printed, 1983. Discussed in Kenneth Bakken, *The Call to Wholeness.* New York: Crossroad, 1985.

———. *Health Promoter Training; Celebration/Mental Depression.* 1983.

Stanger, Frank Bateman. *God's Healing Community.* Nashville TN: Abingdon, 1978.

Stapleton, Ruth Carter. *The Gift of Inner Healing.* Waco, TX: Word Books, 1976.

Stearn, Jess. *The Miracle Workers.* New York: Doubleday (Bantam Books), 1976.

Stein, Murray. *Jung's Treatment of Christianity.* Evanston, IL: Chiron Publications, 1985.

Stringham, James A. *The Mind, Conscious and Subconscious.* Lucknow, U.P., India: Lucknow Publishing House, 1966.

Swami Rama, Rudolph Ballentine, and Alan Hymes, *Science of Breath—A Practical Guide.* Honesdale, PA: Himalayan International Institute of Yoga Science and Philosophy, 1979.

Swartley, Willard M. *Slavery, Sabbath, Women and War.* Scottsdale, PA: Mennonite Press, 1983.

Taniguchi, Masaharu. *The Human Mind and Cancer.* Tokyo: Seicho-no-ie Foundation, 1972.

———. *You Can Heal Yourself.* Tokyo: Seicho-no-ie Foundation, 1961.

Targ, Russell and Harold Puthoff. *Mind Reach: Scientists Look at Psychic Ability.* Delacort Press, 1977.

Tart, Charles T., ed. *Altered States of Consciousness—A Book of Readings.* New York: John Wiley and Sons, 1969.

Thomas, Leo. *The Healing Team: A Practical Guide to Effective Ministry.* New York: Paulist Press, 1987.

Tillich, Paul. *Systematic Theology.* Chicago: University of Chicago Press, 1963.

Tuchman, Barbara. *A Distant Mirror—The Calamitous Fourteenth Century.* New York: Ballantine Books, 1978.

van der Heydt, Vera. *Jung and Religion.* London: Guild of Pastoral Psychology, n.d.

Varieties of Healing Experience: Exploring Psychic Phenomena in Healing. Transcript of the Interdisciplinary Symposium of October 30, 1971. Los Altos, CA: The Academy of Parapsychology and Medicine, 1971.

von Hügel, Baron Friedrich. *Essays and Addresses on the Philosophy of Religion,* first and second series. London: J.M. Dent and Sons, 1931, 1939.

———. *Eternal Life.* Edinburgh: T. and T. Clark, 1929.

———. *The Mystical Element of Religion as Studied in Saint Catherine of Genoa and her Friends.* London: J.M. Dent and Sons, 1927.

———. *The Reality of God and Religion and Agnosticism.* London: J.M. Dent and Sons, 1931.

Wagner, James K. *Blessed to Be a Blessing.* Nashville, TN: The Upper Room, 1980.

Walsh, Roger. "The Consciousness Disciplines and the Behavioral Sciences: Questions of Comparison and Assessment." *American Journal of Psychiatry* 137:6 (June 1980), 663–673.

Watson, Lyall. *Gifts of Unknown Things*. New York: Simon and Schuster, 1976.

———. *Supernature*. New York: Doubleday, 1973.

Webb, Lance. *Onesimus*. New York: Nelson, 1984.

Webber, Robert E. "Healing in the Mainline Church." *Bulletin of Lancaster Theological Seminary* (March 1986).

Webster, Douglas. *What is Spiritual Healing?* Cincinnati, OH: Forward Movement Publications, n.d.

Weil, Andrew. *The Natural Mind*. Boston: Houghton Mifflin, 1972.

Welch, John. *Spiritual Pilgrims*. New York: Paulist Press, 1982.

Wimber, John, and Kevin Springer. *Power Healing*. San Francisco: Harper & Row, 1987.

Winckley, Edward. *The Greatest*. Puyallup, WA: Valley Press, 1977.

Wink, Walter. *Naming the Powers: The Language of Power in the New Testament*. Philadelphia: Fortress Press, 1985.

———. *Transforming Bible Study*. Nashville, TN: Abingdon, 1980.

———. *Unmasking the Powers: The Invisible Forces That Determine Human Existence*. Philadelphia: Fortress Press, 1986.

Zarrow, Susan. "An Orthodox Method of Heart Protection." *Prevention* (1986).

INDEX